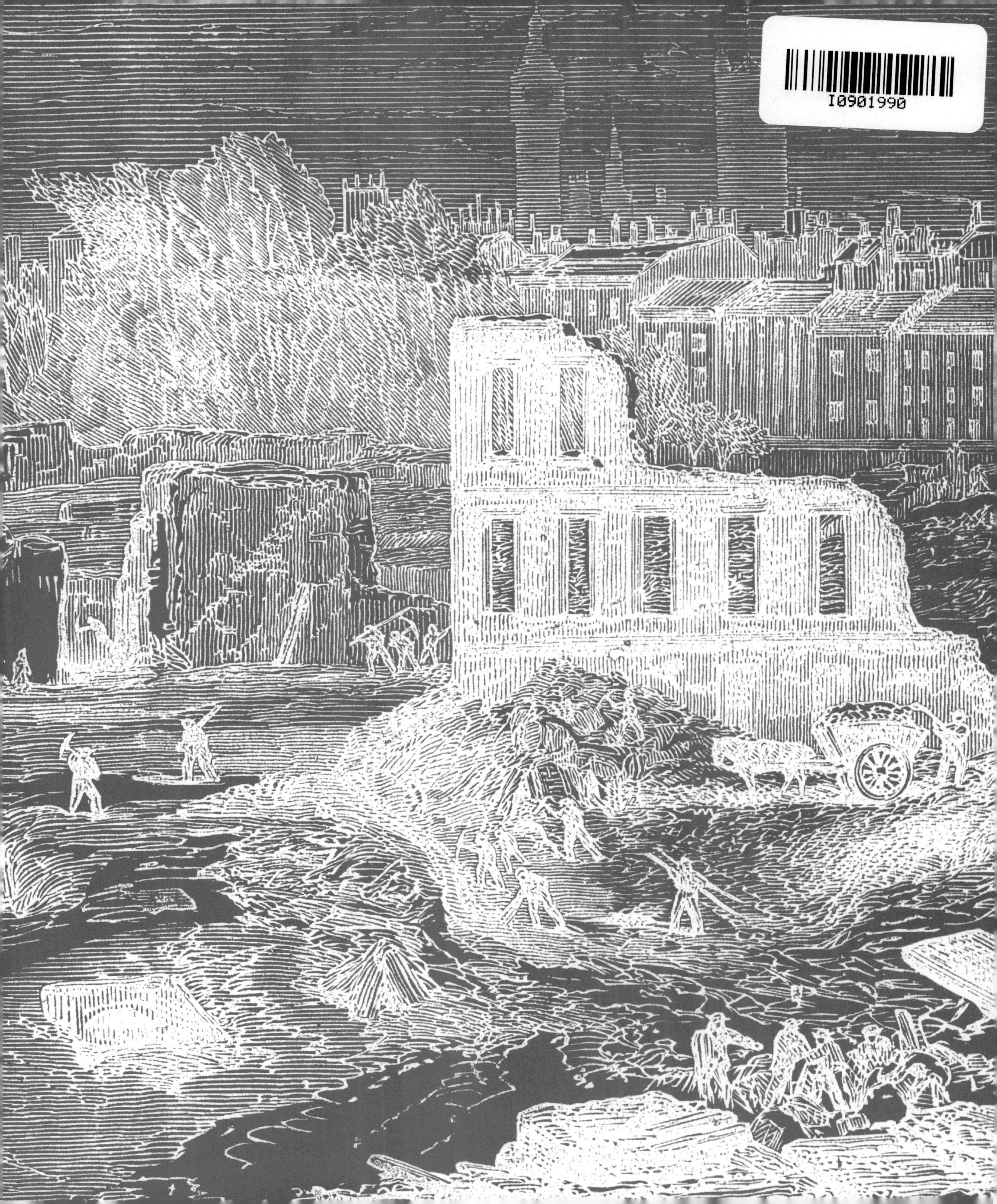

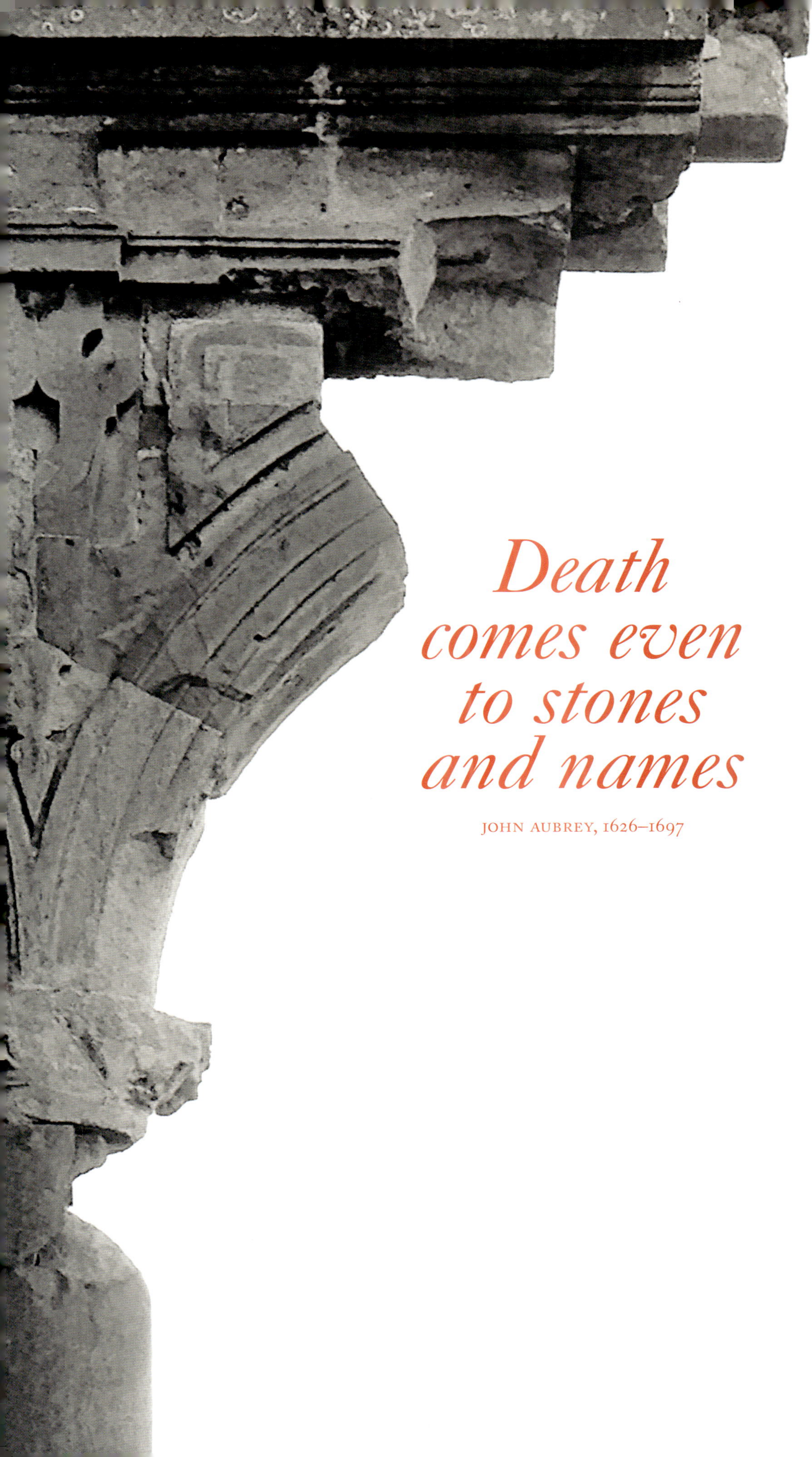

Death comes even to stones and names

JOHN AUBREY, 1626–1697

For my parents

ED KLUZ

THE LOST HOUSE REVISITED

TEXTS BY
Tim Knox
&
Olivia Horsfall Turner

FOREWORD BY
John Harris

MERRELL
LONDON • NEW YORK

CONTENTS

Foreword

John Harris

I first learnt of Ed Kluz's work from a series of nine postcards issued for an exhibition held in 2014 at Mascalls Gallery in Paddock Wood, Kent. They gripped me, for these were powerful re-creations of lost great houses set in invented, stormy landscapes, so as to magnify the effect. My favourite was a rare view of Hamstead Marshall with its cordon of gate piers. On a hitch-hike through Berkshire shortly after the Second World War, I ate my sandwiches at the base of one pier and established the site of the house as bumps in the grass.

Since then, I have discovered more about Kluz's pictures through Tim Knox, who has written a perceptive introductory essay for this book. Most recently, I have been introduced to Kluz in person by Olivia Horsfall Turner, who has composed pen portraits of each house to accompany his images here.

I only wish that I had known Kluz (or, indeed, that he had even been born!) when the Victoria and Albert Museum in London held the *Destruction of the Country House* exhibition in 1974, organized by Marcus Binney and me. What I wrote in the introduction to the exhibition catalogue was succeeded by my two volumes of memoirs, *No Voice from the Hall* (1998) and *Echoing Voices* (2002). In all three publications, I drew on what I could recall from my fieldwork in 1958 and 1959 for the

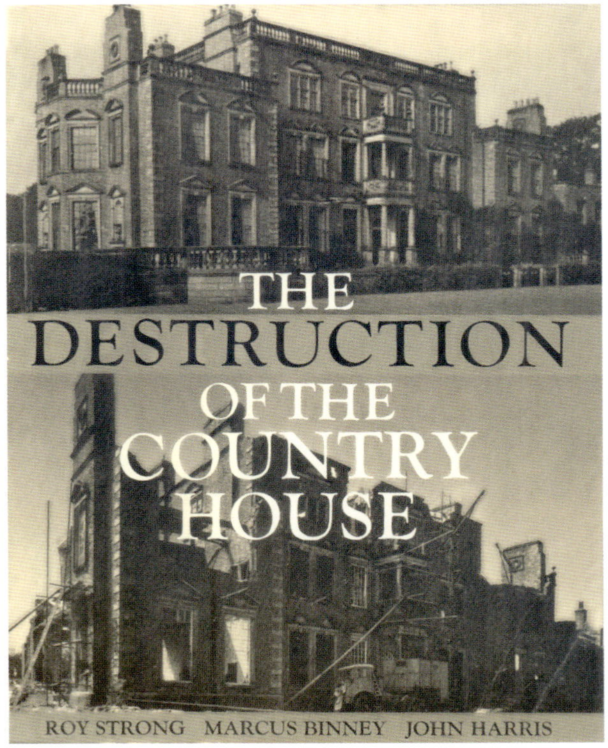

Lincolnshire volume in Nikolaus Pevsner's Buildings of England series, during which I visited the sites of forty-two lost and ruined houses.

To witness a demolition is as painful as losing a child. In 1958 I was at Burwell Hall, a house of 1760, when its gorgeous rococo interiors were ruthlessly torn out and the fabulous stairs thrown on to a bonfire on the lawn. Most heartbreaking was my observation in 1964 of the destruction of Panton Hall, Joseph Gace's noble house of 1720 by William Talman, enlarged by John Carr in 1775. Square yards of superb baroque panelling were being wrenched out, and a crane with a lead ball was ready for the demolition job that I watched at a distance the next day from the Neoclassical stables. These were just two of fifty or more demolitions in the county among the total of nearly 2000 English country houses no longer with us. The death toll is vast and the loss is irreplaceable, but we can find consolation in the fact that, through Kluz's images, some of them live again. APRIL 2017

The catalogue of the influential exhibition at the Victoria and Albert Museum in London, organized by John Harris and Marcus Binney; published by Thames & Hudson, 1974.

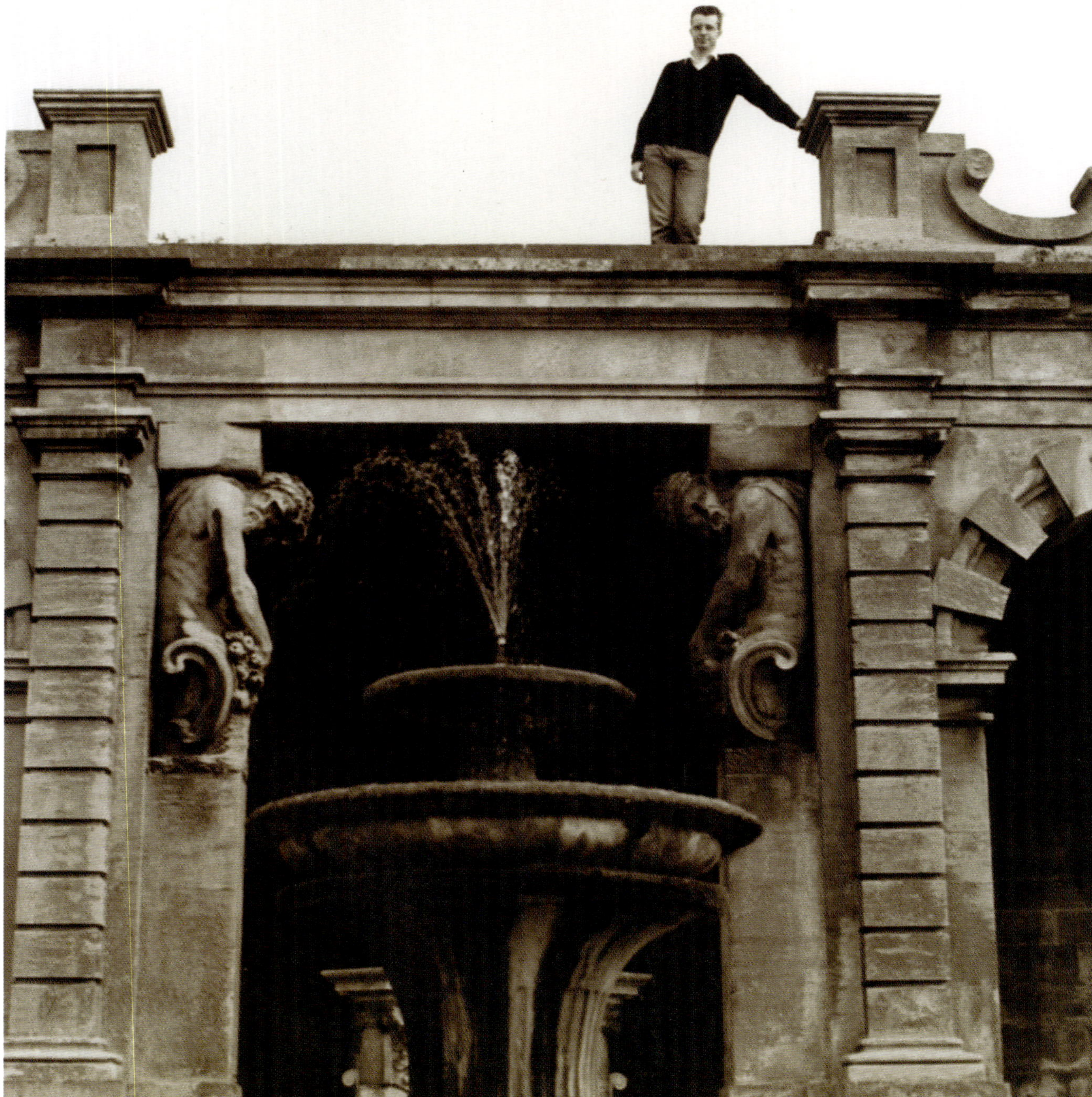

Introduction

Tim Knox

Tim Knox at Harlaxton Manor, Lincolnshire, c. *1989.*

The sixteen large collages of lost country houses that Ed Kluz exhibited in 2014 at Mascalls Gallery in Paddock Wood, Kent, impressed all by virtue of their boldness and originality. These works, Kluz's first 'Lost House' series (pp. 178–83), were intriguing on account of not only their medium – layer upon layer of collage elements on a ground of coloured inks – but also their haunting subject matter. What had led Kluz to depict this group of celebrated houses that had been burnt, abandoned to ruin or deliberately destroyed? The appearance of this series of new works, 'The Lost House Revisited', portraying more much-mourned houses – among them Worksop Manor, Old Campden House, Hamstead Marshall, Coleshill House, Eastbury Park and Hope End – has been eagerly anticipated.

Carefully researched and lovingly re-created, Kluz's 'Lost Houses' conjure up the vanished buildings in all their pomp, perched on stark, treeless plains under threatening skies, as if briefly illuminated in the glare of lightning or the beam of an arc light. There is something temporary and scenographic about them, captured on the verge of dissolution. In their crisp lines and their concentration on the filigree architecture and silhouette of building itself, Kluz's views of houses are, I suppose, heirs to the highly finished perspective drawings produced by professional architectural artists in the early nineteenth century, but they also draw on the bold graphic tradition of Eric Ravilious and Edward Bawden, combined with a brightly coloured, festive quality – like scenery in an old-fashioned toy theatre. What is clear is that they are the latest in a distinguished line of British country-house portraits.

Kluz is a very fresh and distinctive voice in this long tradition, a genre well documented in John Harris's *The Artist and the Country House: A History of Country House and Garden View Painting in Britain, 1540–1870*

(1979, revised edition 1985). From the earliest drawings and watercolours of Henry VIII's palaces by the visiting Fleming Joris Hoefnagel to the crepuscular evocations by the late nineteenth-century painter John Atkinson Grimshaw of damp manor houses engulfed by Leeds suburbia, Harris traces the evolution of house portraits. We encounter meticulous bird's-eye views of Dutch-style houses set within a chequerboard of compartments containing ornamental and useful gardens; Kip and Knyff's famous engravings of houses surrounded by a network of radiating avenues and plantations; the sweeping panoramas of John Wootton and Peter Tillemans, in which the house forms a backdrop to some sporting activity; and the Claudian visions of Richard Wilson and George Lambert. Harris's enthusiasm seems to wane somewhat when confronted with late eighteenth- and early nineteenth-century views of country houses, where the mansion is more often than not reduced to a mere incident in the romantic landscape. Did not John Constable himself describe his painting of Englefield House in Berkshire as 'a picture of a summer morning, *including a house*'?

Indeed, it was as if artists moved away from proud depictions of spanking new properties, delineated with all their amenities, towards atmospheric views of buildings in ruin. J.M.W. Turner's rare forays into country-house painting were specific commissions and, in the case of his views of William Beckford's capricious Fonthill Abbey in Wiltshire, an uneasy collaboration with its architect, James Wyatt. Turner clearly thought that the crumbly, ivy-hung charms of genuine monastic ruins were more rewarding subjects for the pencil than the flimsy pasteboard abbeys erected by his contemporaries. But the real reason for the decline in painted views of country houses was photography, which was embraced by the landowning classes with great enthusiasm. They either commissioned records of their houses from such professional photographers as Bedford Lemere & Co. or, as in the case of the pioneers William Henry Fox Talbot and the 2nd Earl of Craven, took up photography themselves.

It is true that country houses continued to be the occasional subject of paintings by twentieth-century artists: Rex Whistler, Algernon Newton, John Piper, Felix Kelly and Julian Barrow all produced house portraits, but these are almost invariably pervaded by a sense of gentle melancholy – or, in the case of Piper, a slightly sinister foreboding of impending disaster (King George VI famously remarked of Piper's views of Windsor Castle, 'You seem to have very bad luck with your weather,

Mr Piper'). If a tradition of conventional country-house portraits is still maintained today by the likes of Jonathan Warrender and Marcus May, it is photography on which we now more often rely for a visual record of houses.

Ed Kluz's interest in historic, decaying houses was probably first inspired by stories told by his father, who had been brought up in an old property called Kingsley House, in Barnack, near Stamford. More a large rectory than a country house, it had been requisitioned during the Second World War, and so was in deplorable condition when the family moved in. The childhood home of the eponymous author of *The Water Babies*, it was, naturally, a magical place for children to grow up in. An ancient wing, supposedly dating back to the Norman Conquest, was a boarded-up semi-ruin, while the extensive, rambling grounds, with overgrown walled gardens, were full of mystery and adventure. Kluz recalls his father telling him and his siblings about his childhood there, the things the family did, the animals they kept, and the resident ghost: 'We loved these stories. It opened up a way of looking at the past.' In fact, Kluz never knew Kingsley House as it was, for the property had to be sold in the 1960s. It is a sad but all too familiar story: it was subdivided by a developer, a mysterious fire destroyed the medieval wing, and houses were built in the gardens – so, in a sense, it is a lost house, too.

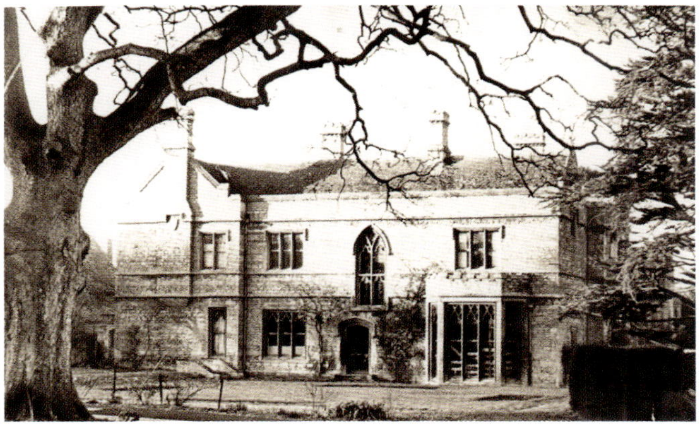

Kingsley House, Barnack, Cambridgeshire, 1949; the childhood home of Kluz's father.

Much later, Kluz's parents bought a ruined eighteenth-century farmhouse at Applegarth in the Yorkshire Dales. It was a forlorn ruin, uninhabited for about ninety years except by the occasional sheep. For two years, as they restored it, the whole Kluz family camped out in a caravan parked in the farmyard. Living next to a ruin was a memorable experience; there were walls painted with oxblood limewash and in the attic a stash of Napoleonic-era newspapers. Neighbours came by with strange stories about life there ages ago. They described how the house had been deliberately slighted

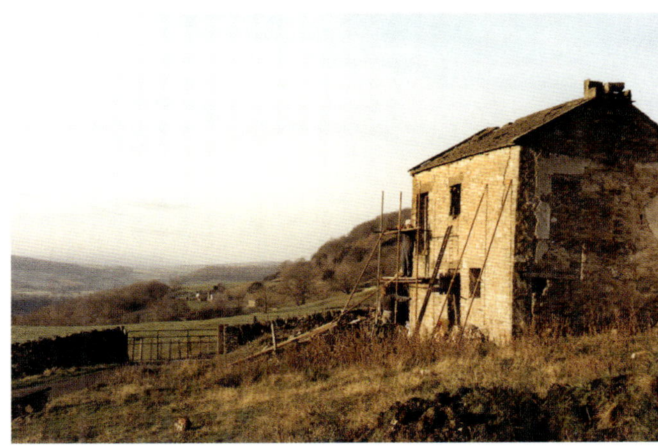

High Applegarth, near Richmond, North Yorkshire, 1985; the Kluz family home.

after a fire, and mentioned the death of a child in the farmyard and curious discoveries in the garden. In that part of Yorkshire there were ruins everywhere, from the great abbeys of Rievaulx and Fountains to the site of Stanwick Park, once owned by the dukes of Northumberland. Only tantalizing traces of Stanwick's elaborate gardens remain. Another favourite haunt was Temple Grounds in Richmond. Although the great house is long gone, demolished in the 1820s, its park – with derelict grottoes and follies – survives.

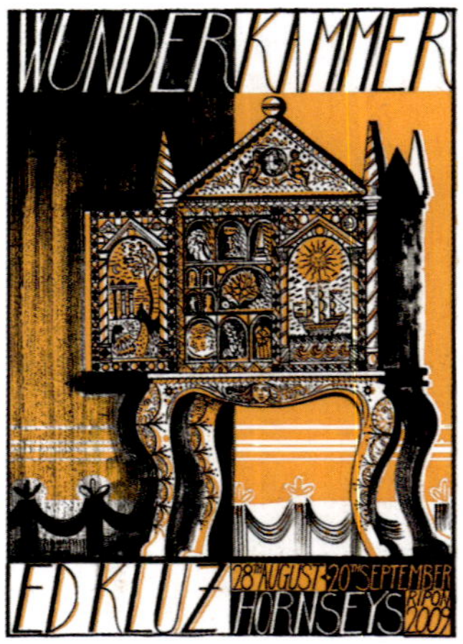

Wunderkammer *exhibition poster, screenprint, 2009.*

Kluz was an artistic boy, always making things, and his parents indulgently encouraged his interest in old houses. No wonder he loved *The Amazing Mr Blunden*, a 1970s film by Lionel Jeffries about some children who become custodians of a large, ruinous country house at the end of the First World War. Kluz admits that he is not a fan of the original book, 'but the film was very evocative, and how we lapped it up'. He was also inspired by his school's art master, Chris Moss, an unconventional young man who sported Edwardian suits and pocket watches. By kind permission of the elderly chatelaine, Lady Serena James, Moss took his pupils drawing in the overgrown topiary gardens of St Nicholas House in Richmond. Kluz remembers that the grounds were wonderful, 'laid out in the early twentieth century with rare trees and shrubs as a series of rooms and corridors with topiary peacocks and hedges. We would wander the gardens and draw. The sense of melancholy decay was heavy, and Chris's ability to encourage us to look beyond the purely visual was extremely formative.'

Kluz went on to study at Winchester School of Art, where his early work was very different, 'all about installations and videos'. However, in subsequent years he gradually forged his own distinctive style, and his obsession with old houses kept inexorably returning. He also read voraciously about the subject. Edward Waterson's books on lost Yorkshire houses were eagerly devoured, while Janette Ray, who runs a bookshop in York that specializes in architecture and gardens, and is herself a garden historian, became a friend. Ray introduced Kluz to the catalogue of the exhibition *The Destruction of the Country House*, which was held at the Victoria and Albert Museum in London in 1974; the catalogue is one of the principal inspirations behind the present series of collages. Kluz tells me that he almost prefers houses in decline or decay, ruins being much more dynamic and romantic, while well-maintained houses have a vaguely static character. 'Maybe it's fine to let things go', he muses.

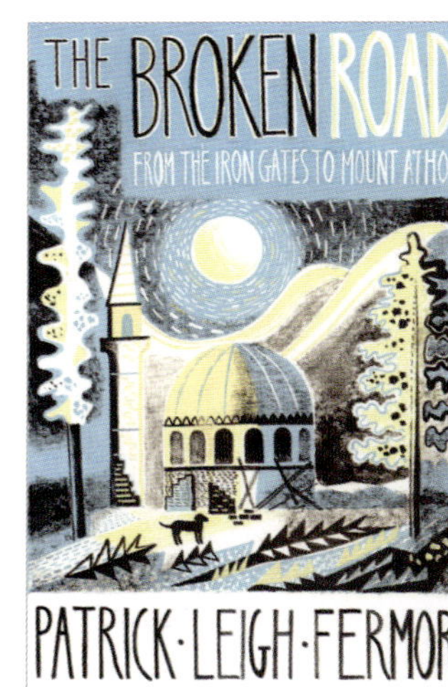

Jacket design for John Murray, gouache on paper, 2013.

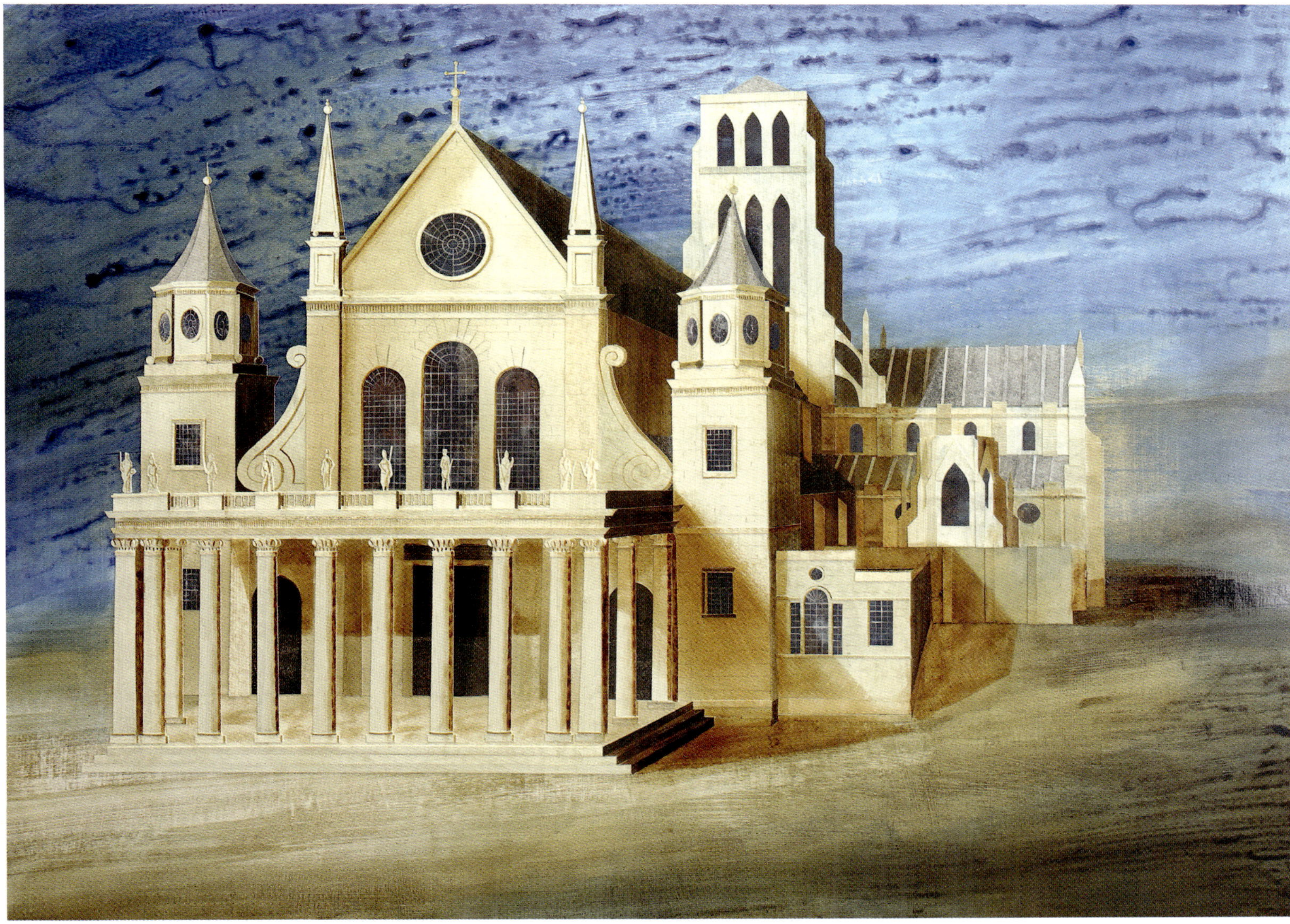

Old Saint Paul's Cathedral, *c.* 1660
Paper collage and mixed media
2015

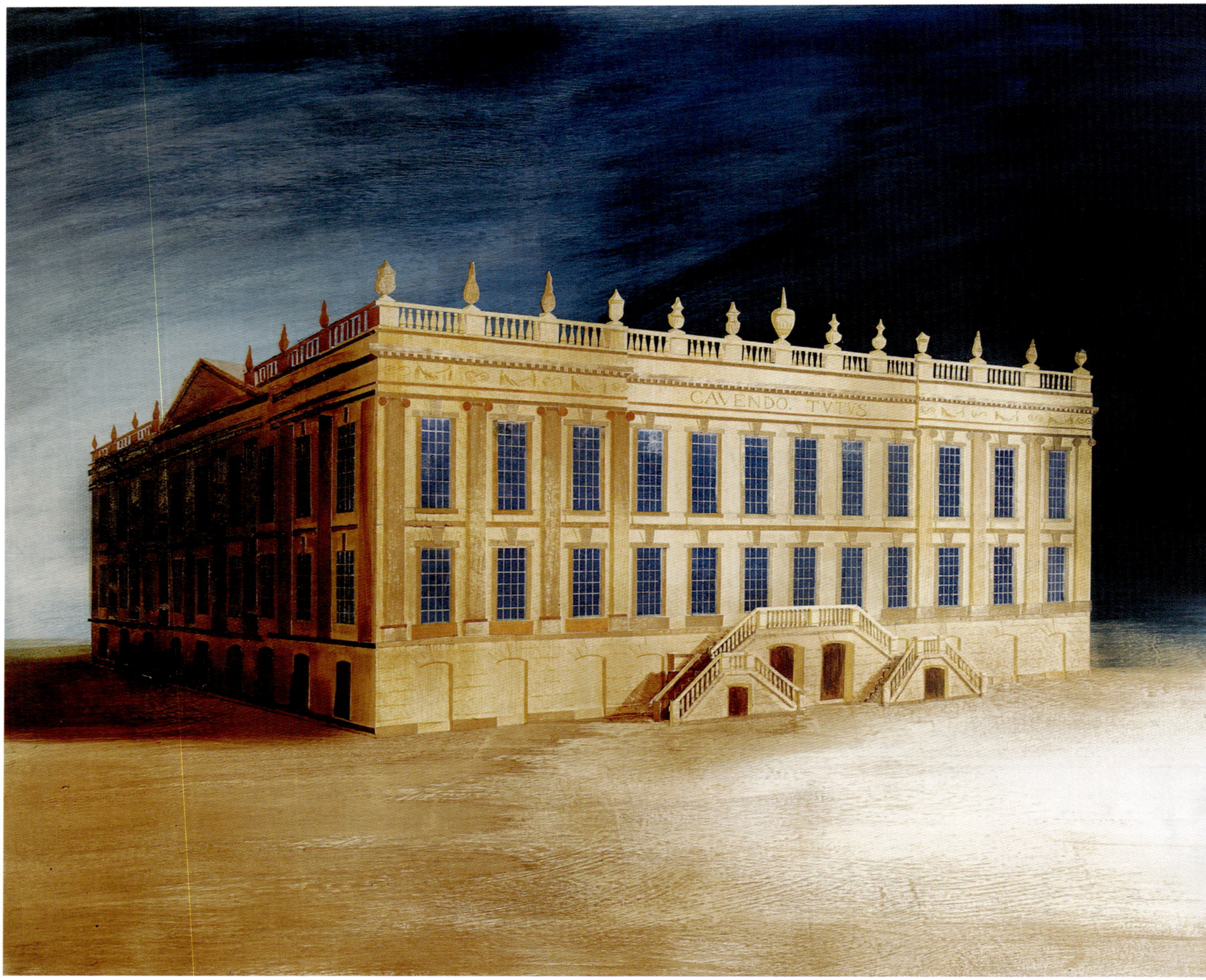

Chatsworth House, Derbyshire
Paper collage and mixed media
2015

Kluz's preferred subjects are Gothic Revival or Neoclassical buildings, structures that are themselves derived from ancient models and earlier architectural forms – 'products of the imagination, now gone, returning to imagination'. The more extravagant and prickly the structure the better, especially such ephemeral, dreamlike buildings as Fonthill Abbey or Eaton Hall. These are buildings that could almost be theatrical scenery or architects' models, sculpted from plaster and wood, or flimsy affairs of painted cloth. When asked why his visions of houses have no landscape setting, Kluz explains that he tends to avoid the 'sentimentality of romanticism, which can seem contrived at times', favouring instead 'a stripped-back, starker setting, brutal and minimal, allowing the architecture to speak for itself'. Kluz's technique is unusual and demands some explanation. First, he prepares a board with a special white gesso ground, which gives the works their distinctive luminosity. He then paints in the background, using expensive coloured inks made by an obscure firm in Thuringia. The inks have very strong, brilliant colours and yet are transparent. Next Kluz applies the collage, cutting up papers of different colours and textures. He builds up the architecture like a model, the largest forms first, then gradually lays down smaller and more delicate features, such as quoins and glazing bars. All architectural elements are of collage, strengthened with ink here and there.

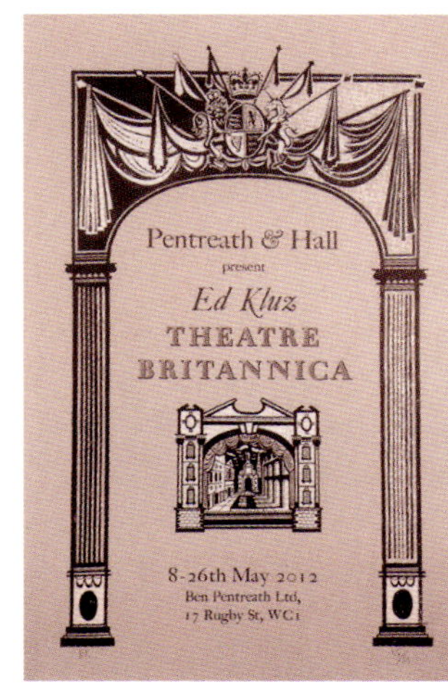

Theatre Britannica
exhibition poster, relief print, 2012.

Kluz favours collage for its expressive texture and three-dimensionality, citing as inspiration nineteenth-century folk art and also the influence of such modernist pioneers as Georges Braque, Pablo Picasso, Wilhelmina Barns-Graham and Ben and E.Q. Nicholson. Bawden, Ravilious and Enid Marx have all contributed to Kluz's artistic ancestry, Piper is an influence, and he likes Felix Kelly, too: 'He was a New Zealander, so has an outsider's eye.' Kluz loves the raw materials of collage, old papers and found objects, prints and ephemera, although he does not incorporate anything 'found' into his own collages, explaining, 'It doesn't quite work.' However, he omnivorously collects early prints from bookshops and barrows, and enjoys the quality of line and the texture and age of paper. A recent find at a car boot sale was an early engraved view of Coleshill House in Oxfordshire (formerly in Berkshire). Kluz speaks movingly of the way in which the old print – now very distressed, foxed and nibbled – has absorbed its history, and of how paper soaks up strong associations.

In conjuring up vanished great houses in his beautiful and ingenious collages, Ed Kluz caters for a strange longing. Why do demolished, burnt or otherwise lost country houses exert a far greater fascination on us than their more fortunate, surviving, counterparts? For some reason, Nonsuch Palace seems far more glamorous than Hampton Court, and Vanbrugh's Eastbury or the burnt-out shell of Seaton Delaval Hall are much more stirring than Blenheim Palace. Were Canons and Wanstead really so grand as to surpass Chatsworth and Wentworth Woodhouse? Why is it that we mourn the loss of Fonthill Abbey, yet somehow take the almost equally extraordinary Ashridge – now a prosaic business college – for granted?

At home I have a sort of dresser, its shelves laden with small scraps of stone, marble and plaster, as well as bits of glass and tile, and a few metal oddments, all neatly labelled in Indian ink with the evocative names of demolished country houses: Sutton Scarsdale Hall, Trentham Hall, Clumber Park, Hamilton Palace, Piercefield Park, Badger Hall, Drakelowe Hall, Panshanger, The Grange. Most pieces are dated, commemorating the countless expeditions I have made to see what is left of these great houses. Interestingly, some of the more impressive fragments – the baluster from the bridge by Sir William Chambers at The Hoo, Hertfordshire, or the brick stamped 'Dalquharran' from the pristine ruin of the South Ayrshire castle by Robert Adam – are from comparatively obscure lost or ruined houses. Most are pocket-sized (for obvious reasons), but I always regret having to forgo an entire column of Warwickshire marble found in the burnt-out shell of Barrells Park, which was too heavy to carry home. Indeed, I am not the first such souvenir hunter, as the sites of many of the really famous lost houses have been well picked over. Who knows if my tiny scrap of masonry really is from Hamilton Palace, rather than later builder's spoil, or if the tile I found at Wanstead is an actual survivor of the great sale of building materials from that house in 1825. In addition to bits of British country houses, there are a few more exotic relics from abroad: a chunk of the Berlin Wall, a tiny cube of onyx from the famous screen in Mies van der Rohe's Barcelona Pavilion of 1929, and an eighteenth-century nail from the roof of the Winter Palace at St Petersburg.

Tim Knox's own collection of architectural fragments.

Some of my most impressive trophies have been presented as gifts, such as a plaster rose, supposedly from Nuthall Temple in Nottinghamshire, given to me by the designer David Vicary. Most, however, are worthless scraps piously collected on very personal pilgrimages, often in the company of those great connoisseurs of lost houses, John and Eileen Harris. I can well remember hours spent with them grubbing around

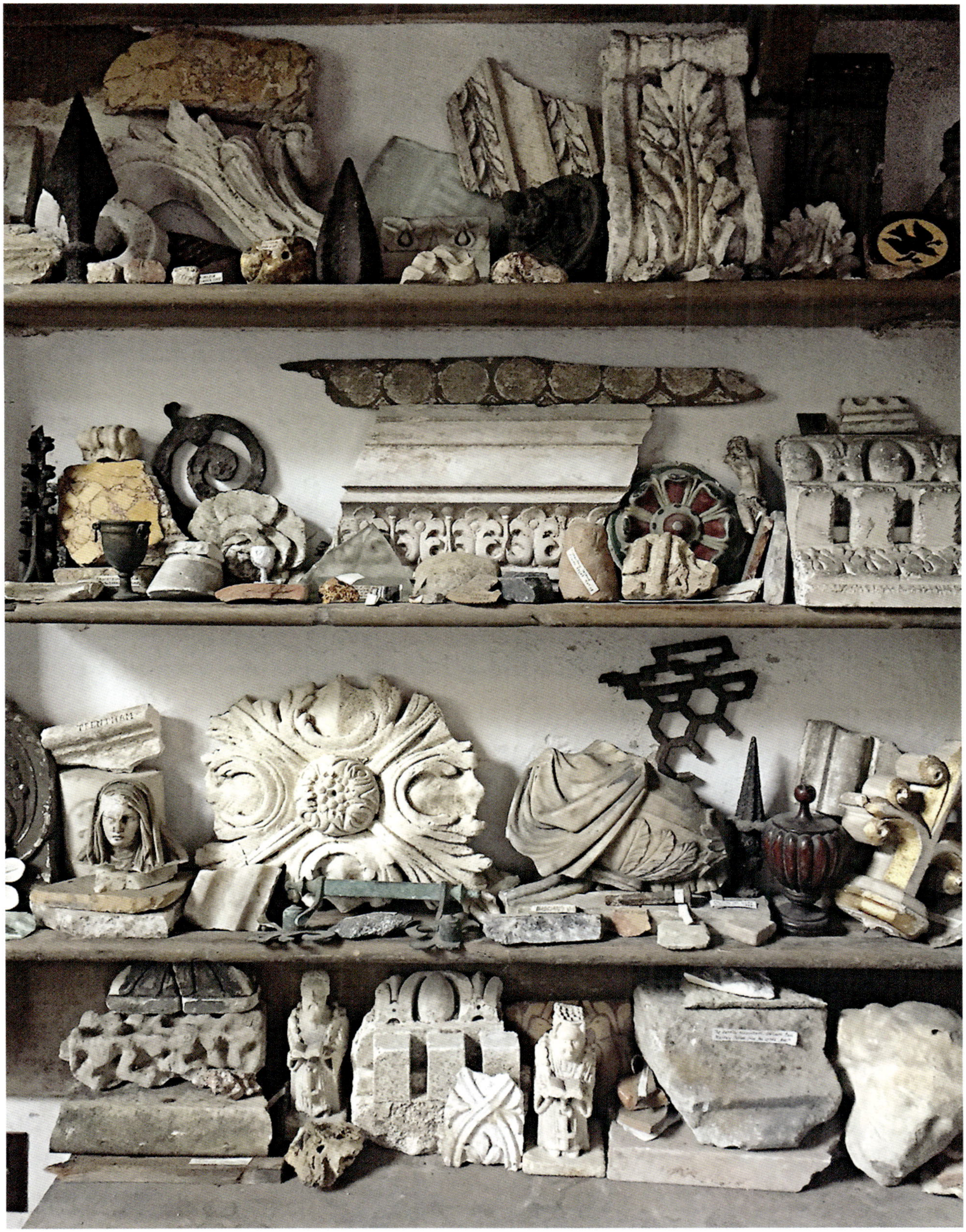

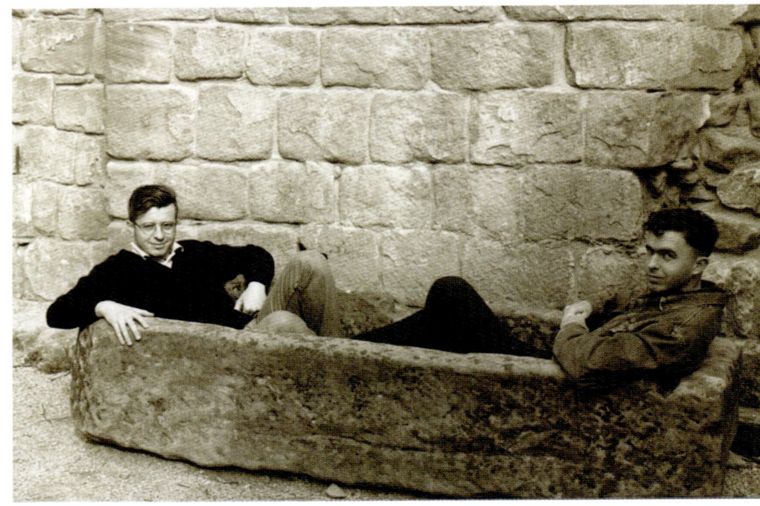

Tim Knox (left) and Todd Longstaffe-Gowan at Fountains Abbey, North Yorkshire, c. 1989.

in dripping rhododendrons in Stanmore, trying to find some trace of Monsieur de Fierville's famous island grotto, which Eileen had seen mentioned in an early gazetteer. We eventually discovered some strangely shaped flints, one of which is proudly displayed on my shelves. There were other adventures, too: at Haynes Grange in Bedfordshire we were menaced with a shot-gun, while at Halswell House in Somerset, inspecting a strange Egyptian bridge, we were pursued by a ferocious horse. We were ejected from the grounds of Stratton Park in Hampshire, chased down the overgrown drive of Syston Park in Lincolnshire, and warned off the site of poor Belhus in Essex – now the tenth hole of the local golf club. One or two of my trophies come from places that have since been restored and undergone a revival, such as a fragment of Sicilian jasper from the Darnley Mausoleum in Cobham Park, Kent, then a squalid, burnt-out ruin.

Tim Knox at the mausoleum, Wentworth Castle, South Yorkshire, c. 1991.

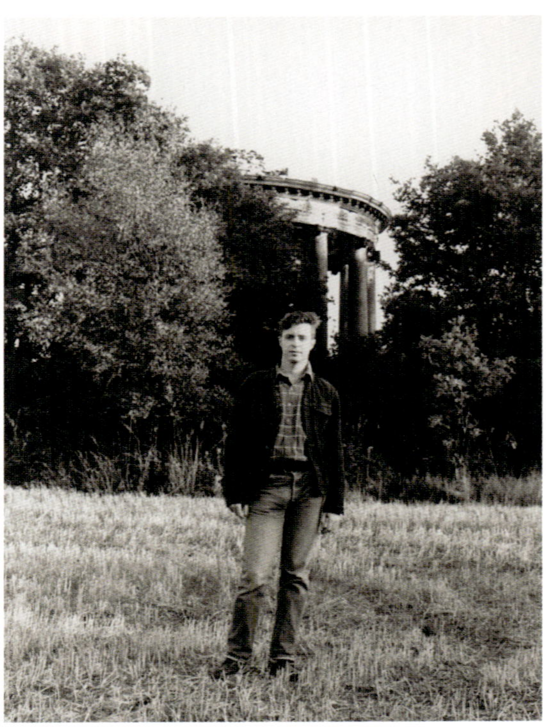

My own interest in lost country houses was sparked by experiencing the romantic decay of the demesne at Gunton Park in Norfolk (now beautifully restored), where decrepit triumphal arches in a variety of whimsical styles patrolled an irresistible combination of overgrown woodland, half-burnt-out house and a church in the form of a perfect Tuscan temple. I also read and re-read Sacheverell Sitwell's account of the decay of Sutton Scarsdale in *British Architects and Craftsmen* (1945). As in Kluz's case, my somewhat ghoulish interest in distressed or demolished mansions was further fuelled by the *Destruction of the Country House* exhibition in the mid-1970s. Incarcerated at the time in a prep school in Sussex – itself installed in a particularly dreary country house – I could not obtain permission to go, so missed this thought-provoking show, with its tolling bell and recorded litany of names of demolished houses. I was, however, able to send off for the catalogue, which I loved; I spent hours poring over the grainy black-and-white images of houses that had been lost. Much later, a job at the Royal Institute of British Architects brought me in touch with John Harris, whose extraordinarily evocative reminiscences of exploring derelict country houses after the Second World War formed the basis of his two volumes of memoirs, *No Voice from the Hall* (1998) and *Echoing Voices* (2002).

With the Harrises I visited many of the sites featured in the V&A exhibition or John's books to see what had become of them. A gate lodge or pairs of old gate piers often survived, as did stables and garden buildings, sometimes converted to domestic use. At Horton Hall, Northamptonshire, the architectural historian Gervase Jackson-Stops rescued the celebrated Menagerie from dereliction. He told me that on his first visit a cow was looking out of the window of the grandiose domed banqueting room. More often, it is only a cluster of trees that give away the precise location of a lost house, as at Hardwick House in Suffolk, where groves of immense yews and champion cedars of Lebanon mark the site in what is left of the degraded park. At Panshanger, Hertfordshire, a roofless orangery still stands, while at Deepdene, Surrey, we discovered the mausoleum of Thomas Hope, deliberately buried up to the apex of its pediment. It has now been heroically exhumed and restored. However, in some places everything seems to have disappeared: a school occupies the site of the celebrated grotto at Oatlands Park in Surrey, while a depressing housing estate

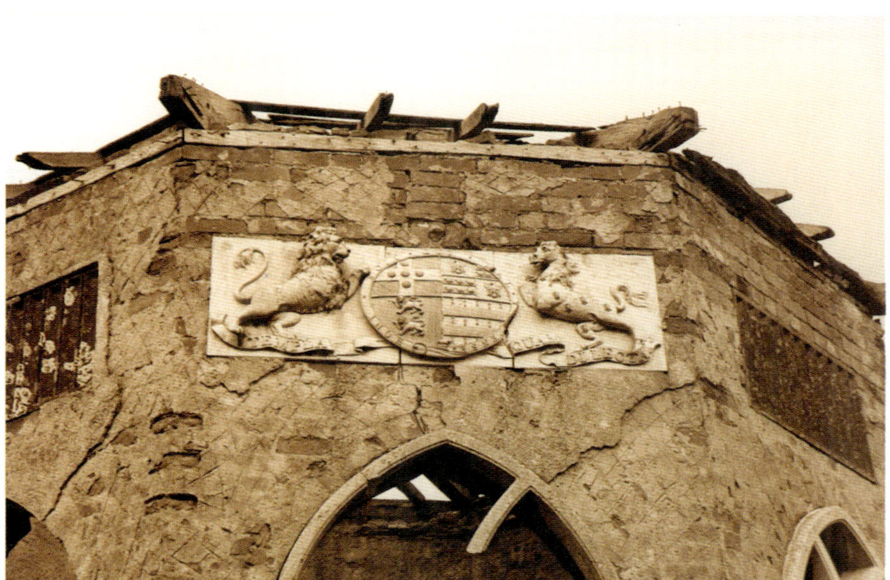

The Gothic Umbrello, Stowe, Buckinghamshire, c. *1992.*

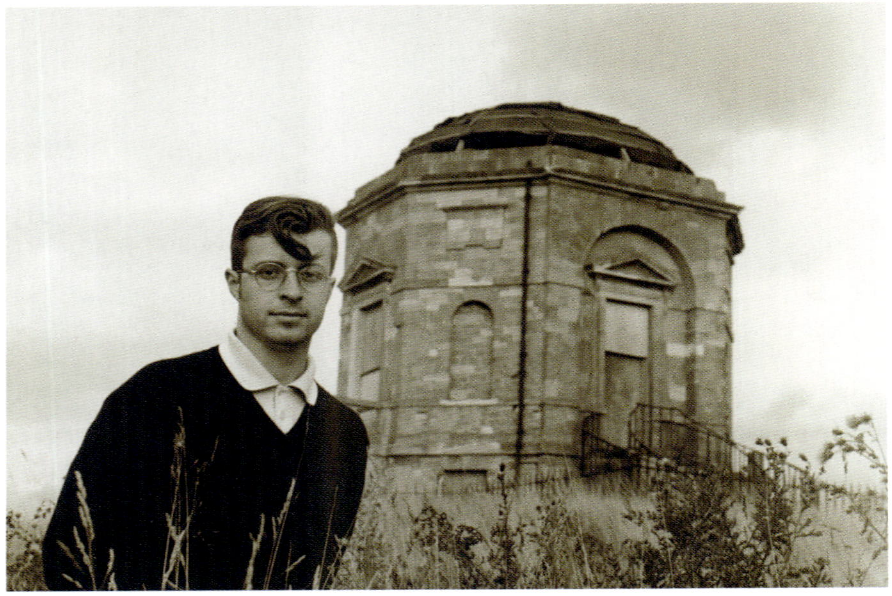

Tim Knox at the Temple of Victory, Allerton Park, North Yorkshire, c. *1989.*

is built over the Thameside terrace once occupied by Sir Sampson Gideon's Belvedere House at Erith.

One memorable expedition was to Felix Hall, Essex, the former home of John Harris's friend Geoffrey Houghton Brown, an antiques dealer. The house had been requisitioned by the Army, but had promptly been burnt out. Houghton Brown had bought it cheaply just before the Second World War, demolished the wings and – typically – sold off the chimney pieces and Chinese wallpaper at a tidy profit. Within its gaunt shell he had created a bungalow, which still survived. It was an extraordinary combination: a tiny weekend retreat entered via an imposing Ionic portico guarded by headless sphinxes, a haunting vision presiding over the surrounding cornfields. In the courtyard was, amazingly, a complete ancient Roman mosaic – a relic of the famous collection of antique sculpture formed here by the house's Regency owner, Lord Western. But the resident at the time, old Mrs Gray, soon sent us inquisitive 'snoopers' packing. Much more amenable was the farmer living in the outbuildings of Bylaugh Hall in Norfolk, who was quite happy for us to explore the gutted pile, 'as long as you don't fall through the floors', or the kindly owner of what is left of Worksop Manor in Nottinghamshire, who showed us the sculpted pediment of James Paine's huge neo-Palladian house for the Duke of Norfolk marooned in a nearby paddock. Exploring the creepy remains of rambling Gwrych Castle in Conwy, North Wales, was even more thrilling, as were assaults on the abandoned shells of Crawford Priory in Fife, the aforementioned

Dalquharran Castle and the brooding basalt mass of the Earl-Bishop's (Frederick Hervey, 4th Earl of Bristol and Bishop of Derry) Downhill House in County Londonderry.

Since the *Destruction* exhibition in 1974, few important country houses have been lost altogether – but many have been stripped of their contents, and one or two, such as Uppark House in West Sussex and Clandon Park in Surrey, have tragically been damaged by fire. Over the years, public interest in lost country houses has been steadily mounting; the ever-growing literature on the subject ranges from scholarly enquiries into the causes of the decline of country houses and their proprietors by David Cannadine and Peter Mandler, through Giles Worsley's poignant *Country Life* picture book, *England's Lost Houses* (2002), to the excellent booklets by local antiquaries devoted to the losses in particular counties. The internet has also spawned entire websites dedicated to the subject. With them, and the emergence of hitherto unknown painted views and photographs, the iconography of the lost country house is much enriched. Almost all these sources have been tapped by Ed Kluz in his search for information about his often elusive subjects.

Kluz's *Lost House Revisited* is a handsome addition to the literature on the lost house. Enjoying these ambitious collages, together with the wealth of supplementary material gathered by Olivia Horsfall Turner on the history of the houses and their respective fates, one yearns to have them all back; but, in a sense, we have, in Kluz's scenographic visions. Thus, the unveiling of this new group of works is a cause for celebration.

Works, 2008–15

Ed Kluz's practice covers a wide range of media and processes: printmaking, painting, drawing and collage. Each discipline and its material character have had a strong and lasting impact on the evolution of Kluz's work. The following selection of pieces plots the visual development of his ideas.

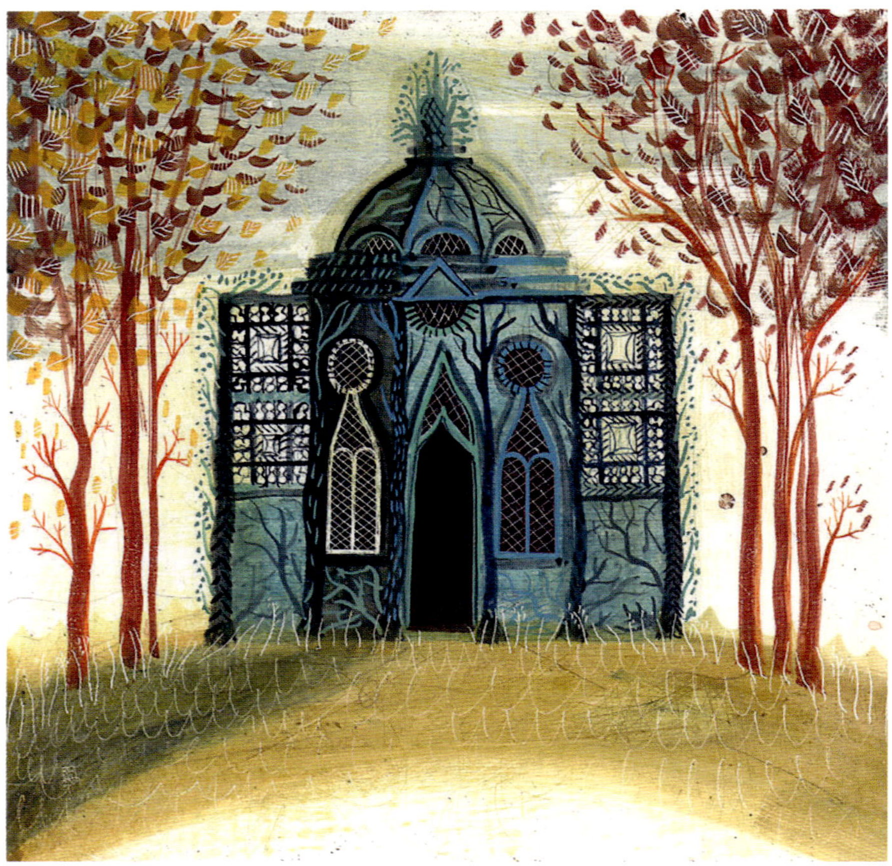

Based on a design by Thomas Wright for an arbour
Egg tempera on gesso panel
2008

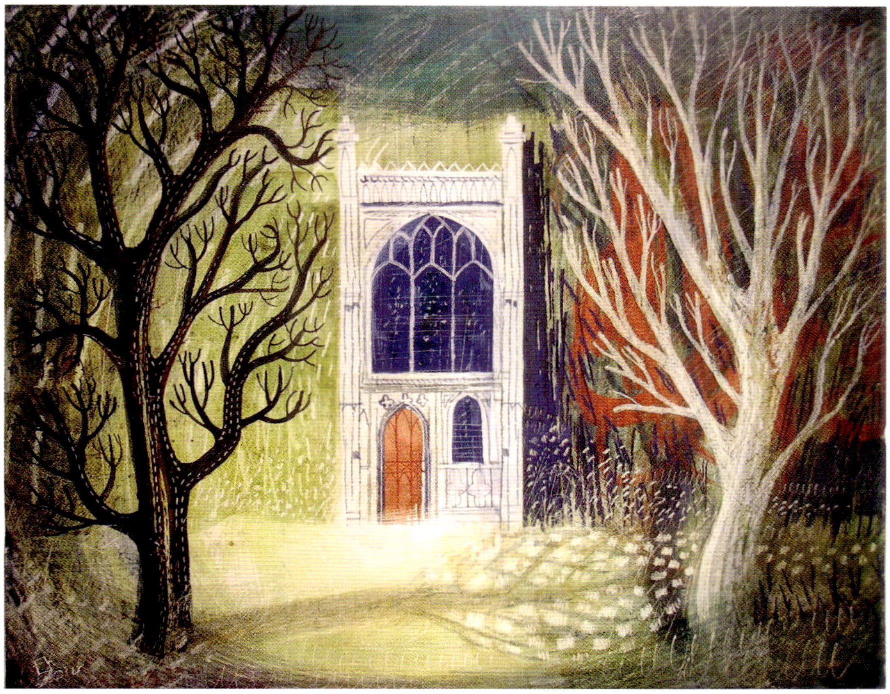

Chapel in the Woods, Strawberry Hill, Twickenham
Egg tempera on gesso panel
2009

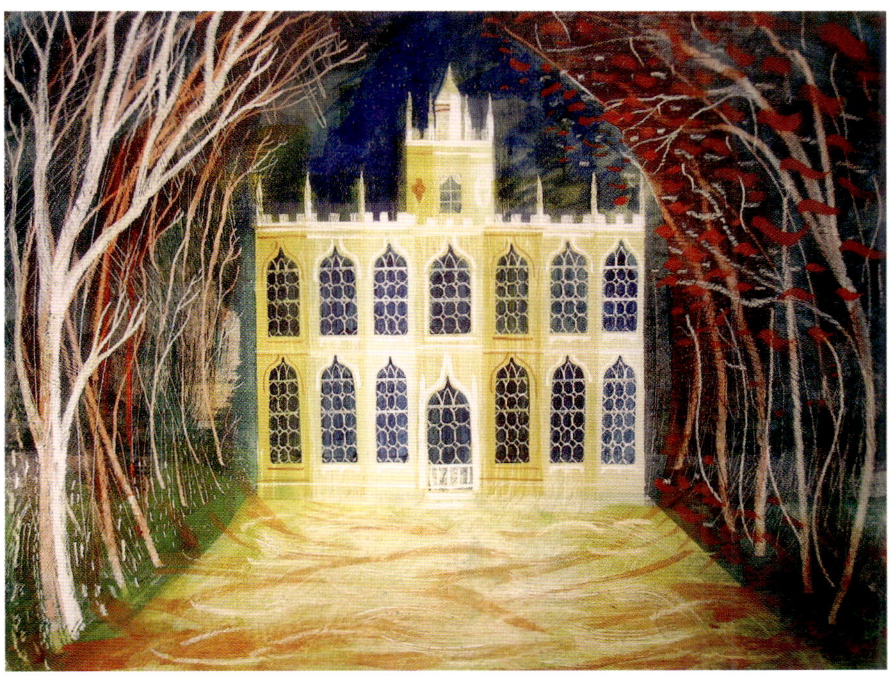

The Orangery, Frampton Court, Gloucestershire
Egg tempera on gesso panel
2009

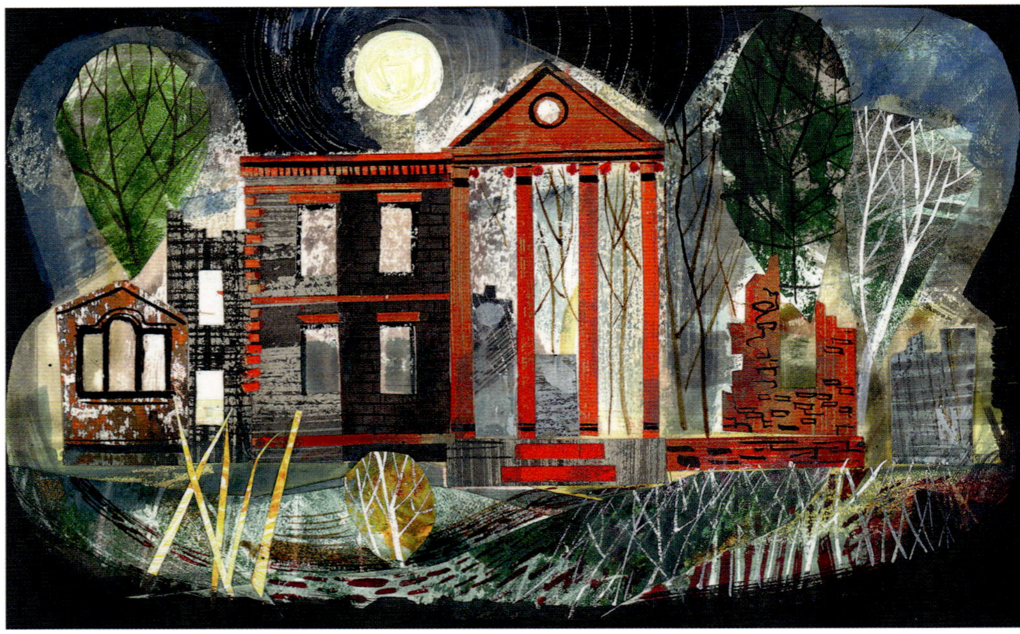

Carclew House Ruins, Cornwall
Paper collage and mixed media
2010

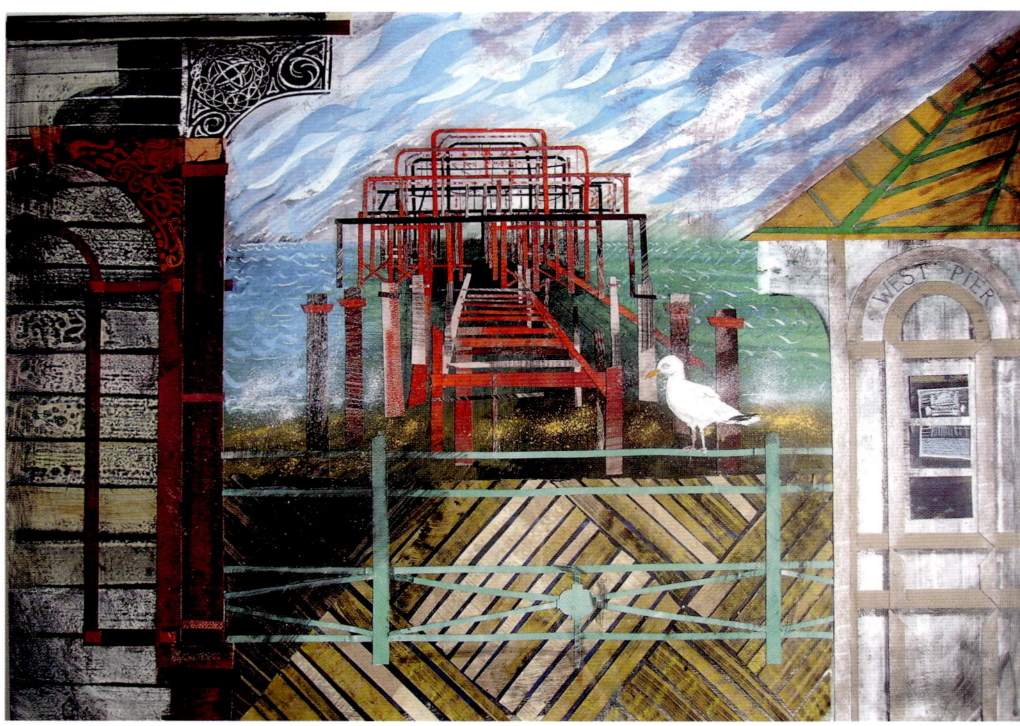

The Ruins of the West Pier, Brighton
Paper collage and mixed media
2010

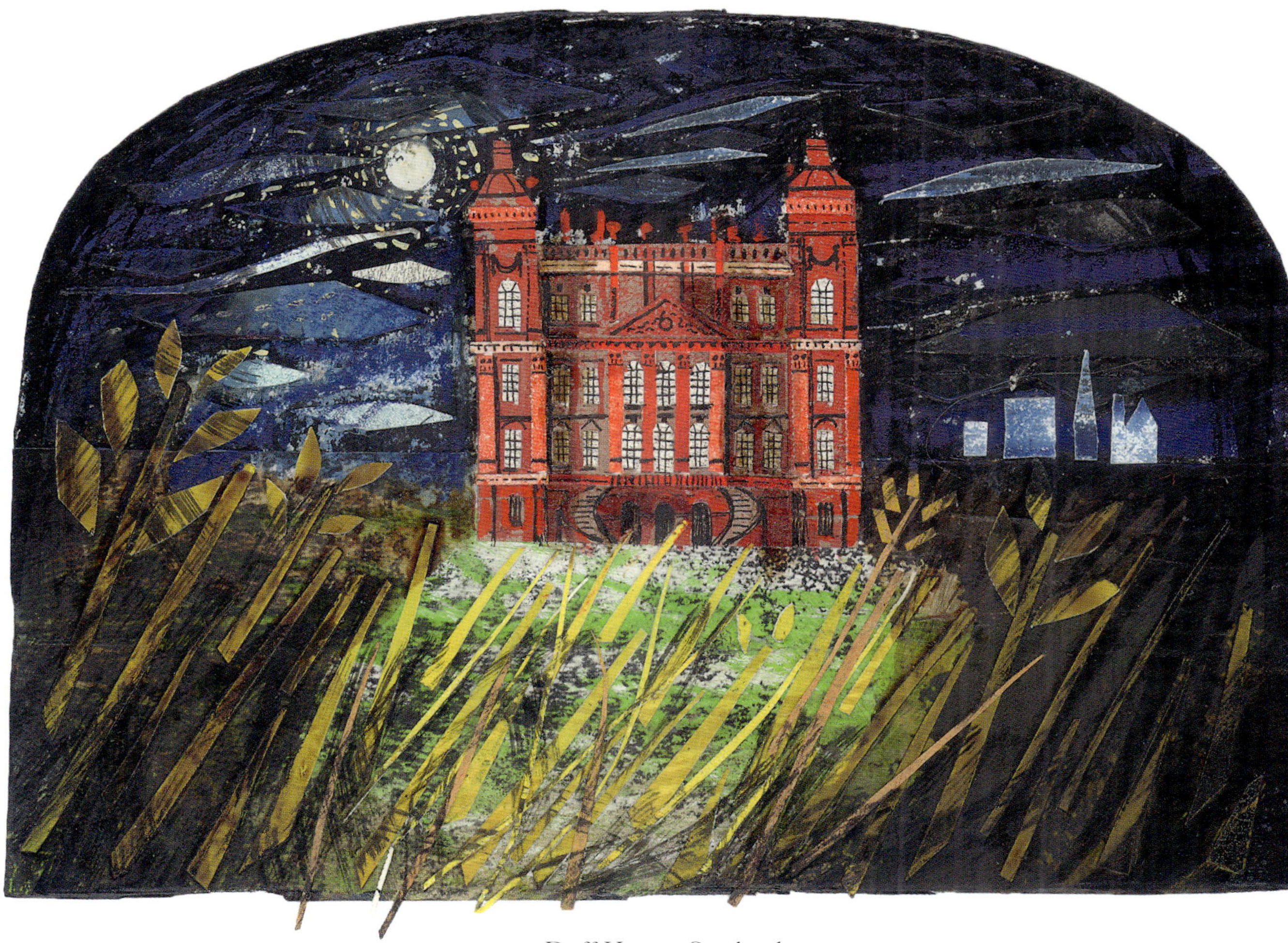

Duff House, Scotland
Paper collage and mixed media
2012

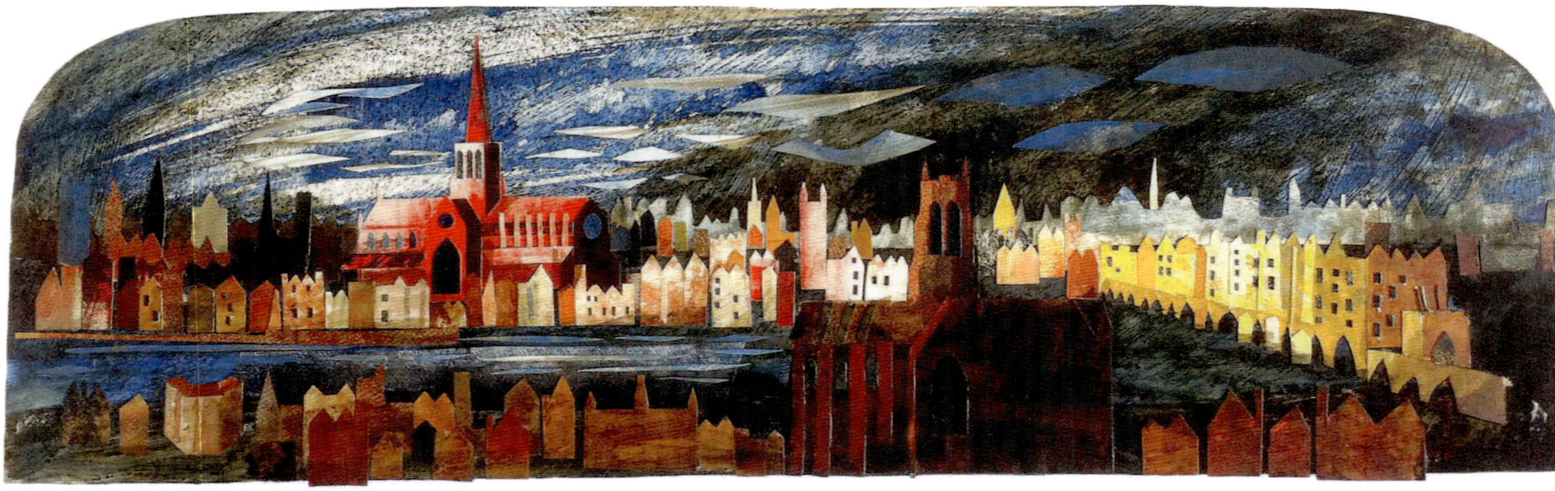

Prospect of Old London, after Visscher
Paper collage and mixed media
2013

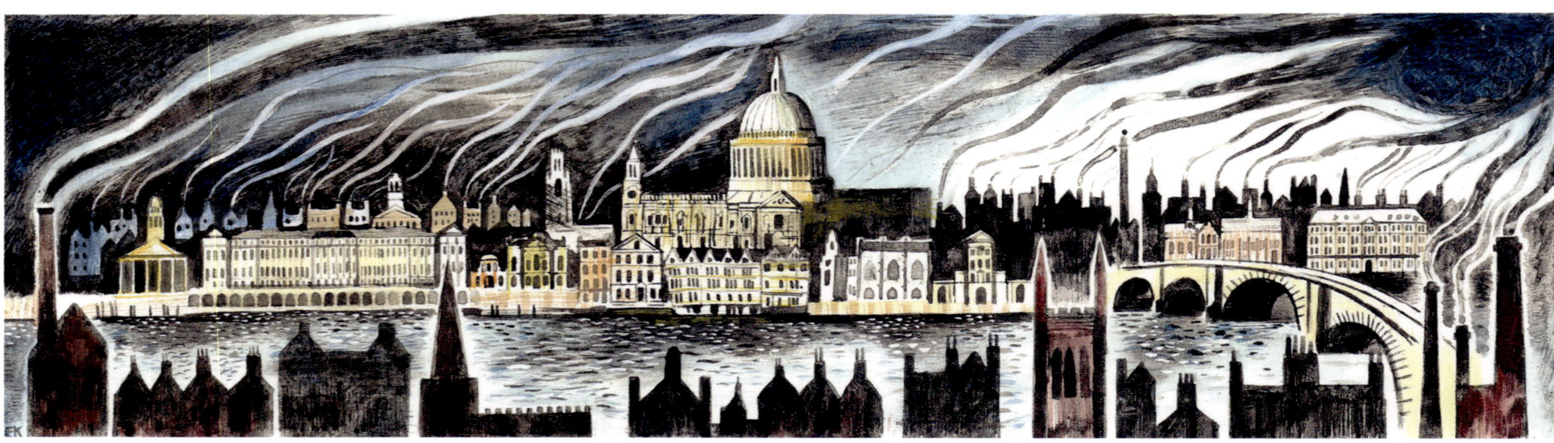

Dickensian London
Watercolour on paper
Commissioned by the Film
and Video Umbrella for the
'Our Mutual Friends' project,
2012

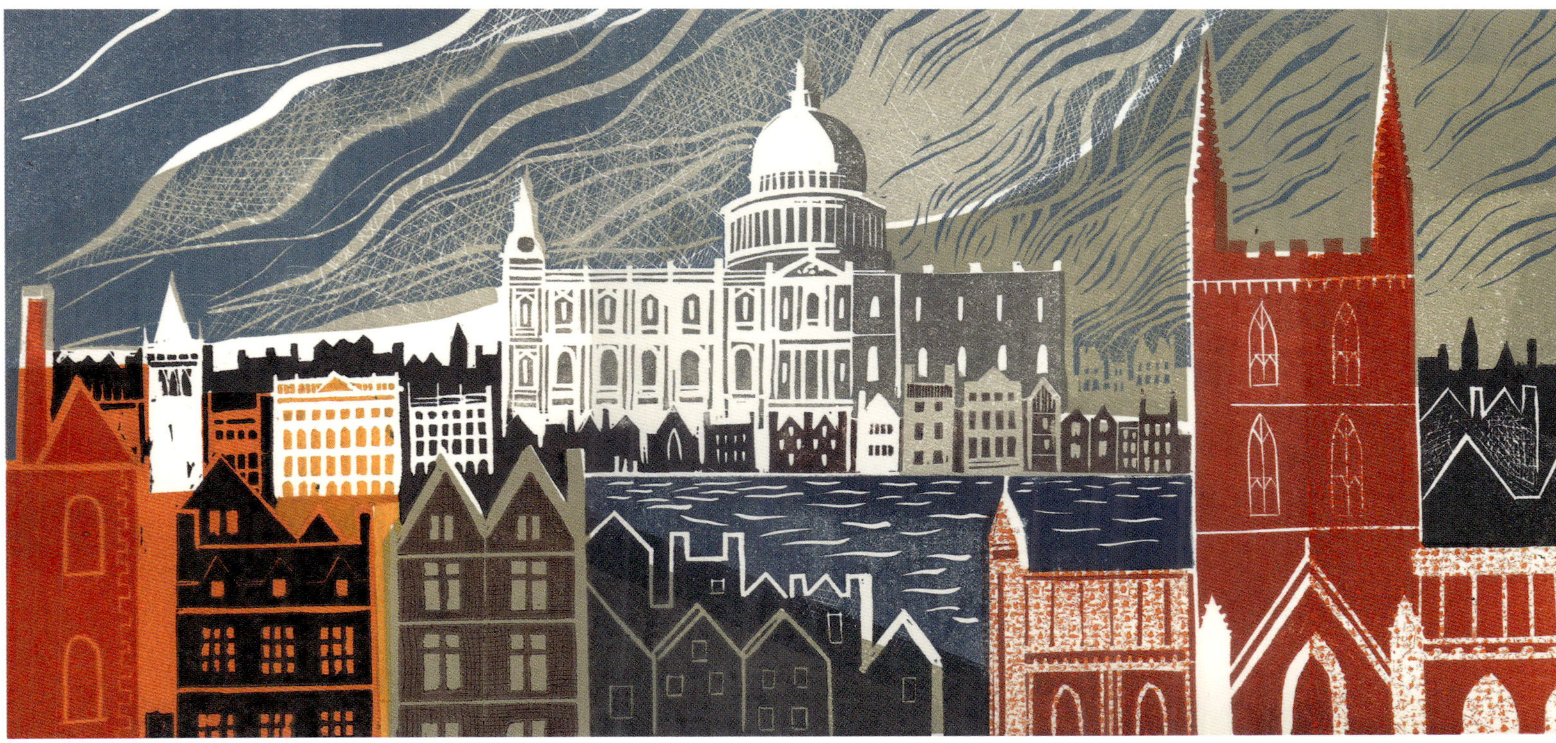

Restoration London
Linocut
2012

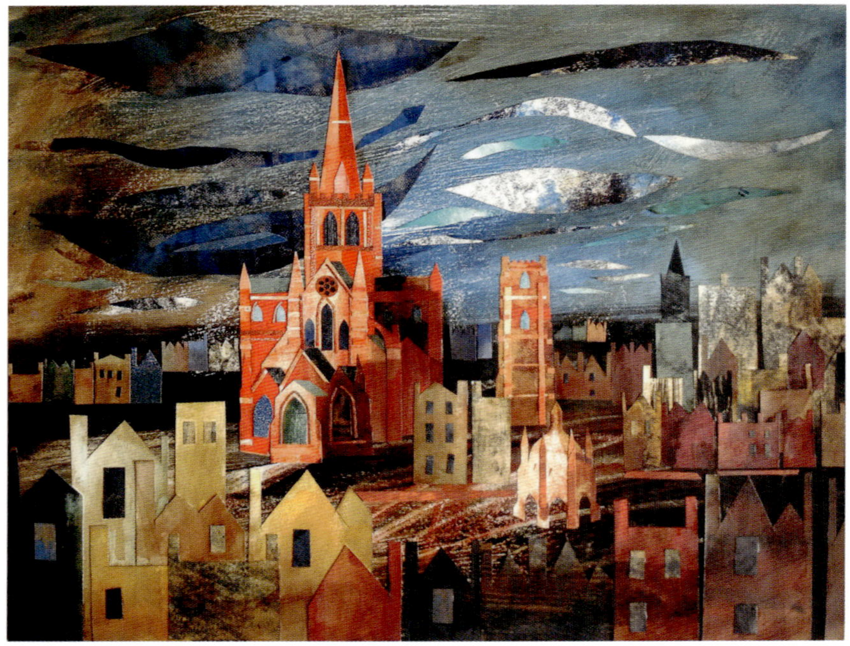

Chichester Prospect
Paper collage and mixed media
2013

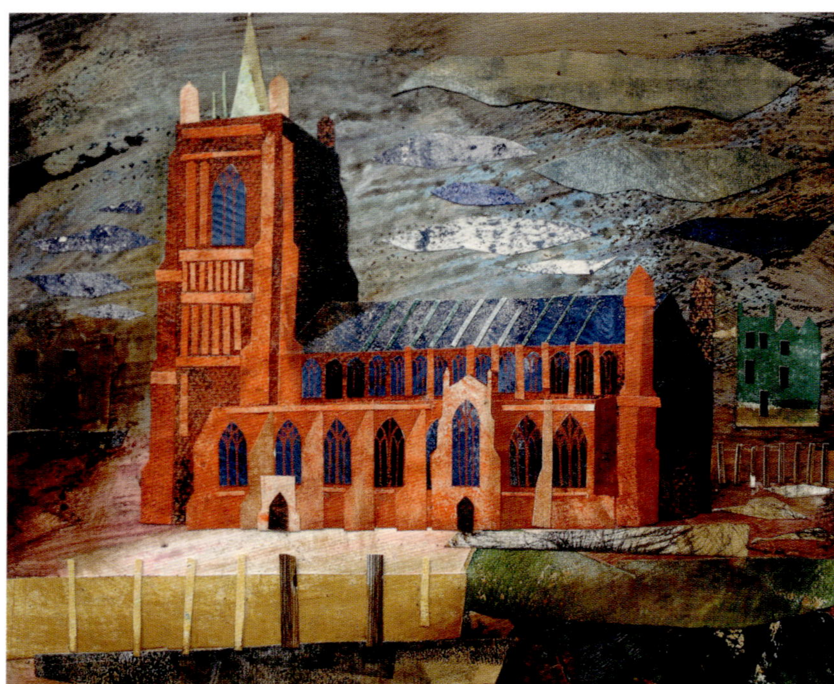

The Church of St Peter Mancroft, Norwich
Paper collage and mixed media
2013

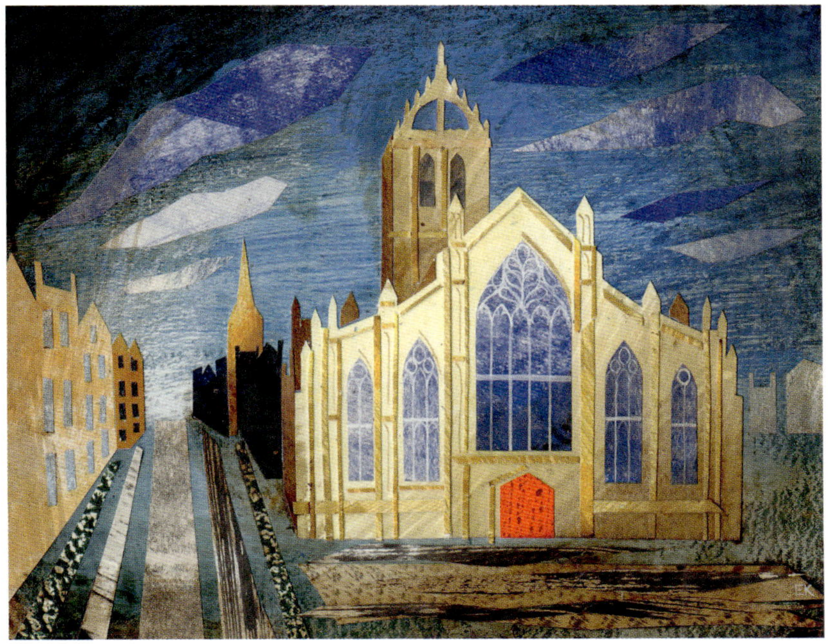

St Giles' Cathedral, Edinburgh
Paper collage and mixed media
2013

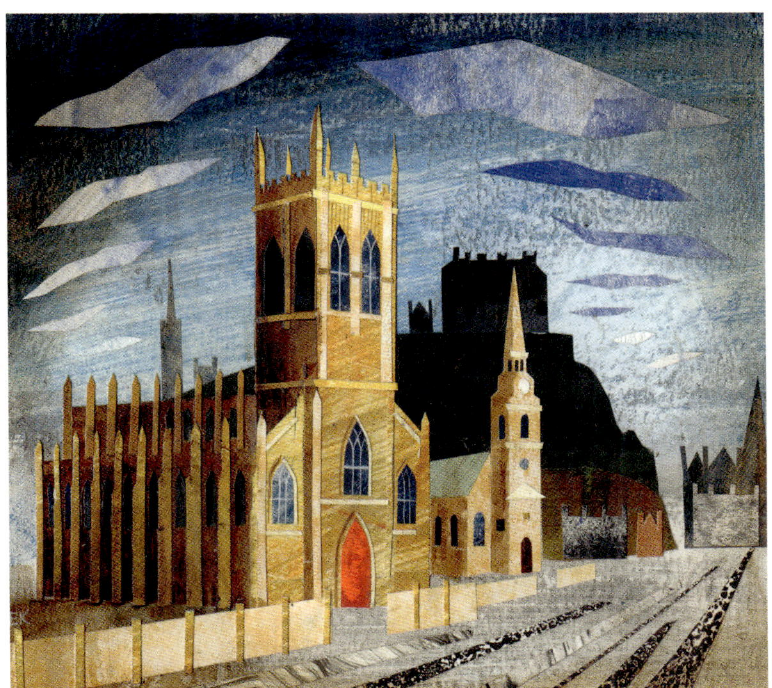

The Churches of St John's and St Cuthbert's, Edinburgh
Paper collage and mixed media
2013

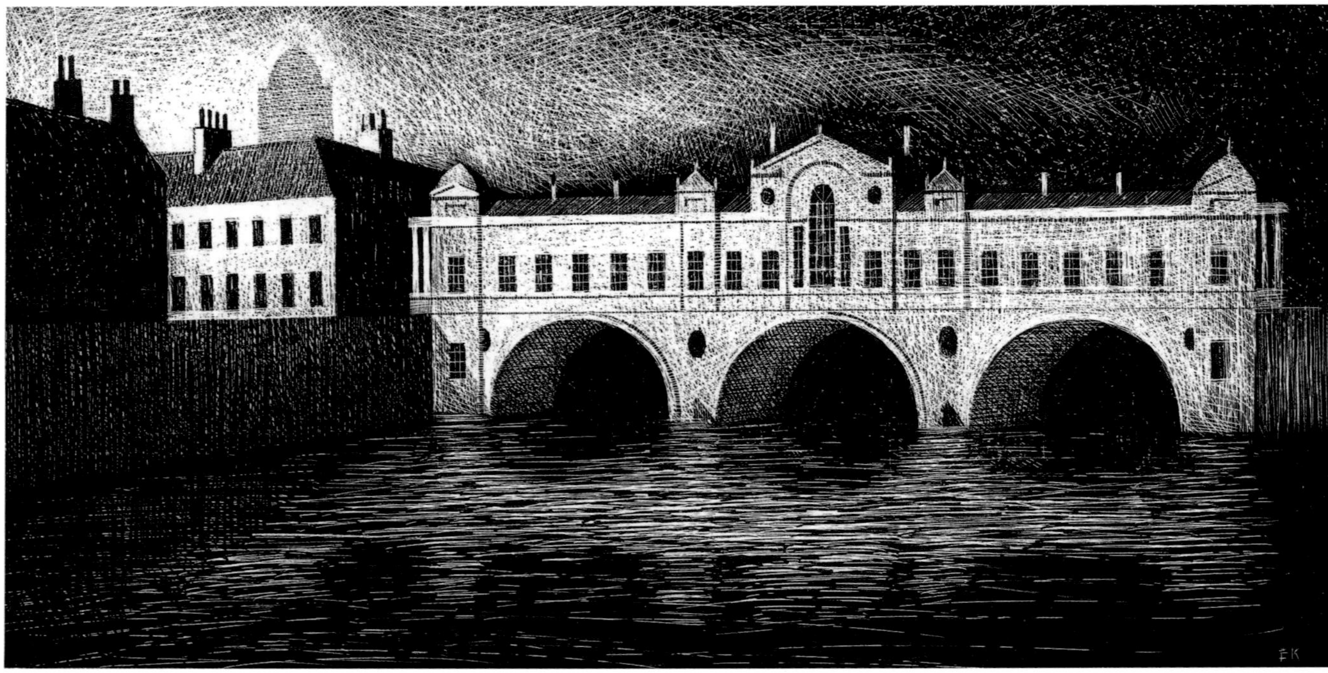

Pulteney Bridge, Bath
Scraperboard
2014

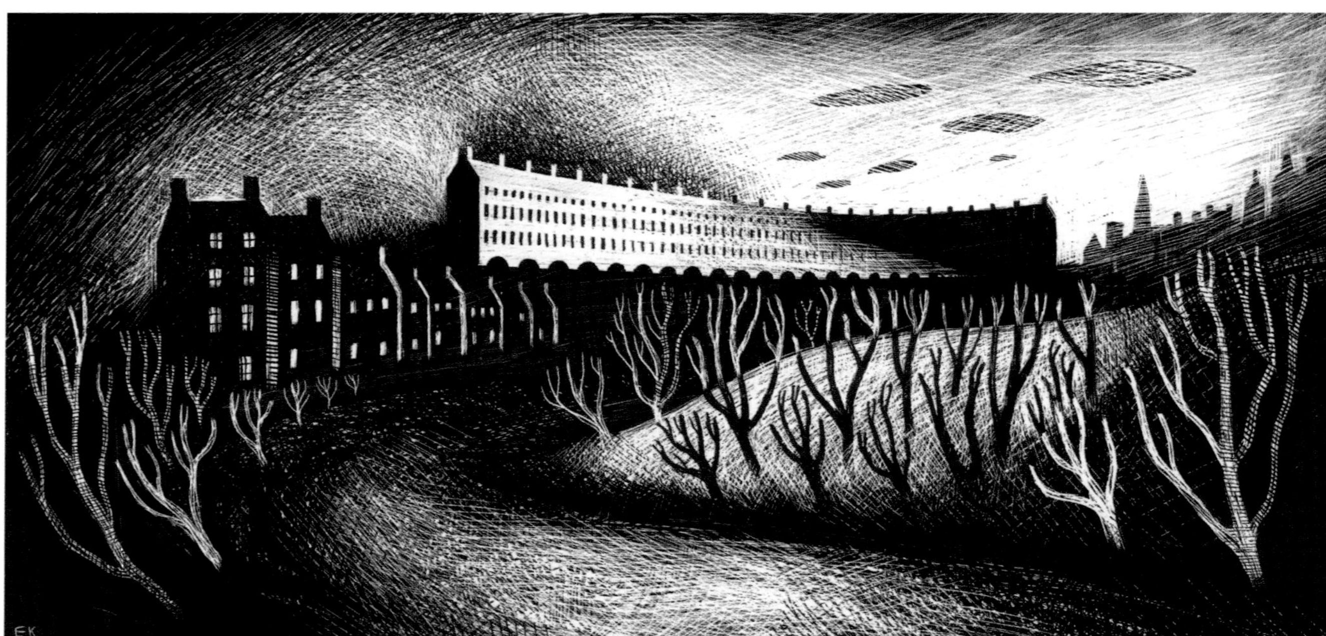

Camden Crescent, Bath
Scraperboard
2014

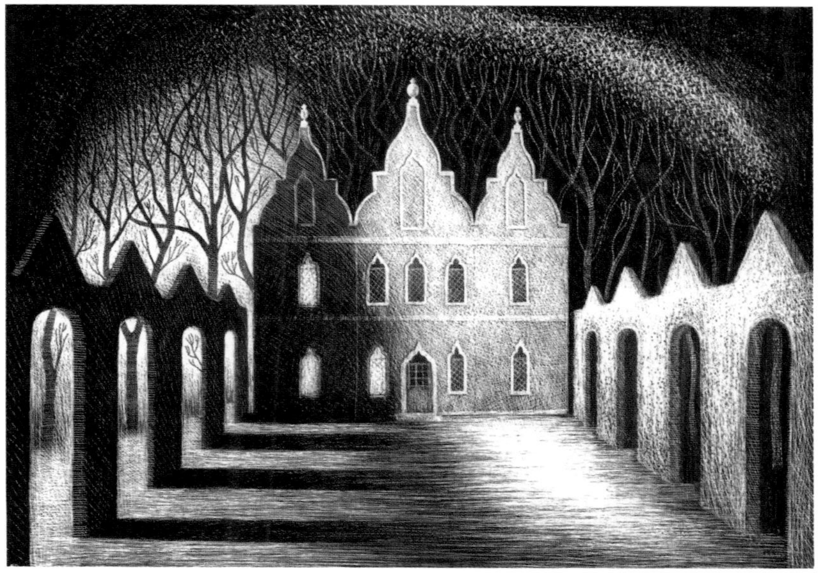

King Henry's Hunting Lodge, Odiham, Hampshire
Scraperboard
2014

Chiswick House
Scraperboard
2014

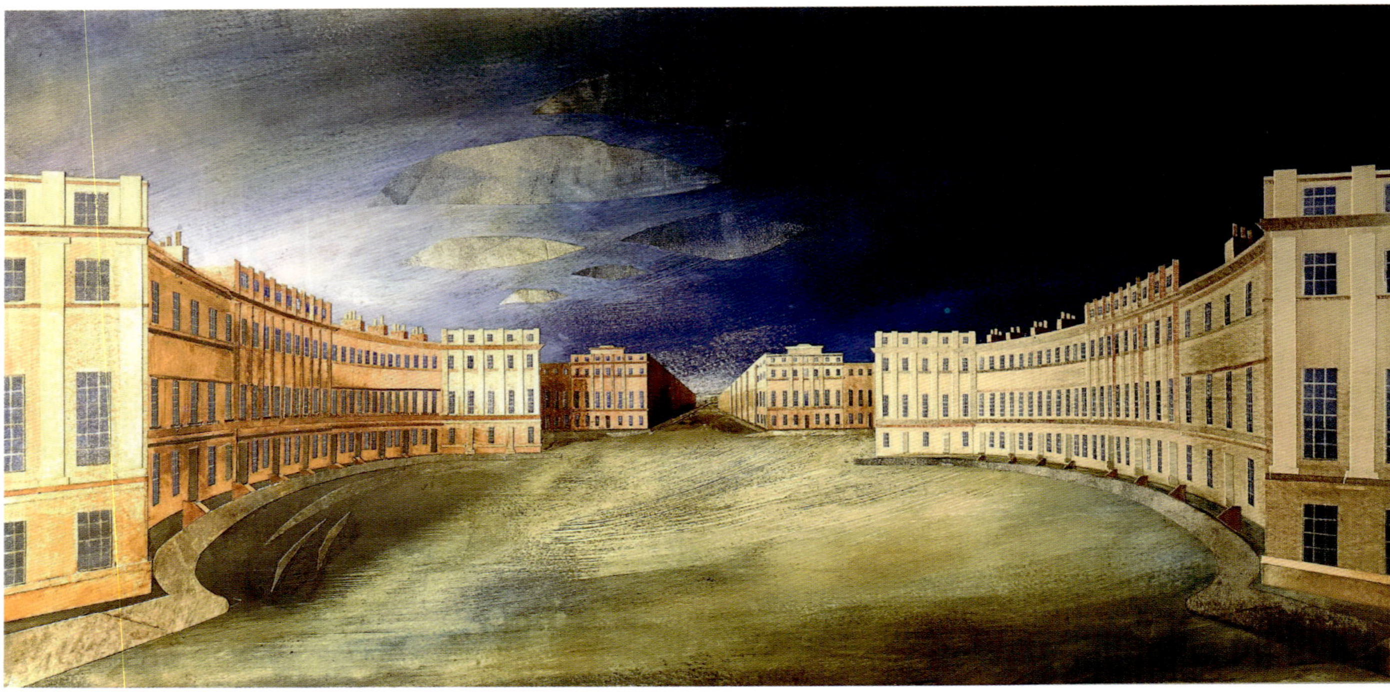

The Royal Circus, Edinburgh
Paper collage and mixed media
2014

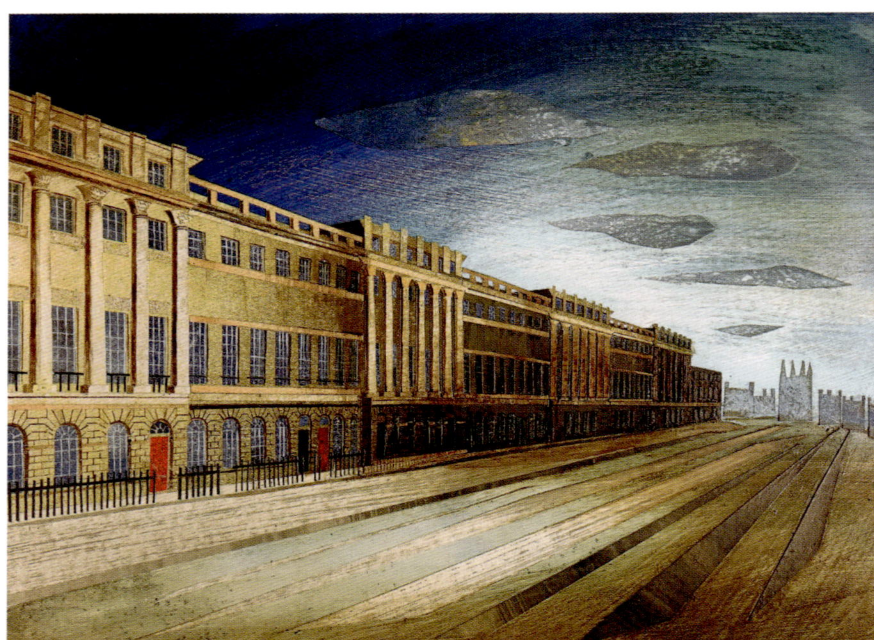

The Royal Terrace, Edinburgh
Paper collage and mixed media
2014

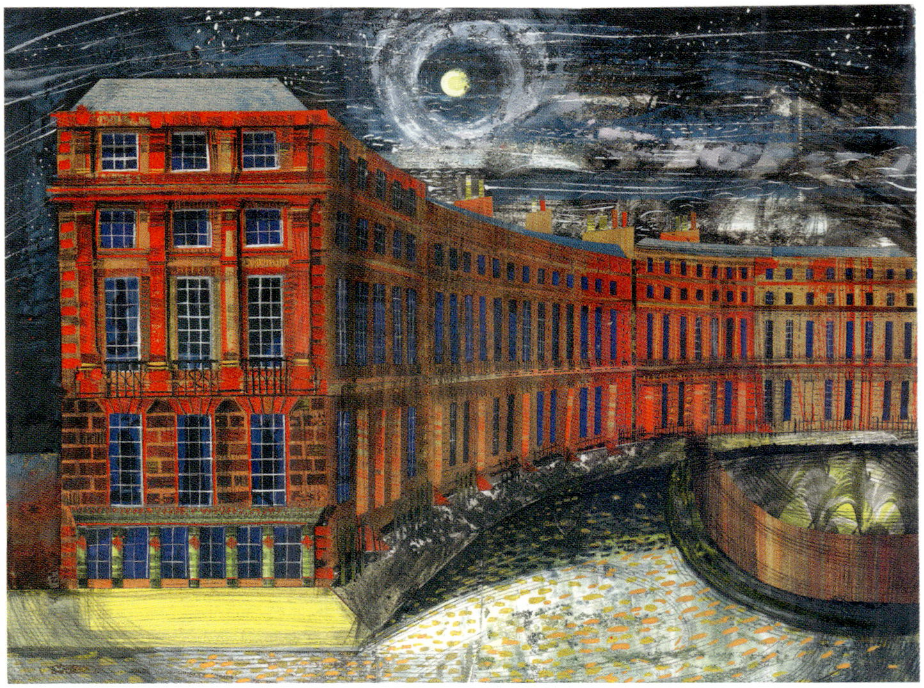

The Royal Circus, Edinburgh
Paper collage and mixed media
2009

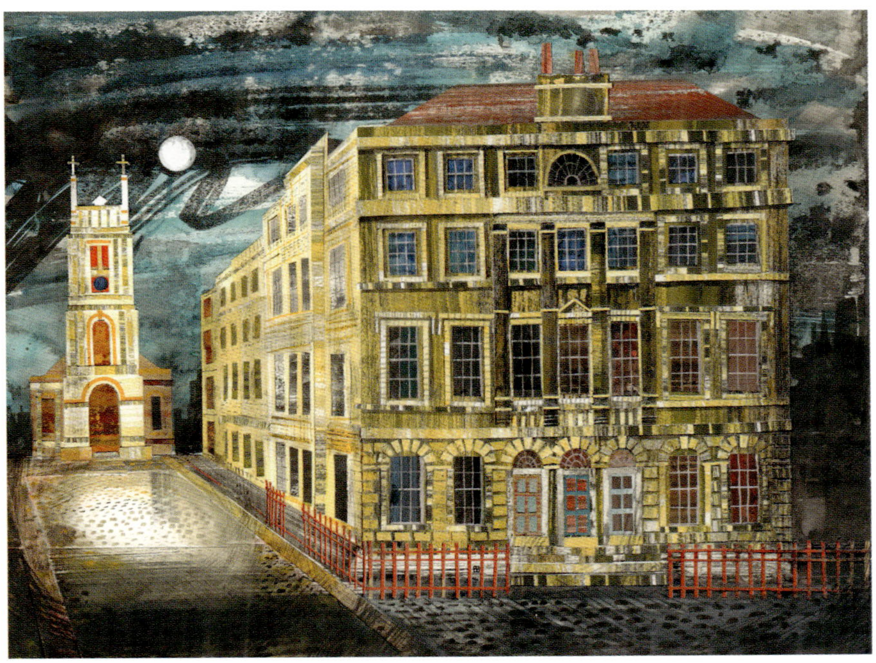

Great King Street, Edinburgh
Paper collage and mixed media
2009

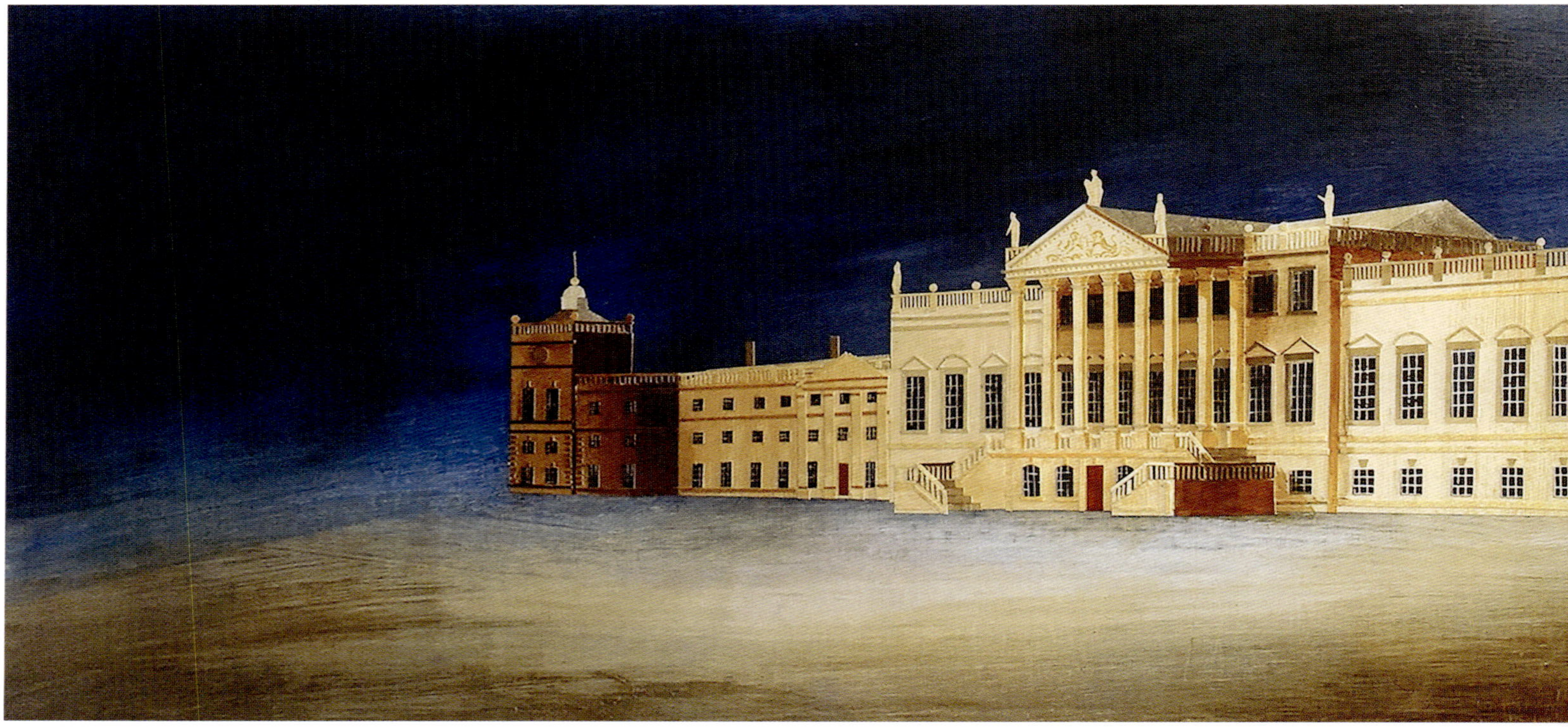

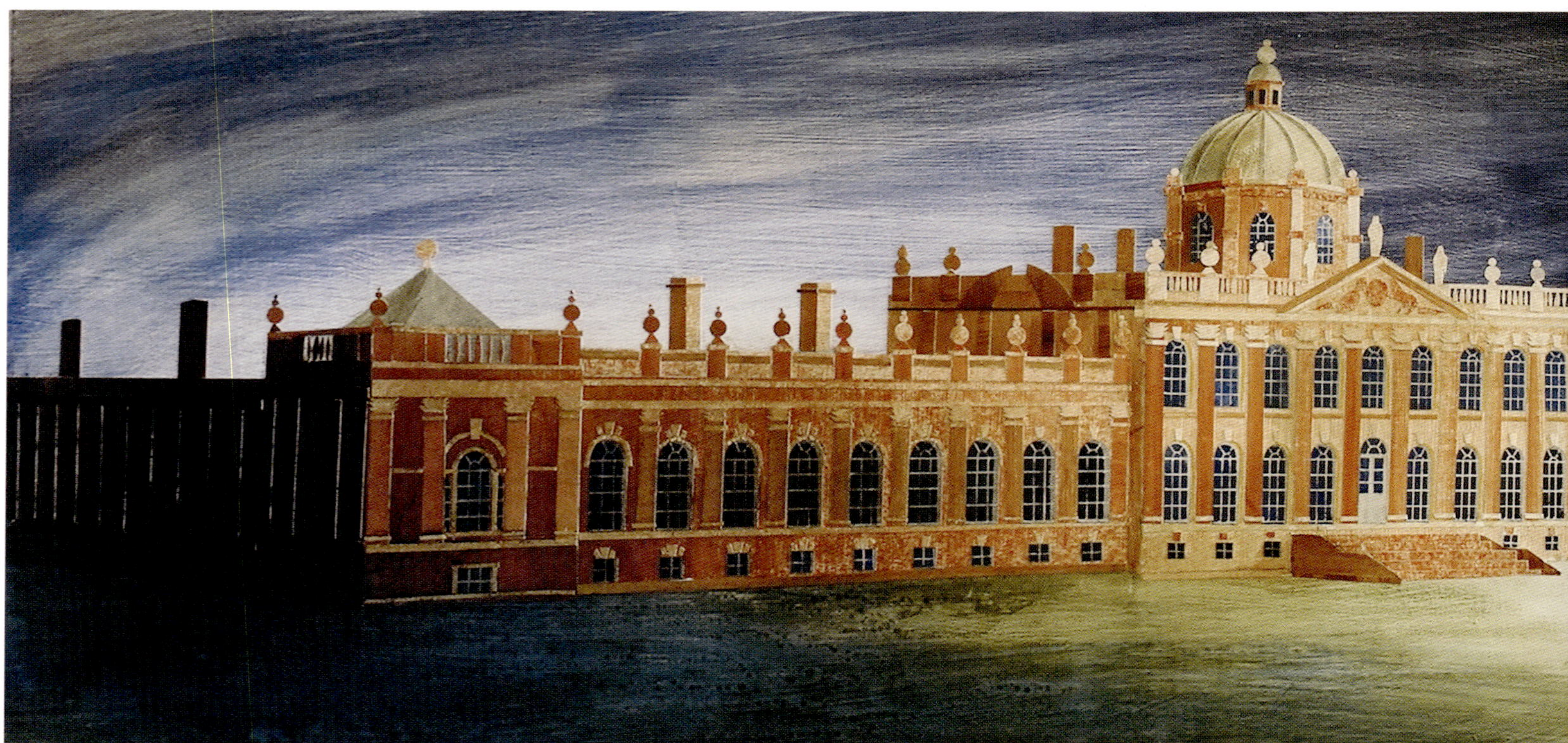

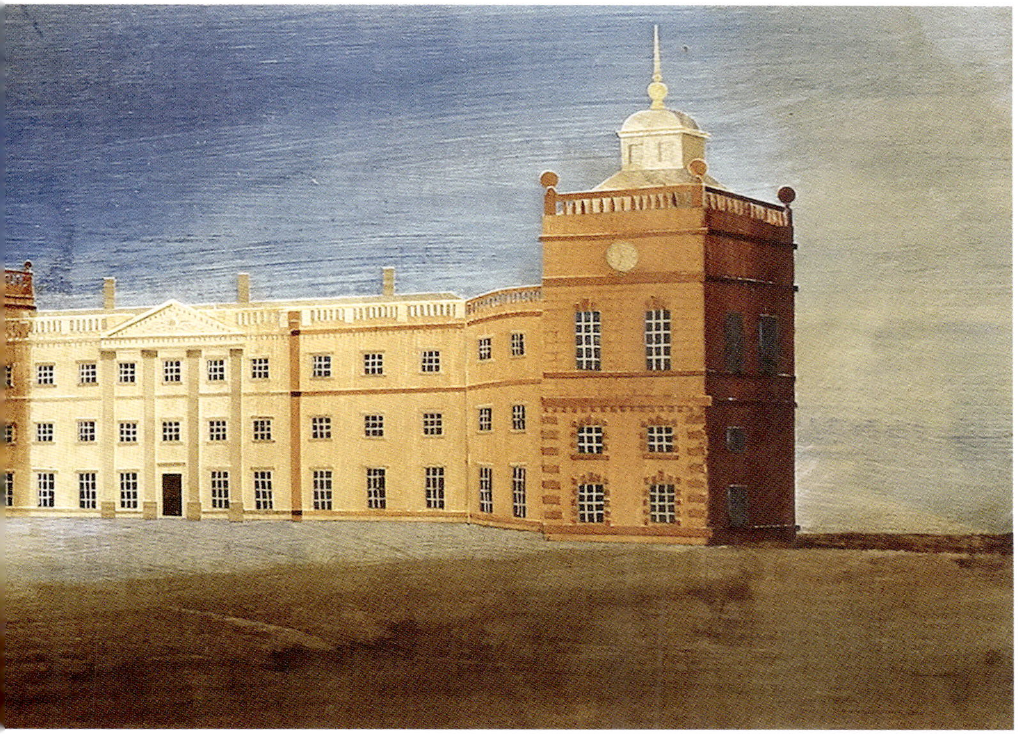

Wentworth Woodhouse,
South Yorkshire
Paper collage and mixed media
2015

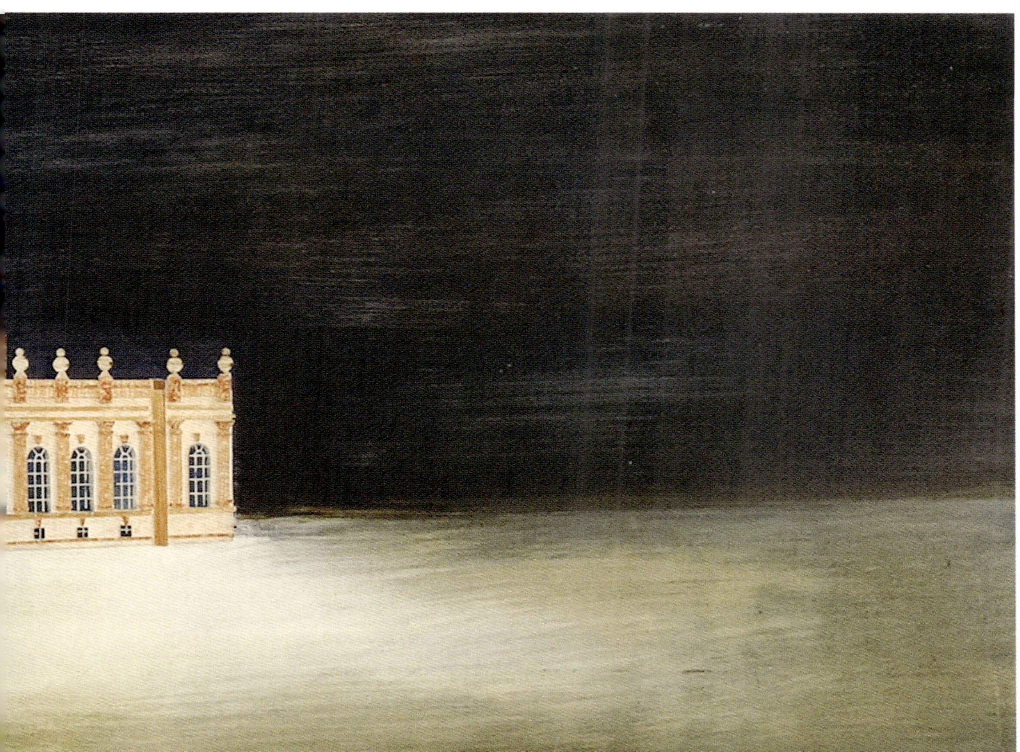

Castle Howard,
North Yorkshire
Paper collage and mixed media
2015

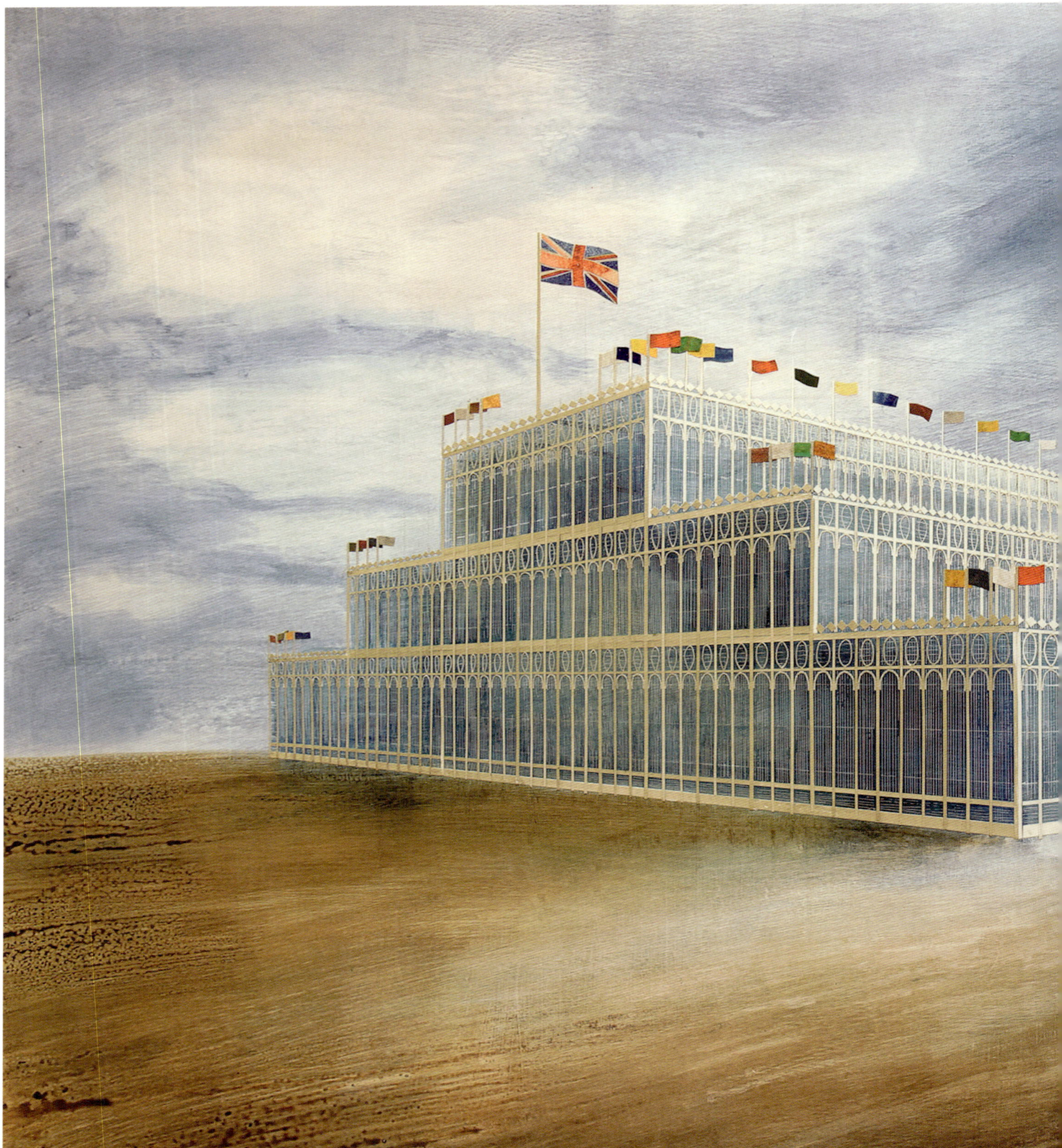

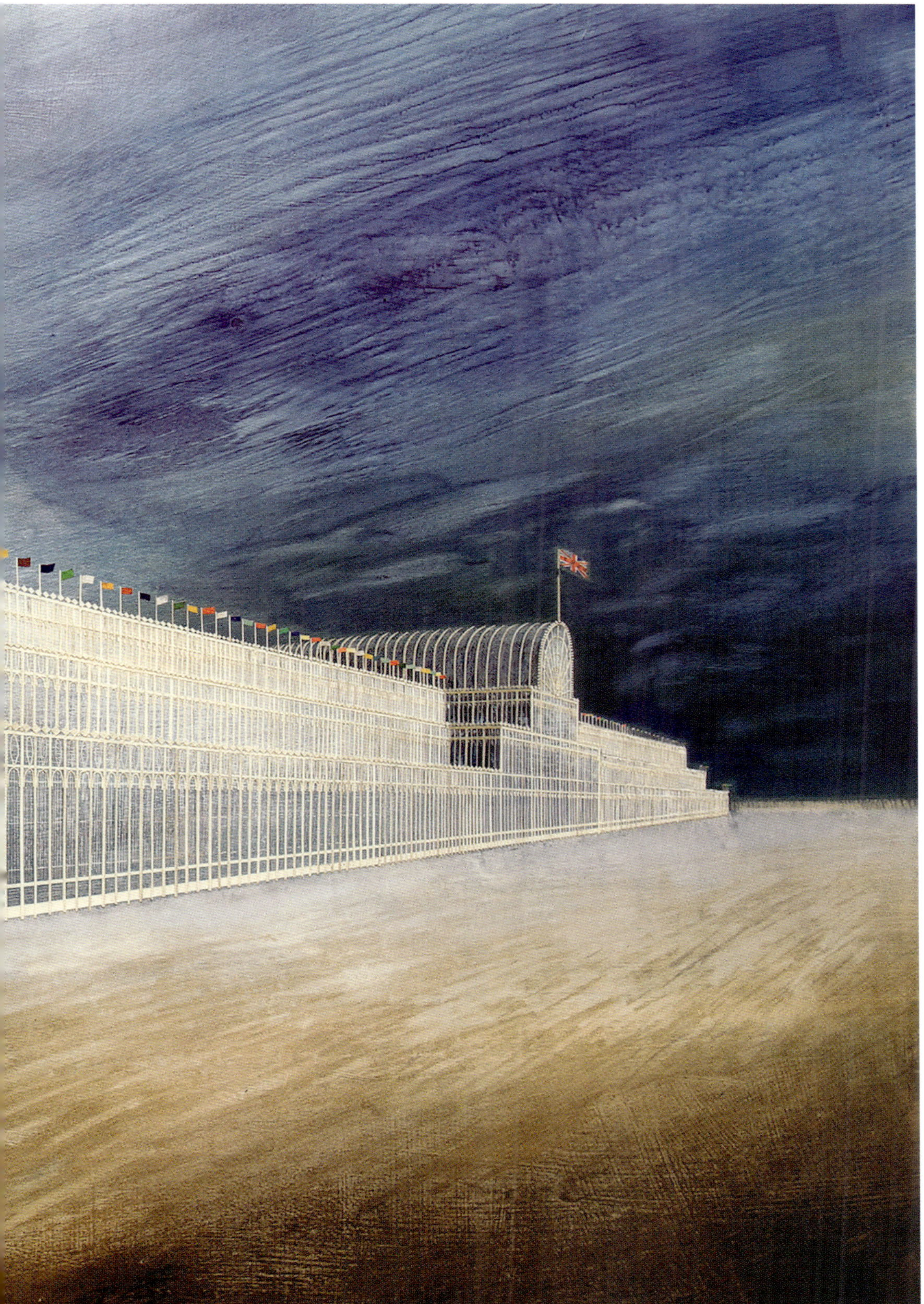

The Crystal Palace,
Hyde Park, 1851
Paper collage and mixed media
2015

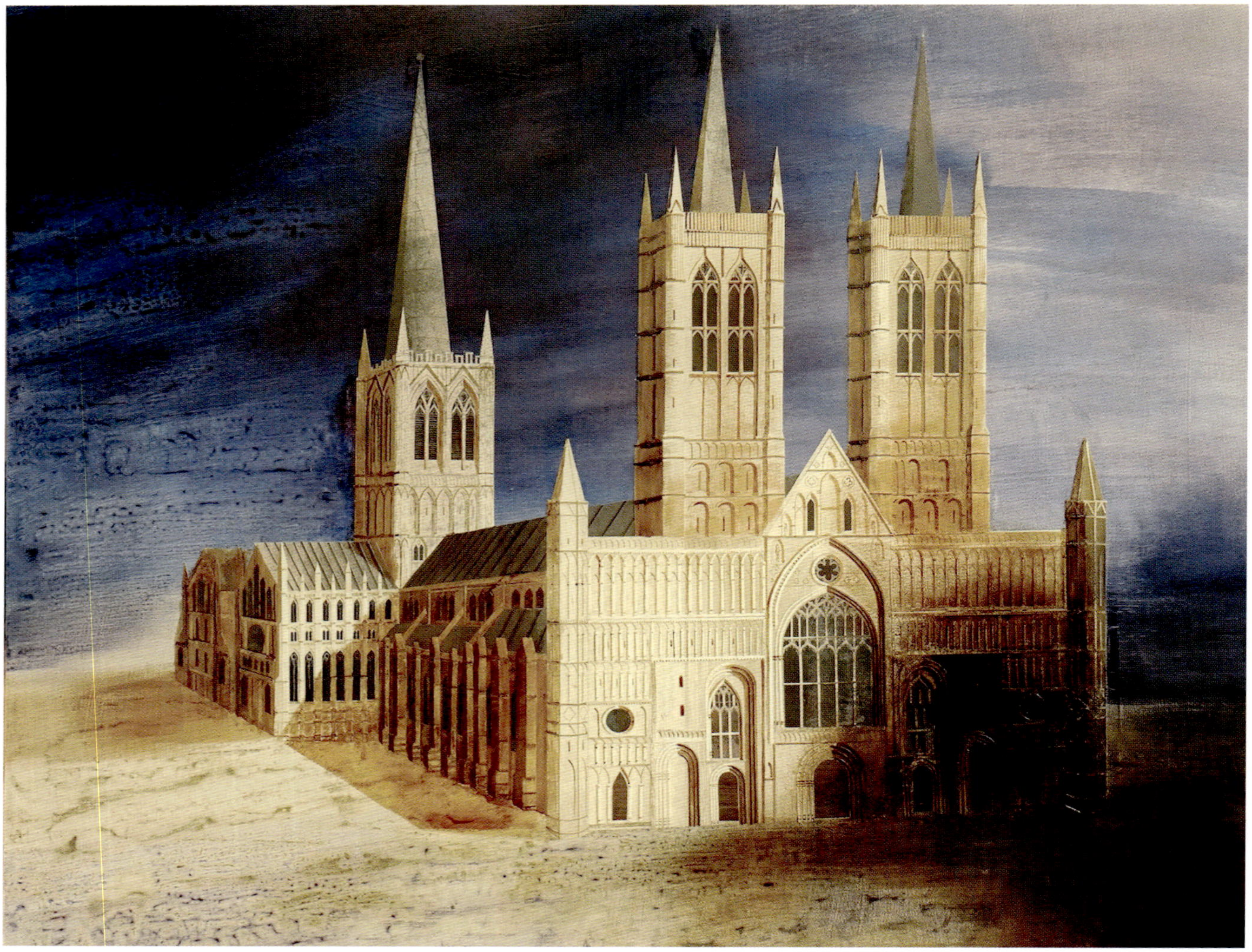

Lincoln Cathedral, *c.* 1500
Paper collage and mixed media
2015

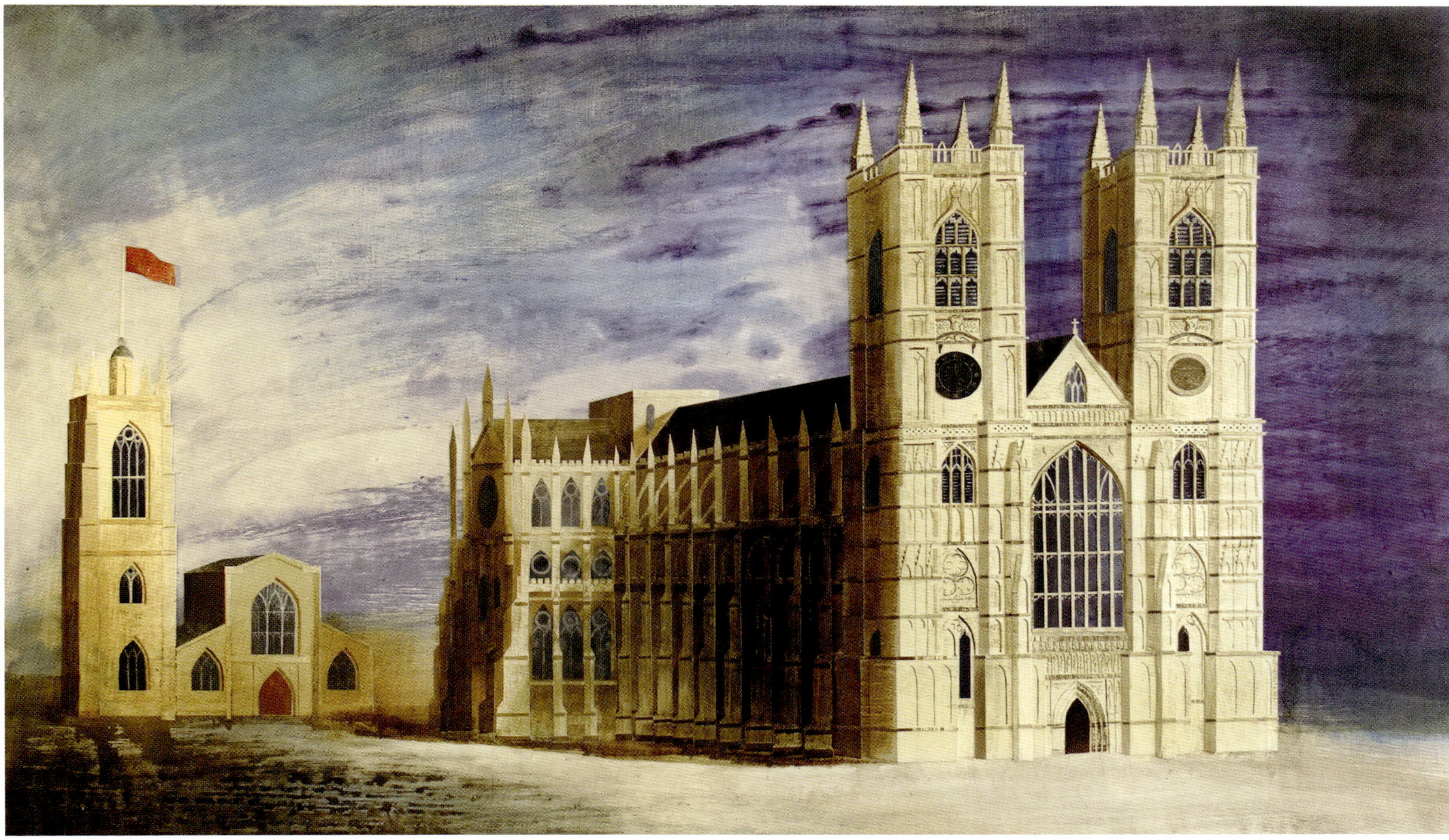

Westminster Abbey
Paper collage and mixed media
2015

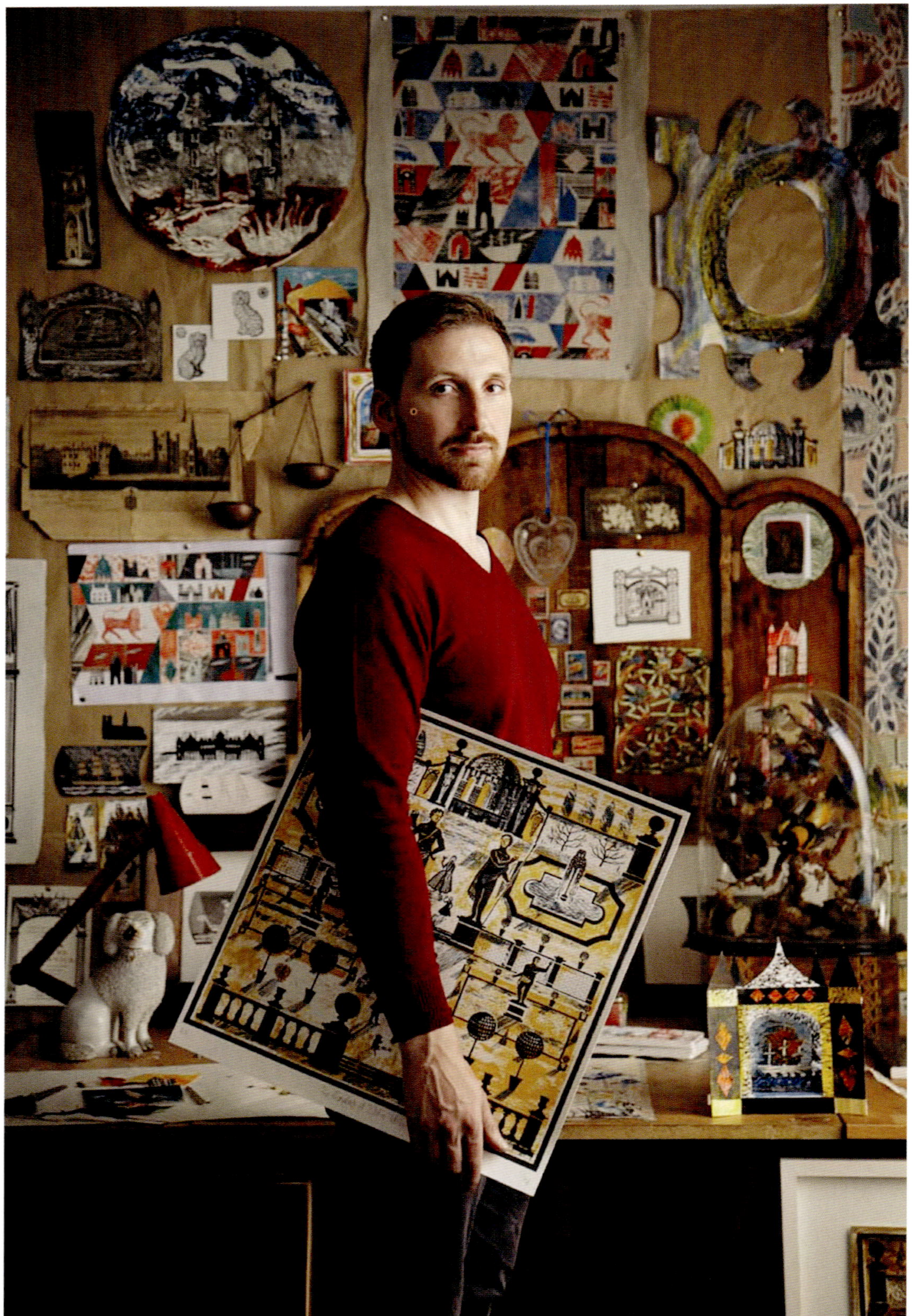

The Lost House Revisited

Ed Kluz

Ed Kluz in his East Sussex studio.

Shortly after 4 pm on 29 April 2015, reports began to surface of a fire at the eighteenth-century mansion Clandon Park in Surrey. Details were scant, but slowly more information trickled into the media. An electrical fault had overwhelmed and ignited a fuse box in the cellars. The spreading flames fanned through the stone vaults and reached hidden cavities within the walls and a modern lift shaft. The fire moved vertically through the house into the wide span of the open attics. While the upper rooms and their contents fed the gathering inferno, a panicked emptying of the floors took place below. Paintings were sliced from their frames, furniture and fragile pieces hurriedly grabbed and passed in relay through the windows; a desperate and brutal act of salvage in the face of imminent loss. Objects that had witnessed almost three hundred years of life within the house lay disinterred on the lawns. The fire was unforgiving, raging through the night. It seemed inevitable that by the next day only the bare brick walls would survive.

I went to Clandon the day after the fire. The National Trust had granted me access to record the extraordinary sight of the smouldering ruin. The site was busy with activity, yet a melancholy hush had fallen. I walked around the perimeter of the house, picking up chunks of charcoal scattered across the lawns. I used these to make drawings. As I looked at

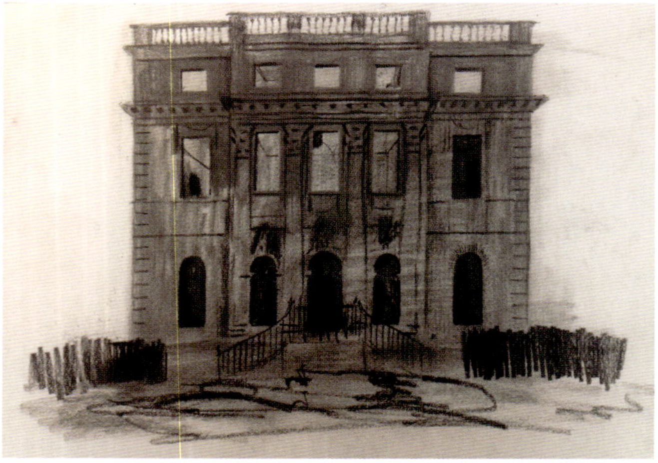

the scorched shell of the building, my eyes began to settle on the newly created spaces within. Fireplaces stood stranded several storeys up on walls picked clean by the flames. Openings framed bizarre vignettes: the great fire-nibbled State Bed of 1710 still in position among fallen beams; singed red plush curtains in glassless windows moving gently in the breeze. Fragments of the once white, celestial interior of the celebrated Marble Hall clung to the walls in defiance – shattered Corinthian columns, intricate plasterwork cracked by the heat, a statue of Venus high up in a niche peering tentatively from her perch. It was as though Clandon, in its ruinous state, imitated the very buildings of classical antiquity that had inspired its architecture. The slow-cooked atmosphere of three hundred years that once infused its rooms had dissipated. It seemed as if the house had been lost. By a miraculous twist of fate, however, one room remained almost entirely untouched by the flames: the Speakers' Parlour, albeit water-damaged, still retained its fragile rococo plaster ceiling and delicate silk wall coverings. It was a tantalizing and surreal fragment among total ruin.

Above, below and opposite: Clandon Park, Surrey, *charcoal on paper, 2015.*

The sight of a charred country house in the wake of fire was, I thought, a thing of the past. In the course of my research I had studied countless early photographs of eerily similar scenes: the minarets of Aqualate Hall in silhouette against the glow of the blaze in 1910; Mells

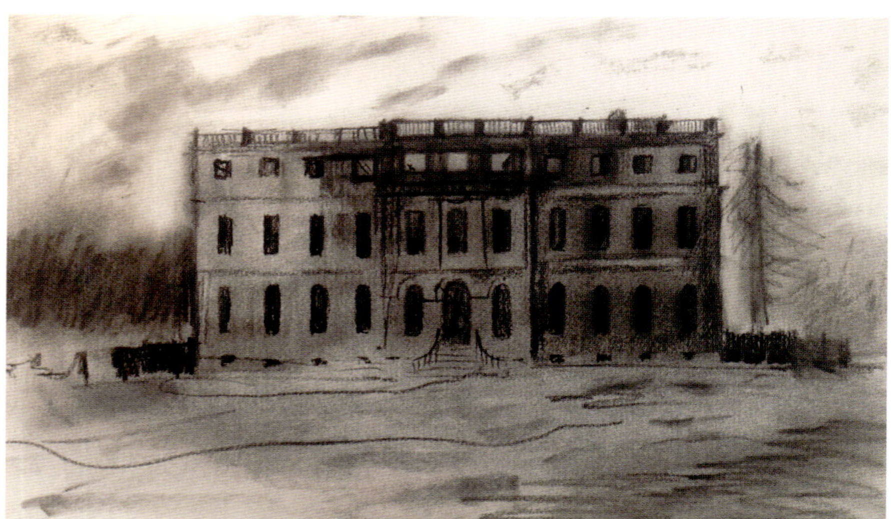

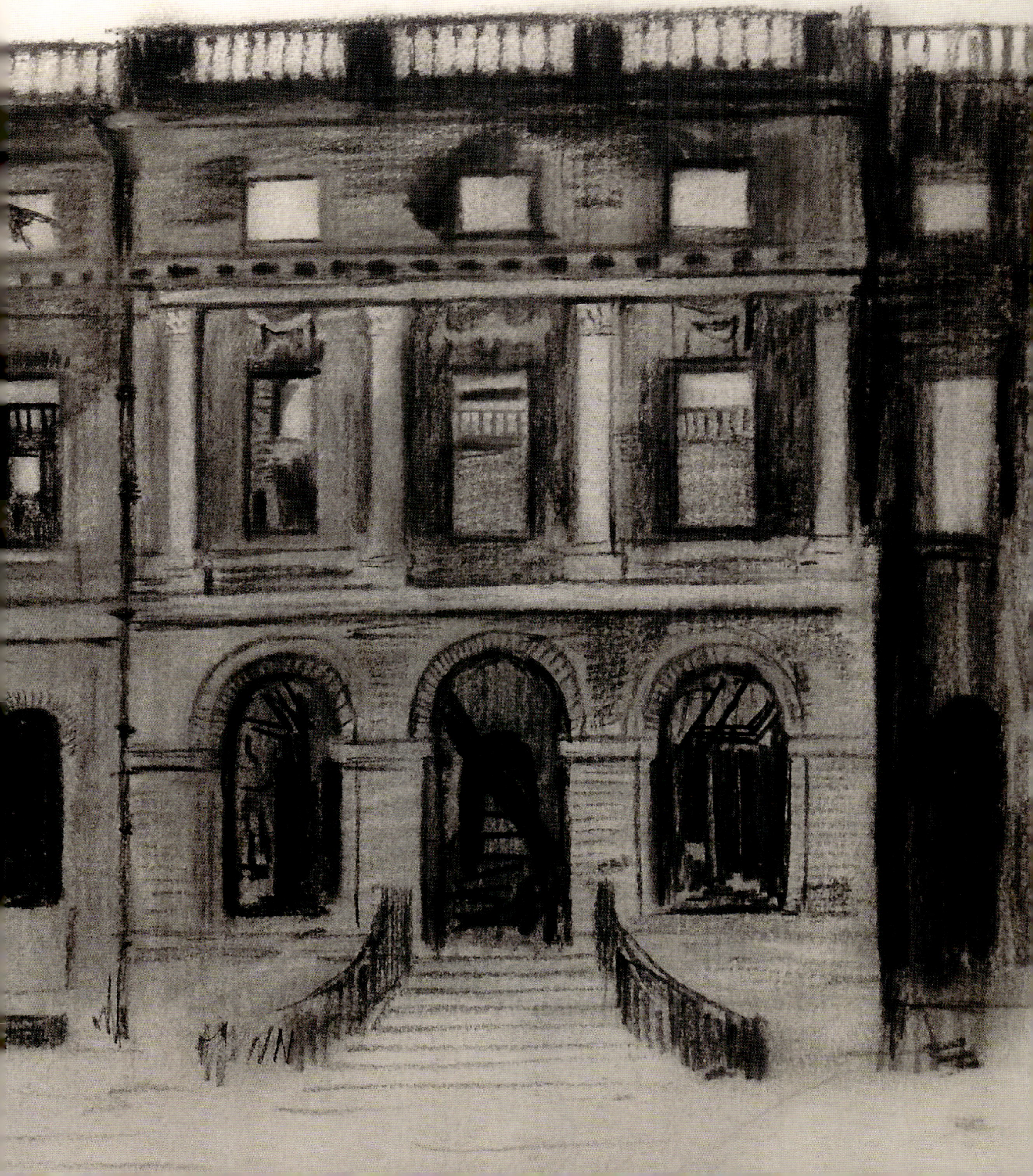

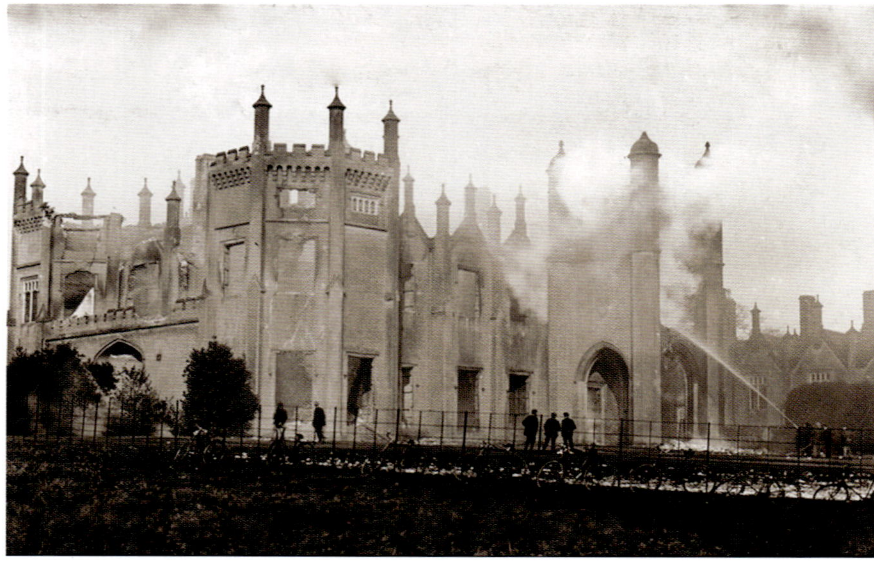

The fire at Aqualate Hall, Staffordshire, 1910.

Park standing gutted and gaunt in 1917; and the uncannily almost premonitory image of the burnt-out central marble hall of Oulton Hall in 1926. I knew of a few rare recent examples that had joined the roll call of burnt houses: Uppark House (West Sussex, 1989), Tangley House (Hampshire, 2000), Liscard Hall (Merseyside, 2008), Northfield Manor House (Birmingham, 2014) and, most recently, Parnham House (Dorset, 2017). To see the aftermath of the destruction at Clandon for myself was at once terrifying and enthralling. Fire and demolition are both spectacles that transfix; like a form of theatre, they are acts that can elicit reflection and contemplation. The unexpected cutting-short of the life of a building is a stark reminder that death and slow decay come to things both living and inanimate.

In many ways, the form and functions of a house echo those of the human body. Arterial corridors and staircases connect rooms; windows and doors look out on to the world; life-sustaining and warming hearths topped by chimneys respire; kitchens provide and distribute nourishment; picture galleries, gardens and chapels house the spiritual and creative needs. Houses are also material projections of the personalities and aspirations of their creators. They are theatrical displays of architecture that reflect the discernment and enlightenment of the owners, and stand as a physical monument to their lifetime's achievements. Fashionable styles of the period shape their outward and inner appearance. Towers, porticos, pediments and halls raised in a classical, Gothic or exotic style tap into the architectural language of the past. As old generations die out or new owners take possession, a house will evolve and morph with changes in taste and the swell or loss of fortunes. New wings will be raised, others torn down; interiors will be ripped out and remodelled, old façades re-clad. As the building ages, time-worn idiosyncrasies slowly become part of its character: woodwork warps, brick cracks, stone weathers, paint and gold leaf become dull and faded. There are also the more transient acts of living that seep into the fabric – smells, voices, music, events happy and sad. Layer upon layer, a house acquires its own unique history. It becomes a palimpsest in which relics, vestiges of times gone, and the almost imperceptible acts of lives lived, co-exist. They are rich spaces that connect and surround us with the past. When visiting a historic house, I try, where possible, to switch off the more rational part of my brain and open my senses to the quieter, less immediately tangible qualities of a place. If it is a public place, the end of the day is often the best time, when the last visitors are trailing through the rooms ahead and the usually eager stewards are too tired to recite an endless monologue of facts. At these times the still, melancholy state of a house will often slowly reveal a different character.

Abstract notions of the past are, for me, more resonant than yearnings to re-create, restore or relive. If we were able to travel back to a chosen point in history, how would we react and how would our perceptions be challenged? Would the smells, sounds and sights be familiar or alien? Would it be a comforting or an unnerving experience? The opening line from L.P. Hartley's 1953 novel *The Go-Between* offers something of a possible answer: 'The past is a foreign country: they

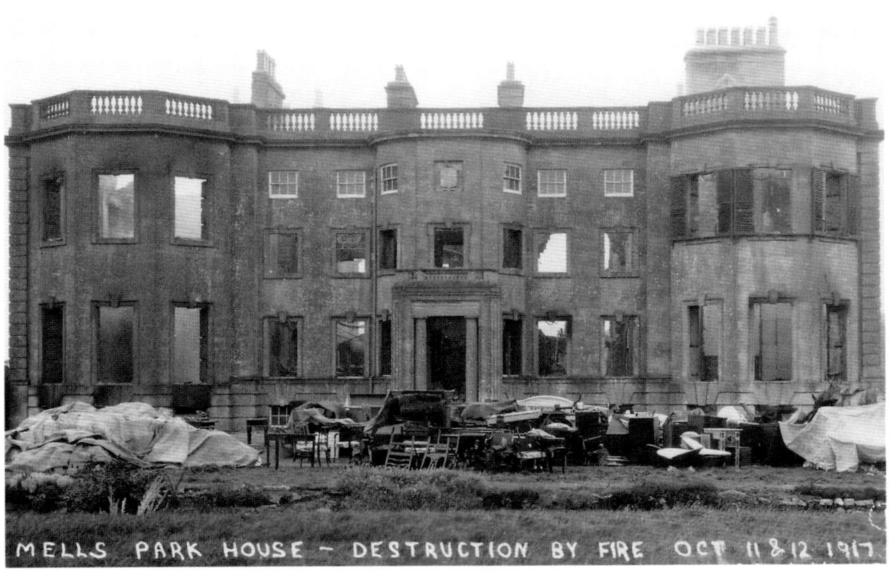

Mells Park, Somerset, after the fire of 1917.

do things differently there.' The sites of lost houses are charged and uncanny places where acts of the past and the reality of the present collide. In their destruction an immaterial presence is created. The allure of the long-gone is a powerful attraction for me, and the unseen sparks my imagination far more than the seen. In this sense, lost houses are far more fascinating than a building that stands complete.

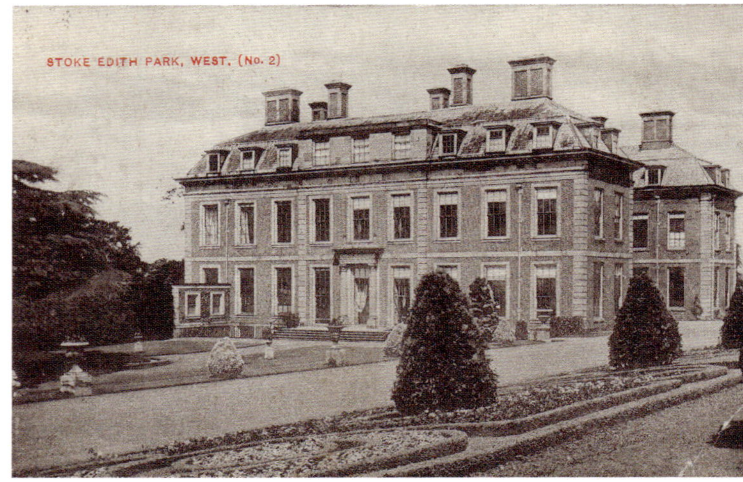

Above: Stoke Edith House, Herefordshire.

Opposite: The Gardens at Stoke Edith, *screenprint, 2012.*

I have visited the sites of many vanished houses, often as unplanned detours while driving along country back roads. A telltale avenue of trees heading off into the distance or the distinctive planting of a stately parkland is usually the first sign that something of interest may be close by. Where a house still exists, a long roofline or large façade usually comes into view and gives up its location. However, on the odd occasion my curiosity is piqued when a building does not materialize. A glance at a map will confirm the absence of a 'big house', but the landscape never fails to point to where one once stood. A derelict gate lodge, a neglected dirt track leading from a farm gate to strange lumps and bumps in the middle of a field, overgrown walled gardens, bits of park wall and fencing in a state of disrepair, maybe even a fine stable building or an eye-catcher; these all once played their part in the setting of a stately house, and often remain long after its demolition.

The fire at Stoke Edith House, 1927.

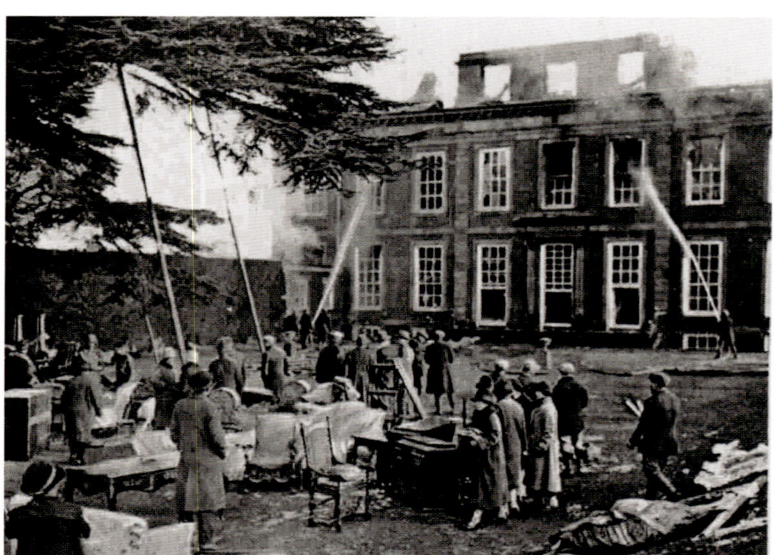

A few years ago, on a trip through Herefordshire one November afternoon, I spotted a sign for Stoke Edith. I had seen pictures in books of the fine late seventeenth-century house set high on a hill among elaborate gardens, and of the sumptuous baroque interiors with celebrated painted walls and ceilings by James Thornhill portraying scenes from classical history. The house

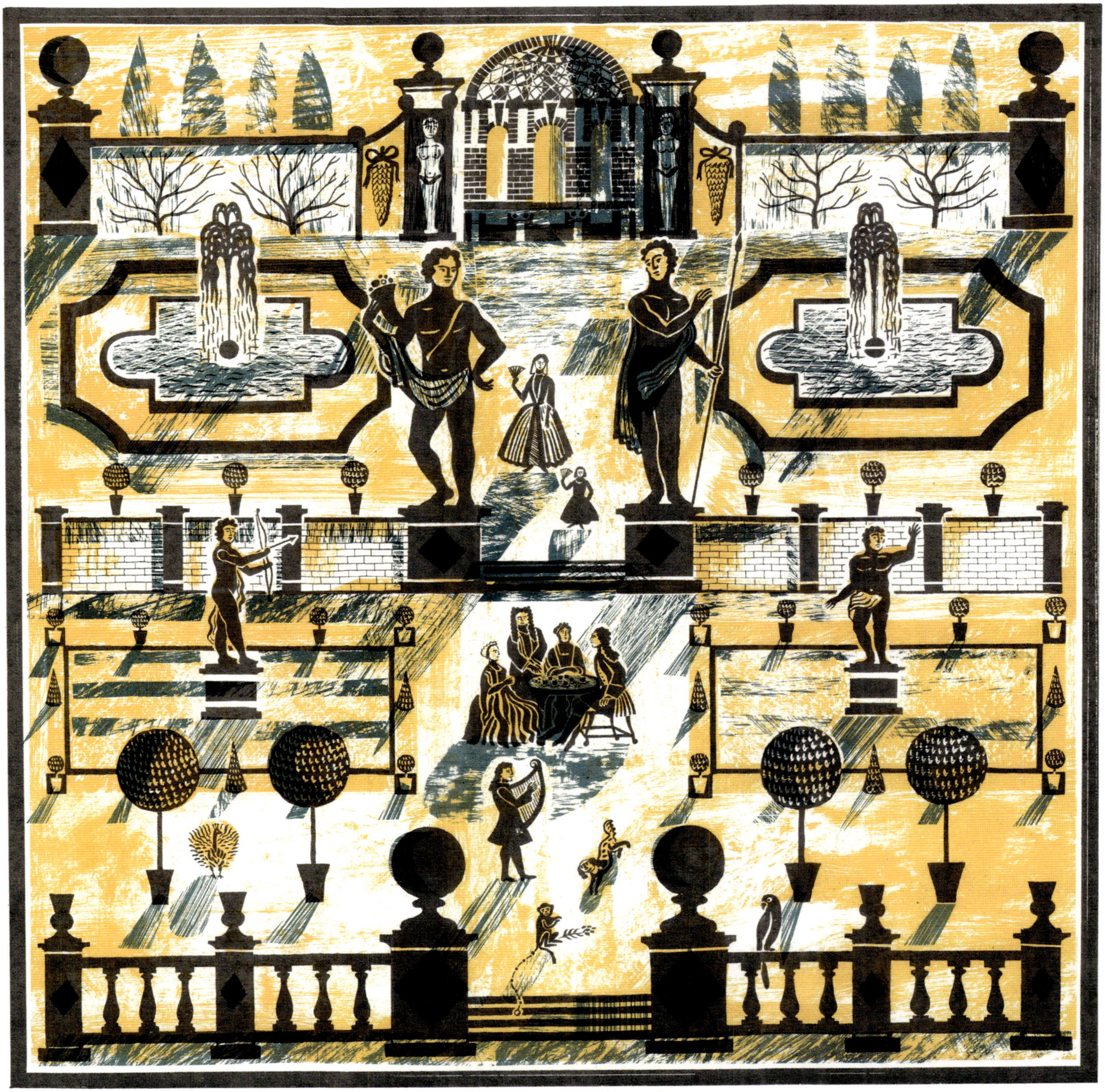

had caught fire on the night of 15 December 1927 – the owners narrowly escaping the flames in their night clothes – and had been left a gutted shell. Newspaper articles at the time featured photographs of scenes similar to those I saw at Clandon, with firemen dousing the smouldering ruin, and piles of furniture scattered on the lawn. Many times I had sat transfixed by the huge eighteenth-century Stoke Edith wall hanging in the British Galleries at the Victoria and Albert Museum, one of a pair rescued from the burning house, depicting the elaborate gardens as they had been in 1710. These extraordinary survivors, which once hung in the Green Velvet Chamber, display peculiarly haunting scenes. In one, a young girl mimics her adult chaperone on a walk through the parterres, a spaniel runs towards a pet monkey, and a harpist serenades a fashionably dressed group taking tea. I had longed to see the site of their former home for some time.

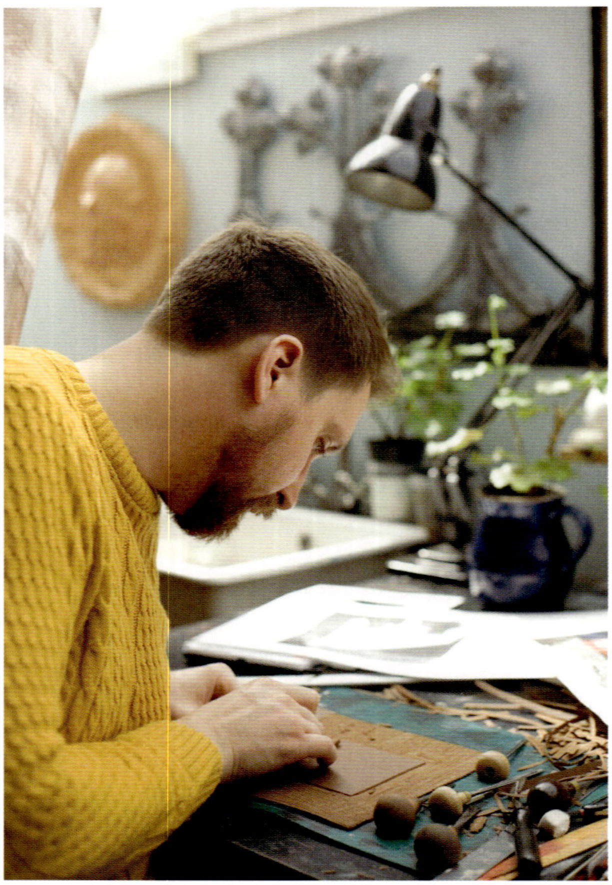

Ed Kluz at work in his studio.

As I drove up the single-track road towards Stoke Edith, a group of buildings with a church at their centre came into view. Aside from its medieval tower, the church had been remodelled in the baroque style, presumably to match the architecture of the main house, which must have stood nearby. As I parked the car I noticed a pair of padlocked, long-disused gates, behind which stretched an overgrown drive heading into dense scrub. I knew that the house must have been somewhere ahead. A gap in a disintegrating, ivy-clad fence at the end of the churchyard provided the point of entry into the grounds. Brambles and young ash trees crowded in from either side. A collapsed roof, a red-brick wall and rotting sash windows emerged behind a tangle of bare trees and shrubs. This had been the stables. An uncanny quietness hung over the site, occasionally punctuated by a bird call and the rustle of unseen movement deep within the clogging, leafless, thorny undergrowth. The sense of abandonment and stillness was alarming. I walked onwards with a little apprehension. Stretches of crumbling walls indicated where kitchen gardens had once been, and here and there lay piles of dressed stone. Eventually a clearing opened up in front of me, with bits of ancient rusting farm machinery unceremoniously dumped at the sides. At this point I noticed that strange walled terraces rose above me on three sides. As my eyes adjusted, I peered deeper into the brambles that cloaked the brickwork. Low, dark openings seemed to head into murky subterranean spaces. I realized that I was now standing at the spot where the house had once stood. The strange terraces were in fact the last remaining fragments of the lower parts of the building, and the uninviting black spaces, the cellars. Had I been at the same spot ninety years previously, a symmetrical double-flight stone staircase would have led up to the front door of a tall, handsome, four-storeyed façade crowned by a fine pediment. Standing before the footprint of the house, I felt a powerful sense of absence in this eerie and forgotten landscape – a feeling of the past within the present. To visit a site and revisit a house in the imagination and sense its scale and form is a creative act in itself. It is a form of longing to be enveloped by the rooms, to witness the light from tall windows fall across floors, to view pristine gardens through rippled glass panes, and to hear the echo of domestic sounds play within the volume of the house. It is not nostalgia that motivates me, but more a wish to sense the past as a performance, as a theatrical and peculiar act.

The creation of this series of collages depicting lost houses is underpinned by the experience of the house site. I will often rely on words rather than sketches to document my impressions. As the series

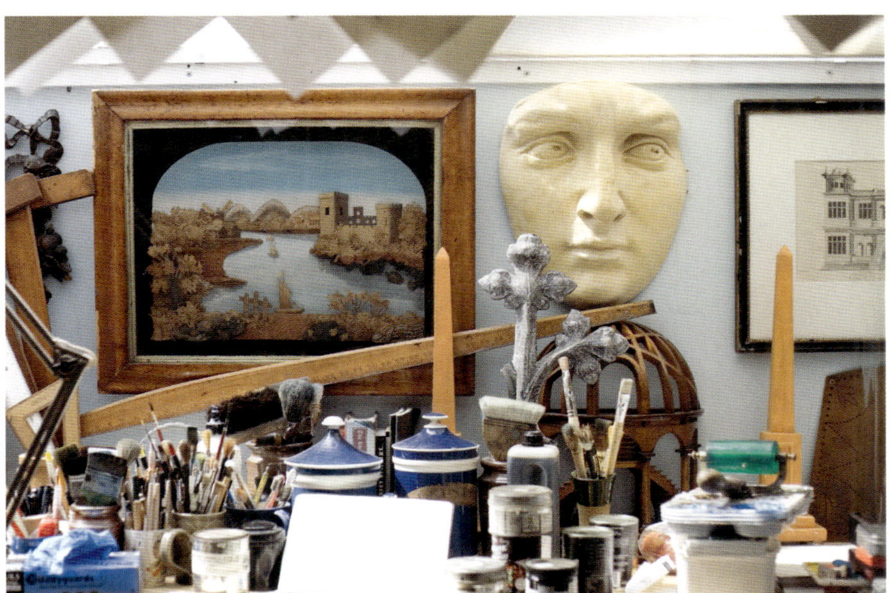

The wall of Kluz's studio.

has evolved, my ideas about memory and the past have become more central than the desire to render an accurate re-creation of the building surrounded by its landscape. I have chosen to show the houses more like ghosts, existing in surreal, dreamlike landscapes illuminated by theatrical lighting. In this way, I am also able to present the buildings as purely architectural ideas. In fact, a lost house is rather like an architect's plan; it is a product of the imagination, without physical form. The composition and scaling of the structures within the pictures are deliberately ambiguous; some could be architects' models, others stage sets. The act of creating a collage is akin to that of model-making, each element meticulously cut from paper and glued one on top of another. Research is also a crucial part of the process, enabling me to flesh out the forms of the buildings. Our libraries and archives hold vast amounts of material, and the possibility of making a new discovery relating to a particular house is always exciting. I will pore over old engravings, drawings, plans and descriptions in order to build a full mental picture. Often a house will have vanished without proper documentation; plenty of houses dating from between the sixteenth and the nineteenth centuries exist almost only in name. The name of an architect is also invaluable in creating a faithful likeness of a house. Their stylistic flare, sense of proportion, decorative taste, architectural massing and material sense can all be distilled from other examples of their work. I will seek out fragments of the buildings themselves where they exist. The demolition of a house dissipates a huge number of architectural relics. Pillars, pediments, plasterwork, staircases, panelling, carved stone, stained glass and fireplaces frequently find reincarnation in other buildings. Aerial photographs will often add more to the story. Parch marks in dry grass will reveal wall lines and garden features, as in the case of the spectre of a baroque parterre that appears in the playing fields of the North London Collegiate School during hot weather, marking the site of the famed Canons House. Where possible, I collect engravings, drawings, paintings and photographs; unexpected treasures have turned up in the least likely of places. Some years ago on a popular internet auction site I found a rare engraved ticket to the auction viewing in 1823 of Fonthill Abbey and its contents, and junk shops and car boot sales regularly present finds. Similarly, the individuals who created these great country houses also collected objects and fragments of the past. They, too, were fascinated by notions of the monumental in ruin or the fallibility of their predecessors. It is almost the ultimate irony that many of their names and houses are now also confined to memory, and the fragments of their existence now likewise collected by modern-day antiquaries.

It is virtually impossible for houses to disappear entirely, as their names and the memories associated with them persist in writing, print and folklore. Artists, writers and musicians have always contemplated and responded to the more destructive moments of history. It is possible that the products of their creativity can persist longer than stones and mortar, and therefore become valuable and powerful conduits to the past. We are ghoulishly fascinated by ruination and things passing out of existence, time and memory. The scorched ruin of Clandon was one of the most horrifying and yet thrilling sights I have witnessed. To see a house rapidly slip out of existence as it is destroyed by fire, blown up by dynamite or smashed by a wrecking ball is to observe perhaps the most perfect end to an extraordinary life – almost as if a curtain falls on a centuries-long performance. Throughout the creation of this 'Lost House' series the words of Prospero in act 4, scene 1 of *The Tempest* have been pinned on the wall of my studio. In many ways, they express the notions behind this book far more succinctly than I am able:

The cloud-capped towers, the gorgeous palaces,
The solemn temples, the great globe itself –
Yea, all which it inherit – shall dissolve,
And like this insubstantial pageant faded,
Leave not a rack behind.

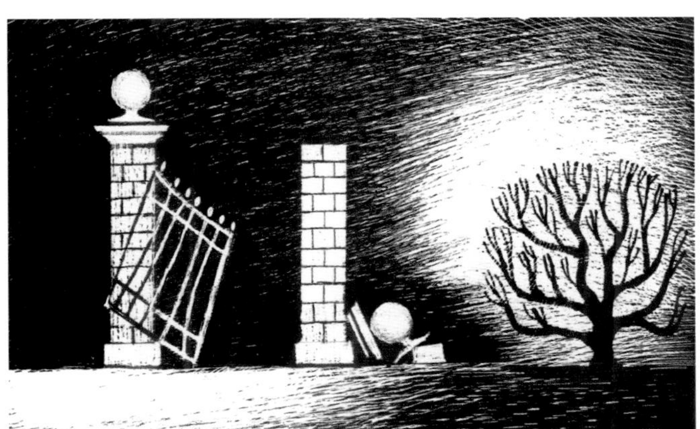

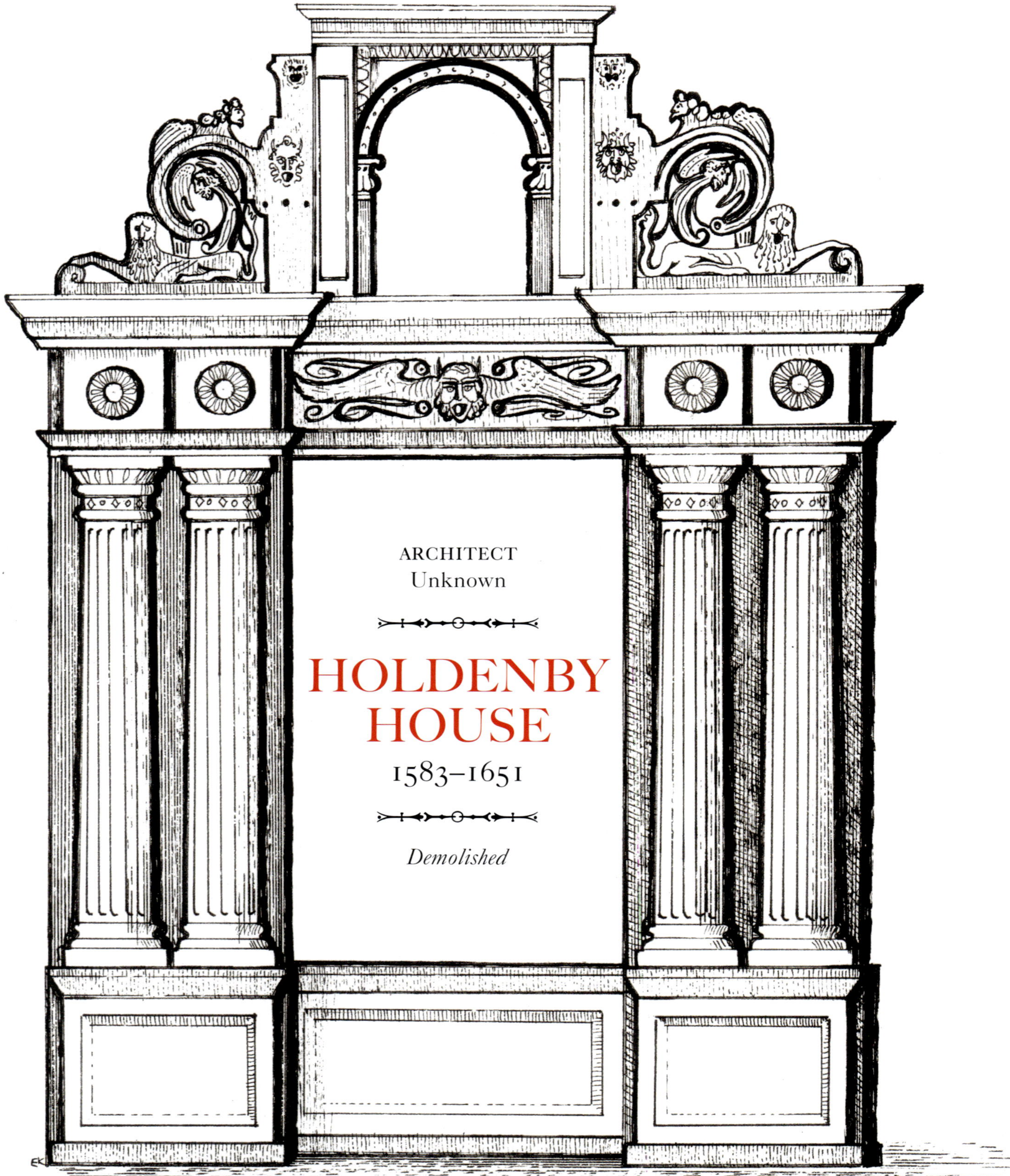

ARCHITECT
Unknown

HOLDENBY HOUSE

1583–1651

Demolished

So definitive was the sight of Sir Christopher Hatton's glittering house that it gave rise to a Northamptonshire proverb: 'It shines like Holdenby.'[1] Completed in 1583, it was not only unique for its extensive glazing, but also claimed the prize for the largest house in England. Although Holdenby was intended as a 'shrine' to accommodate Hatton's 'holy saint',[2] Queen Elizabeth I, she never visited, and it was not until her favourite and she were both dead that it was finally used as a palace – and a royal prison.

Hatton (1540–1591) came to Elizabeth's attention owing to his dancing prowess; thereafter, his rise depended on his aptitude as well as her favour. In 1577 he became Vice Chamberlain and was knighted. A decade later, until his death in 1591, he was Lord Chancellor. No building accounts or papers survive to reveal when construction started at Holdenby (a manor Hatton's family had held since at least the thirteenth century), but it was certainly underway in 1578 and substantially finished by 1579, when Lord Burghley, Elizabeth's chief adviser, visited. The date of 1583 on the surviving forecourt arches suggests the year of its completion; work on the extensive gardens continued until 1587.

The identity of the architect is also unknown. Although surviving drawings by John Thorpe point to his involvement, they are, in fact, records made after the completion of the house. In a letter to Lord Burghley, Hatton self-deprecatingly requested 'your opinion to the Surveyor of such lacks and faults as shall appear to you in this rude building'.[3] Who this surveyor was remains a mystery.

Opposite: Edward Blore, Remains of the Palace at Holdenby, *engraving, 1845.*

Pages 56–57: Samuel and Nathaniel Buck, The South View of Holdenby Palace, in the County of Northampton, *engraving, 1729.*

Holdenby comprised two courtyards with towers at each corner and at each end of the cross-range. The main approach was through a gatehouse into a forecourt with elaborate archways to either side. Inside the first court, the focus was the central tower of the classical orders positioned midway along the cross-range and flanked by an arcade. The most innovative feature was the south front: a 350-foot (107-m) length of glinting windows that gave a novel effect both inside and out. Holdenby was lavishly praised by all its visitors. Burghley lauded its 'great magnificence', the 'stately ascent' from the hall to the great chamber, and the 'lightsomeness' of the rooms.[4] Sir Thomas Heneage averred it was 'the best house that hath been built in this age', and John Norden praised it as 'erected with such uniformity … as … not to be matched in this land'.[5]

After the death of Hatton, Holdenby passed successively to two of his descendants before James I bought it in 1607. It became a royal retreat – as well as a place of imprisonment for Charles I in 1646–47. In 1651 it was seized by Parliament and sold to Adam Baynes, MP for Leeds, who demolished the house and sold off the materials. He retained the offices, which he turned into a small hall for himself, and the forecourt arches, one of which he inscribed with the date 1659. A portion of façade endured, as did one of the distinctive obelisks that had stood in the hall in place of a screen. To John Evelyn in 1675 these remnants looked 'like a Roman ruin',[6] and in the early eighteenth century James Thornhill, William Stukeley and the Buck brothers all drew the remaining fragments.

After the Restoration, the Crown sold the estate and Baynes's residence became a farmhouse. During the mid-1870s and again in the 1880s it was extended, on the latter occasion by R.H. Carpenter and William Slater, who incorporated salvaged elements, including the original chimneys. Elizabethan Holdenby has disappeared, but its fascination endures, perhaps because, as Thomas Fuller observed, Holdenby's fate is our own, 'being the Embleme of human happiness, both in the beauty and brittleness, short flourishing, and soon fading thereof'.[7]

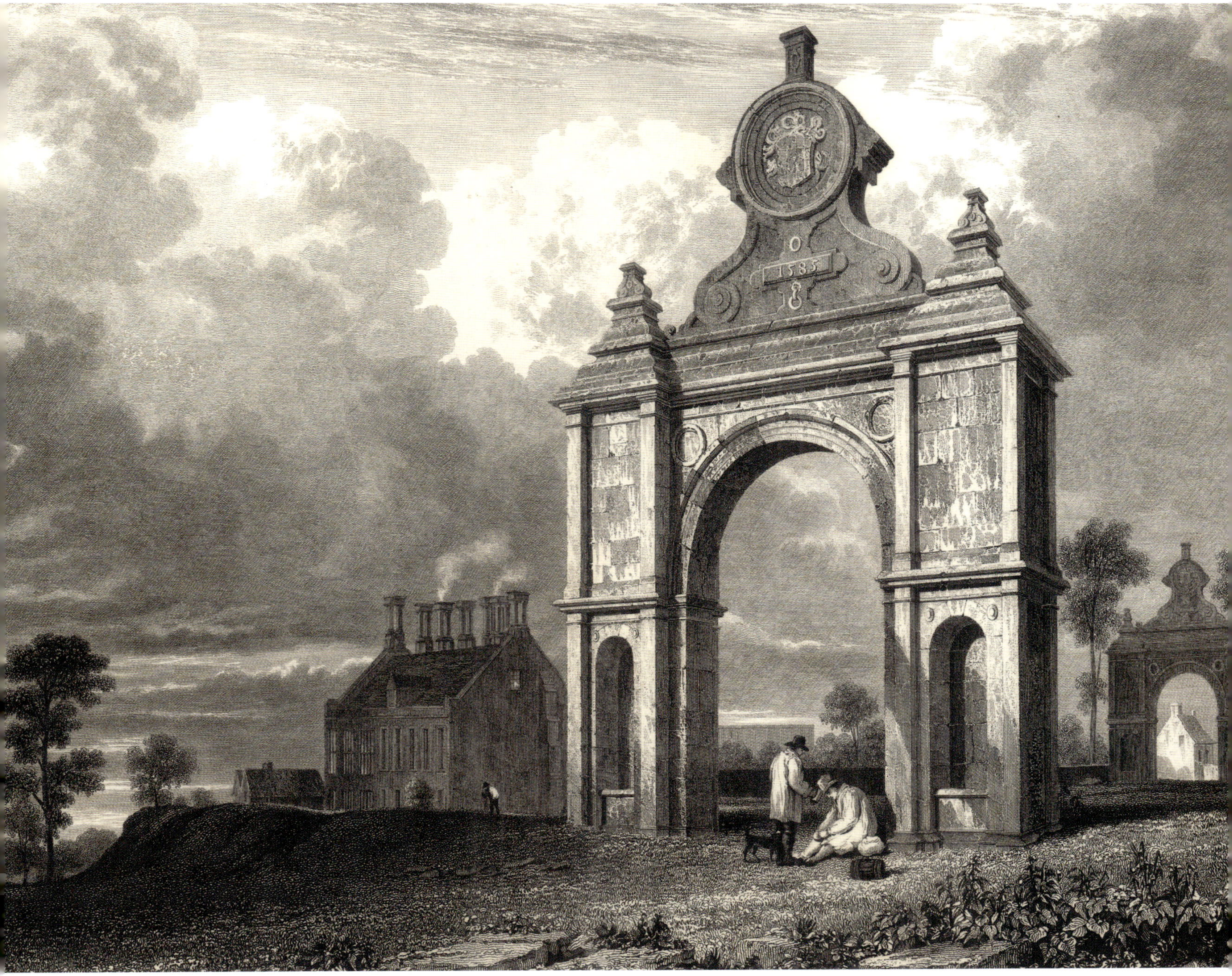

HOLDENBY HOUSE

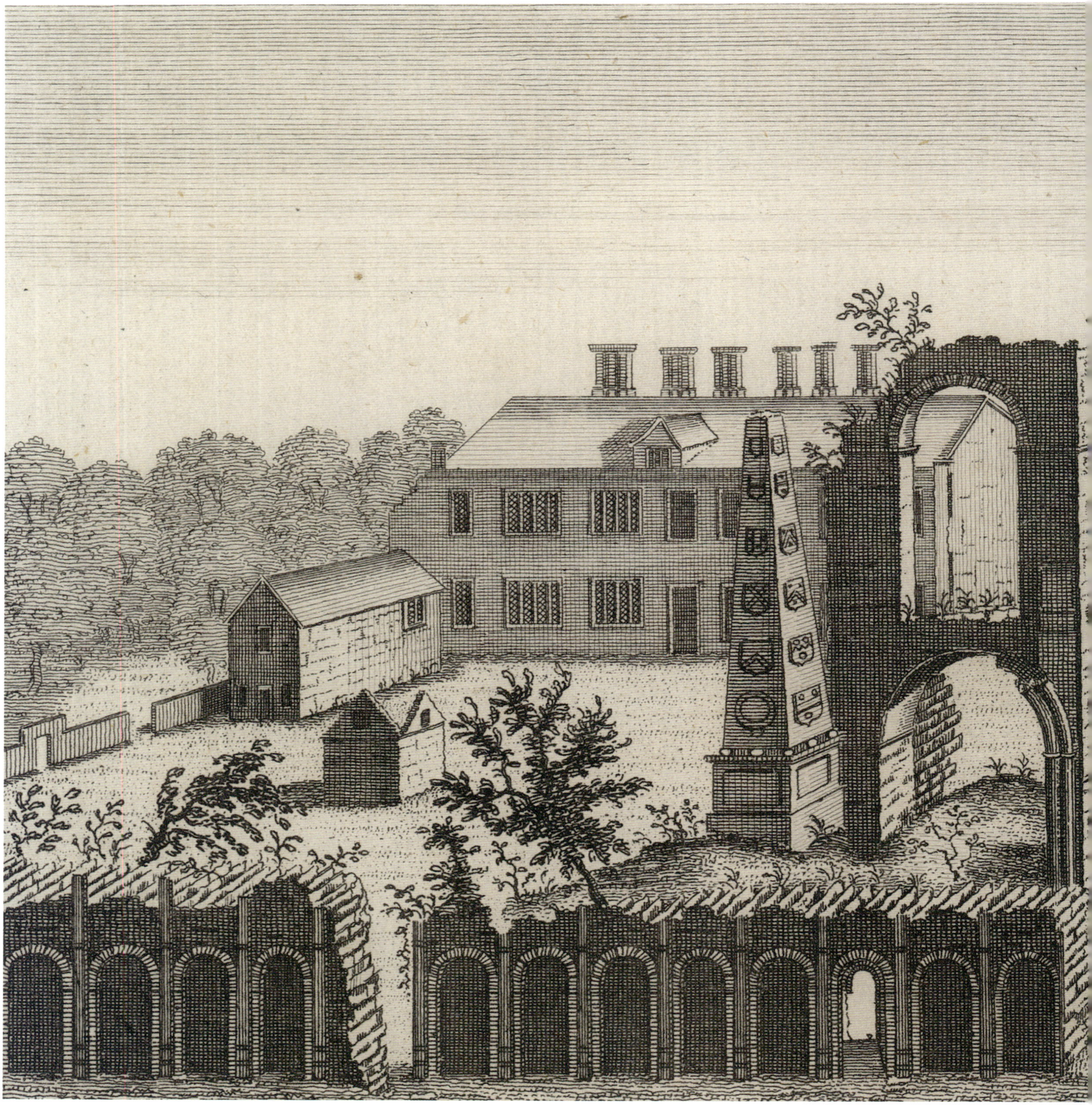

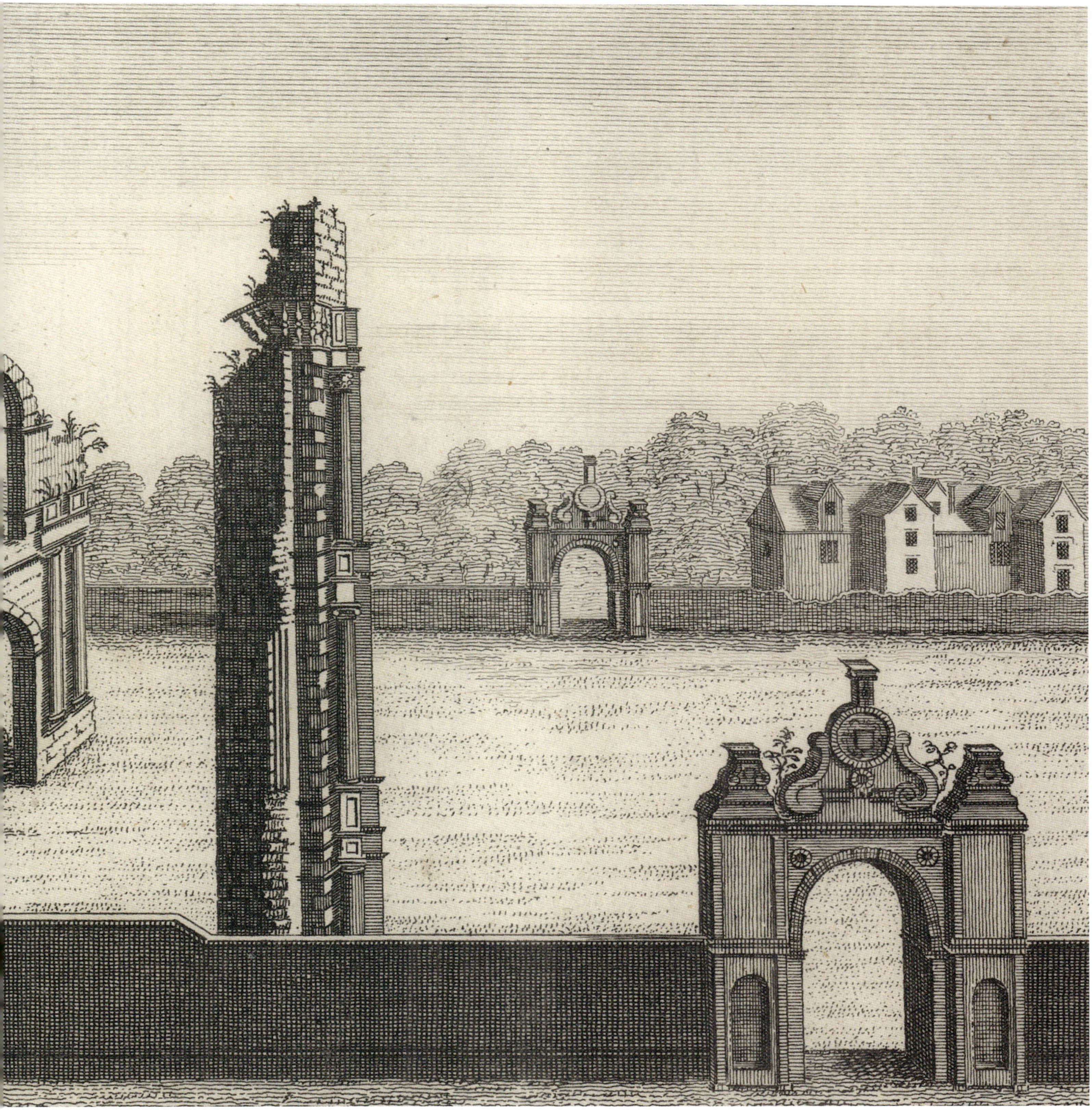

HOLDENBY HOUSE

… a very beautiful building erected with such uniformity, and so answerably contrived as for the quantity and quality is not to be matched in this land.

JOHN NORDEN, ESTATE SURVEYOR, 1610,
SPECULI BRITANNIAE PARS ALTERA; OR,
A DELINEATION OF NORTHAMPTONSHIRE, 1720

View of the Inner Courtyard of Holdenby House, *scraperboard, 2017*.

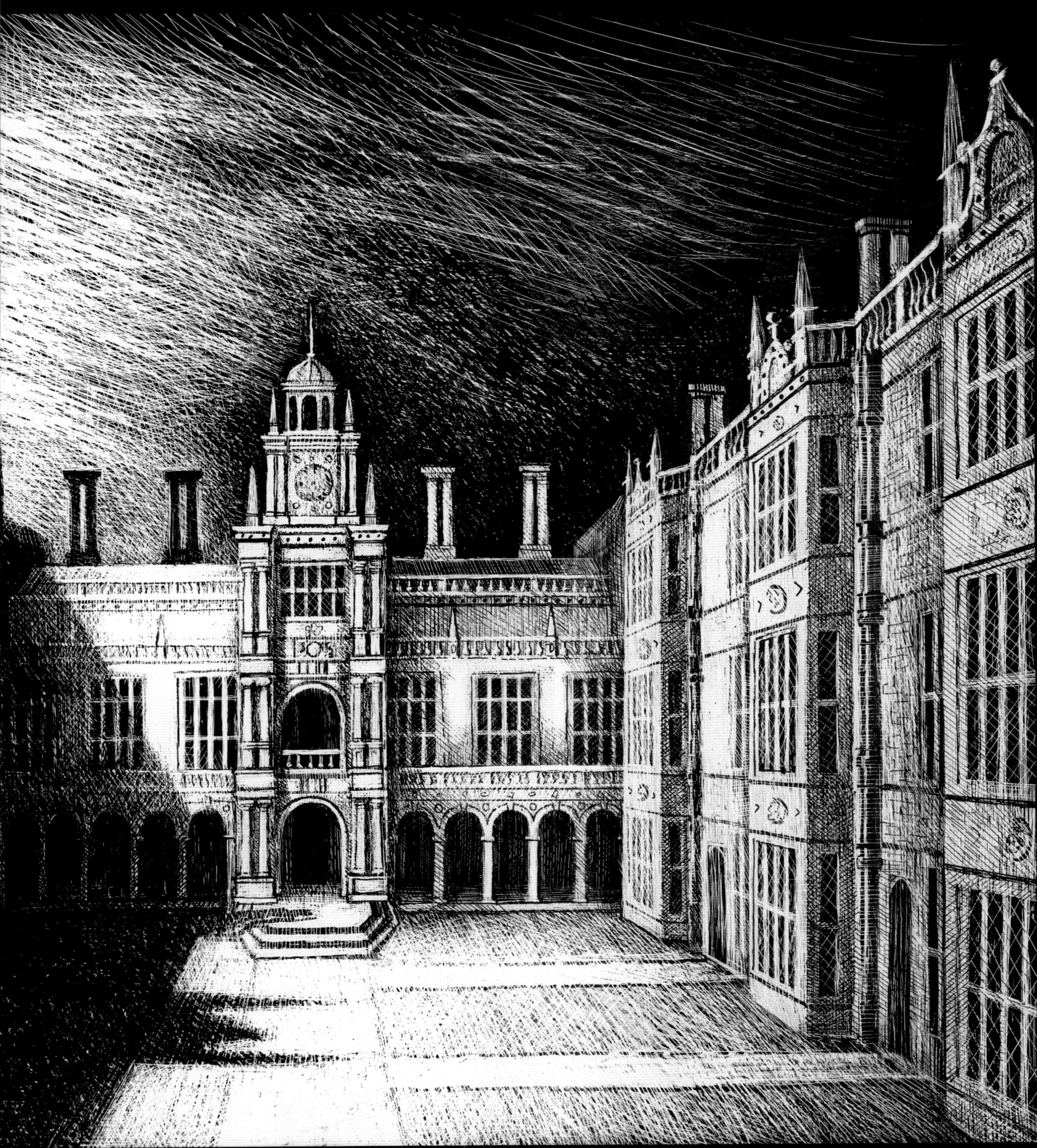

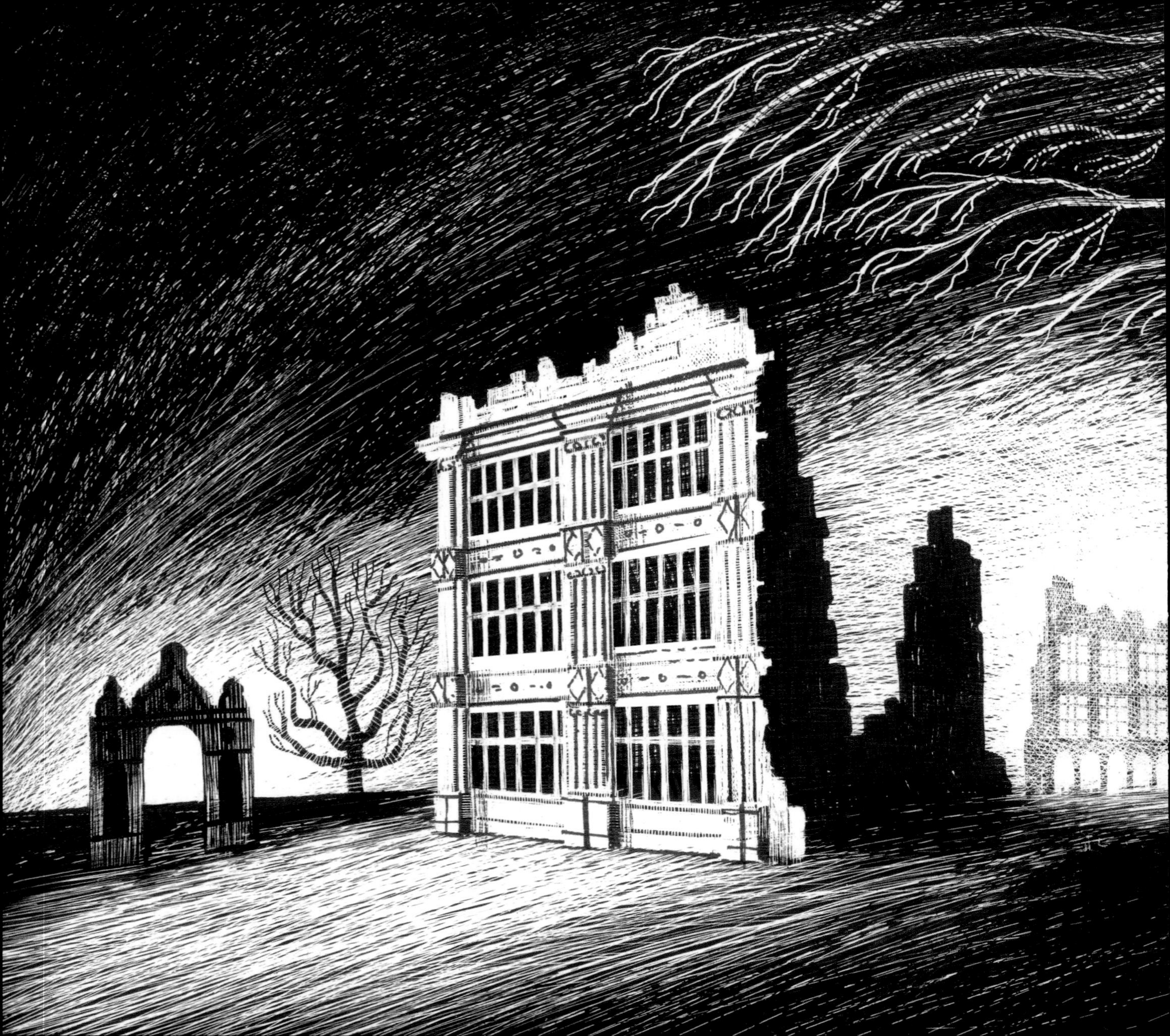

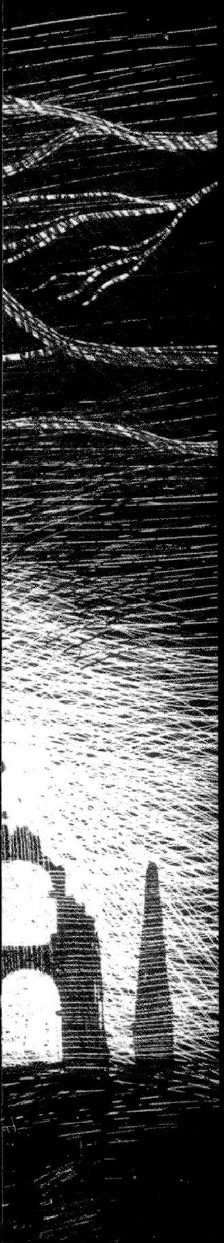

... and from it a prospect to Holmby House, which being demolished in the late civil wars, shows like a Roman ruin shaded by the trees about it, a stately, solemn, and pleasing view.

FROM AN ACCOUNT OF A VISIT TO ALTHORP IN 1675, IN WILLIAM BRAY (ED.), *THE DIARY OF JOHN EVELYN*, VOL. II, 1901

EK

View of the Ruins of Holdenby House, *scraperboard, 2017*.

For my own opinion Holdenby is altogether even the best house that hath been built in this age; and it more showeth the good judgment and honour of the builder than all the charge that hath been bestowed upon stones by the greatest persons and the best purses that hath been in my time.

SIR THOMAS HENEAGE, 1583,
QUOTED IN EMILY SOPHIA HARTSHORNE,
MEMORIALS OF HOLDENBY, 1868

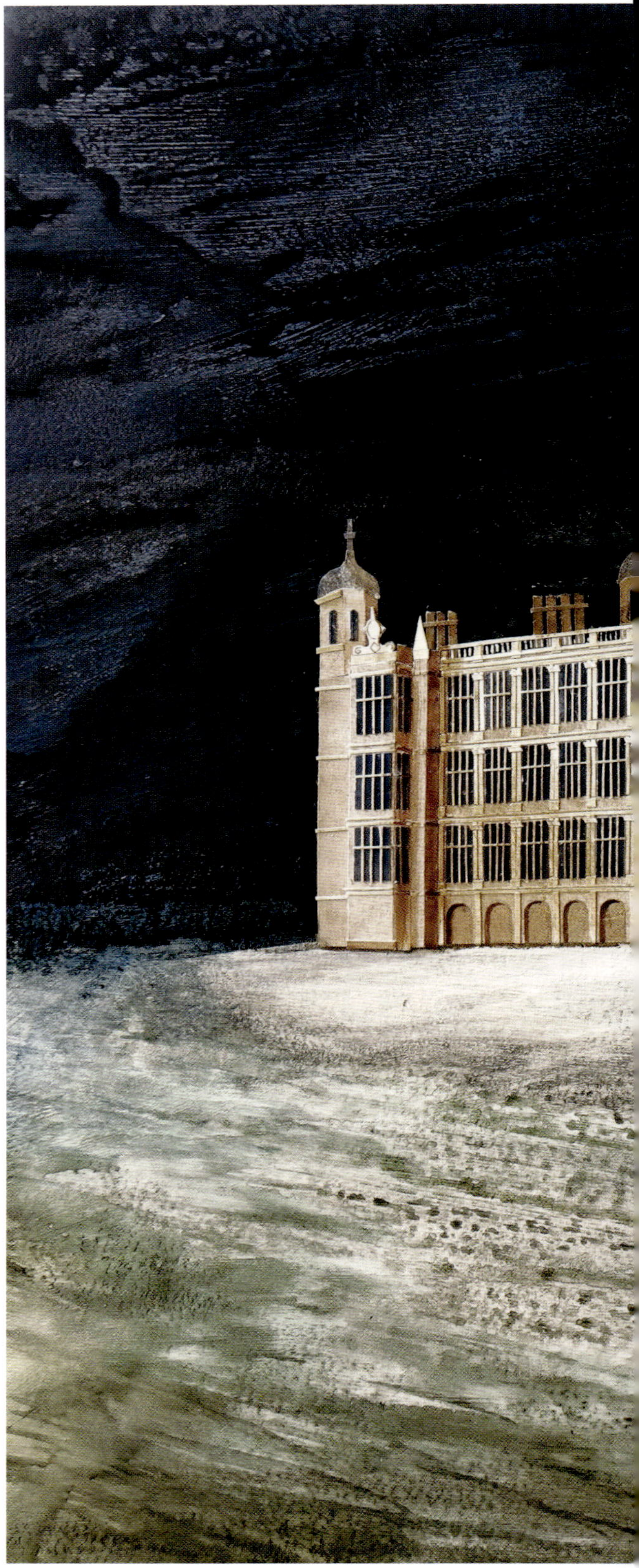

Prospect of Holdenby House, *paper collage and mixed media, 2014.*

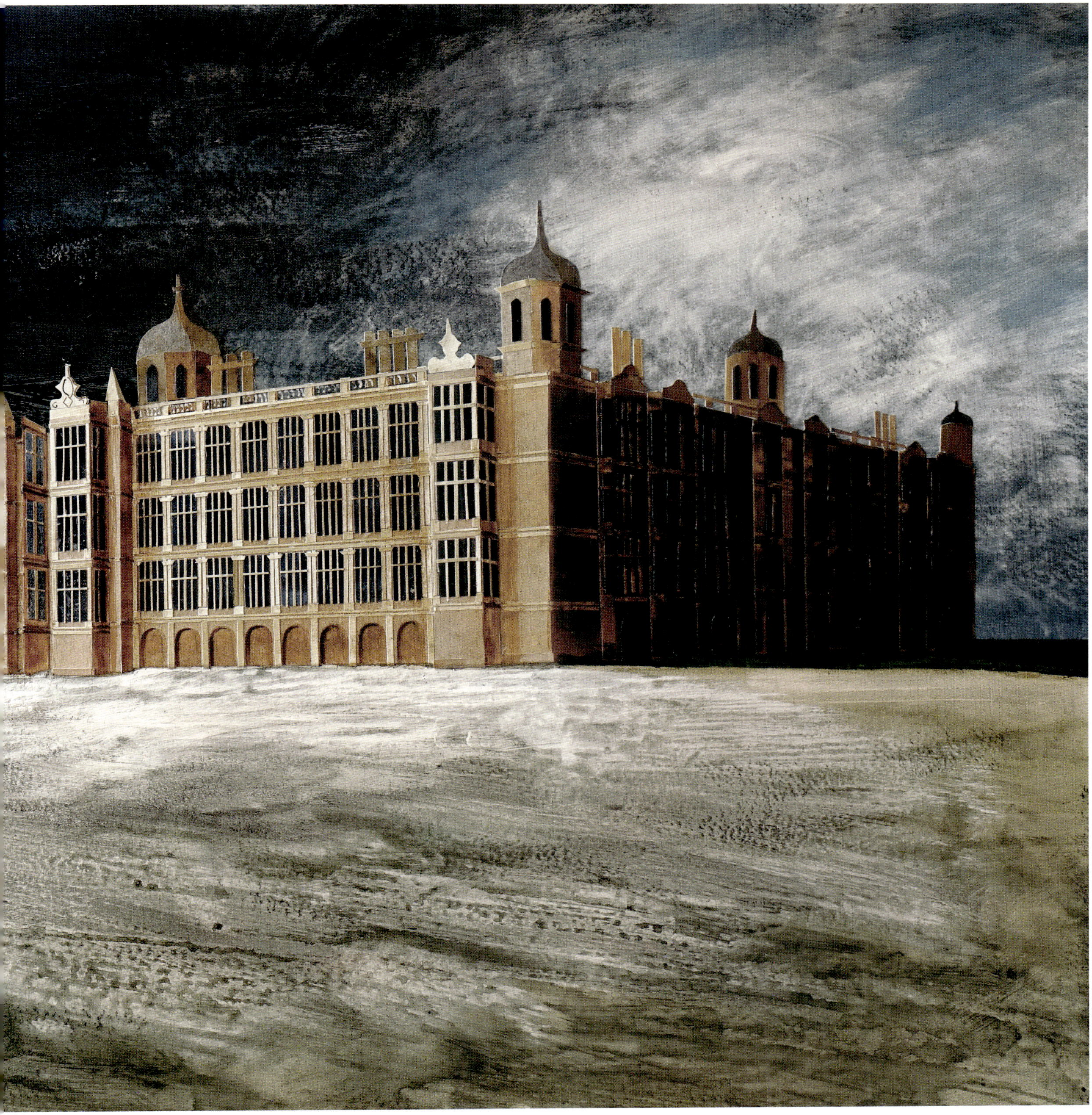

HOLDENBY HOUSE

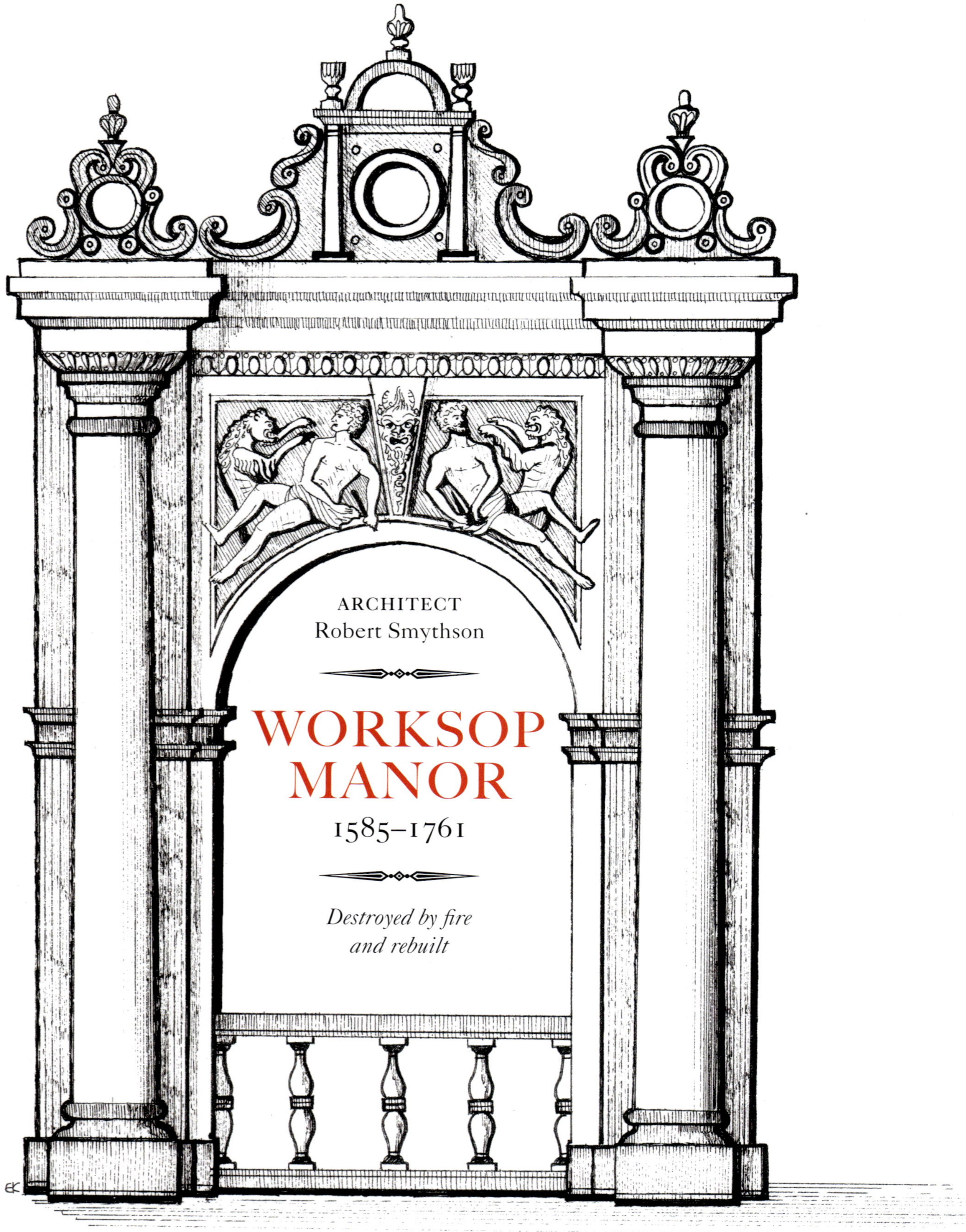

ARCHITECT
Robert Smythson

WORKSOP MANOR

1585–1761

Destroyed by fire and rebuilt

The most prodigious feature of Worksop Manor was its loftiness, as praised in a local rhyme about seats in the region:

Hardwicke for hugeness, Wor[k]sope for height,
Welbecke for use, and Bols[ov]er for sighte.[1]

Worksop, in Nottinghamshire, was almost 90 feet (27 m) tall from ground to parapet. Its chimneys, turrets and domed lanterns rose even higher. Positioned atop a sloping site, the house had a relatively small footprint – about 180 feet (55 m) across and 40 feet (12 m) deep – which served to accentuate its vertiginous elevation. Outside, as one looked towards the building, the multitude of windows glittered. Inside, looking out through the uninterrupted glazing of the rooftop prospect rooms, one was rewarded with a continuous panorama of the Dukeries. It was a quintessential Elizabethan country house.

The owner of Worksop, George Talbot (1528–1590), 6th Earl of Shrewsbury, came from an ancient and esteemed family, and held the powerful office of Earl Marshal of England. From the late 1560s to 1584, he was entrusted with the guardianship of Mary, Queen of Scots – a troublesome honour that cost him financially and personally. His second marriage was to Bess of Hardwick, a formidable figure who had been married three times previously, and who was herself an indefatigable builder of houses.

Lord Shrewsbury's Worksop was not completely new. The existing house on the site was the lodge referred to by the poet and antiquarian John Leland in his *Itinerary* (*c.* 1535–43) as 'the fair lodge in Wyrksoppe Park not yet finisshid'.[2] The remodelling commenced in the early 1580s and was completed in 1585, when the ceiling in the gallery was finished; the same date was emblazoned above a fireplace noted by George Vertue when he visited in 1727. The probable architect was Robert Smythson (1535–1614), who also designed Wollaton Hall in Nottingham (1580–88) and Hardwick Hall, Derbyshire (1590–97), the latter for Shrewsbury's widow, Bess. Although no designs for Worksop survive, there is a drawing by Robert Smythson for a screen 'to bee Builte at Worsope Manner' and a survey drawing of the completed ground floor by his son, John Smythson.[3]

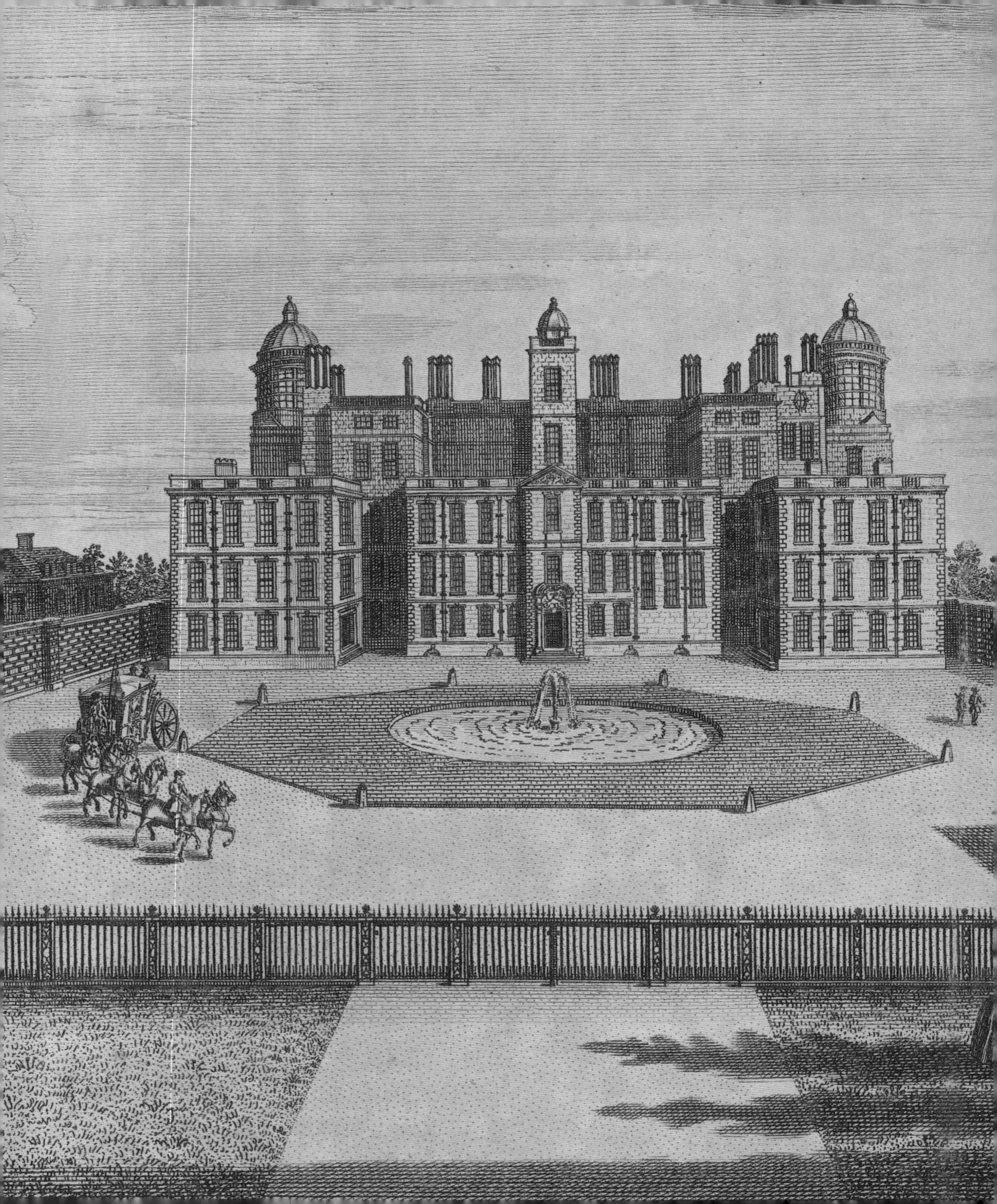

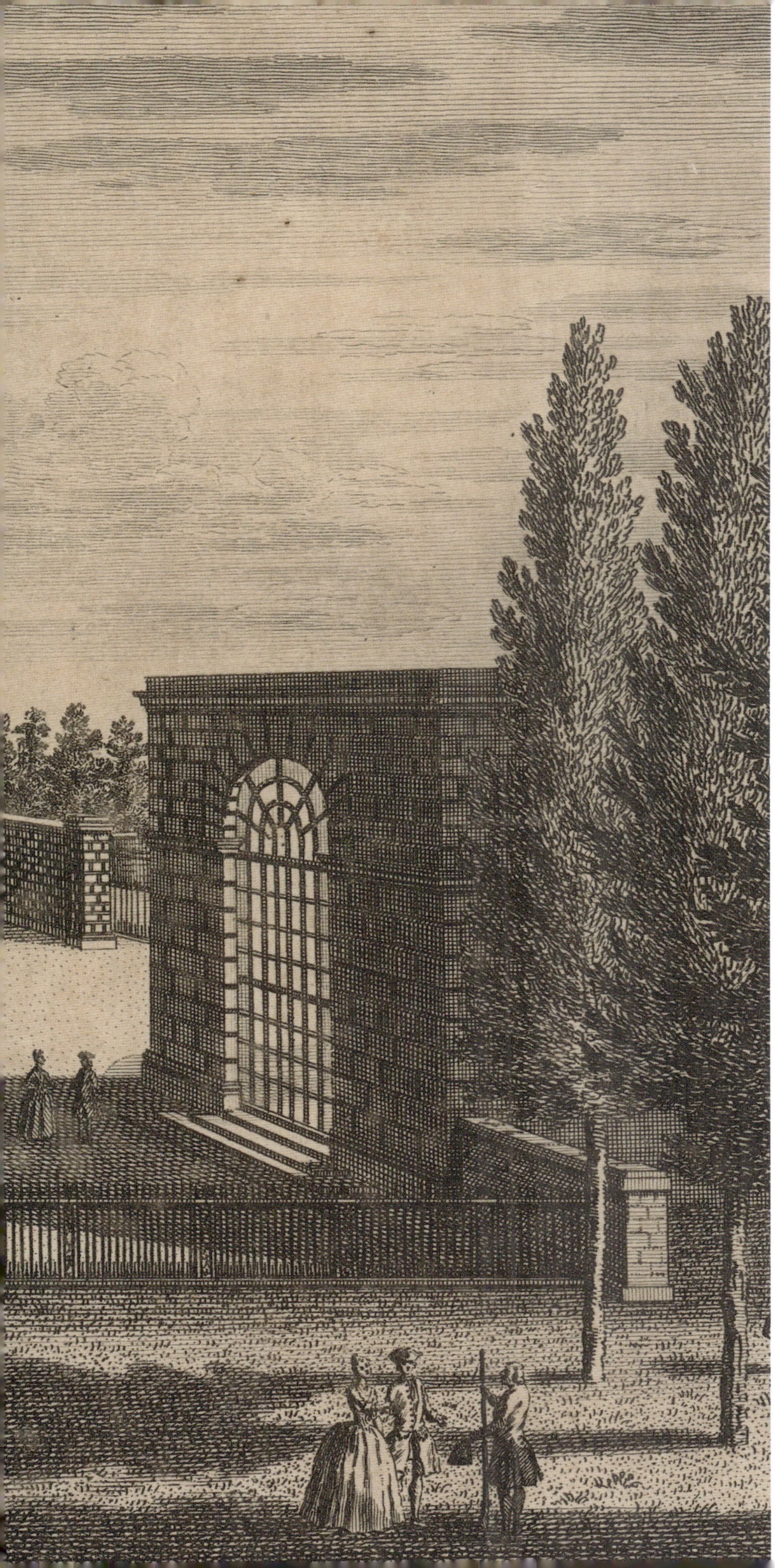

We were first brought up to the great chamber … and after to the gallery, who for the bigness and beauty thereof exceedeth most that I have seen. It is fourscore and fifteen of my paces long … The house is as goodly as I have seen both for the height, situation and form of building.

FROM AN ANONYMOUS ACCOUNT OF A VISIT IN 1618, QUOTED IN JAMES LOXLEY, ANNA GROUNDWATER AND JULIE SANDERS (EDS.), *BEN JONSON'S WALK TO SCOTLAND*, 2014

A Perspective View of Worksop Manor, a Seat of the Duke of Norfolk, *engraving published in* Universal Magazine, *1755*.

Shrewsbury's decision to transform Worksop was surprising given that, according to his personal correspondence, he was already feeling financially burdened. He owned several other houses, so he certainly did not lack alternative accommodation. The project did, however, offer him the opportunity to keep up appearances by building a house as impressively modern as nearby Wollaton. It also allowed Shrewsbury to distance himself from Chatsworth House in Derbyshire (built by Bess's second husband, Sir William Cavendish), where marital relations were increasingly strained.

The resulting house had remarkably plain façades, probably to show the fineness of the local stone. What animated the design were the several bays and towers that projected from the wall plane and above the parapet level to create a lively and dramatic composition. Worksop Manor was renowned not only for its height but also for its second-floor long gallery. At a length of 212 feet (65 m), it became the measure for all others: revealing the competitive nature of Elizabethan building, the builders at Berwick for Lord Dunbar claimed that their gallery would make Worksop's 'but a garret'.[4]

Worksop's history during the seventeenth and early eighteenth centuries was quiet, but in 1761 the press reported news of a 'dreadful

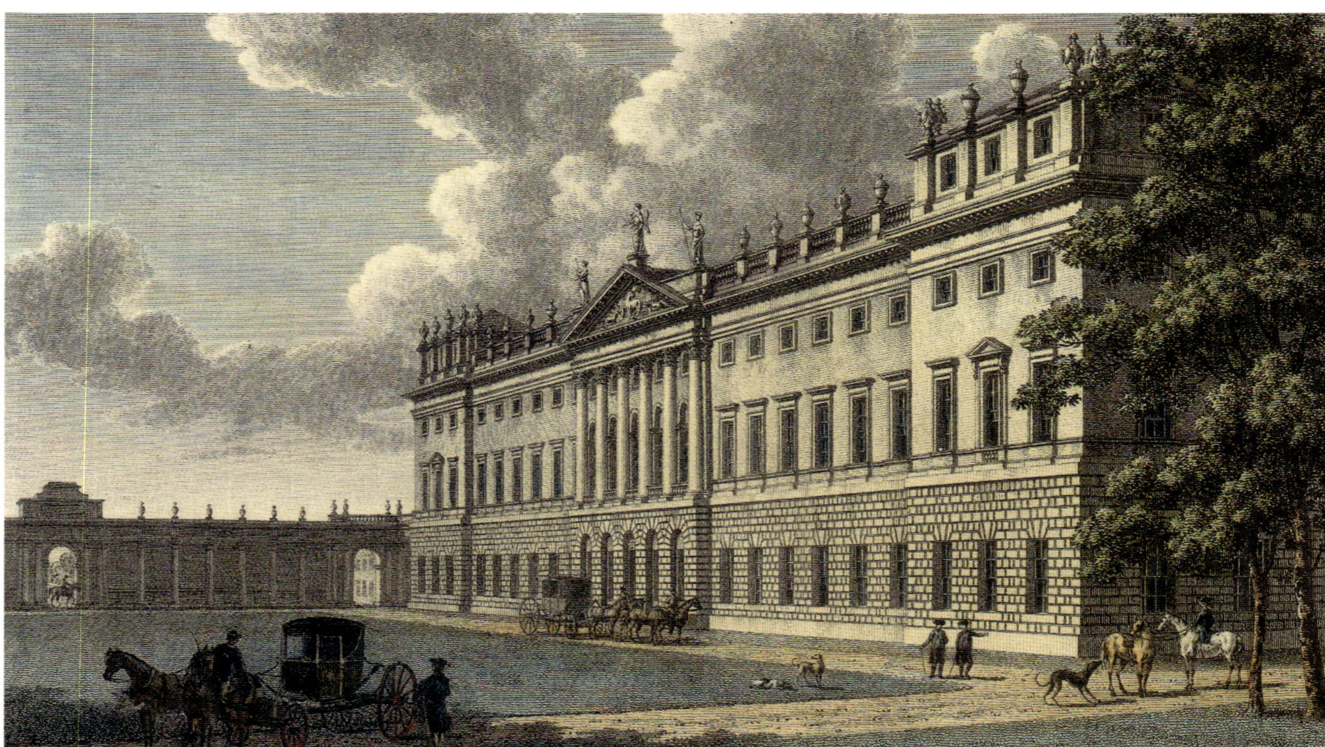

William Watts, Worksop Manour House, in Nottinghamshire, the Seat of the Duke of Norfolk, *hand-coloured engraving, 1780.*

fire'.[5] The fine limestone fabric burnt readily, sparing just the chapel and part of the east wing. The report lamented the loss of the library, 'the magnificent furniture' and one man's life. The Duke and Duchess of Norfolk, the then owners, took the news stoically, worrying principally about 'how many besides us are sufferers by the like calamity': they typically paid £12,000 each year in wages to staff, who suddenly found themselves without employment.

The duke and duchess commissioned James Paine (1717–1789) as architect for the rebuilding, and the duchess took a notably prominent design role, sketching plans and devising interiors, including marble chimney pieces. The intention was to build an overwhelmingly impressive neo-Palladian courtyard house with ranges over 300 feet (91 m) long. Joining the ranges was to be an Egyptian Hall measuring 140 feet by 70 feet (43 × 21 m). The foundation stone for the north range was laid in 1763, and this range was roofed by July 1764. More than 500 workmen were employed under the constant on-site supervision of the duchess. The fitting-out continued until early 1767. At this point, however, the duke and duchess's nephew and heir suddenly died. Work stopped, never to be resumed, and the south, east and west ranges remained unbuilt.

In 1838 Worksop was purchased by the Duke of Newcastle, who shortly afterwards sold the fittings at auction and demolished the house, keeping only the stable court, which he adapted and leased to tenants. Fragments of Paine's Worksop survive in the grounds, most notably the reconstructed pediment, also designed by the Duchess of Norfolk. It portrays animals representing the family alliances, as well as a distant view of the Elizabethan house – a remnant of the second Worksop containing a faint echo of the first.

Prospect of the First
Manor House on Fire,
scraperboard, 2017.

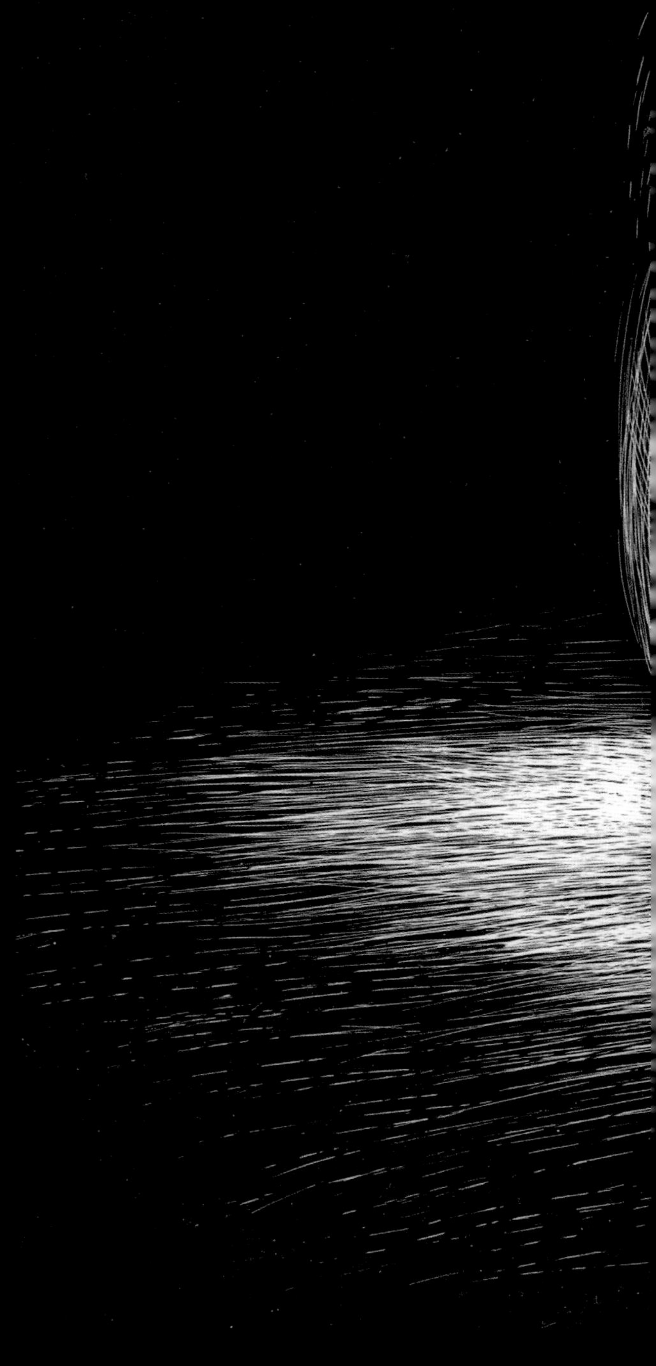

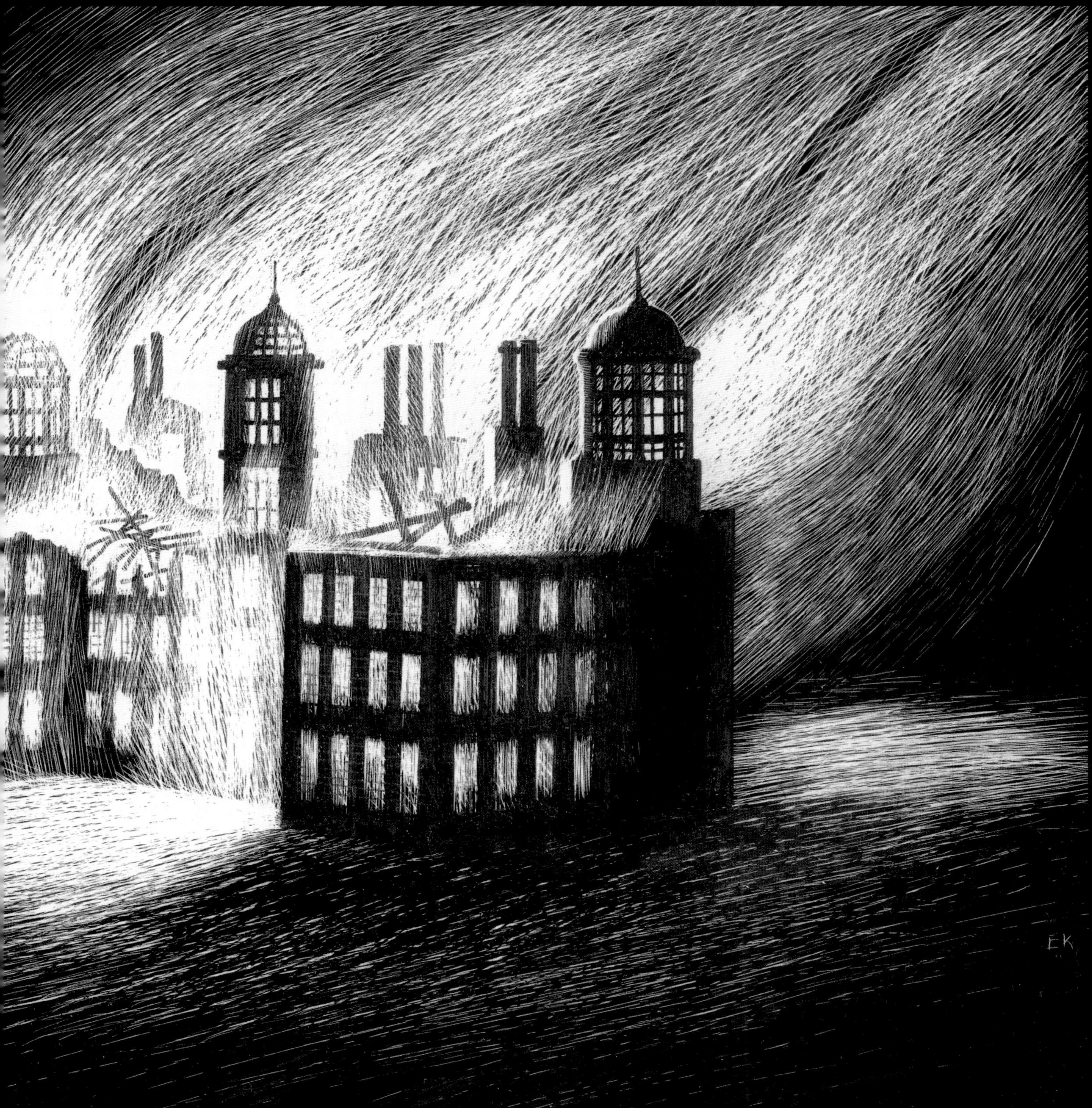

WORKSOP MANOR

The house continued to be admired, embellished, and inhabited, by successive descendants of this noble family, till beyond the middle of the last century, when a destructive event removed the mansion and its magnificence, and robbed the county of Nottingham of one of its proudest ornaments.

JOHN HOLLAND, *THE HISTORY, ANTIQUITIES, AND DESCRIPTION OF THE TOWN AND PARISH OF WORKSOP, IN THE COUNTY OF NOTTINGHAM*, 1826

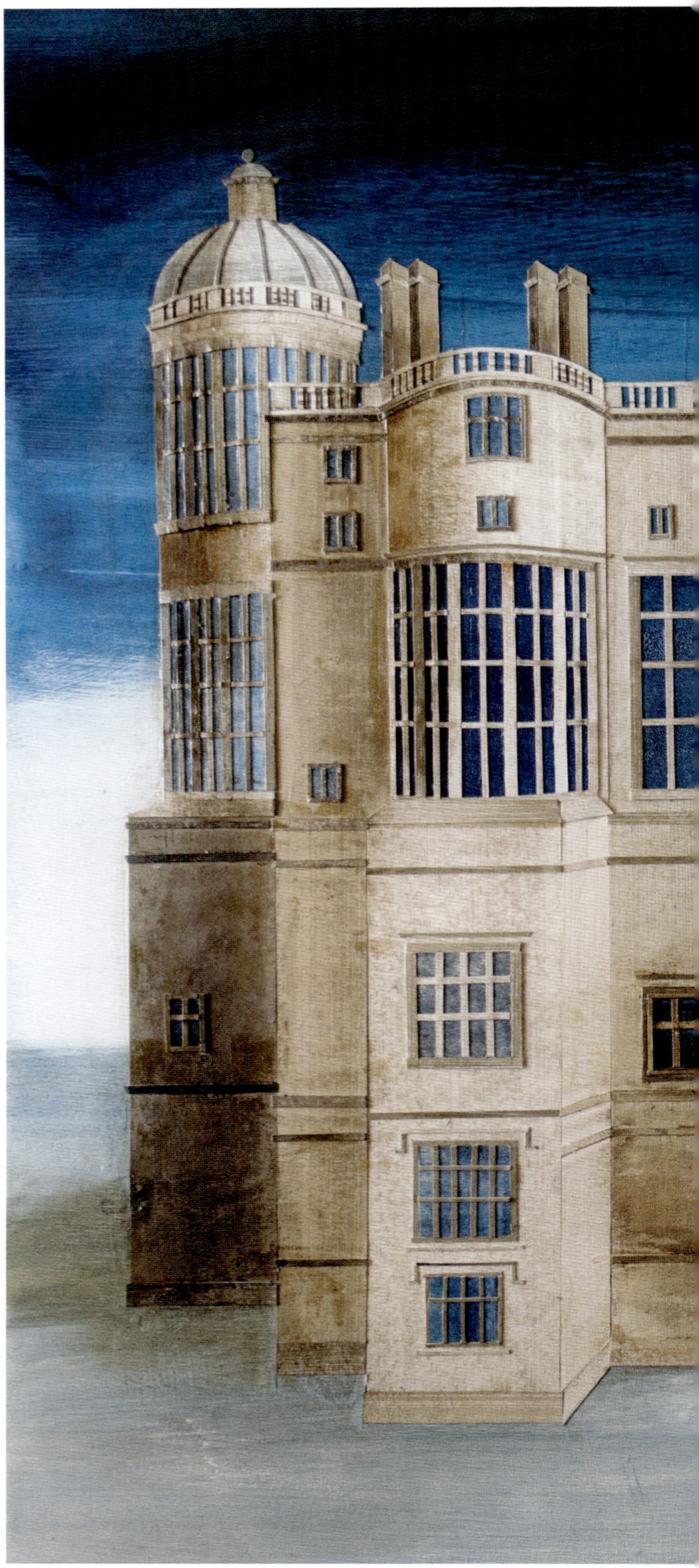

The First Worksop Manor in the Late 17th Century, *paper collage and mixed media, 2017. Detail shown pages 74–75.*

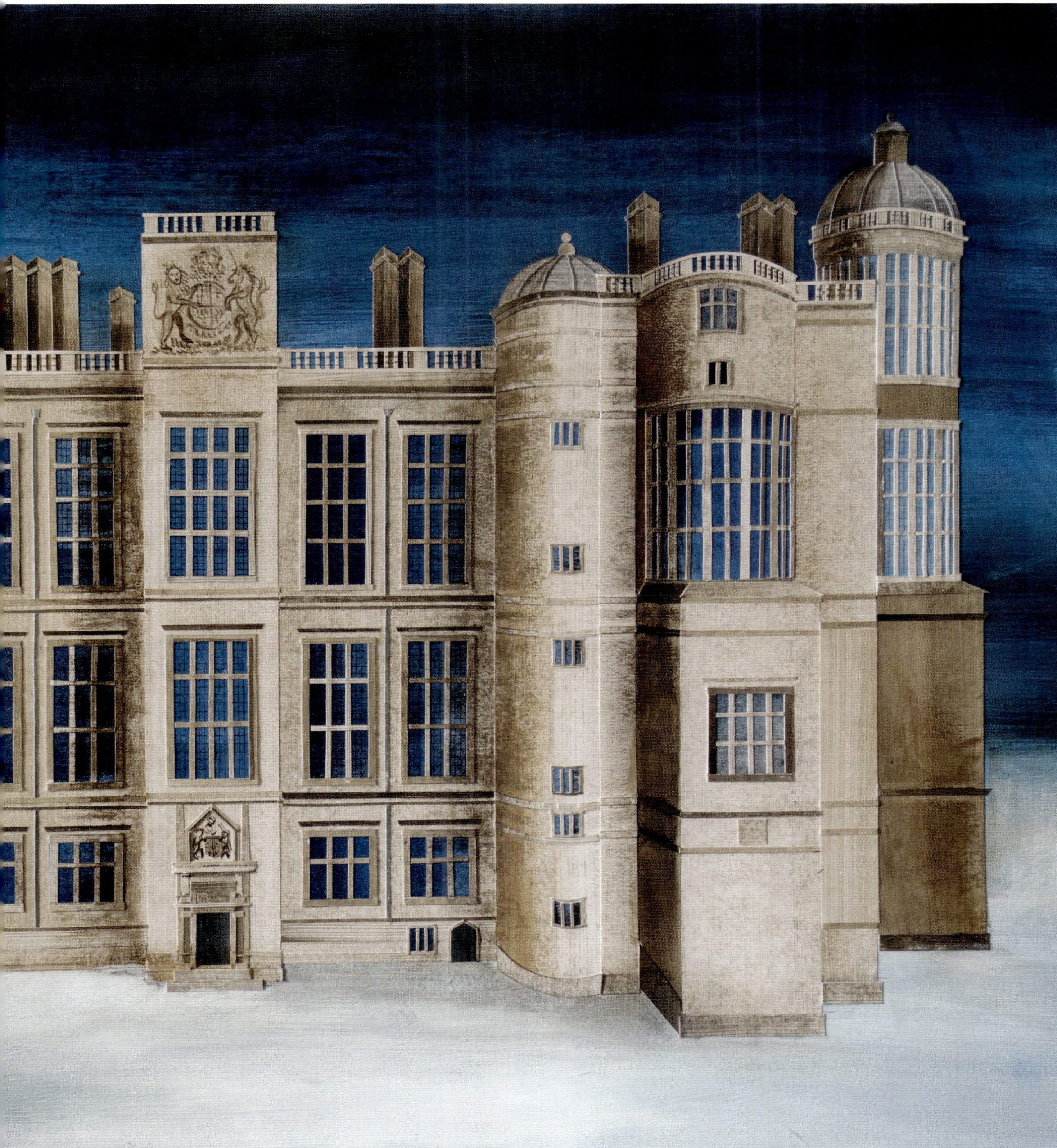

WORKSOP MANOR

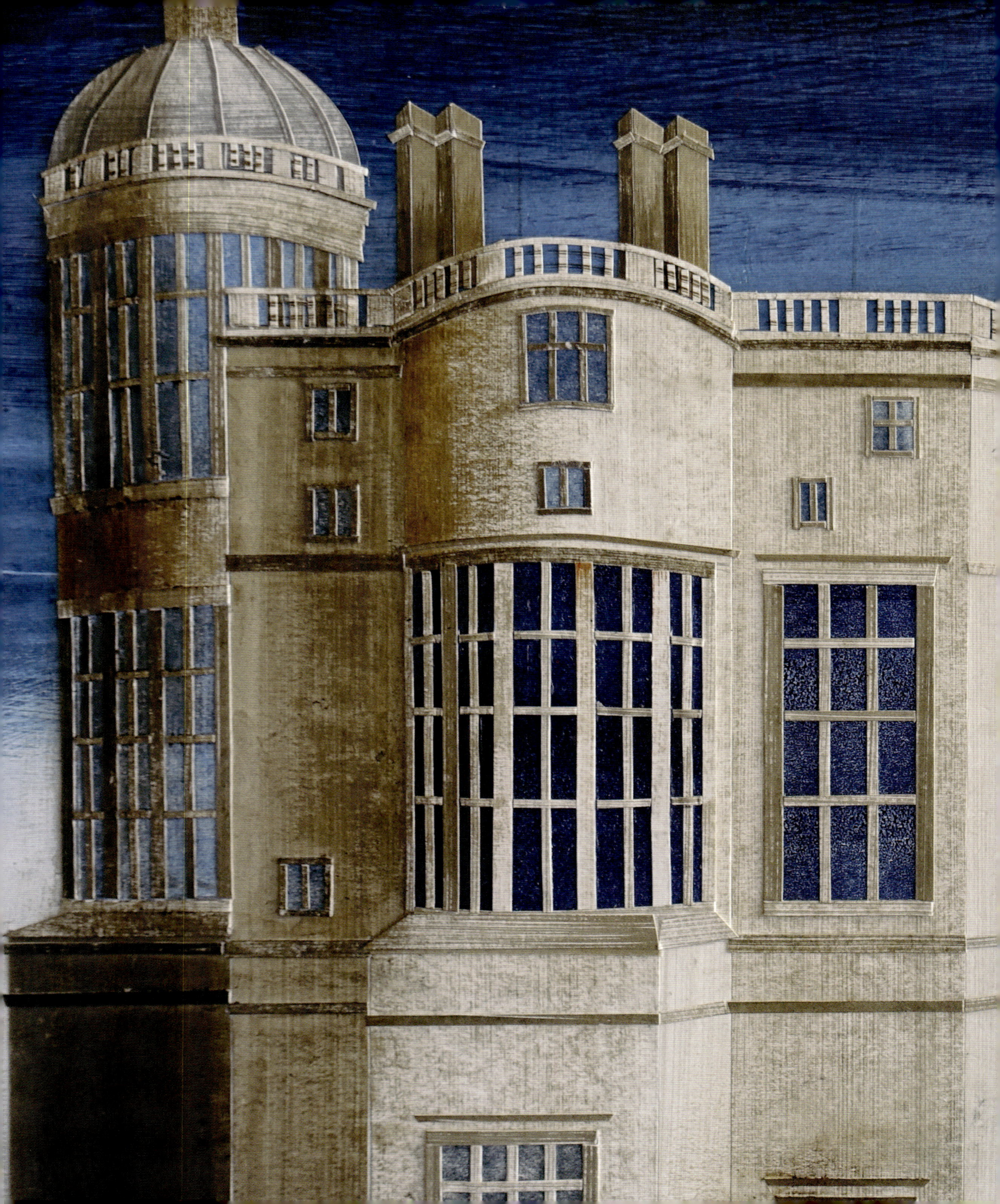

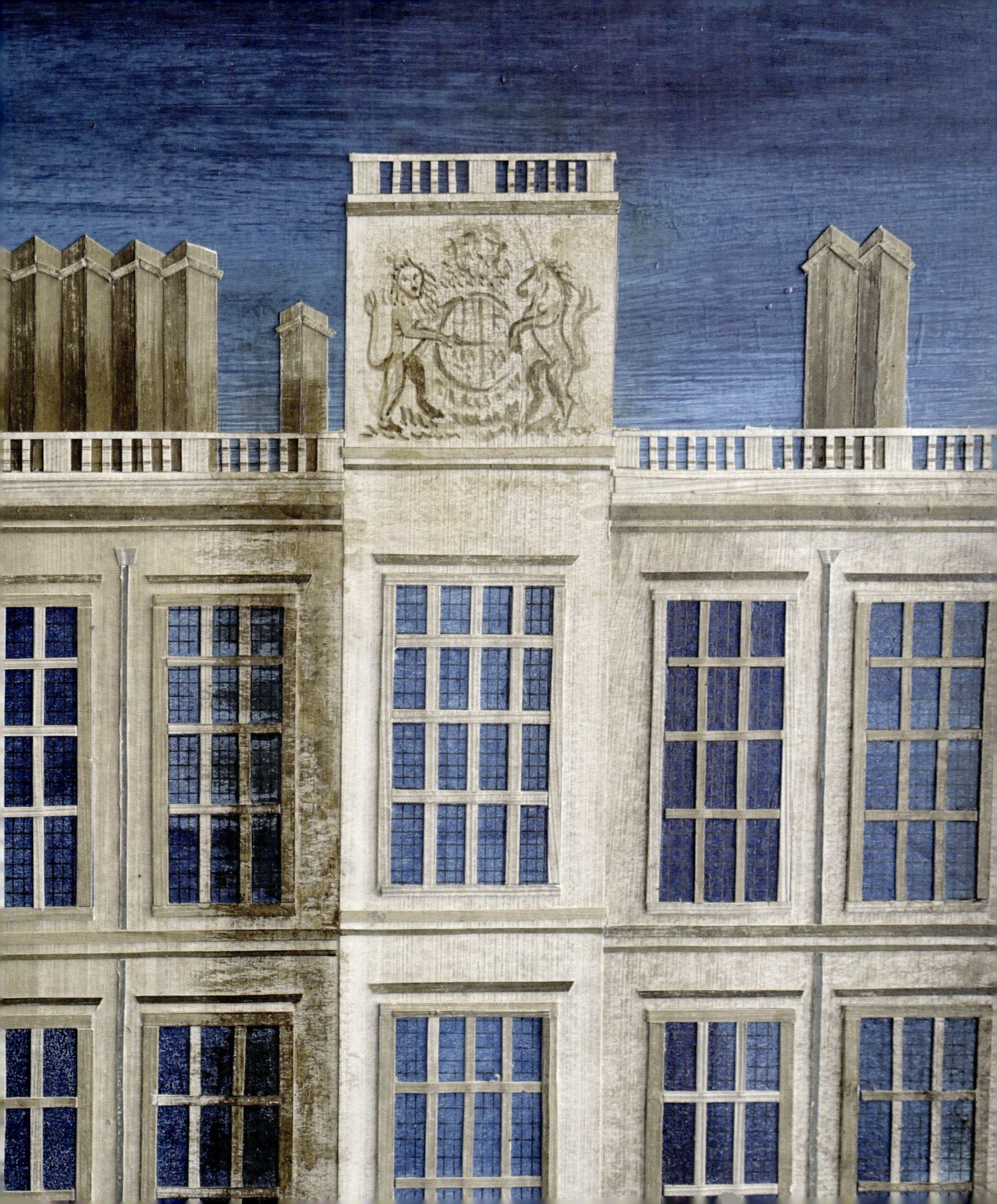

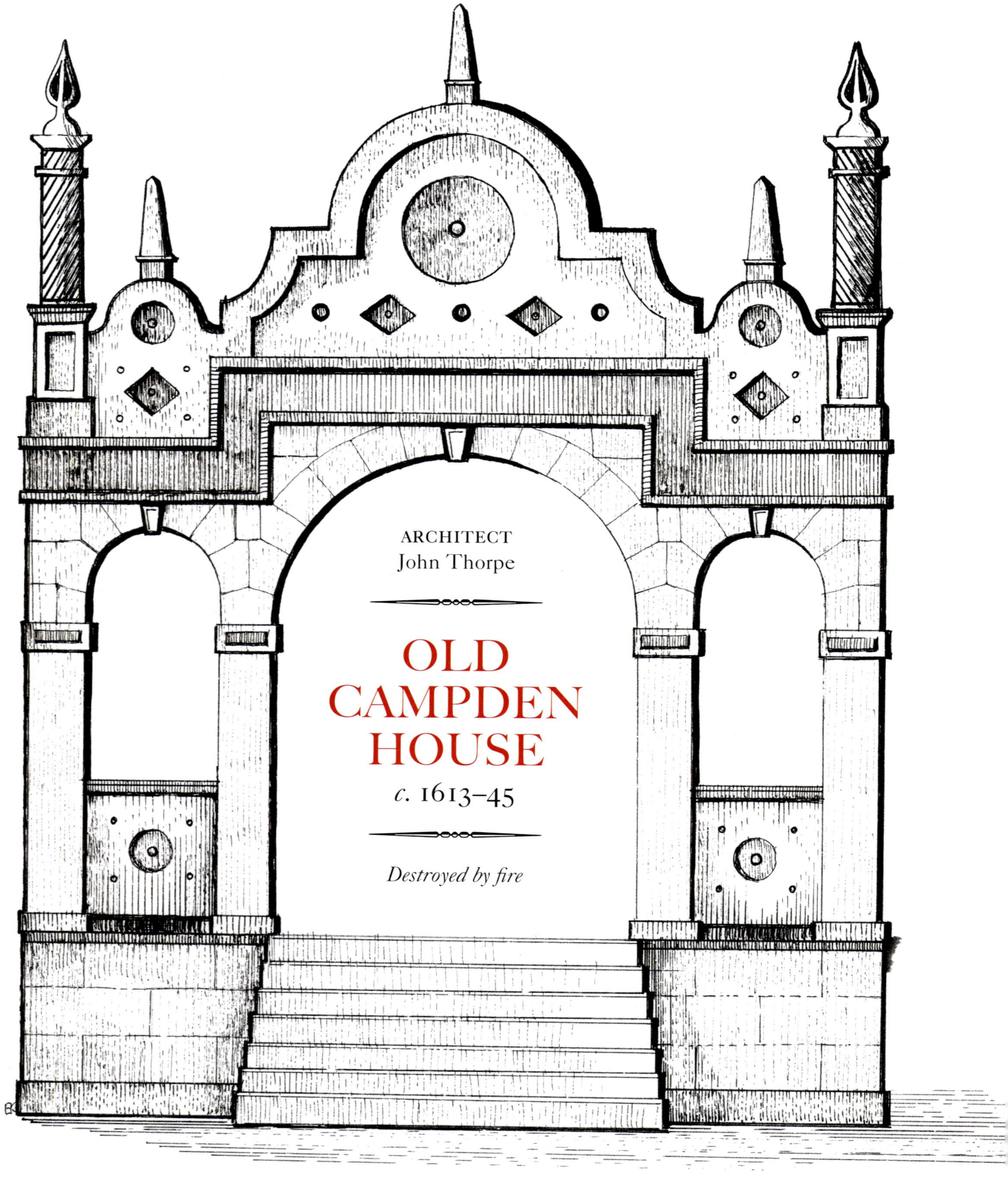

ARCHITECT
John Thorpe

OLD CAMPDEN HOUSE

c. 1613–45

Destroyed by fire

Since the destruction of Old Campden House in 1645, images of it have been handed down like relics. When the architect Charles Robert Cockerell visited Chipping Campden in 1825, he made a sketch of a historical canvas in the possession of a local painter.[1] Likewise, a drawing made by the amateur artist William Hughes around 1750 is likely to be based on an earlier view (pp. 80–81).[2] Although naive, Hughes's image shows the principle features of the house in detail: ornate gables, a domed central lantern, tall chimneys, canted bays and substantial mullion and transom windows, refined by a ground-floor loggia and a three-storey frontispiece comprising a tower of the classical orders. To both the east and west of the house, on the garden side, stands a delightful banqueting house, each one bristling with strapwork gables similar to those atop the main house. These pavilions, together with the gateway lodges, survive intact; today the house itself is a fire-scorched fragment.

The speed with which the house was built around 1613 surprised local commentators, whose critique of the patron's equally swift social ascent was thinly veiled. Baptist Hicks (1551–1629) was, like his father, a mercer, but his family enjoyed close ties with the royal court through their connections with the Cecils of Burghley House in Lincolnshire. Like many of his generation with means and ambition, Hicks also ran a profitable sideline as a moneylender. In 1603 he was knighted by James I, but chose to continue his business, despite the censure of the City of London. He commissioned a large house on the edge of the capital – Campden House, Kensington, completed around 1612 (see overleaf) – and in 1611 bought land at Chipping Campden. Contemporaries such as Henry Peacham were contemptuous about social climbers who had 'shot up with the last nights Mushrome'.[3] New money and ostentatious building went hand in hand.

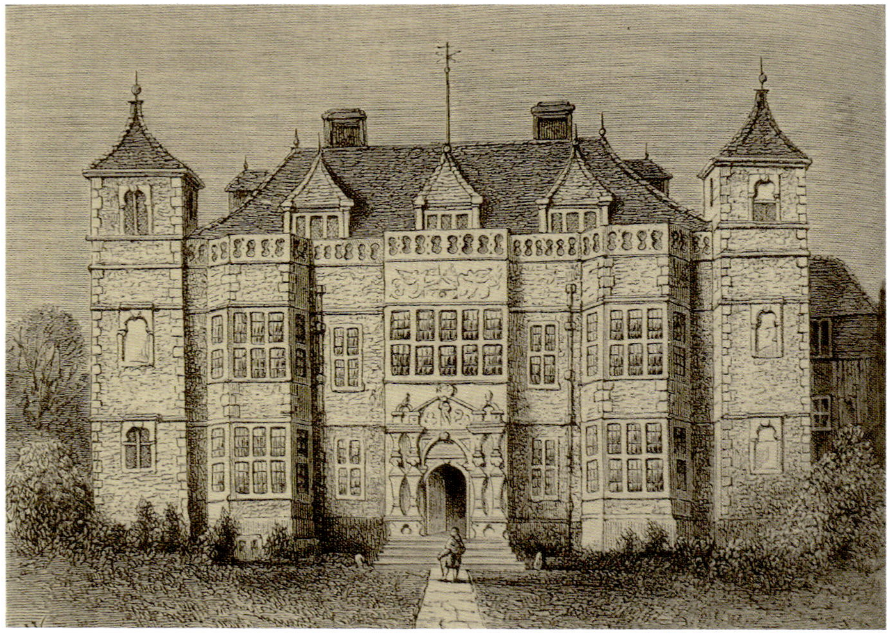

Above: Campden House, Kensington, 1720, *engraving published in Edward Walford,* Old and New London, *vol. V, 1878.*

To set his new social status in stone, Hicks chose the architect John Thorpe (*c.* 1565–1655). His plans for Hicks's Kensington house survive in a sketchbook in Sir John Soane's Museum in London. One includes a marginal sketch that corresponds to the Gloucestershire seat. Thorpe, himself ambitious, was the perfect match for the newly minted aristocracy; his sketchbook contains designs for eleven of those who were knighted in 1603.

Opposite: The remains of Old Campden House, photographed by Ed Kluz, 2017.

In 1645, only sixteen years after Hicks died, Old Campden House was wantonly destroyed in one of the English Civil War's typically bleak power calculations. In 1643 and again from 1644, the house served as a Royalist garrison. When Charles I ordered his men to quit Chipping Campden and join him at Oxford, they torched the house to prevent it being used as a Parliamentarian stronghold. On 10 May 1645, the Royalist colonel Sir Henry Slingsby wrote coolly in his diary: 'I set on a light fire before we marched off. A house, as my lord Campden says, that hath cost £30,000 in building and furniture.'[4] Two days later, a newspaper report described the troops setting out 'by the light of Campden House':[5] a ghastly parody of how, in Hicks's day, the domed lantern was illuminated to shine across the Gloucestershire valley.

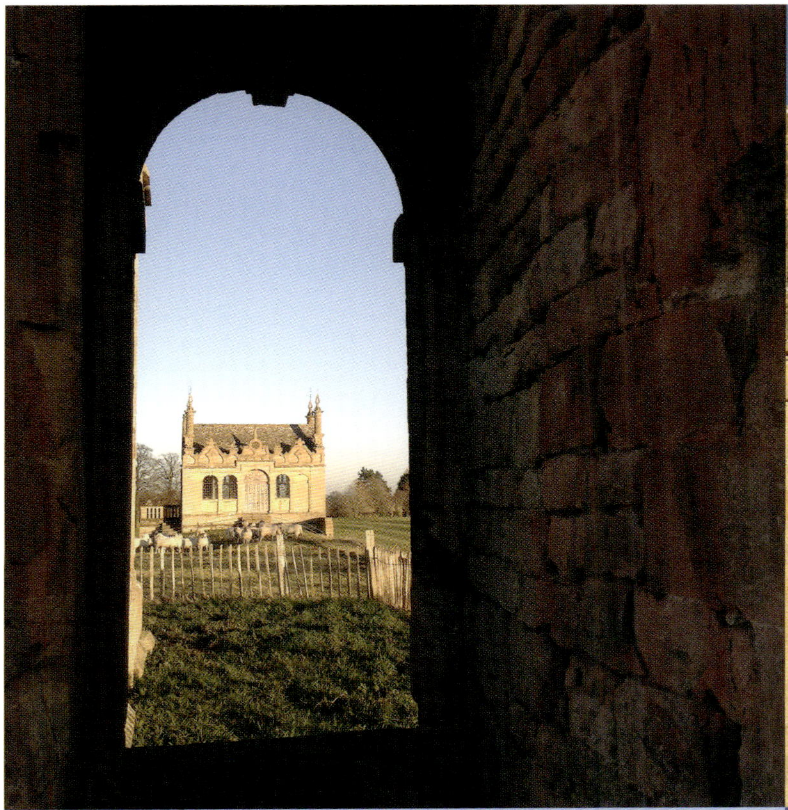
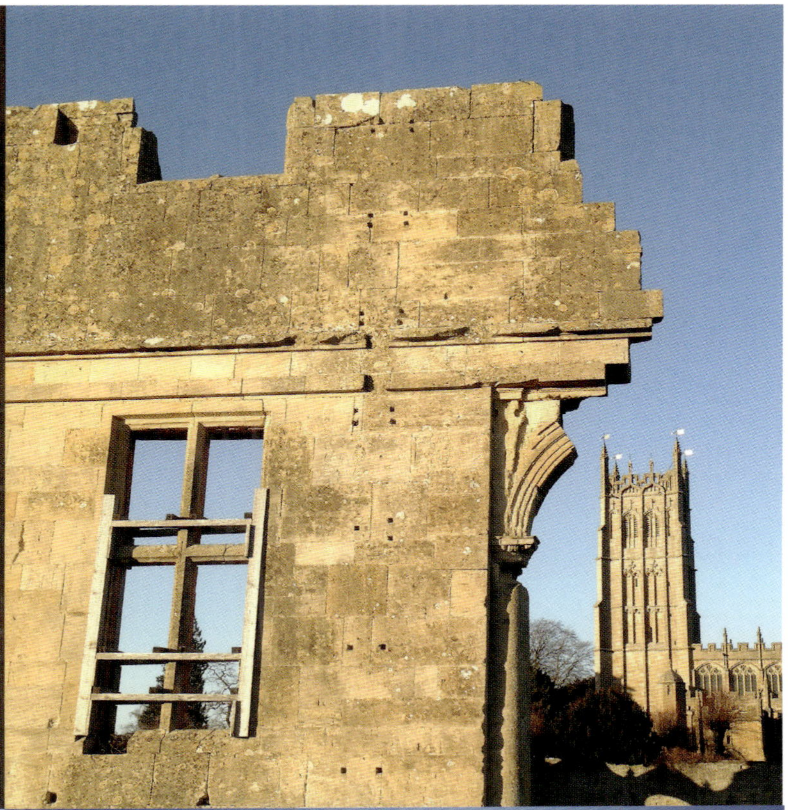
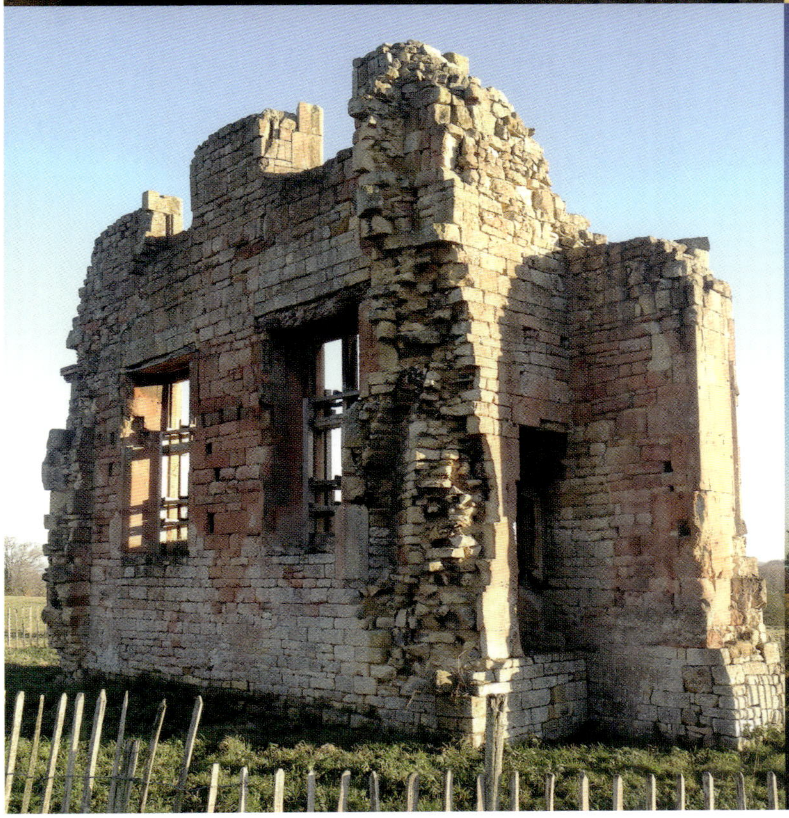
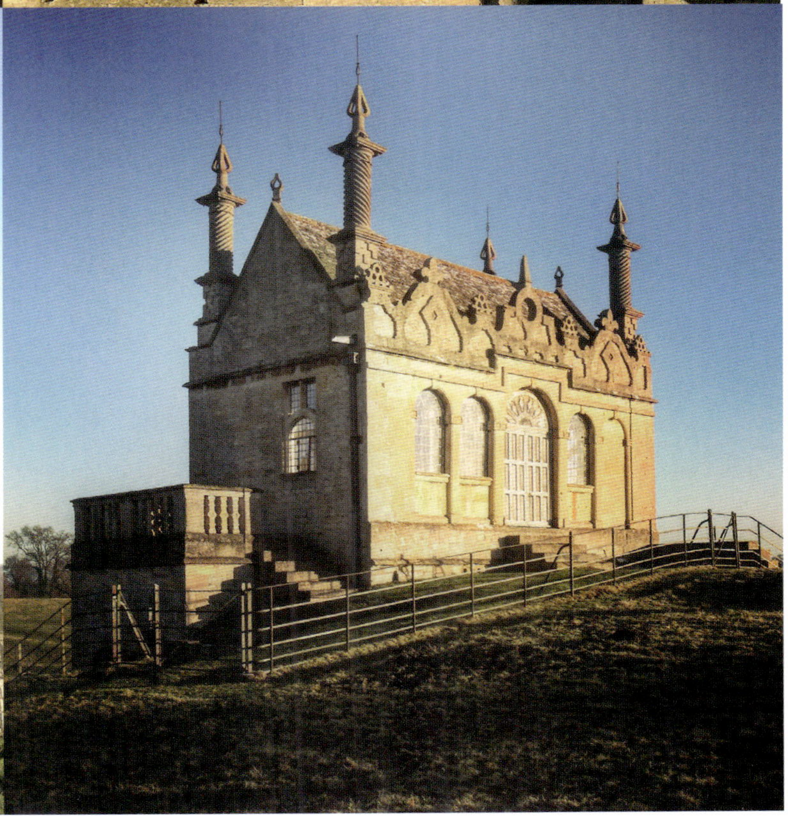

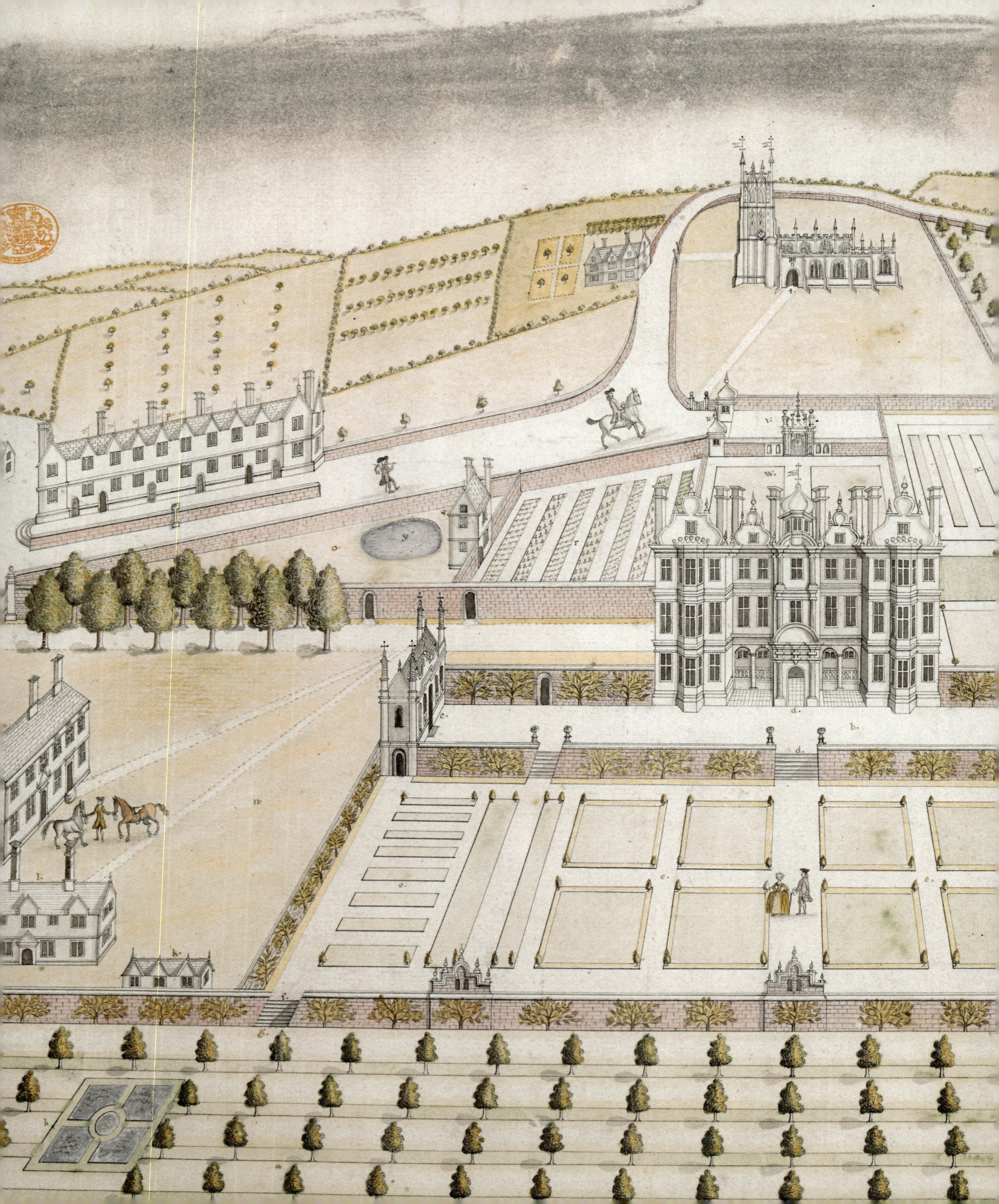

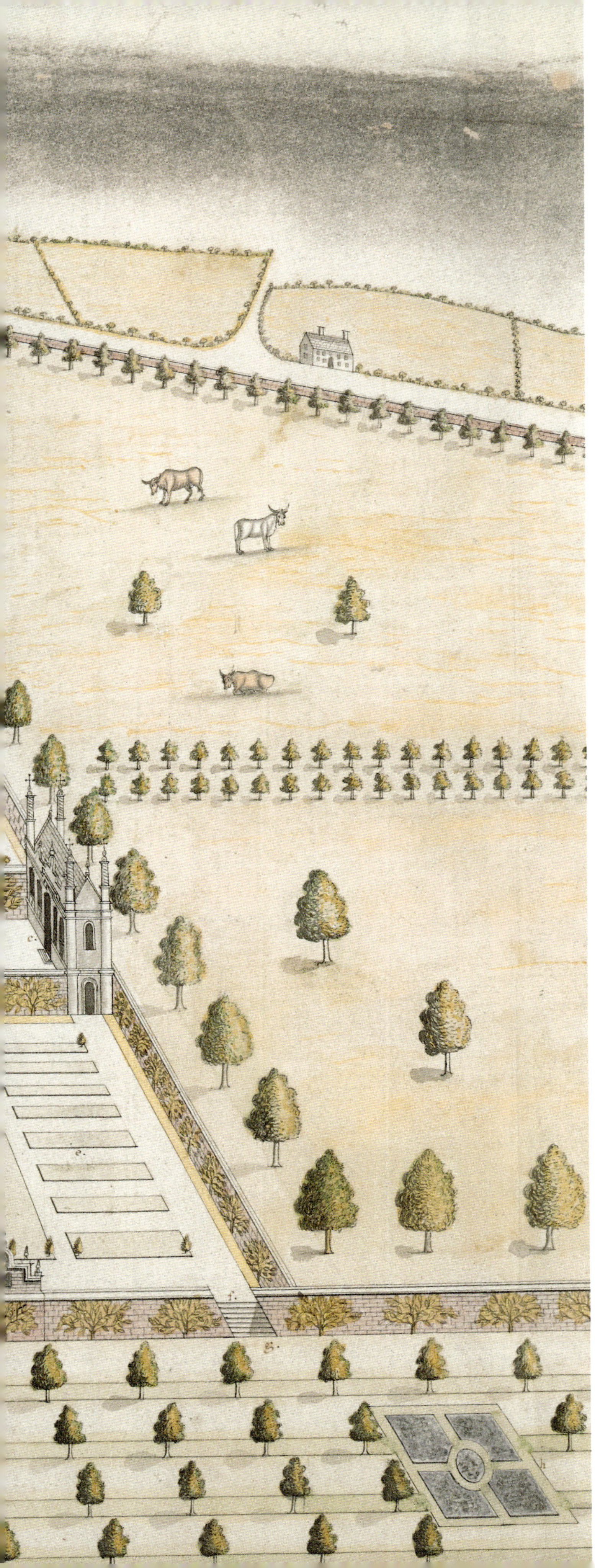

[O]ur late Wars laid a finger on Barkley [Berkeley], their arme on Sudeley Castle ... But their loynes [loins] have been laid on Cambden House (one of the newest and neatest in England; built by Baptist Hicks Viscount Cambden), pressed down to the very foundation.

THOMAS FULLER, *THE HISTORY OF THE WORTHIES OF ENGLAND*, 1662

William Hughes, Bird's-Eye View of Old Campden House in Gloucestershire, *pen and ink with watercolour on paper*, c. *1750*.

Old Campden House on Fire, *scraperboard, 2017.*

Pages 84–85: The site and remains of Old Campden House with its banqueting houses, photographed by Ed Kluz, 2017.

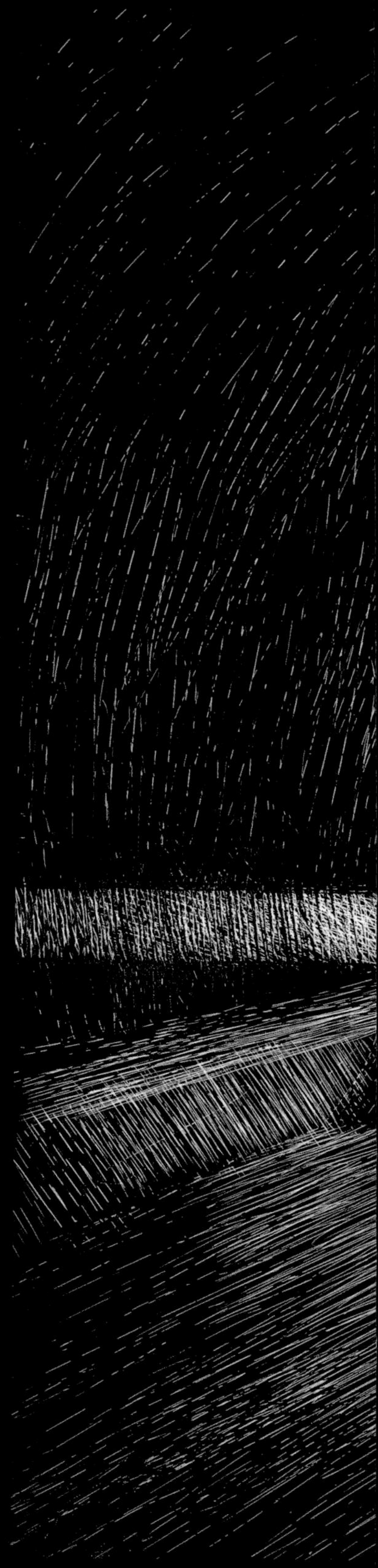

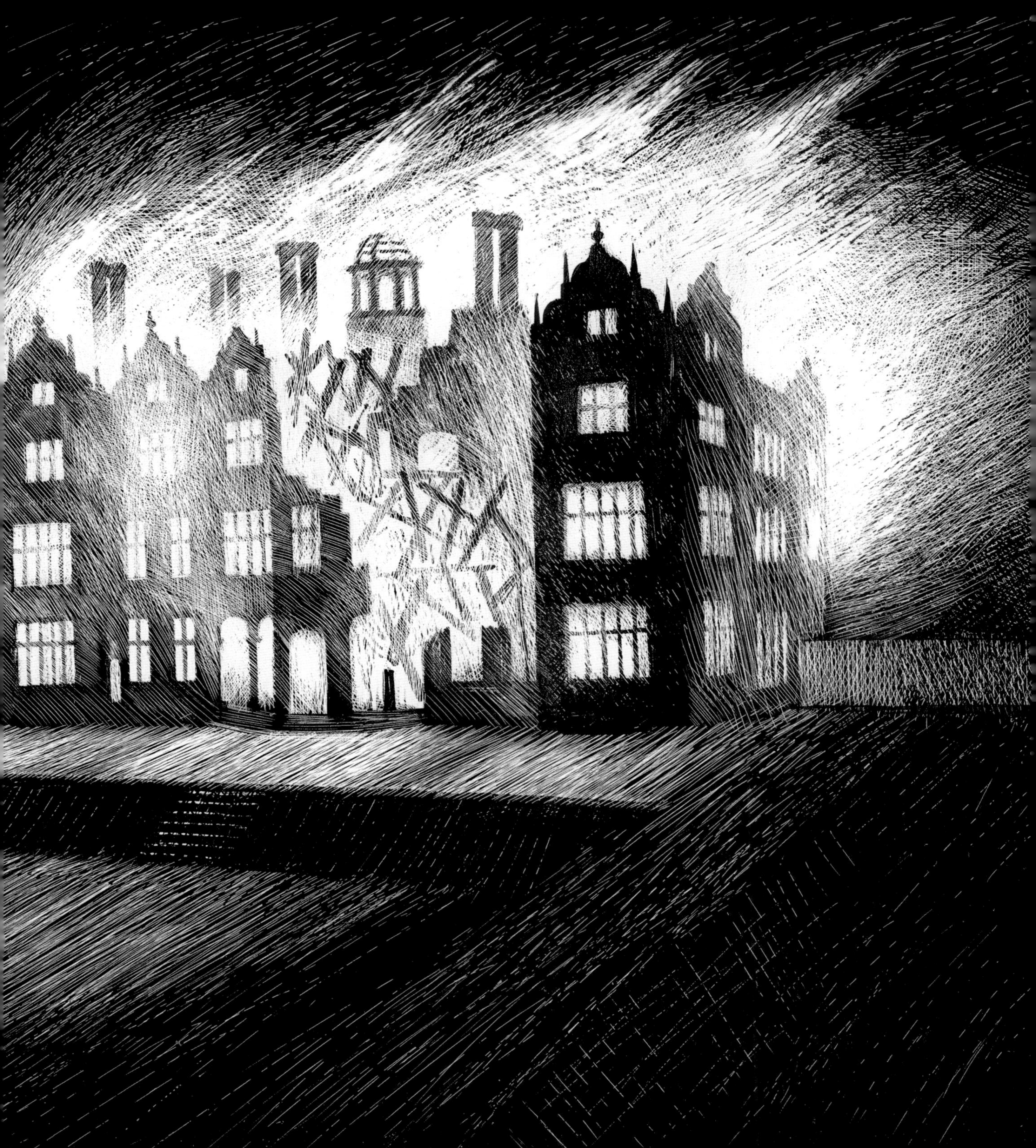

OLD CAMPDEN HOUSE

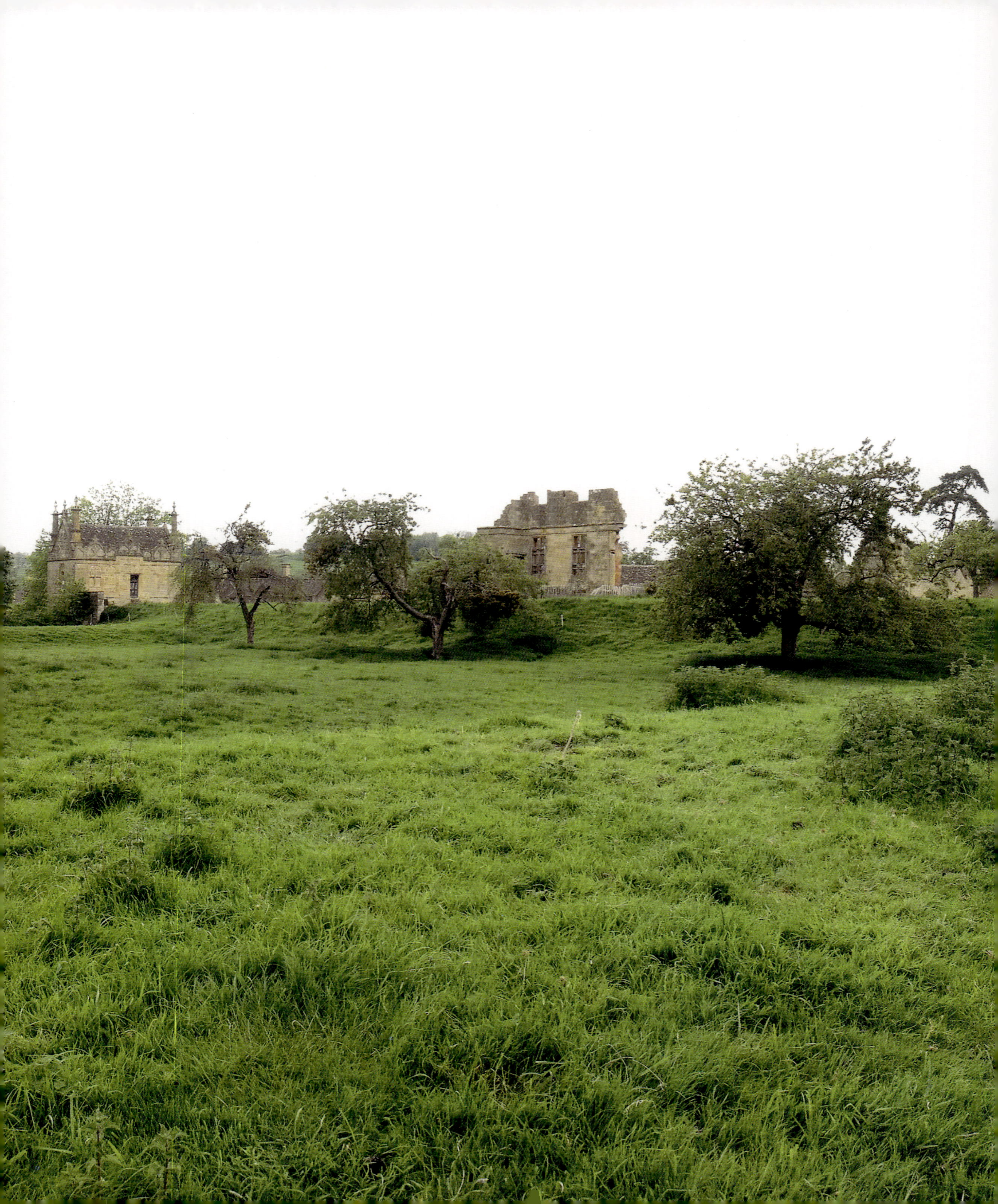

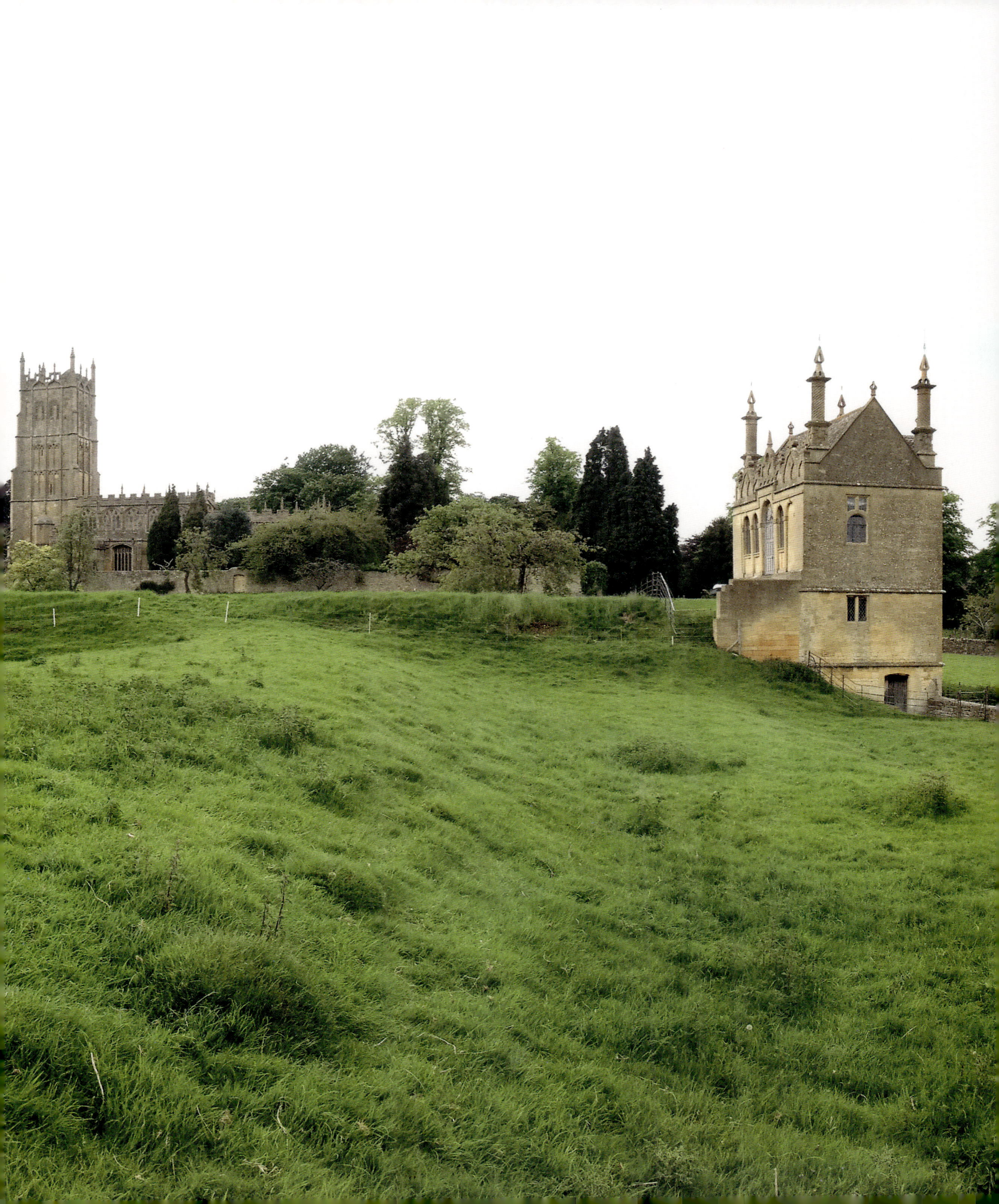

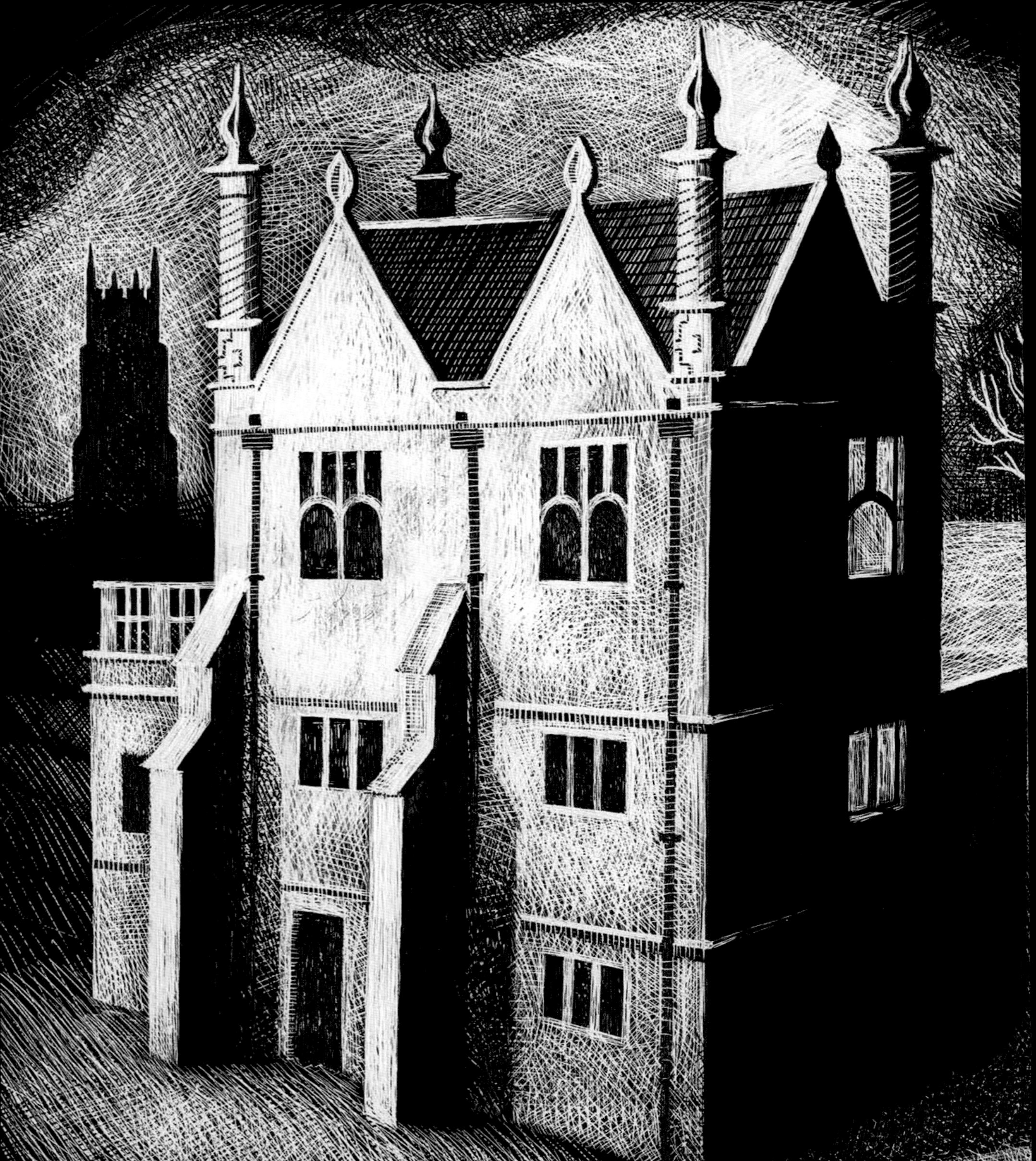
KLUZ

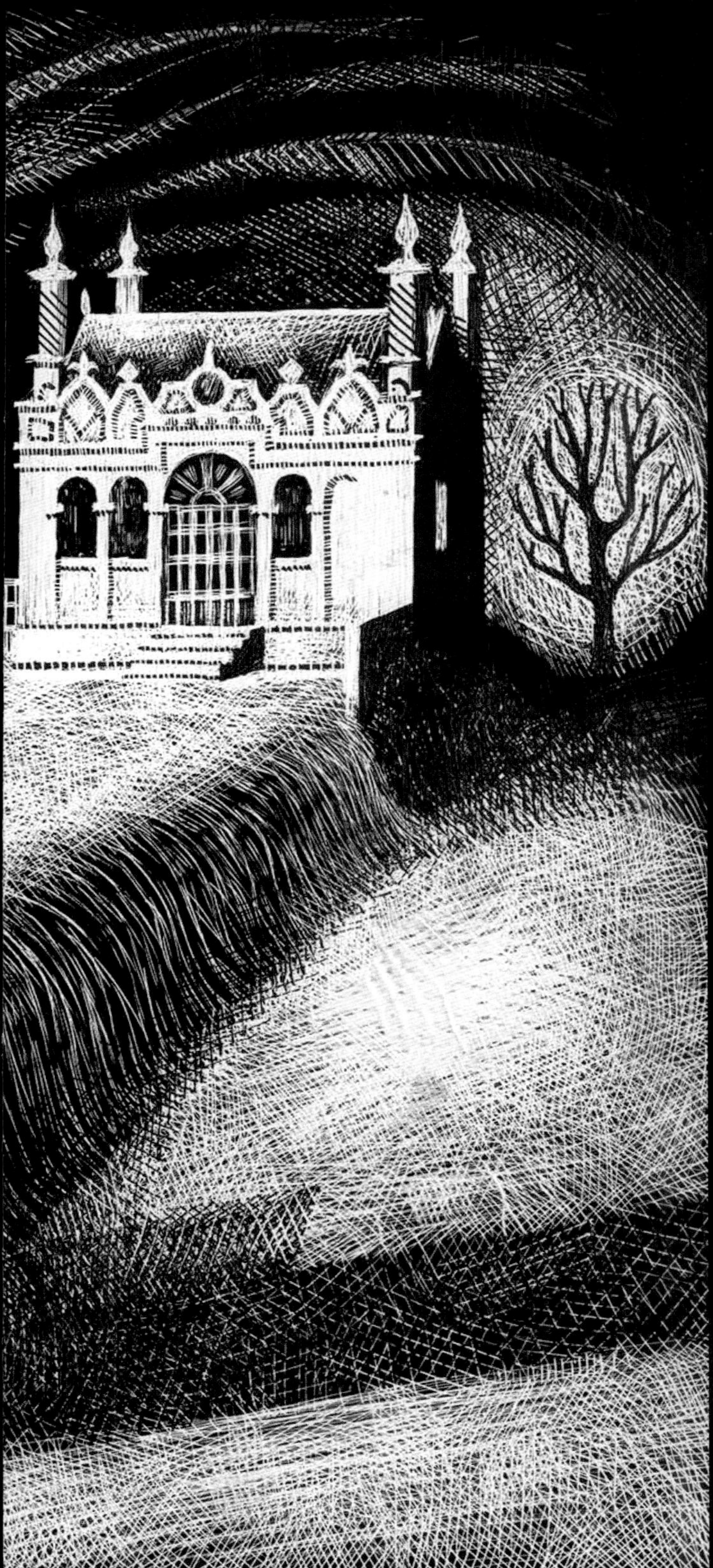

The Banqueting Houses, Chipping Campden, *scraperboard, 2014.*

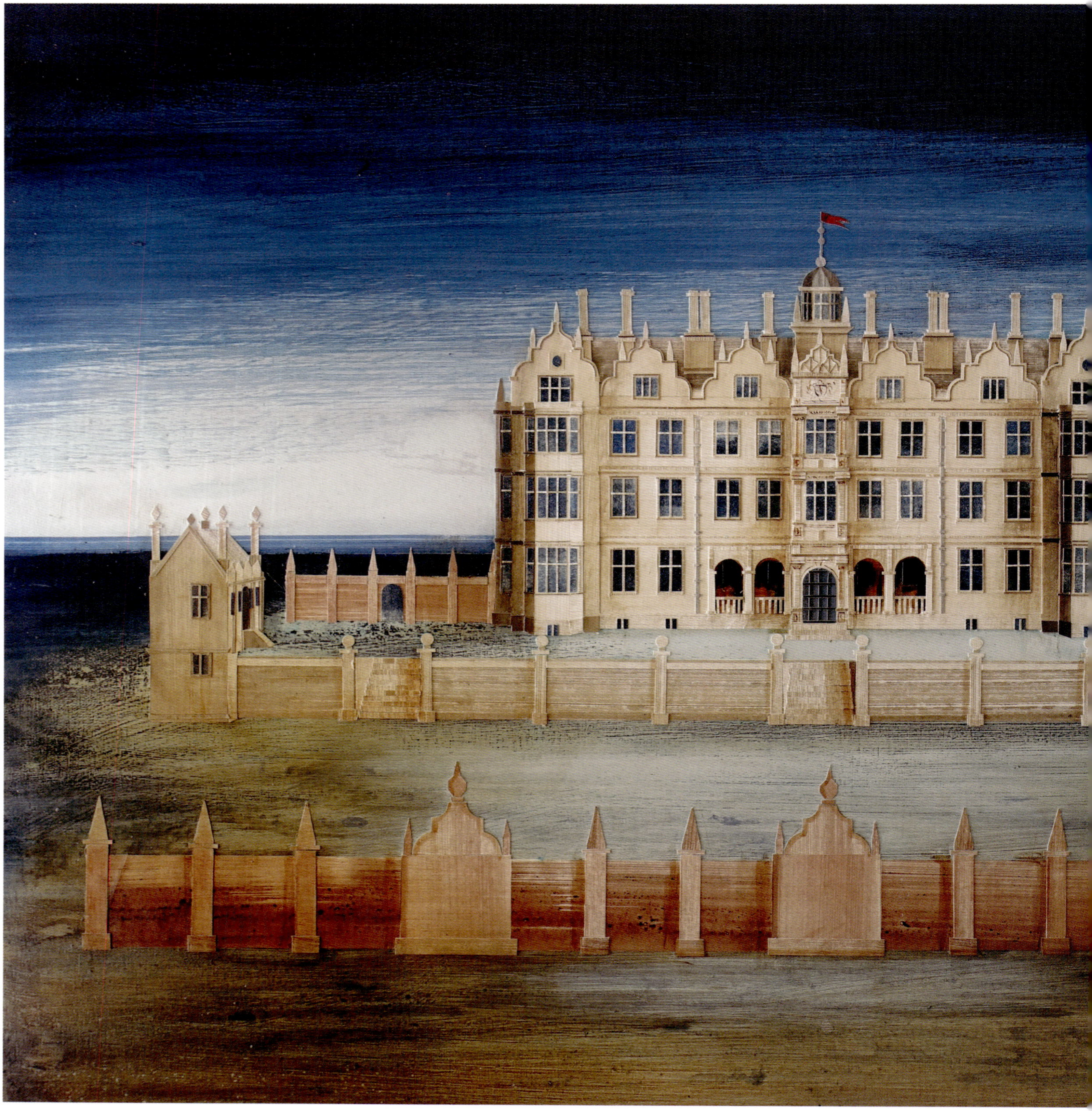

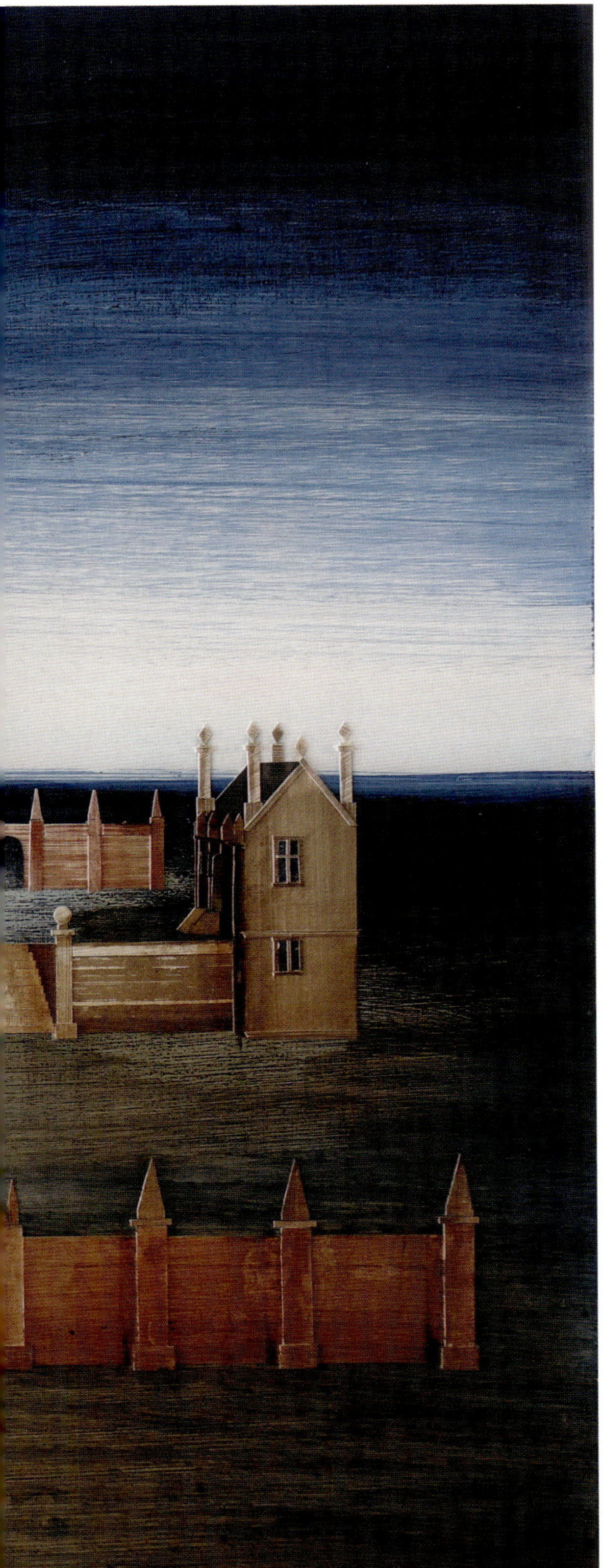

Prospect of Old Campden House, *paper collage and mixed media, 2017. Detail shown overleaf.*

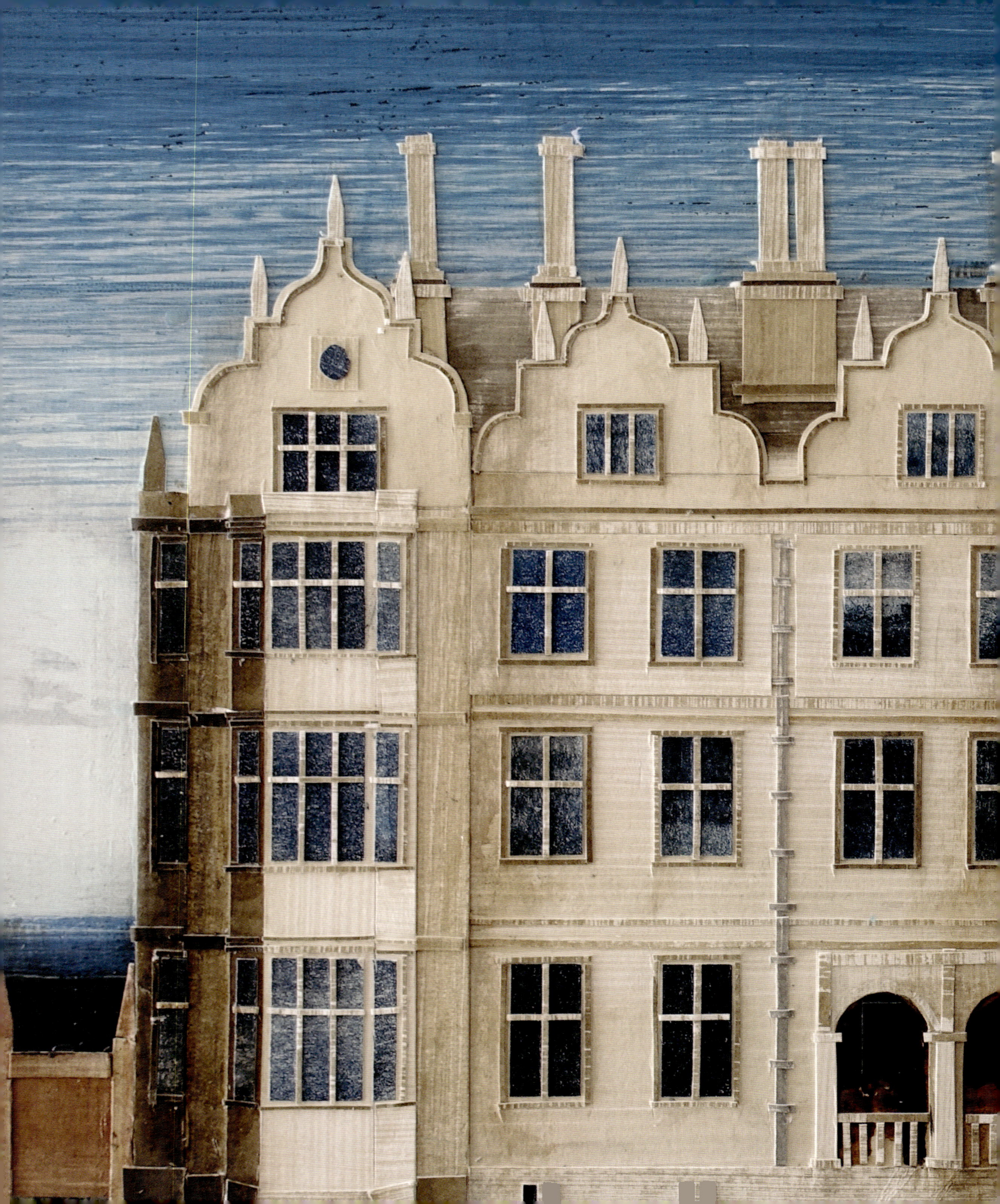

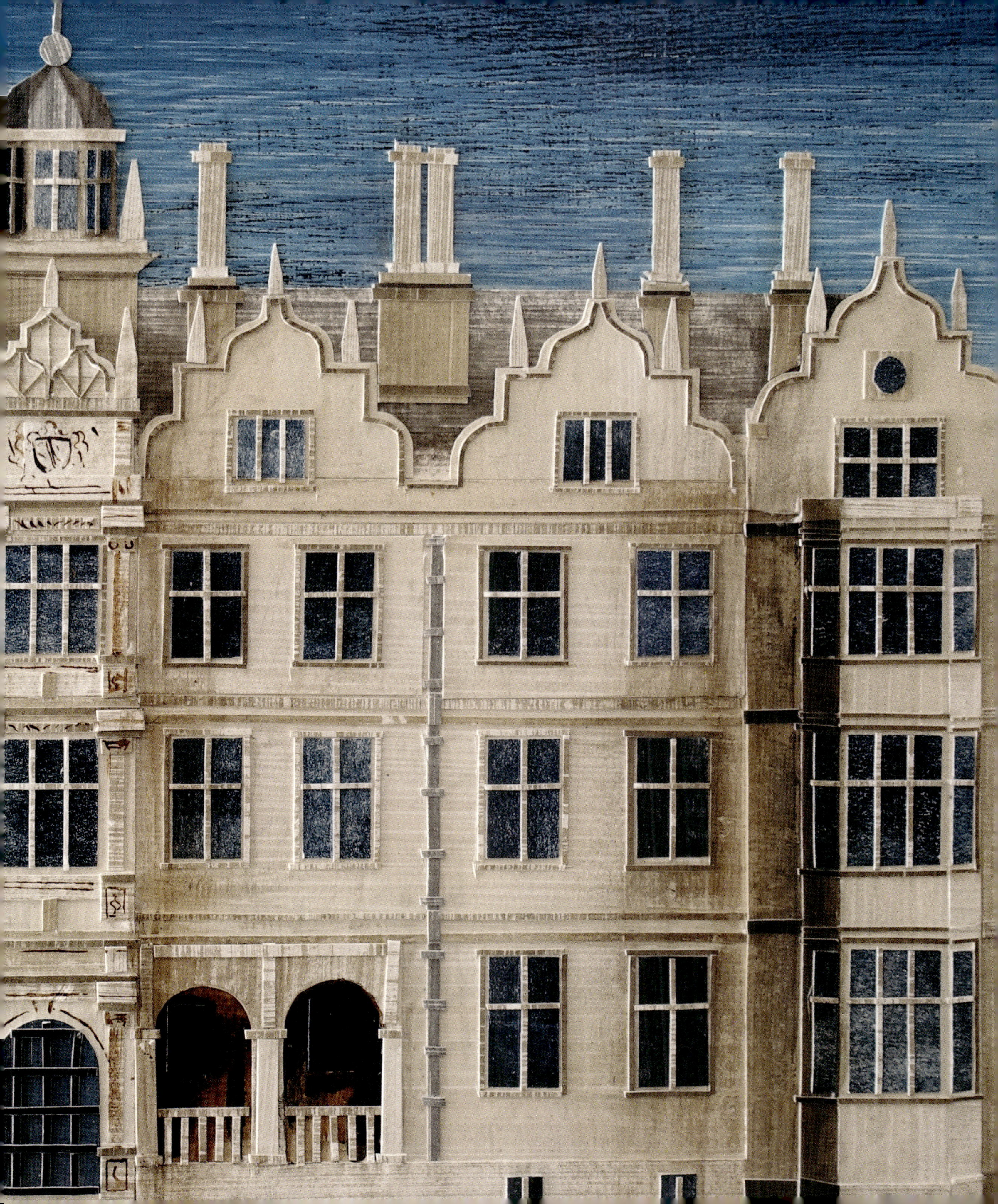

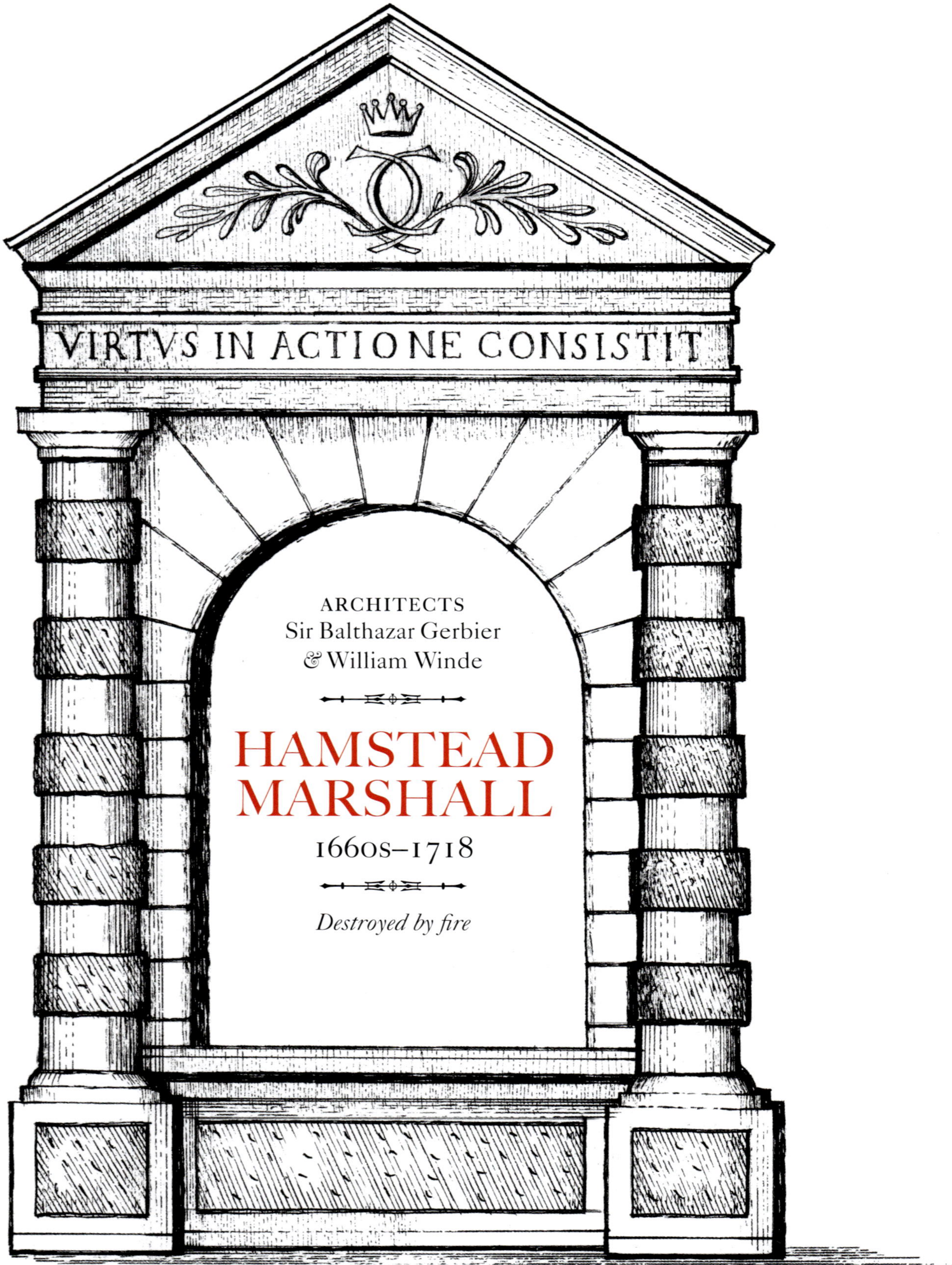

ARCHITECTS
Sir Balthazar Gerbier
& William Winde

HAMSTEAD MARSHALL

1660s–1718

Destroyed by fire

It is appropriate that the design for the great gateway at Hamstead Marshall is the only surviving drawing that bears the signature of Sir Balthazar Gerbier (1592–1663; pp. 98–99), for grand entrances were his speciality.[1] It was probably Gerbier who collaborated with the architect Peter Mills to design the temporary arches for Charles II's ceremonial entry into London in 1661, but for political reasons he 'desired to have his name conceal'd'.[2] Such projects were ideally suited to the artist turned architect, collector and spy, who described himself as skilled 'in sciences, as mathematics, architecture, drawing, painting, contriving of scenes, masques, shows and entertainments for great princes'.[3] Despite his self-professed prowess, however, almost nothing of his work survives on paper or in stone.

Born in a Dutch province to Huguenot émigré parents, Gerbier came to England in 1616 and was soon serving the Duke of Buckingham and Charles I in artistic and diplomatic business. As his espionage on behalf of the Spanish government of The Netherlands remained undetected, he was knighted in 1638. Finding himself out of favour at court by the early 1640s, he then dabbled in banking, teaching and gold speculation. By the 1660s he was touting for business via two architectural treatises, one of which at least Samuel Pepys judged 'not worth a turd'.[4] Nevertheless, at about this time, the 1st Earl of Craven commissioned Gerbier to remodel his house at Hamstead Marshall, Berkshire.

William, Baron Craven (1608–1697) was a courtier and soldier who ardently supported Charles I, was devoted to the king's sister – Elizabeth, Queen of Bohemia – and financially supported the Royalist cause during the English Civil War. His loyalty led to prosecution for conspiracy under the Commonwealth; he was eventually cleared, but his estates were confiscated. After the Restoration he was rewarded for his trouble by an earldom and the return of his house at Hamstead Marshall, which his widowed mother had purchased for him in 1620.

The evidence of Johannes Kip's *Britannia Illustrata* (1707; overleaf), as well as a cache of designs relating to Hamstead Marshall preserved in an album in the Bodleian Library in Oxford,[5] suggest that Gerbier extended the existing Jacobean house rather than erected a new one: the earlier façade, with its central porch and two projecting window bays on either side, is still visible, embedded in the eastern range of the augmented house. As well as adding two storeys, Gerbier devised additional ranges to create a courtyard house. A plan in the Bodleian shows that four ranges, each two rooms deep, were originally intended.

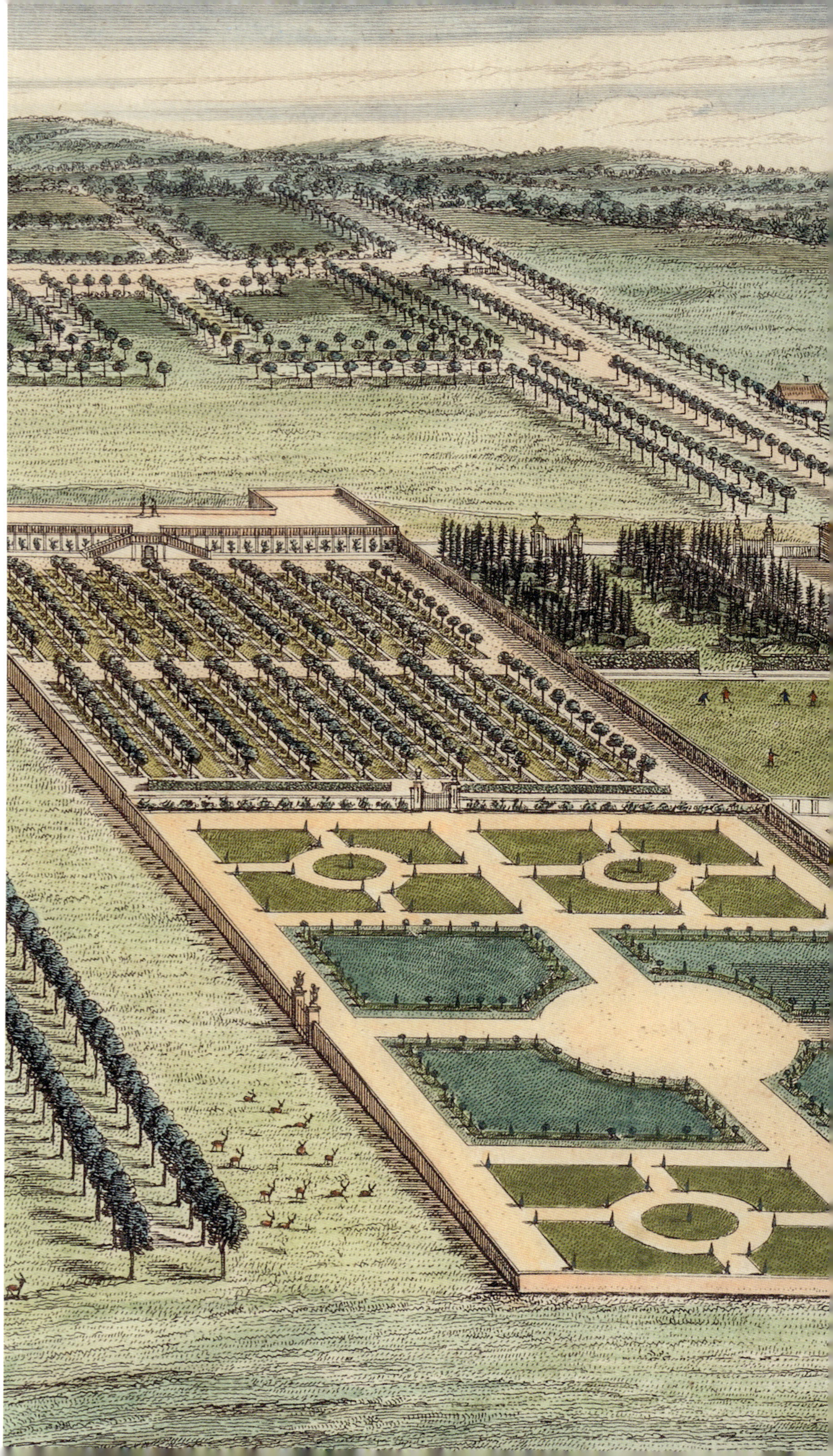

Johannes Kip, after Leonard Knyff, Hamstead Marshall in the County of Bercks, *hand-coloured engraving, originally published in* Britannia Illustrata, *1707.*

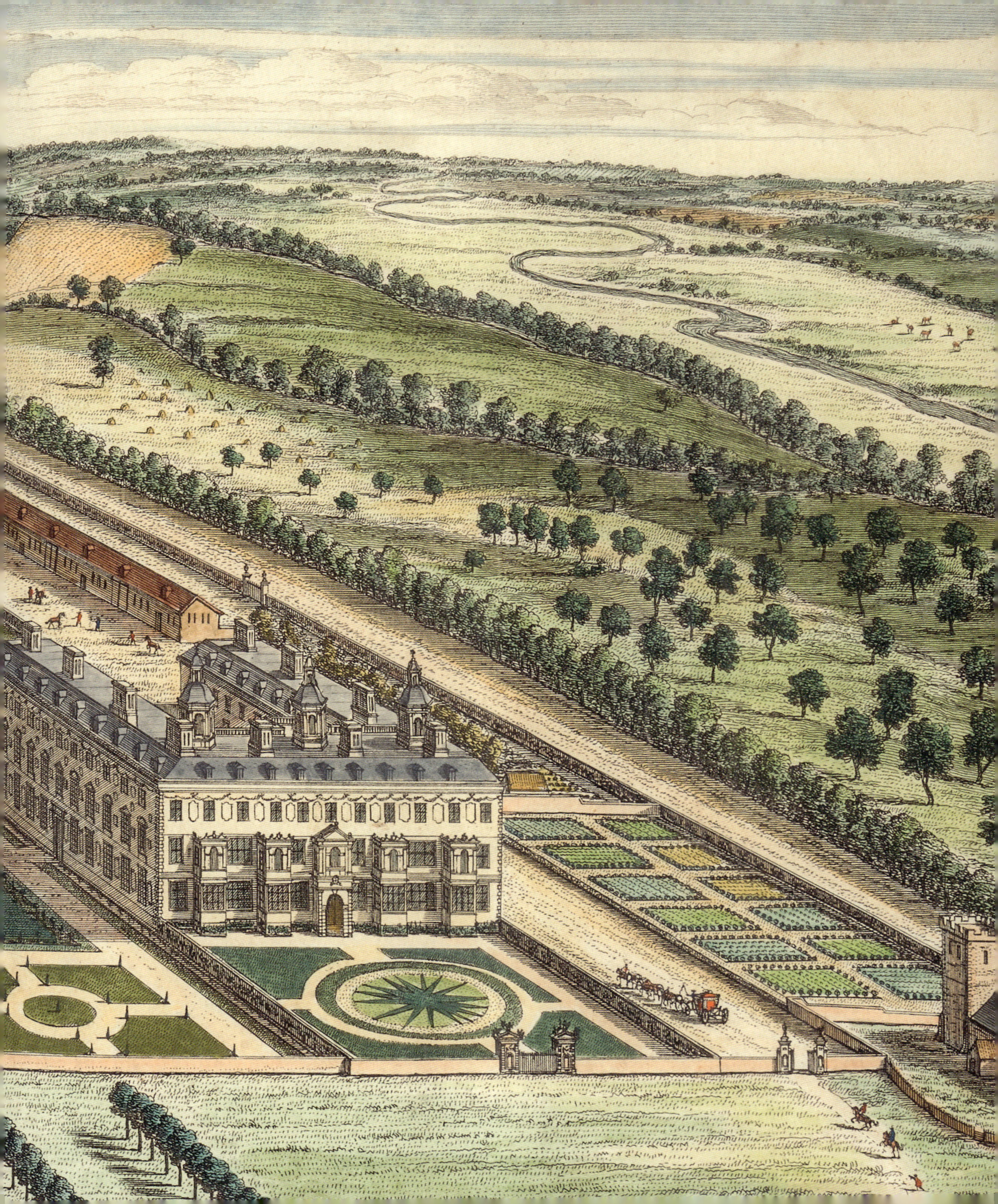

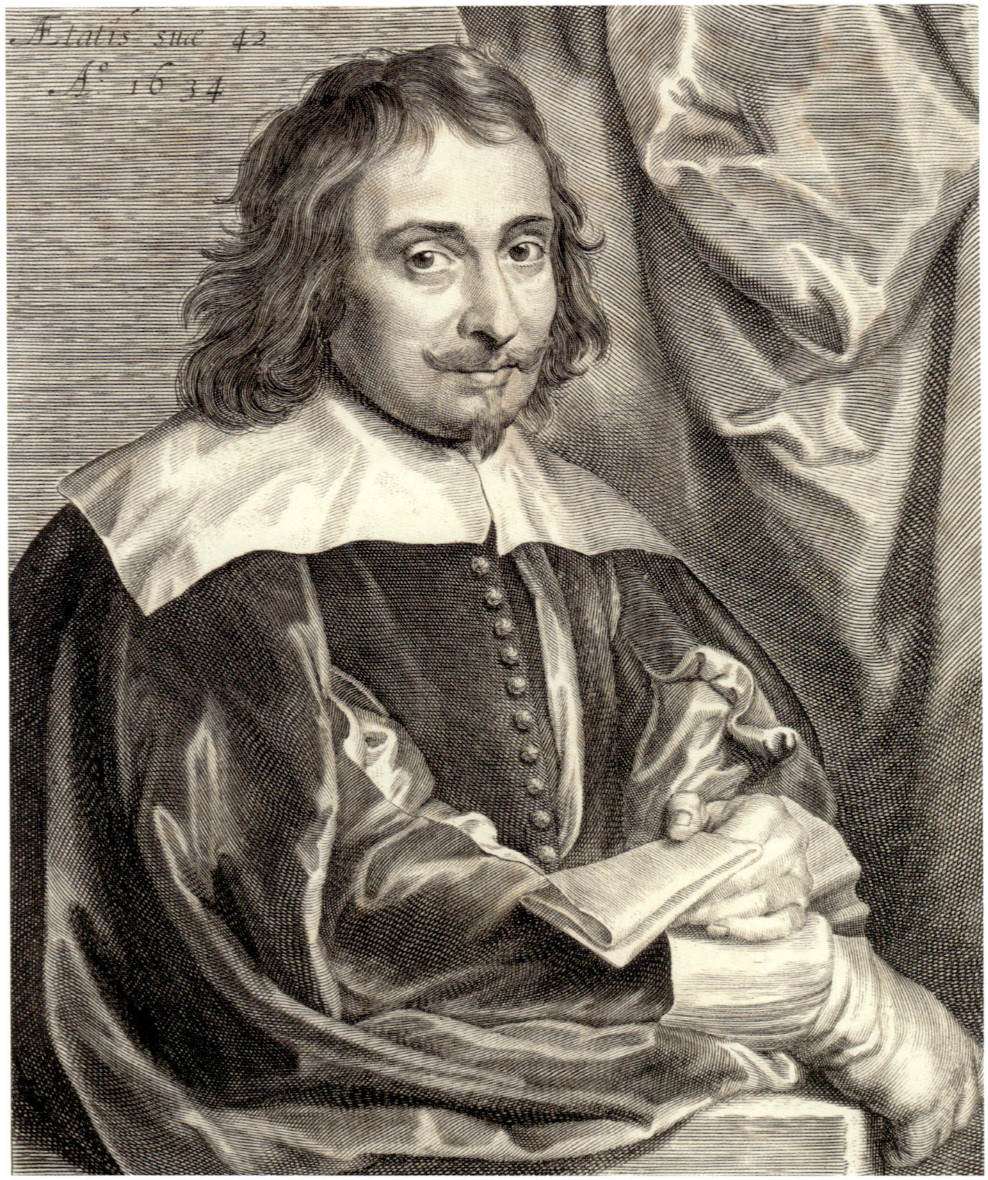

Hempsted-Marshall, the seat of Lord Craven, since destroyed by fire, was the last production of Gerbier. He gave the designs for it, and died there while it was building, and was buried in the chancel of that church.

HORACE WALPOLE, *ANECDOTES OF PAINTING IN ENGLAND*, VOL. I, 1762

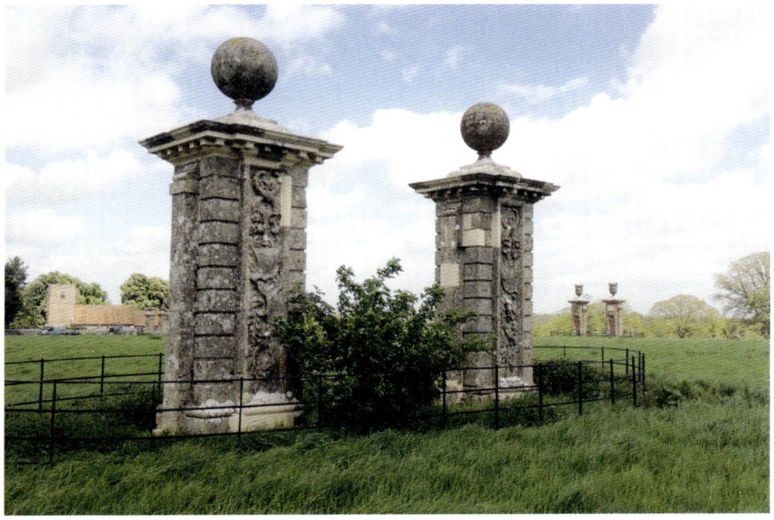

Kip's engraving indicates that the western range was not realized. Although that side of the house is obscured in Kip's view, another design in the Bodleian suggests that it ultimately took the form of a classicizing screen with central portico, much as had been created at Castle Ashby, Northamptonshire, in the 1630s.

Opposite: Paulus Pontius (Paulus Du Pont), after Sir Anthony van Dyck, Sir Balthazar Gerbier, *engraving, 1634.*

Above: The gate piers at Hamstead Marshall, photographed by Ed Kluz, 2017.

Craven's devotion to the Queen of Bohemia was well known, and it was said that Hamstead Marshall was modelled on Heidelberg Castle for her pleasure, but she died while it was under construction. Gerbier, too, did not live to see the house's completion. He died on a visit to the site in 1663 and was buried in the parish church (where the long-posthumous inscription on his monument incorrectly dates his death to 1667). This left William Winde (*c.* 1642–1722), whose signature is on many of the Bodleian drawings, to finish the commission. Exactly what elements can be ascribed to each architect is unclear: the drawing for the western screen is in Winde's hand, but it could have been suggested by Gerbier. The fact that work did not begin on the first additional floor until July 1664 and that several designs for ceilings are dated in the 1670s and '80s indicates there was still much to be done after Gerbier's death. The earl himself died in 1697, and the house passed to his kinsman, also William Craven.

Below: A date stone set into the churchyard wall at Hamstead Marshall, photographed by Ed Kluz, 2017.

Overleaf: Sir Balthazar Gerbier's design for the gate piers at Hamstead Marshall, early 1660s.

In 1718 the house was almost entirely destroyed by fire, an end that commentators found notable on account of the 2nd Baron Craven being renowned for his firefighting efforts. He always attended conflagrations on horseback, so that it was said 'his horse smelt a fire as soon as it happened'.[6] The ruins of the house were gradually dismantled, leaving only a faint depression in the ground. The piers of the great gates were taken to nearby Benham Park to do new service, while remaining pairs of additional piers encircle the former site of Hamstead Marshall like graveside mourners.

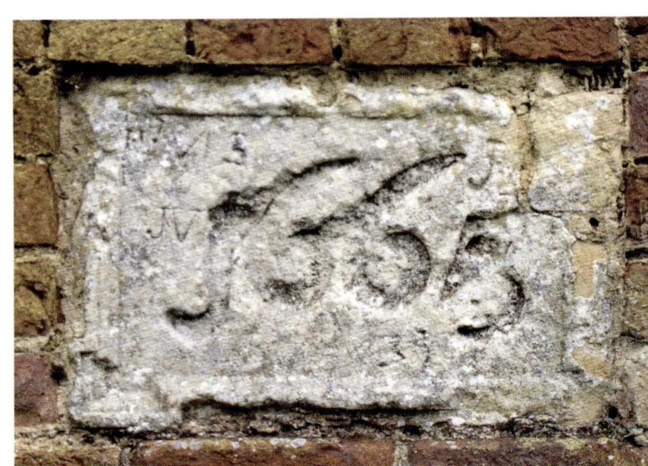

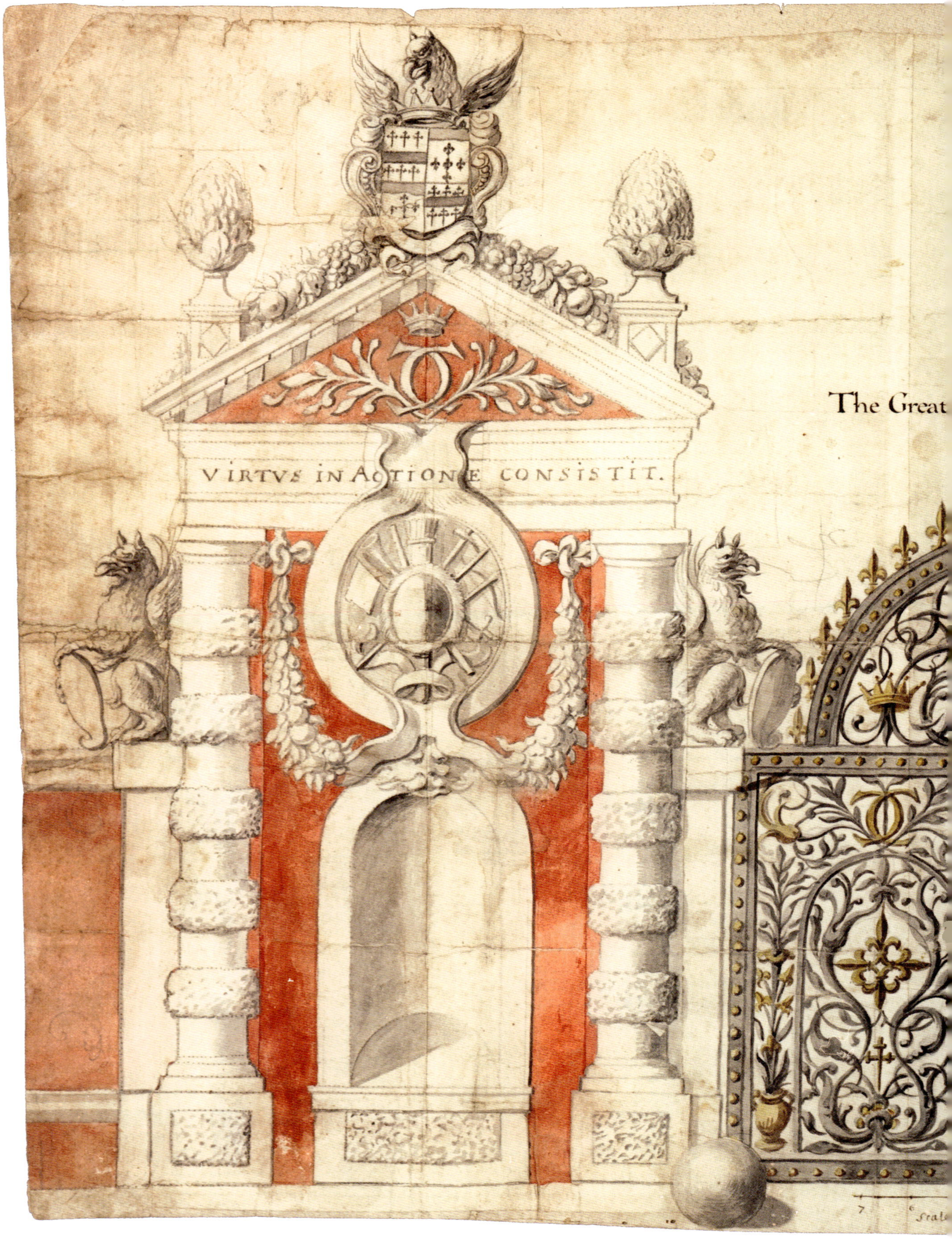
VIRTVS IN ACTIONE CONSISTIT.
The Great

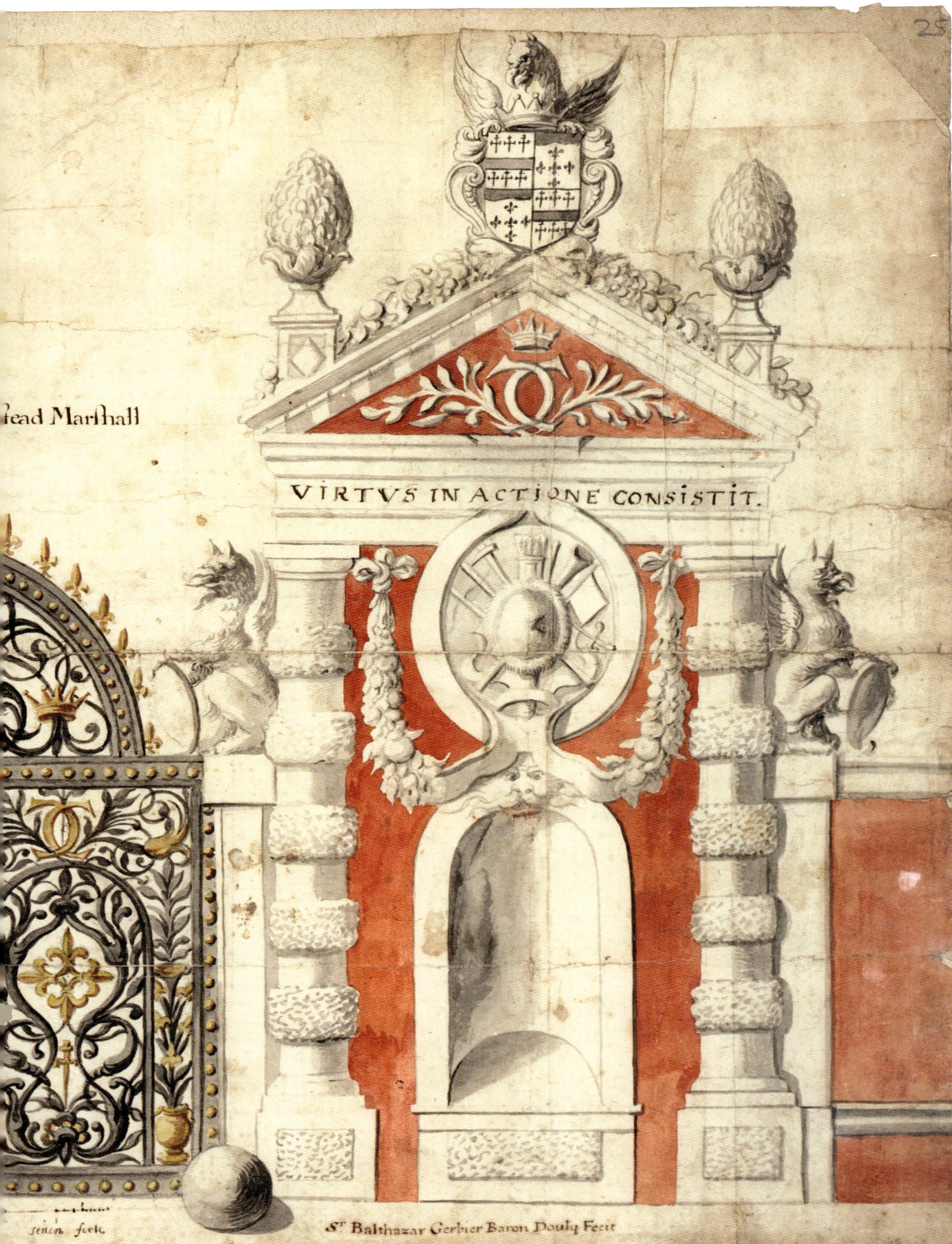

25
…stead Marshall
VIRTVS IN ACTIONE CONSISTIT.
…seven feete
Sr Balthazar Gerbier Baron Douly Fecit

Hamstead Marshall on Fire, *scraperboard, 2017*.

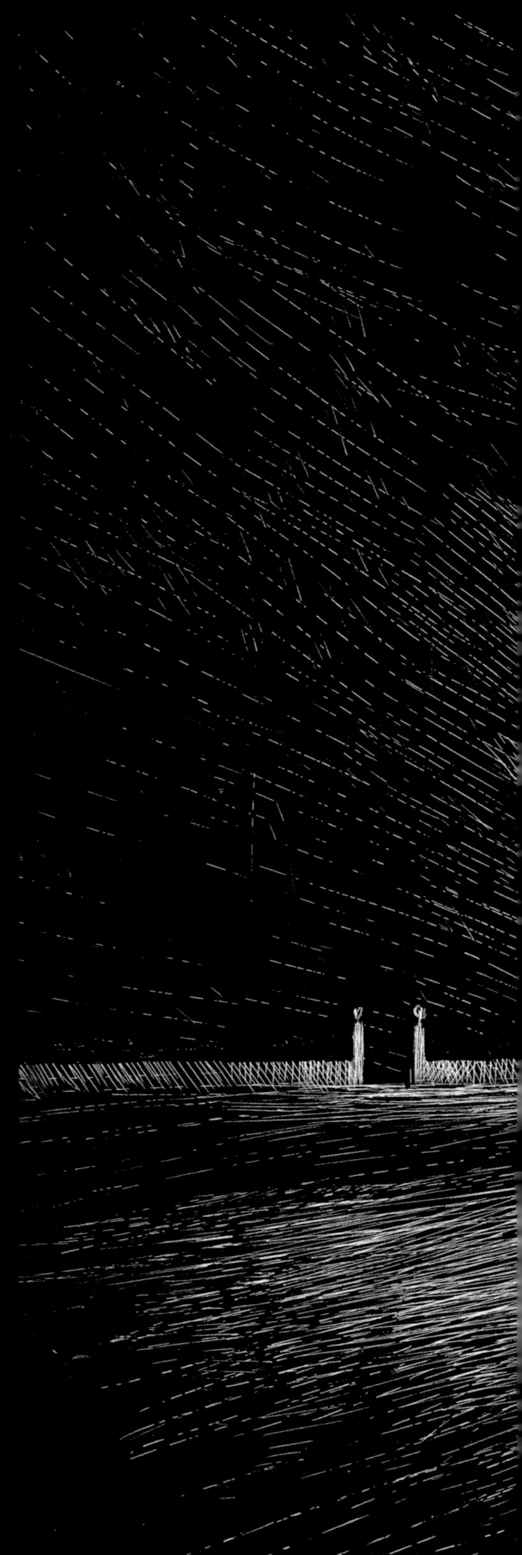

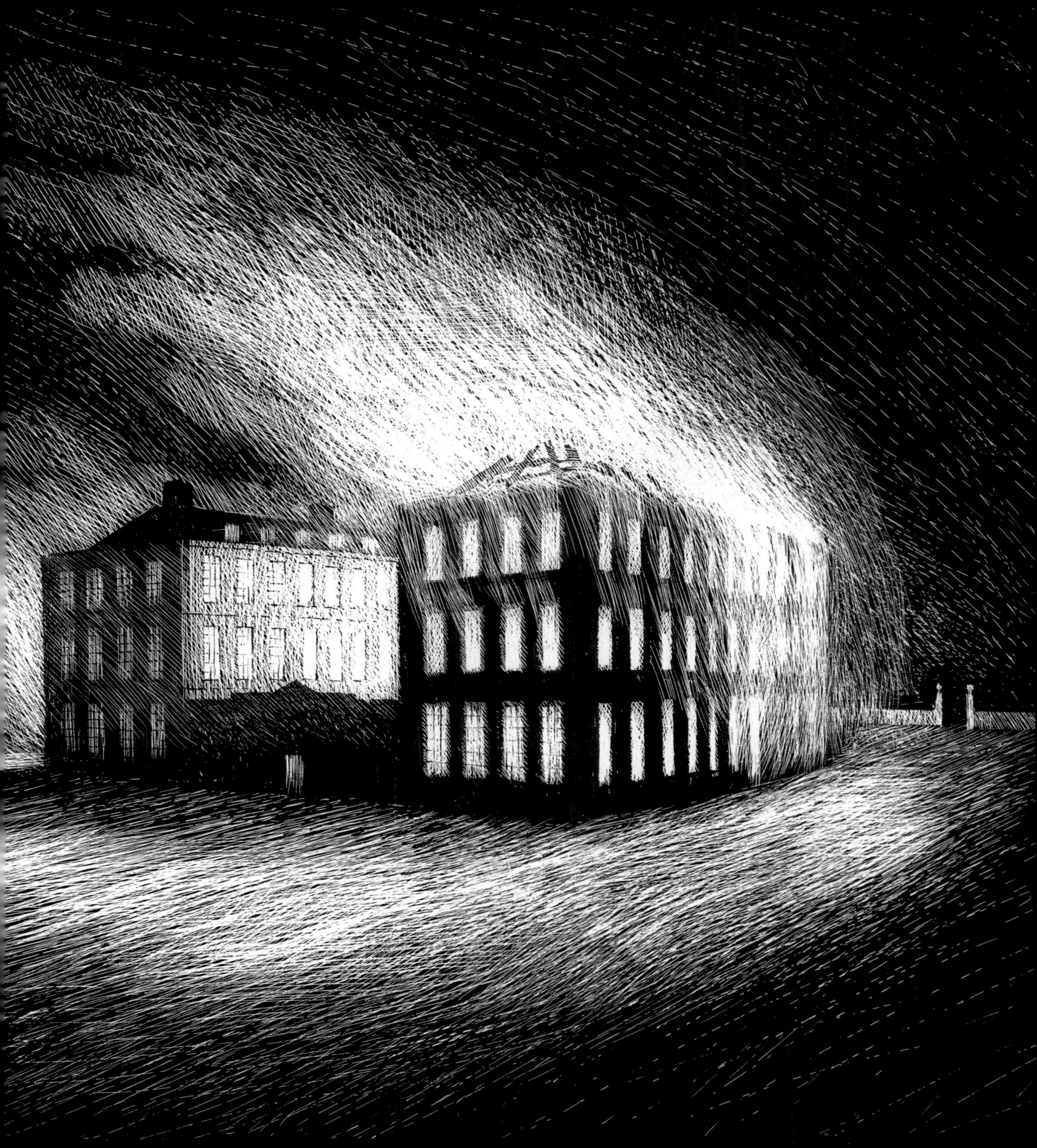

HAMSTEAD MARSHALL

View of the East Façade
of Hamstead Marshall,
scraperboard, 2017.

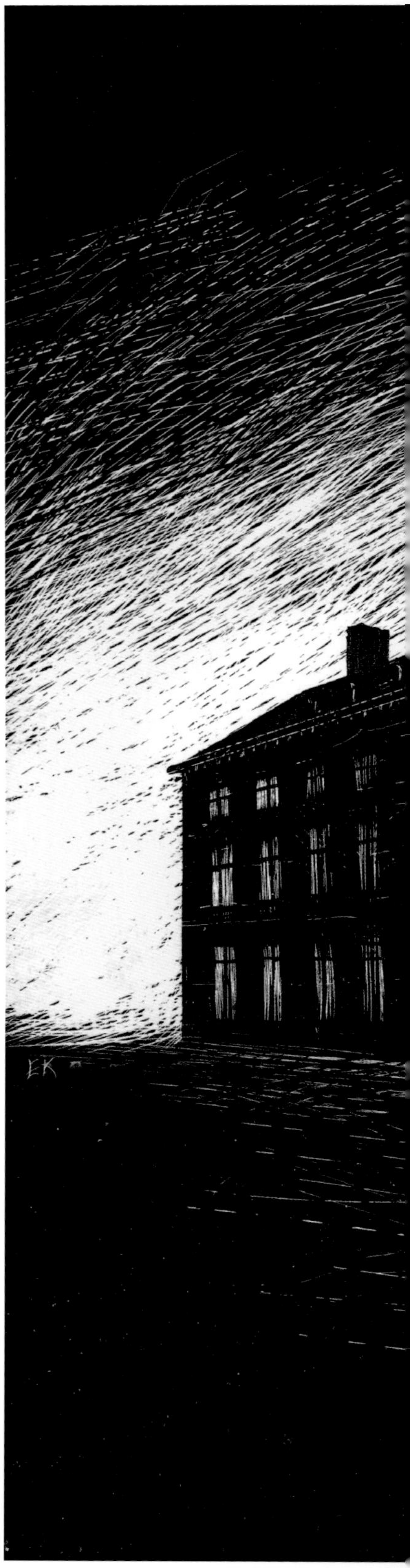

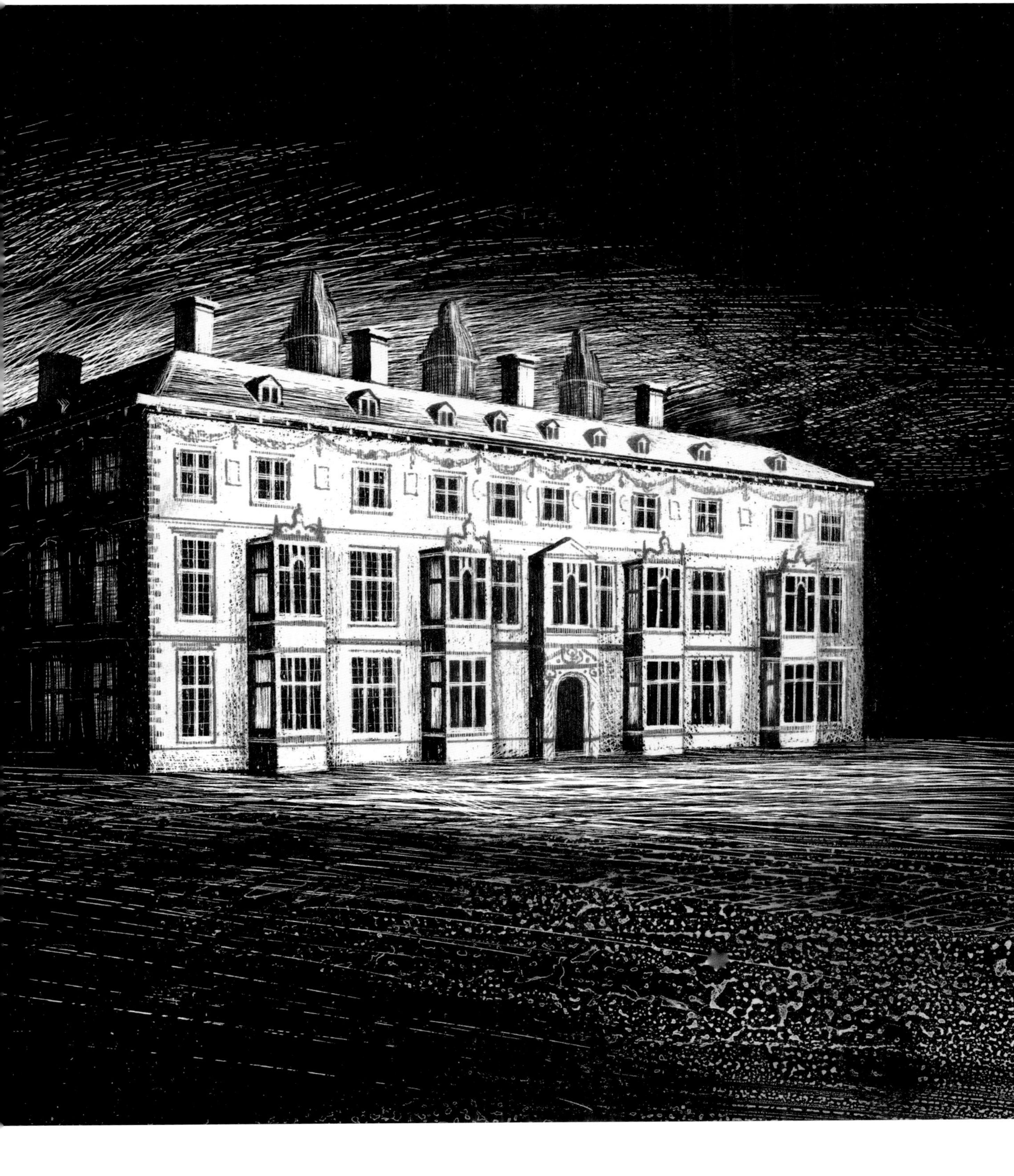

HAMSTEAD MARSHALL

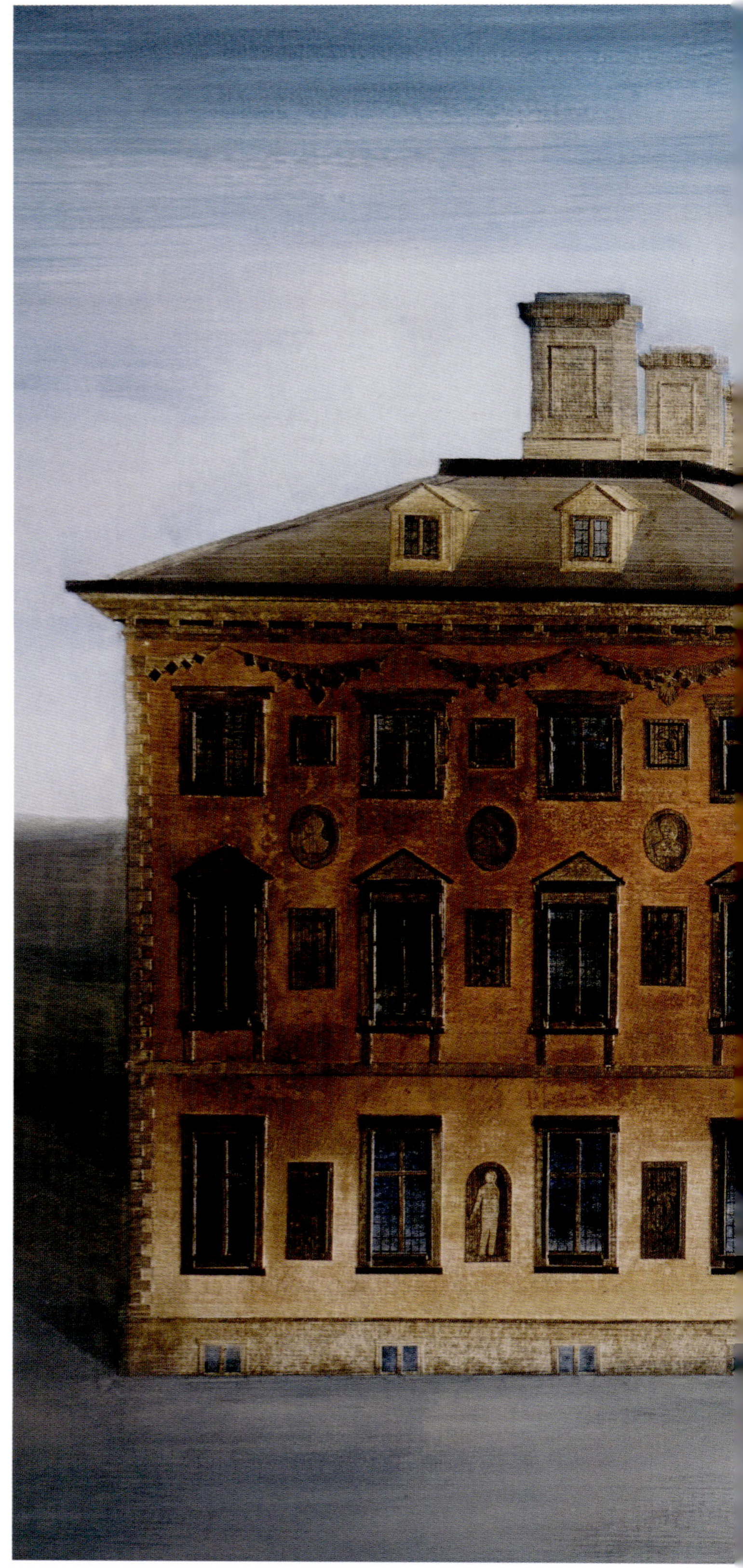

View of the West Façade of Hamstead Marshall, *paper collage and mixed media, 2017. Detail shown pages 106–107.*

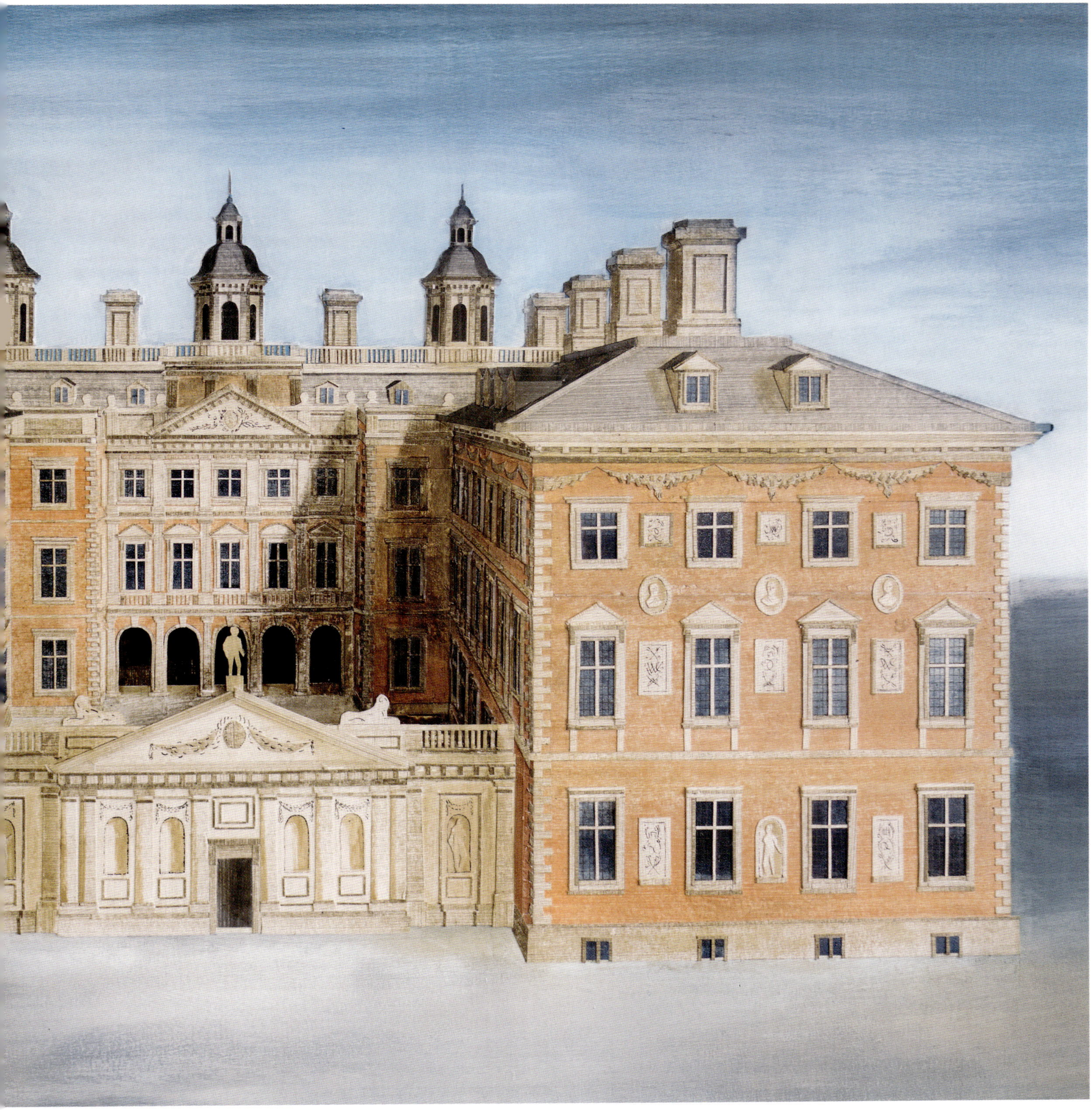

HAMSTEAD MARSHALL

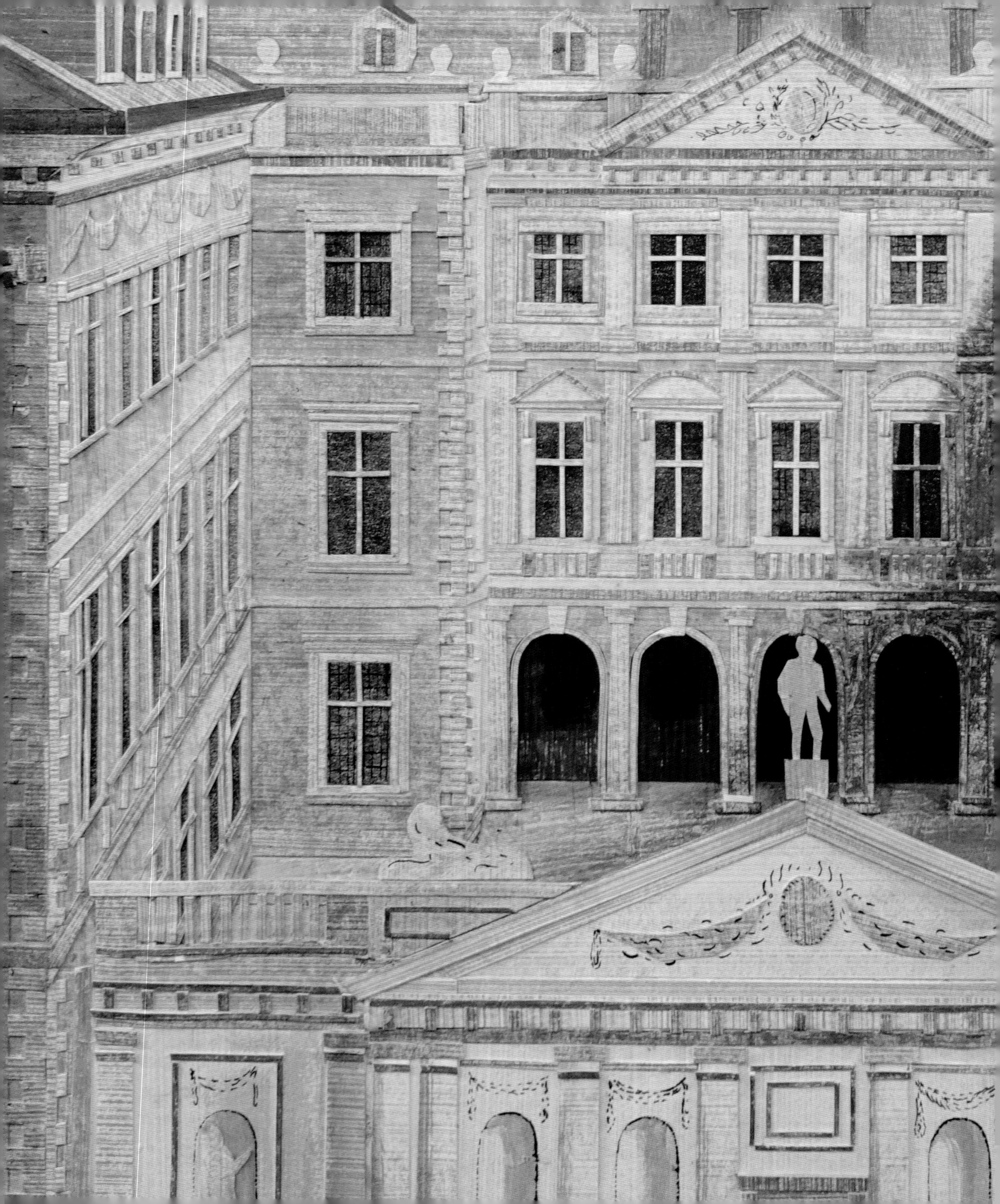

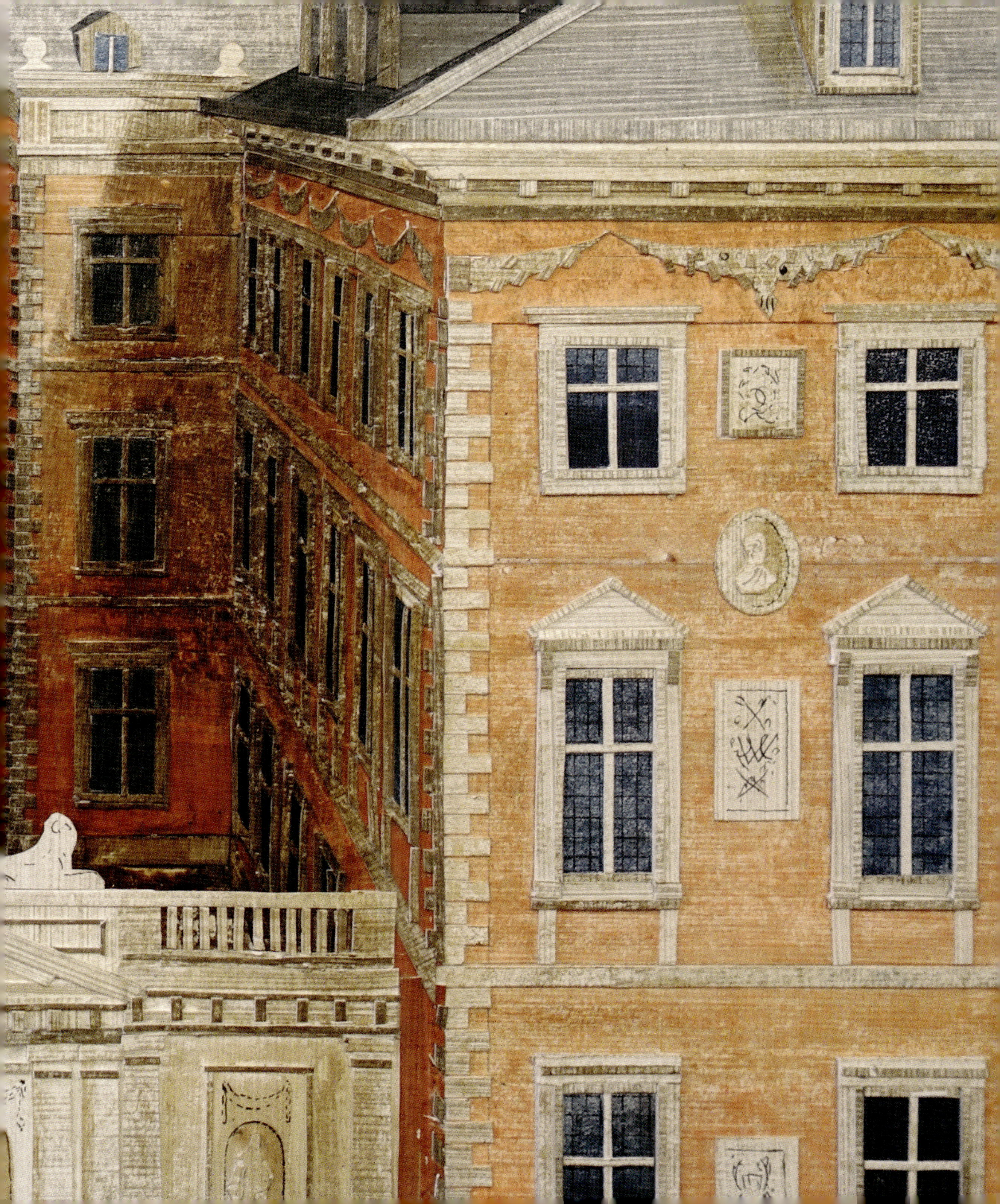

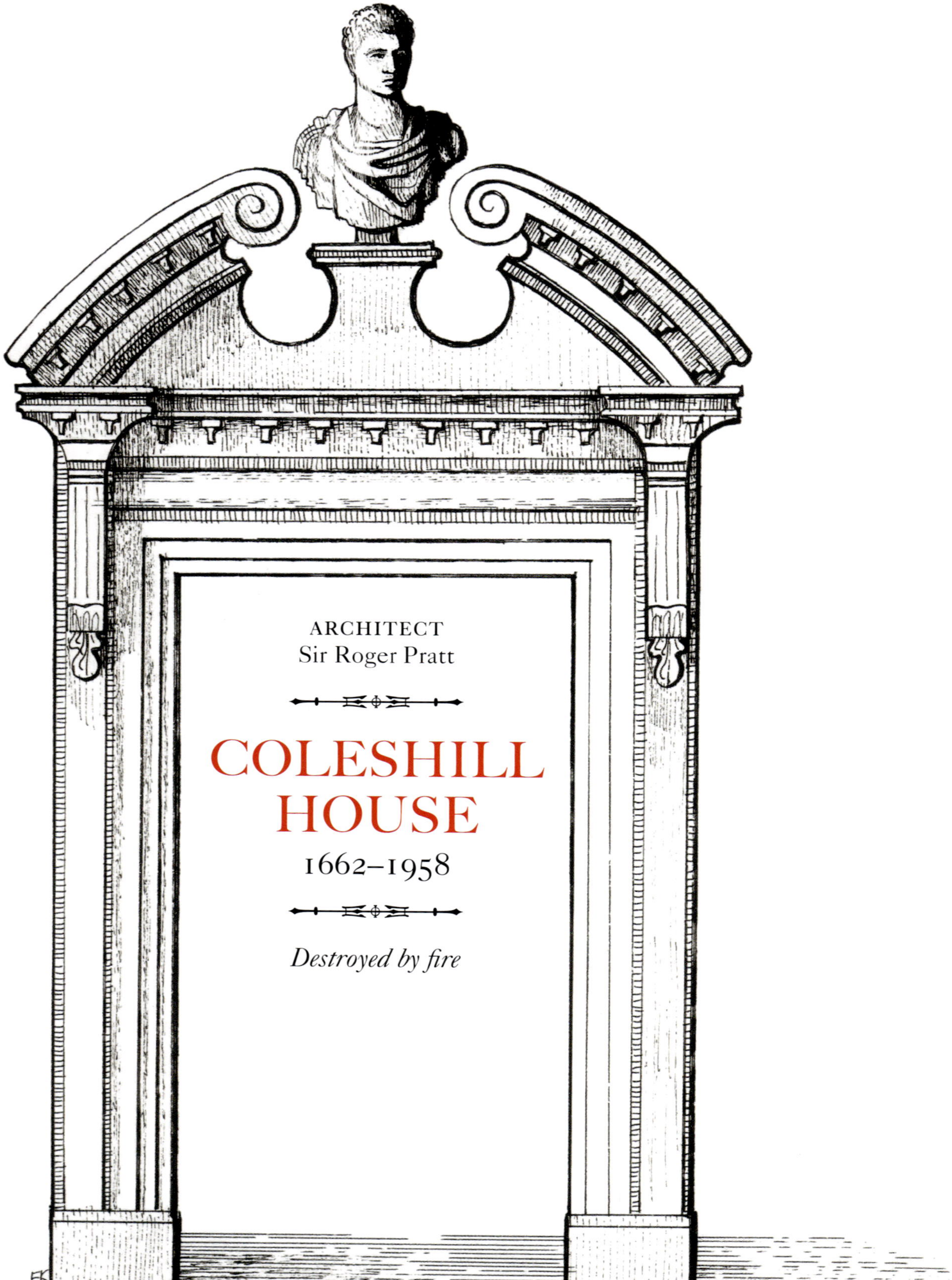

ARCHITECT
Sir Roger Pratt

COLESHILL HOUSE

1662–1958

Destroyed by fire

There are three lost houses at Coleshill, Oxfordshire (formerly in Berkshire): the first burnt down in the late 1640s, the second reached only ground-floor level before it was dismantled, and the third was consumed by fire in 1952. The last of these was England's first completely classical country house, and acquired mythical status in the eighteenth century thanks to its supposed links with Inigo Jones. Its astylar interpretation of classical ideals and pioneering compact plan made it one of the most influential houses of the late seventeenth century.

The estate at Coleshill was acquired by the Pratt family in 1626, when Henry Pratt, an alderman of the City of London, purchased it from Sir Thomas Freake. Little is known of the early house on the site, for it burnt to the ground not long after Henry's death in 1647. Having just inherited the house, Henry's son, George, had to rebuild it.

John Buffin, who served as the estate joiner for fifty years, passed on his recollections of Coleshill's genesis. He claimed that George Pratt had raised a new house to 'one Story' before his cousin, Roger Pratt (1620–1685), returned from several years' sojourn in Italy and persuaded him to abandon it.[1] Roger had extensive theoretical knowledge of classical architecture and, the story goes, called on the practical advice of the former Surveyor to James I and Charles I, Inigo Jones. During the eighteenth century, Jones's role at Coleshill was greatly overstated; although he was involved in a consultative position and his pupil, John Webb, supplied unexecuted designs, Roger Pratt's diaries demonstrate that he himself was responsible for the project. Around 1650, construction of a new Coleshill began on a different plot, and it was finally completed in 1662.

Approached through a series of fine gate piers that still survive, the house was a plain, four-storeyed building, twice as long as it was wide, with a hipped roof. Its sober façades were alleviated by window heads supported on consoles, bold pediments over the doors, and eight soaring, symmetrically placed chimneys. A domed cupola provided access to the rooftop, where Pratt intended that his visitors should enjoy 'ye Pleasure of ye prospect'.[2]

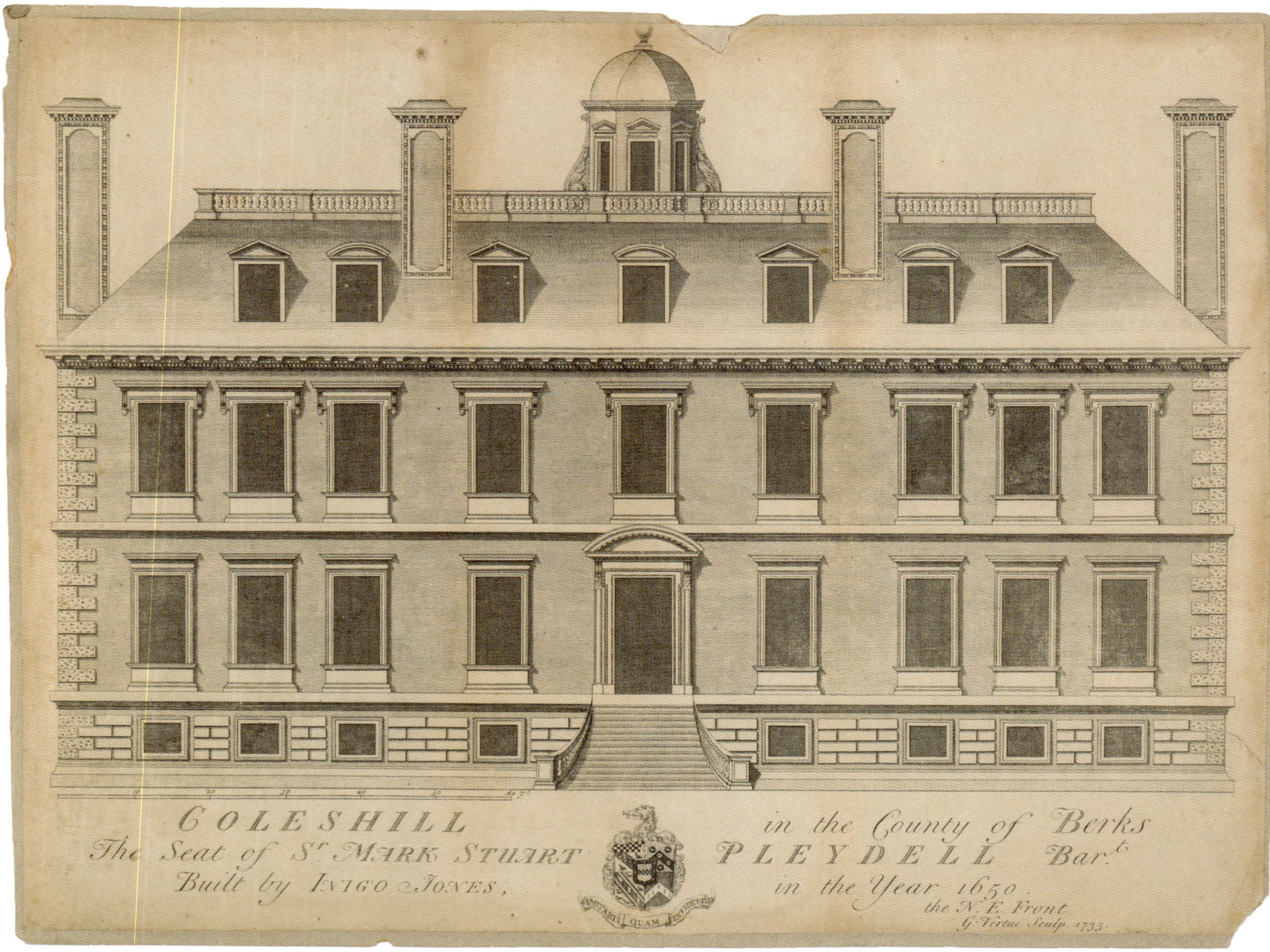

George Vertue, Coleshill in the County of Berks … the N.E. Front, *engraving, 1733.*

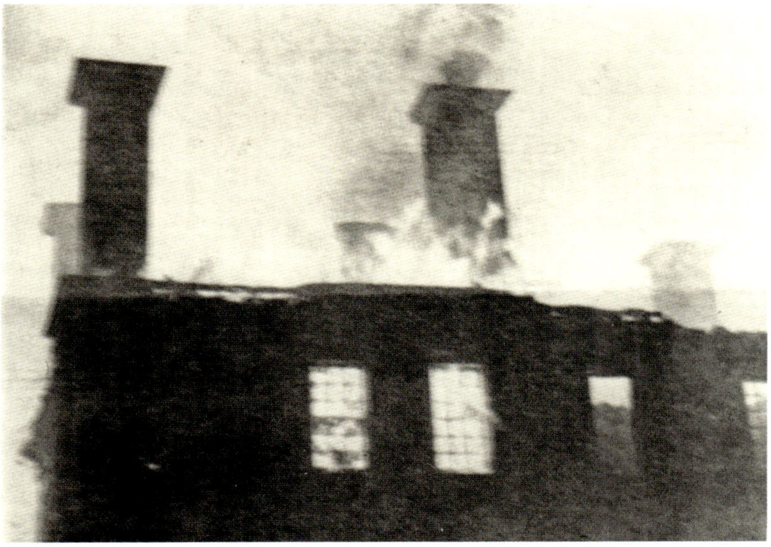

Coleshill House on fire, 1952.

The austere elevations gave little hint of the impressive interiors. When the traveller Celia Fiennes saw the house in 1690, she was struck by the 'lofty' triple-height entrance hall, with its 'spacious and handsom' twin staircase; she admired how 'all the walls are cutt in hollows where statues and heads carved finely are sett'.[3] The lavish plasterwork ceilings, on which Jones had consulted before his death, were so fine that when Lord Burlington visited in 1730, he commissioned Isaac Ware to draw them.

Coleshill descended through daughters into the possession of the earls of Radnor, who lived there for more than two centuries. Unlike some country seats, it survived its period of military service during the Second World War, when it was the training headquarters for the British resistance network. After the war, the Earl of Radnor sold the property to Ernest Cook, grandson of the travel agent Thomas Cook, whose plan was to leave it to the National Trust. In the course of renovations in 1952, however, a dormer window ignited under the heat of a blowtorch, and fire gutted the house. The shell remained until early 1958, when – despite a preservation campaign led by Sir John Betjeman – it was taken down. The site is presently an ornamental garden: box hedging delineates the plan of the building, and architectural fragments gather moss in the undergrowth.

The fire at Coleshill, as reported in the Swindon Evening Advertiser, *24 September 1952.*

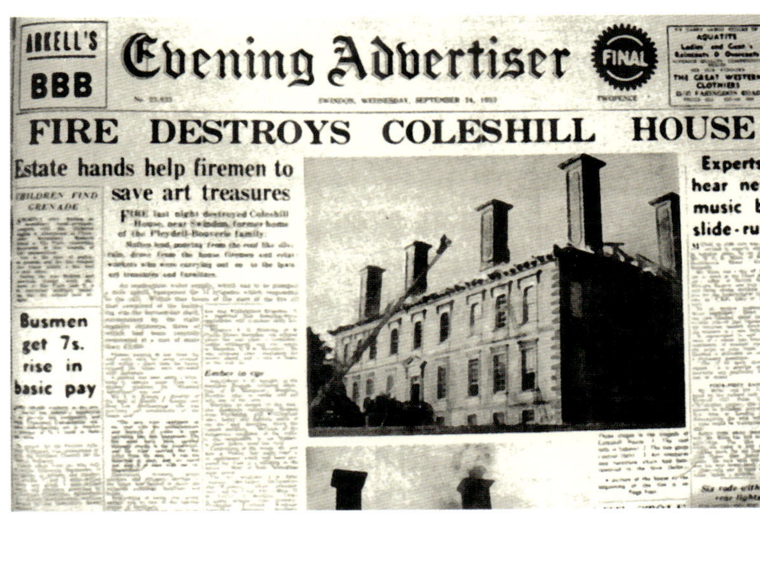

Evening Advertiser

FINAL

FIRE DESTROYS COLESHILL HOUSE

Estate hands help firemen to save art treasures

Busmen get 7s. rise in basic pay

Experts hear new music by slide-rule

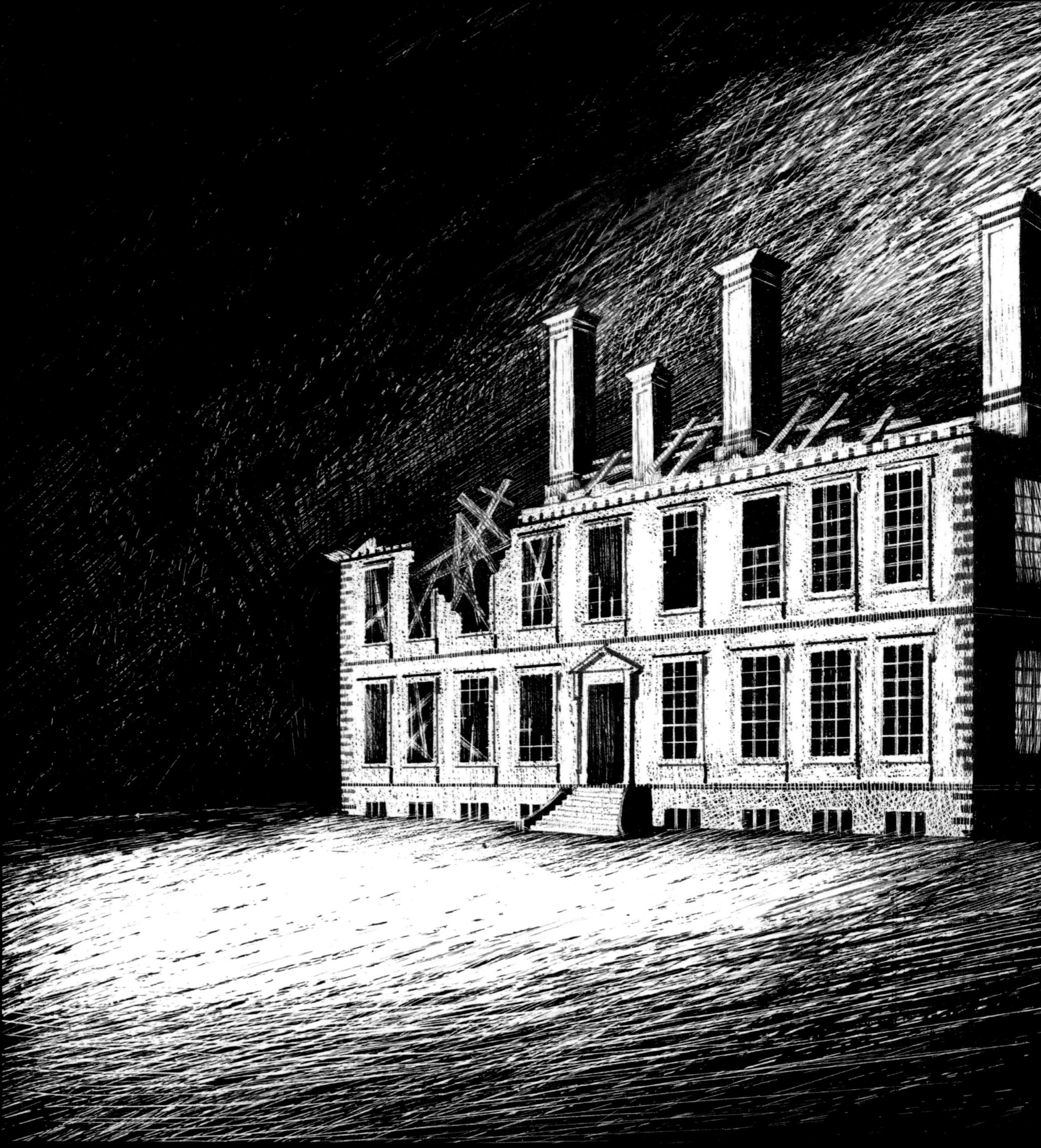

ED KLUZ: THE LOST HOUSE REVISITED

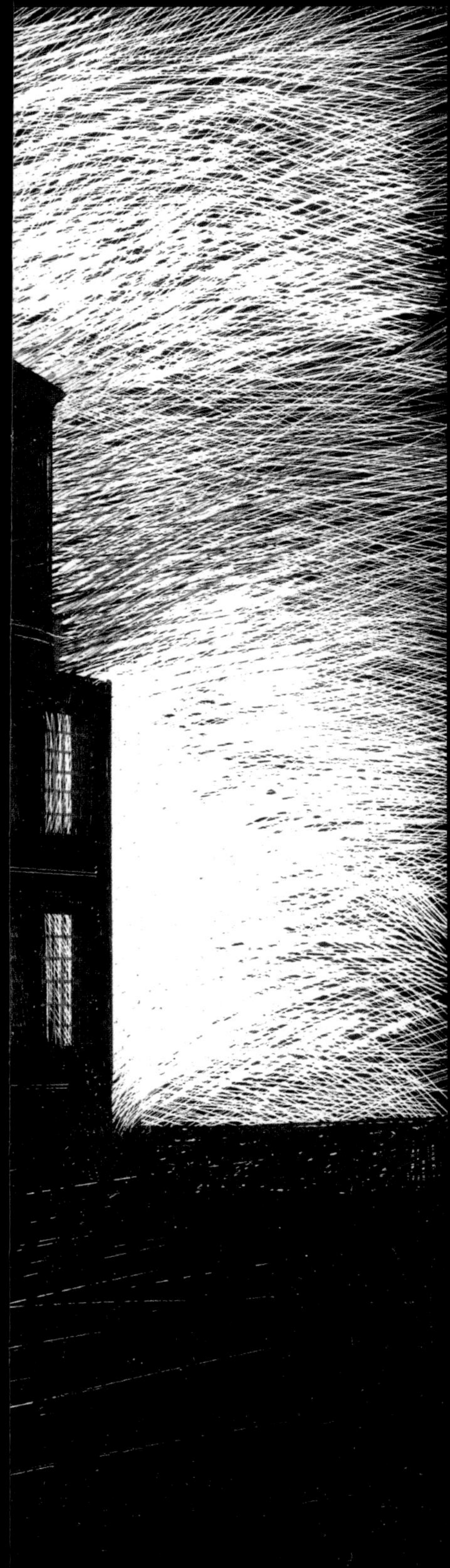

Coleshill House Ruins,
scraperboard, 2017.

The house is new built with stone …
The entrance of the house is an ascent
of severall steps into a hall so lofty
the roof is three storyes, reaches
to the floore of the gallery …

CELIA FIENNES, ACCOUNT OF A VISIT IN 1690,
THROUGH ENGLAND ON A SIDE SADDLE
IN THE TIME OF WILLIAM AND MARY, 1888

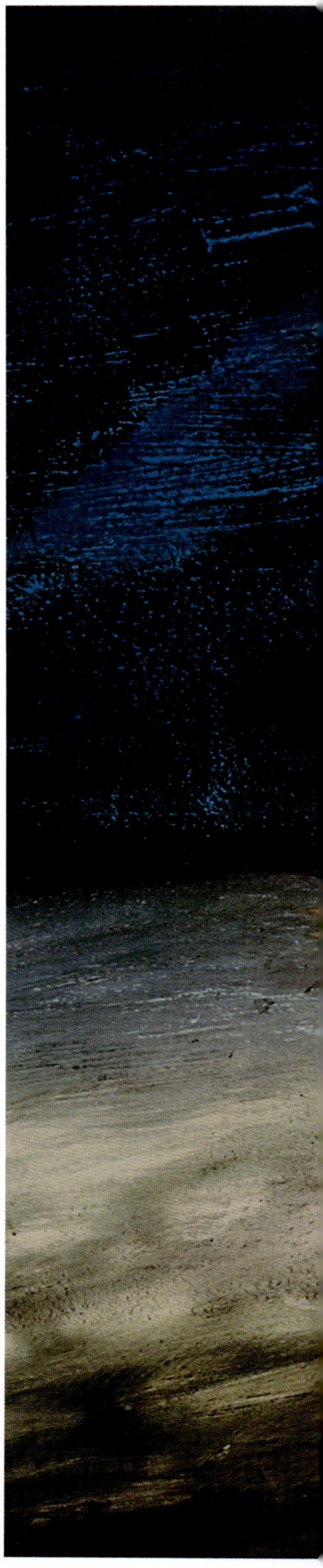

Prospect of Coleshill House, *paper collage and mixed media, 2017. Detail shown pages 116–17.*

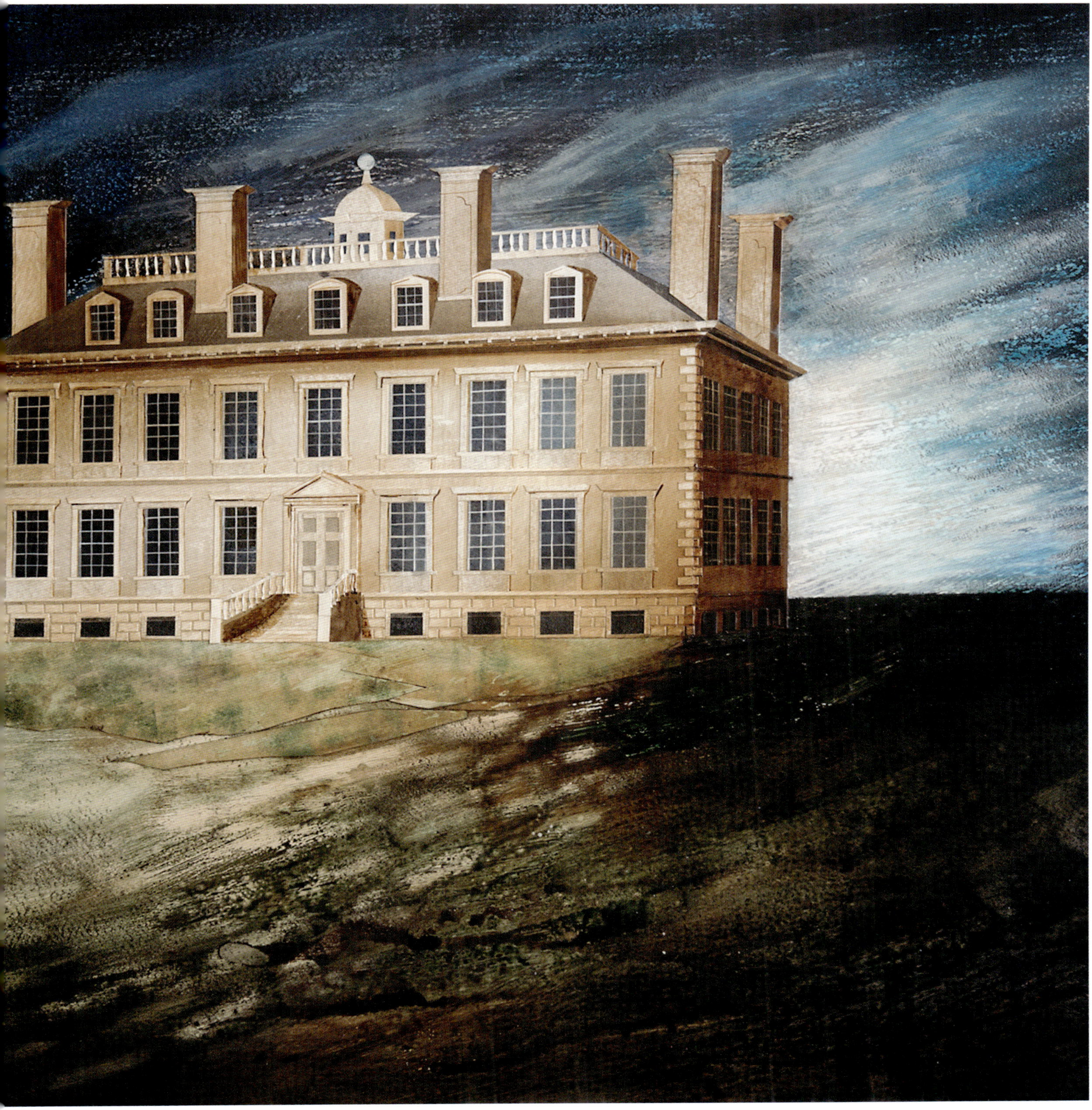

COLESHILL HOUSE

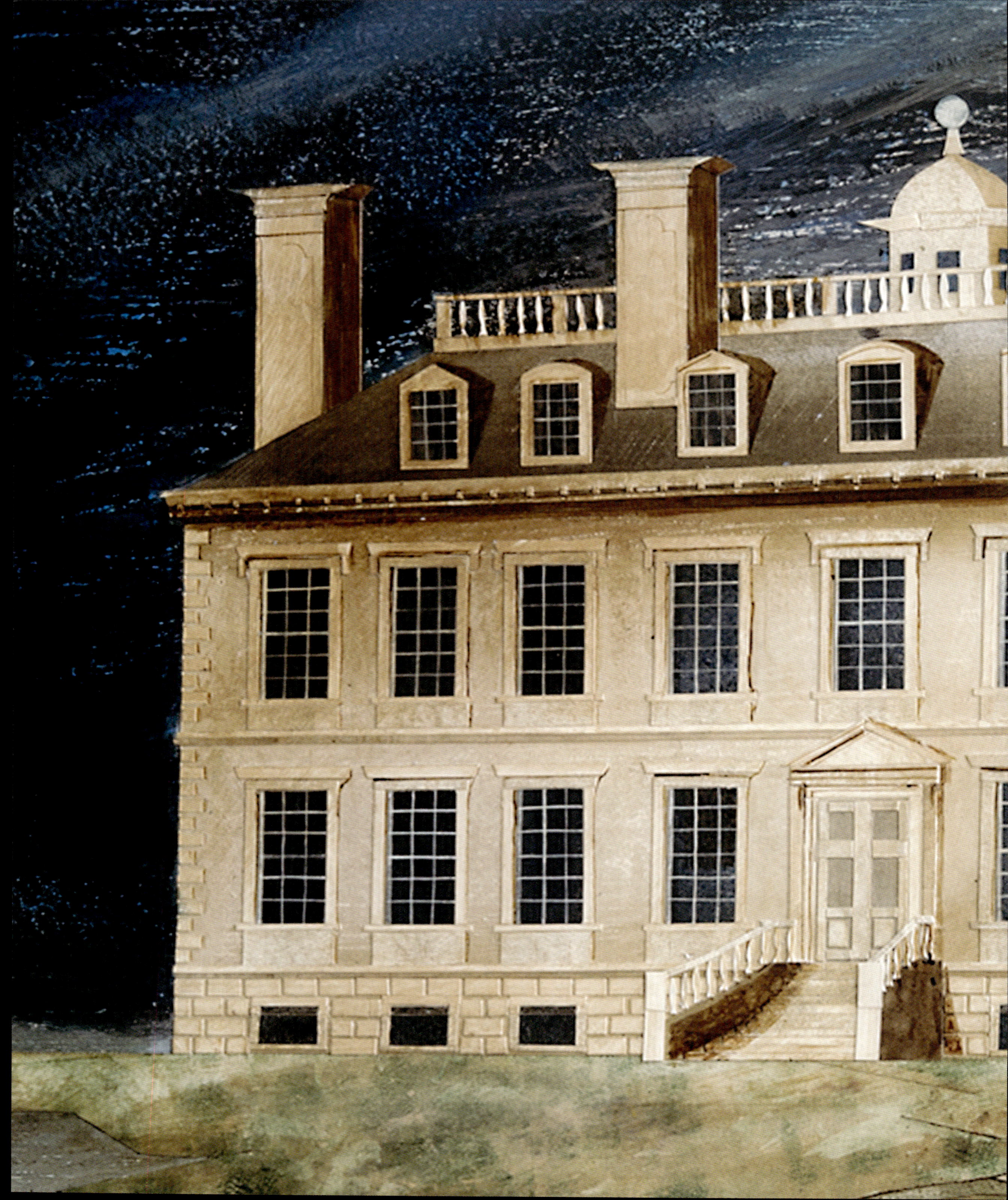

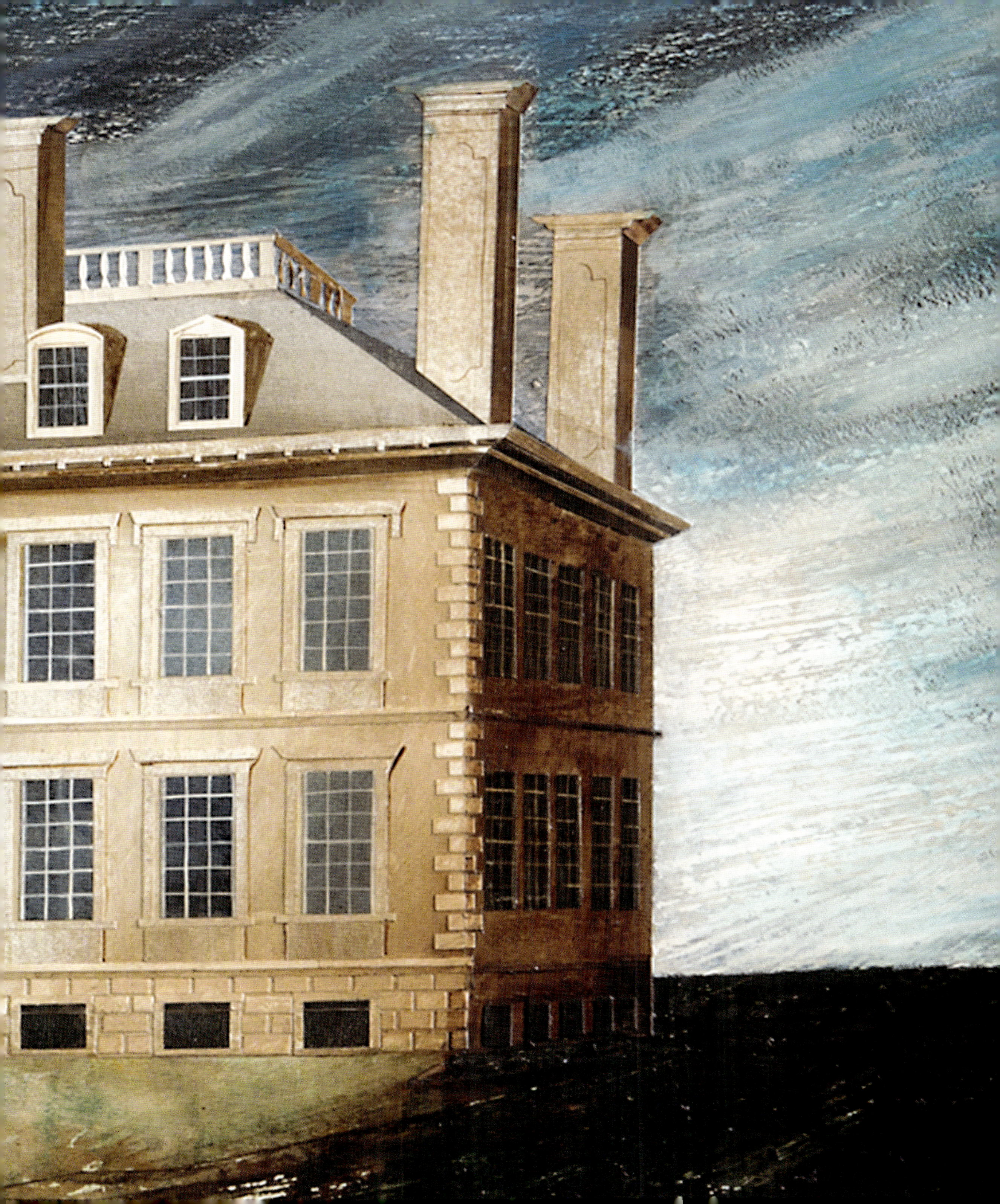

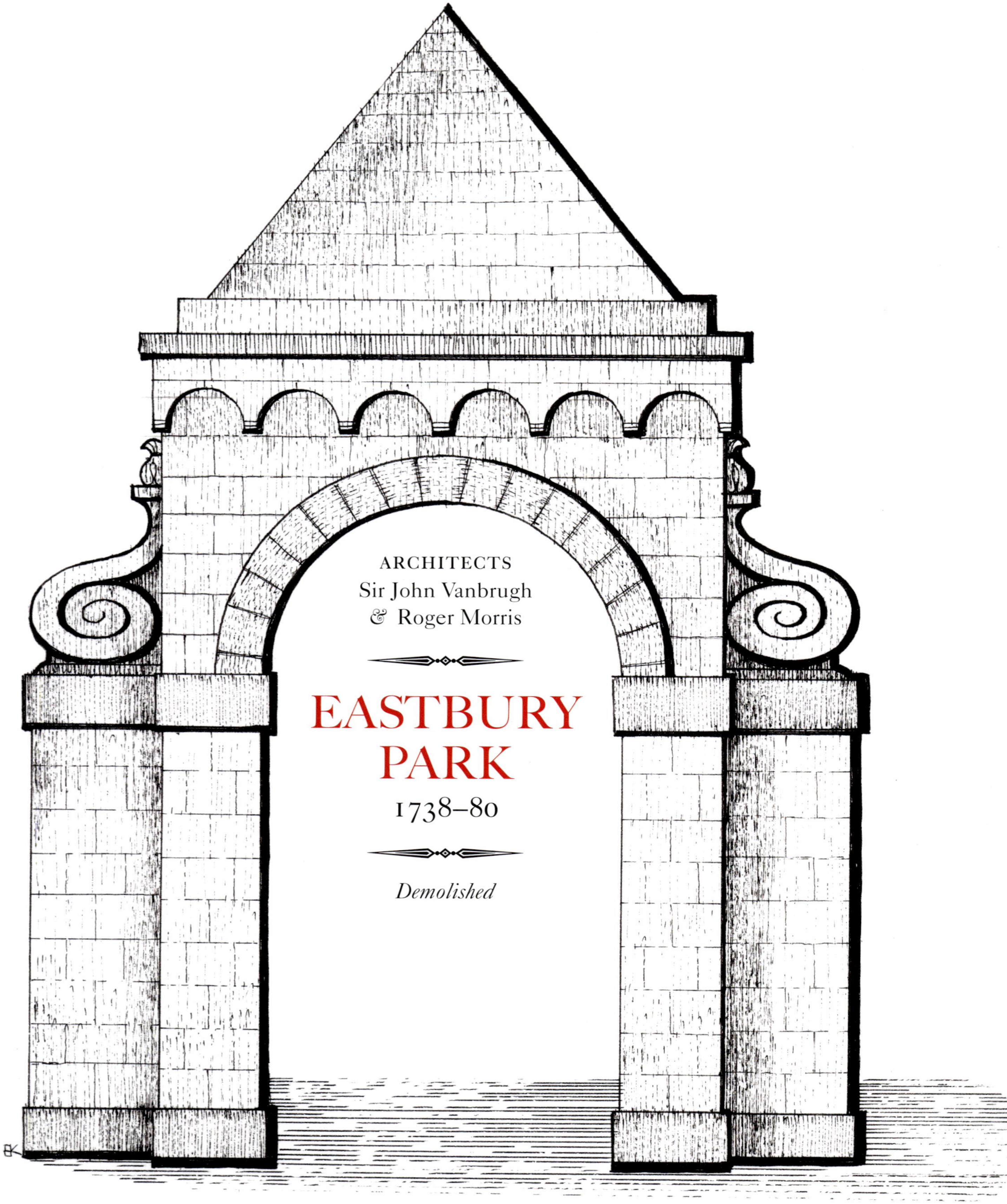

ARCHITECTS
Sir John Vanbrugh
& Roger Morris

EASTBURY PARK

1738–80

Demolished

'Lie heavy on him, Earth, for he/Laid many a heavy load on thee.' So runs the satirical epigram penned by Abel Evans on Sir John Vanbrugh (1664–1726). The playwright-turned-architect was notorious for his monumental designs in which weight was celebrated as an essential quality of architecture. In Eastbury Park, Vanbrugh designed a behemoth of a house, smaller only than his Blenheim Palace and Castle Howard. Part of the north wing and a solitary, heavily corbelled gateway survive to hint at its original scale, which, though awe-inspiring, also occasioned its undoing.

Plans for Eastbury Park were published in volume II of Colen Campbell's *Vitruvius Britannicus* (1717), and described as 'A New Design for a Person of Quality in Dorsetshire'. That individual was Sir George Dodington, a wealthy financier, MP and Lord of the Admiralty. The house was to comprise a central block with a grand forecourt and flanking service courts. Only the forecourt wings and the base courts, however, were complete by Sir George's death in 1720. His nephew, George Bubb, who adopted the surname Dodington, was heir to the building site, as well as £30,000 to complete the house. The son of an apothecary, Bubb Dodington (1691–1762) had experienced a modest upbringing, but he had attained the station of MP and was socially ambitious.

Vanbrugh's revised plans for his new patron were published in volume III of *Vitruvius Britannicus* (1725; p. 121). The central block was given corner towers and its roofline was raised, creating an outline reminiscent of Wollaton Hall in Nottingham and a dramatic, typically Vanbruggian roofscape. Two estate portraits, however, show that the finished house differed from all the designs: Bubb Dodington's purse had been severely tested, and Vanbrugh died in the mid-1720s. From 1733 Roger Morris (1695–1749) oversaw the remaining works, making significant changes, including the introduction of a pediment above the portico instead of Vanbrugh's unconventional arcade of chimneys. By 1738 the house was complete, its total cost a staggering £140,000 – half as much as Blenheim.

Eastbury enjoyed its heyday under Bubb Dodington, who was known for being 'ostentatious in his person, houses and furniture'.[1] Making it a rural salon, he gathered around him a circle of writers and poets that included George Lyttelton and James Thomson. Their verses record it as a place where they found inspiration, quaffed burgundy and even mused on Vanbrugh's architectural models. In 1761 George III elevated Dodington as Lord Melcombe. He had little time to enjoy this new title, for he died the following year.

Eastbury became the property of Richard Grenville-Temple (1711–1779), 2nd Earl Temple, whose family seat was Stowe in Buckingham. The astronomical running costs of Eastbury were unsustainable and, having tried unsuccessfully to rent it by offering £200 per year to anyone willing to take it on, Temple decided to reduce the house. A watercolour of about 1780 depicts its dismemberment (pp. 122–23). Marble was taken to Stowe and other building materials were sold off. Eventually, the remaining shells were demolished with dynamite to defeat Vanbrugh's sturdy structure. Only part of the north wing was preserved and rented out; ultimately it was sold.

Colen Campbell, Elevation of the Bagnio in the Garden at Eastbury in Dorsetshire *(top) and* Elevation of Eastbury in Dorsetshire *(bottom), engravings published in* Vitruvius Britannicus, *vol. III, 1725.*

It is bizarre that less evidence survives regarding this desperate act of demolition than about the connected suicide in 1786 of the Earl Temple's steward, William Doggett. He had embezzled funds from the sale of the building materials and, when discovered, shot himself. The incident was ghoulishly celebrated in a history of haunted houses published in 1897, which recorded that for years afterwards a headless Doggett could be seen riding about the estate in a spectral coach and four. The local expert on the subject, one Miss Billington, mused on his motives: 'No doubt,' she reflected, 'the troubled spirit derived a bitter satisfaction from contemplation of the decayed grandeur of the once proud house, now reduced to scarcely a shadow.'[2]

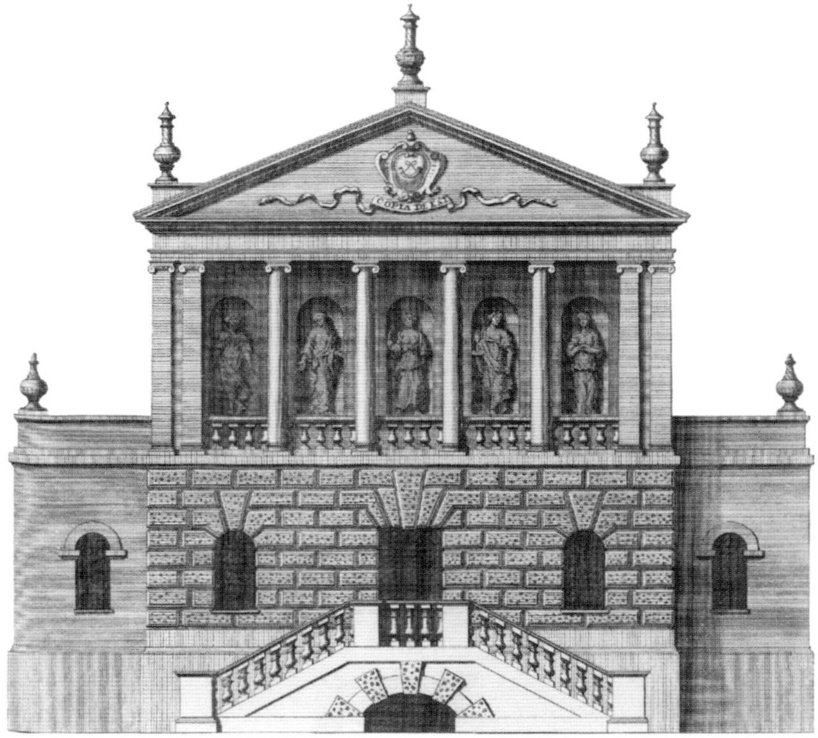

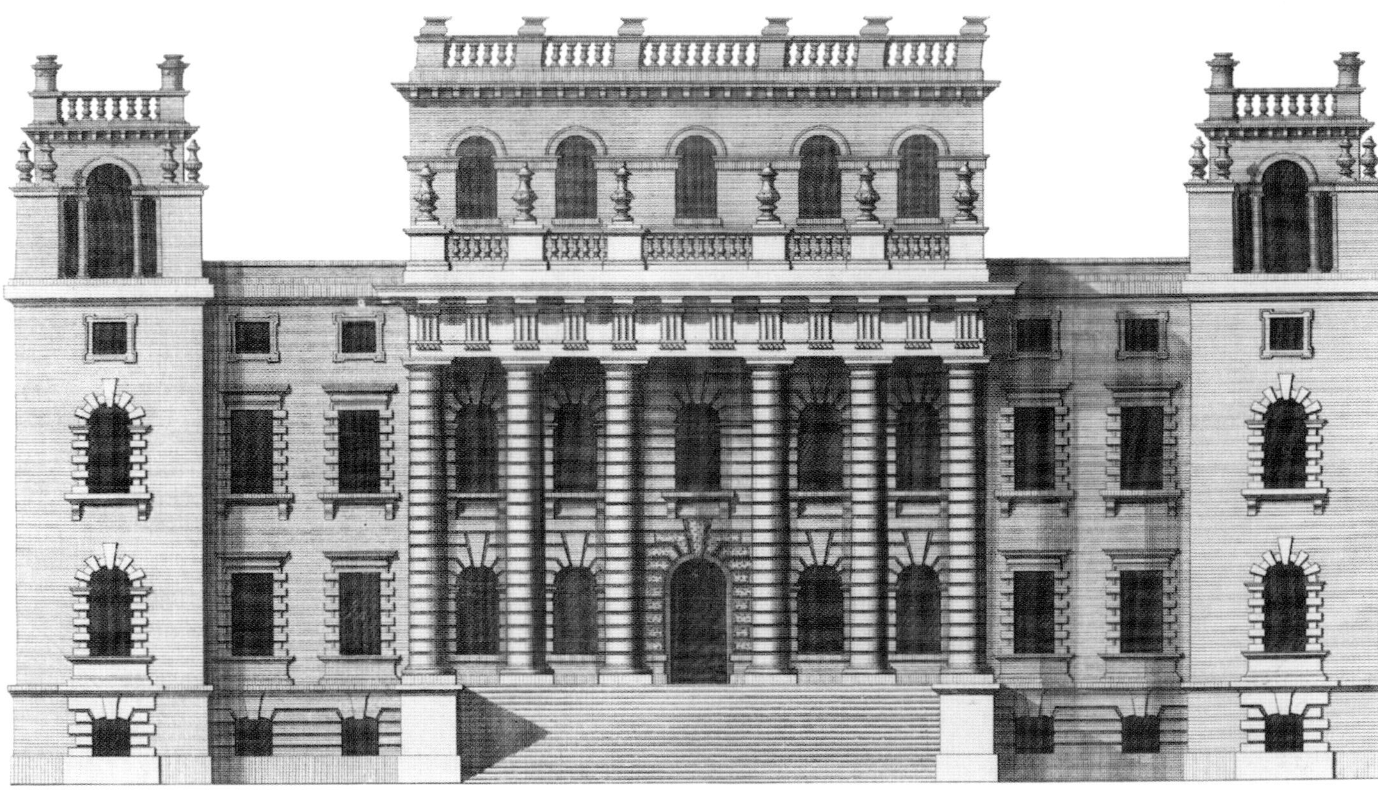

EASTBURY PARK

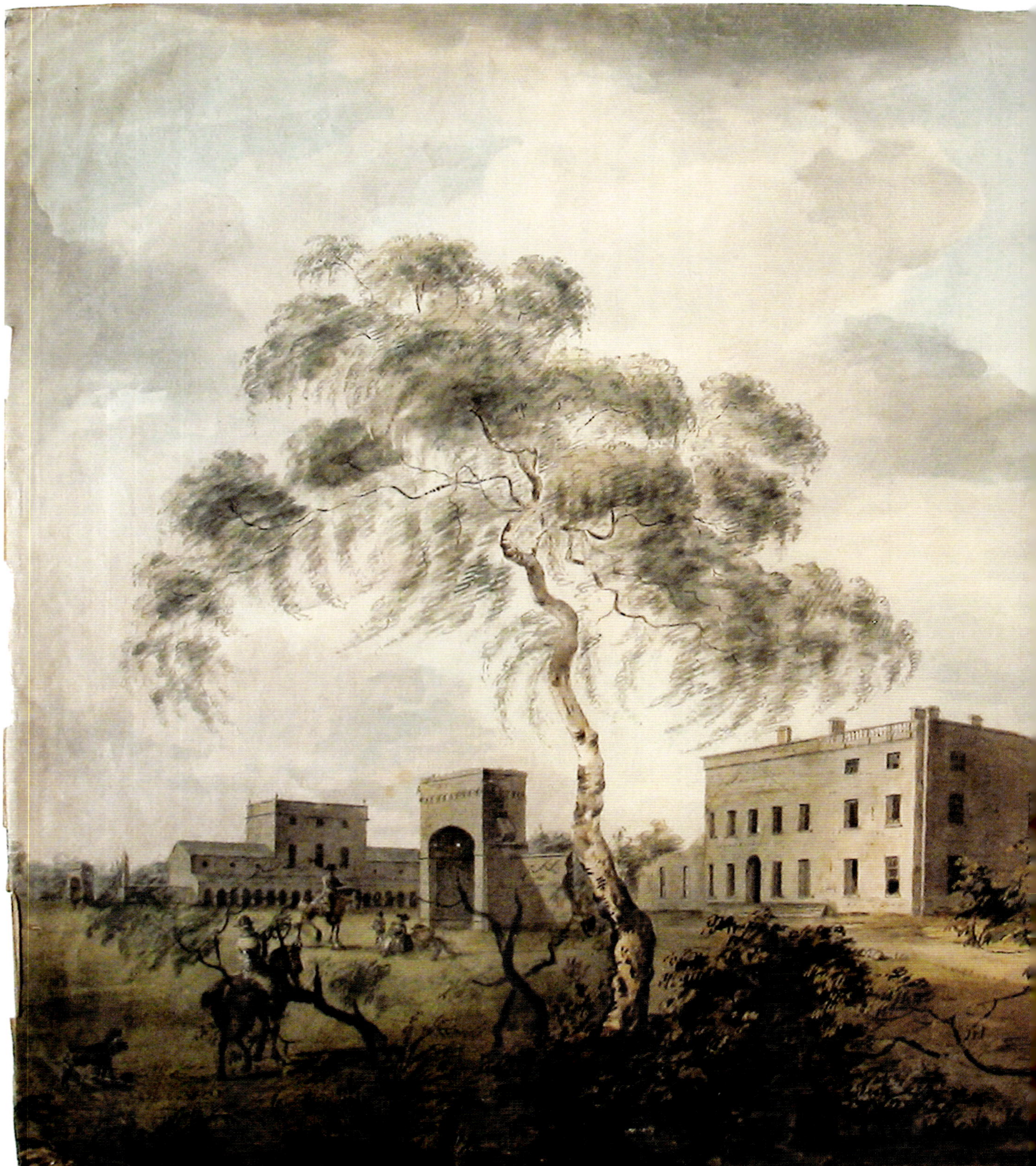

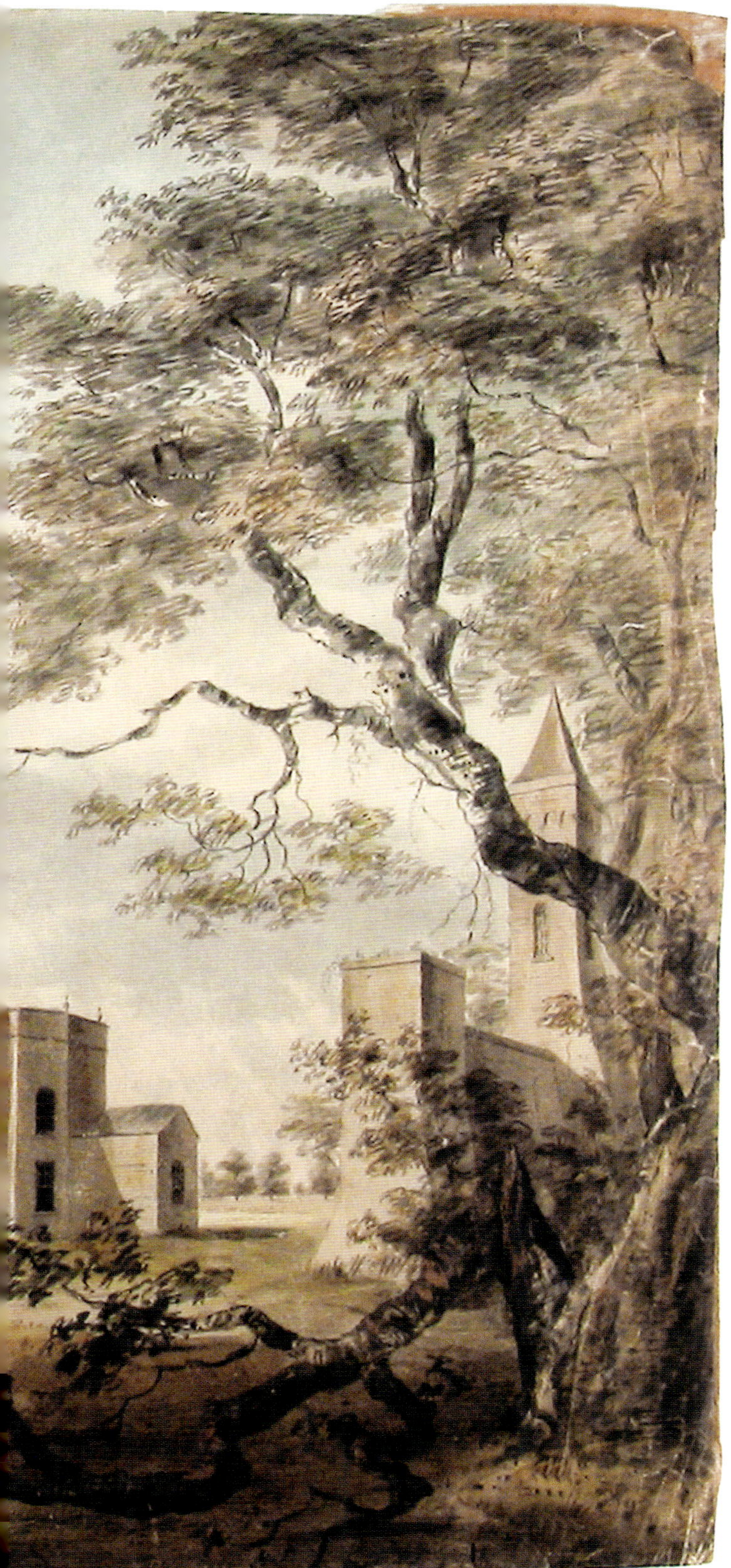

And Eastbury – where Thompson's name,
Gave to thy Downs a tuneful fame.
Where are the Bowers once so sweet
For Druid Bard – a lov'd retreat!
Dismantled now, without a trope you see
'Gone to the dogs' – in stern reality.

FROM REV. W. SMITH MARRIOTT, 'A TRIBUTE TO DORSET', 1831

W. Grant, Eastbury Park, Dorset, in the Course of Demolition, *watercolour*, c. *1780*.

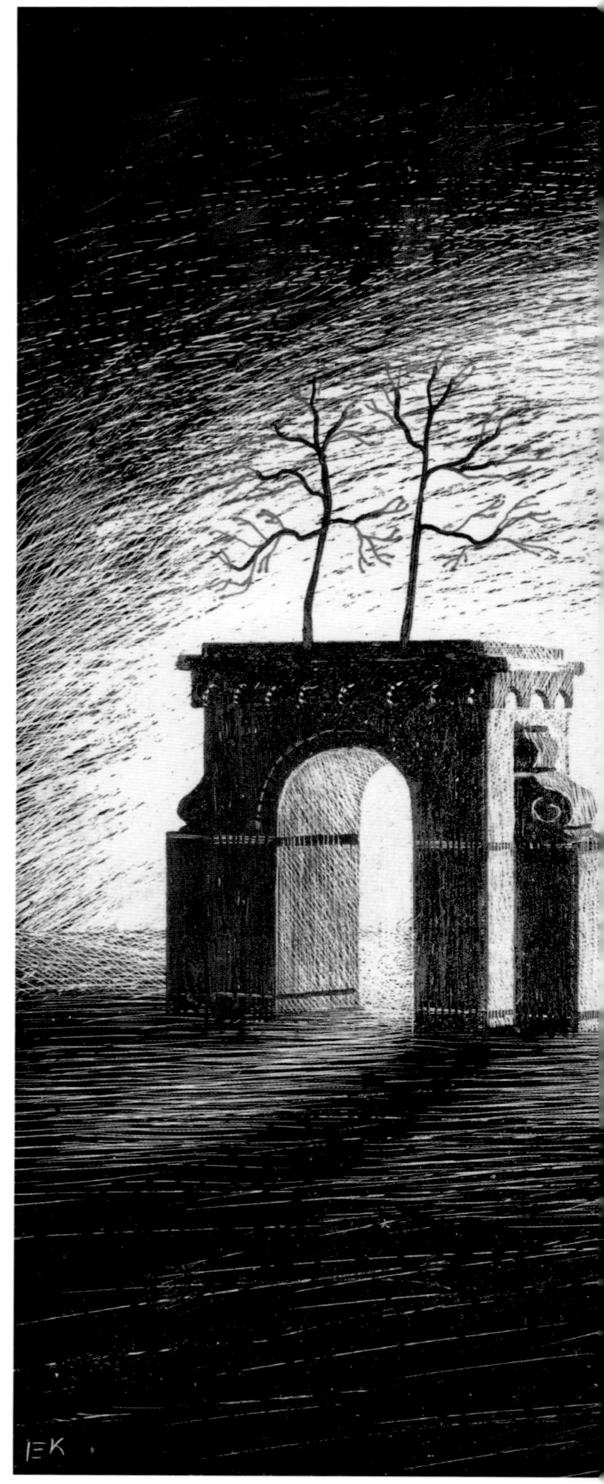

View of the Last
Remaining Portion
of Eastbury Park,
scraperboard, 2017.

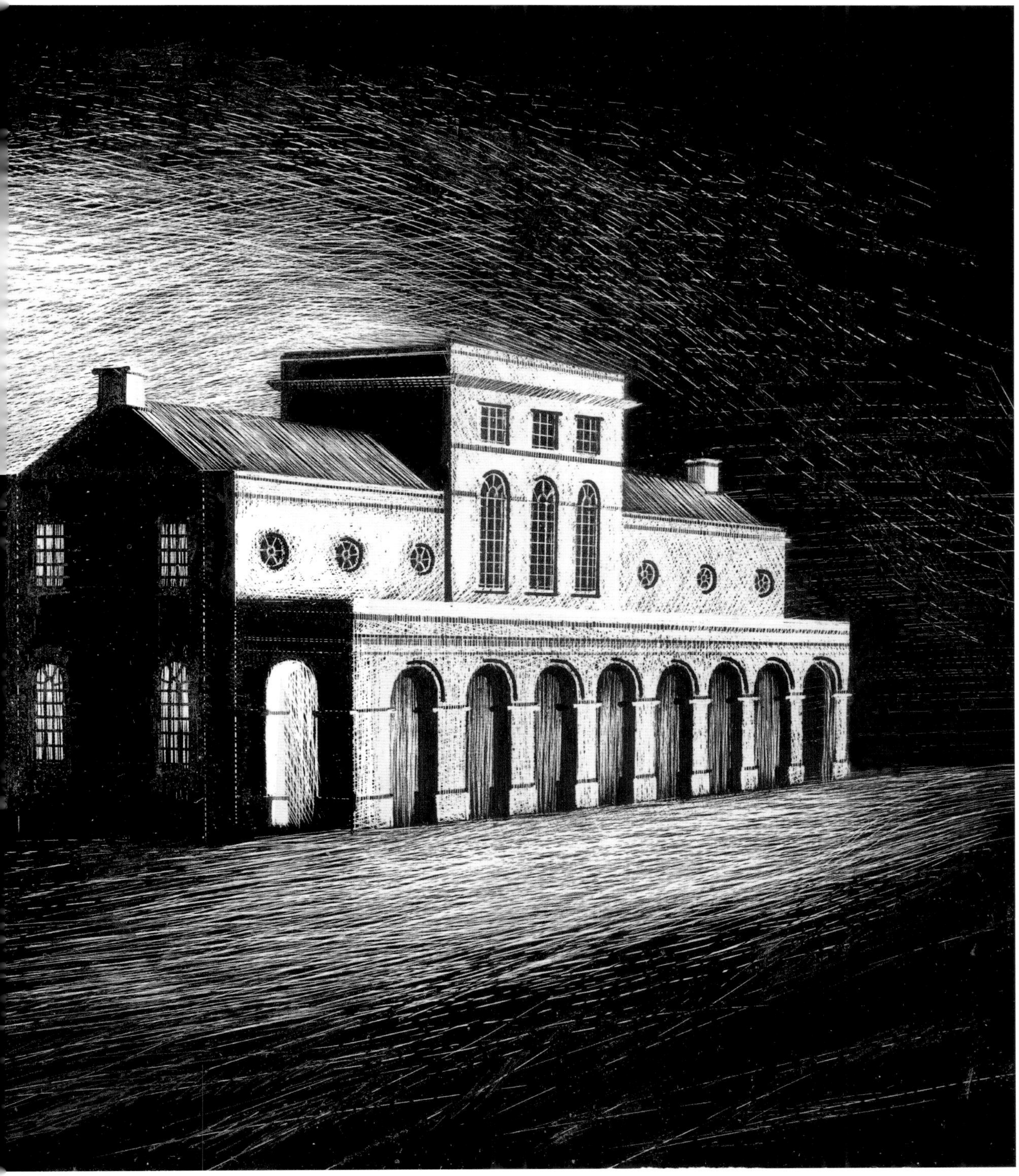

EASTBURY PARK

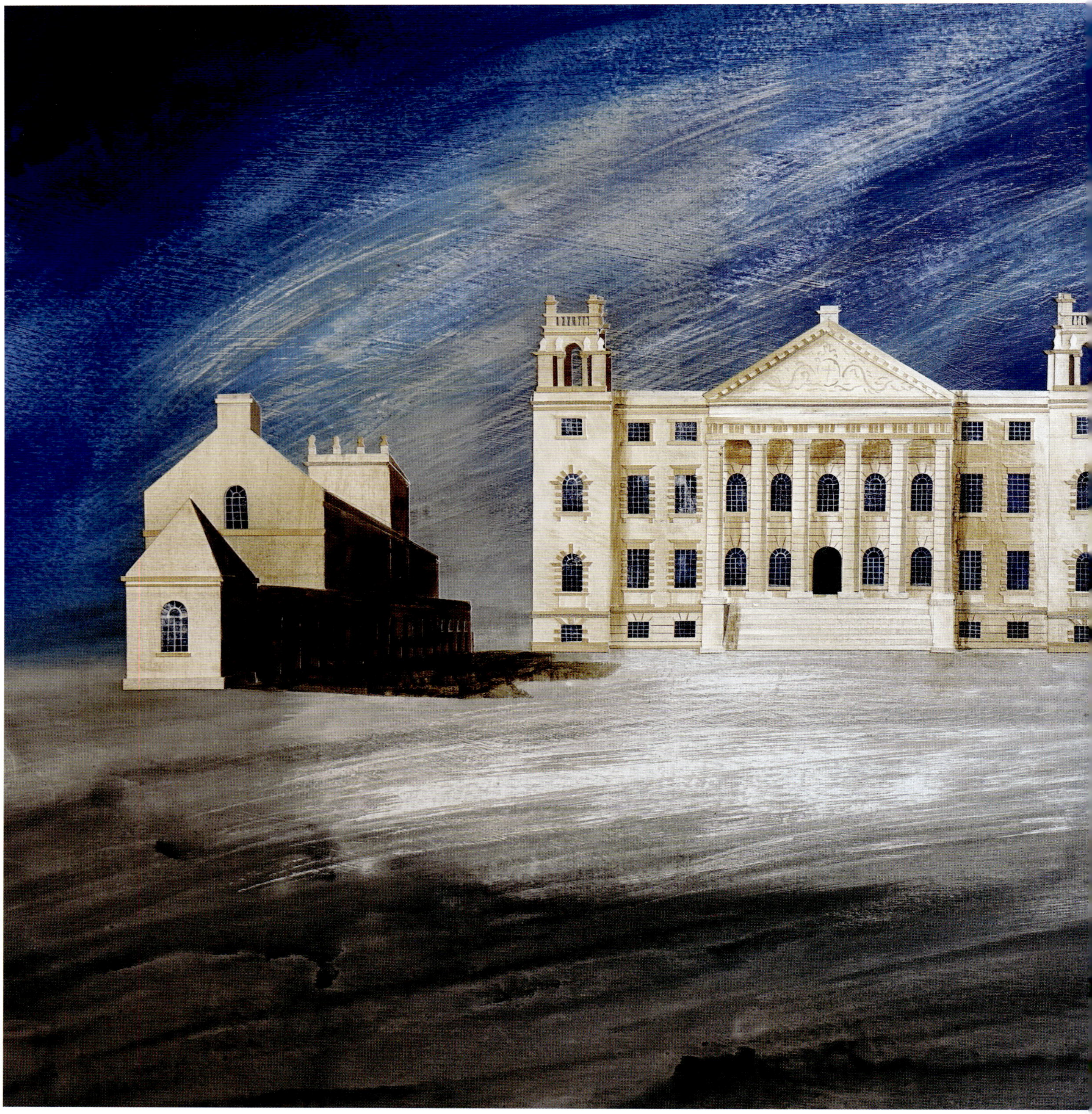

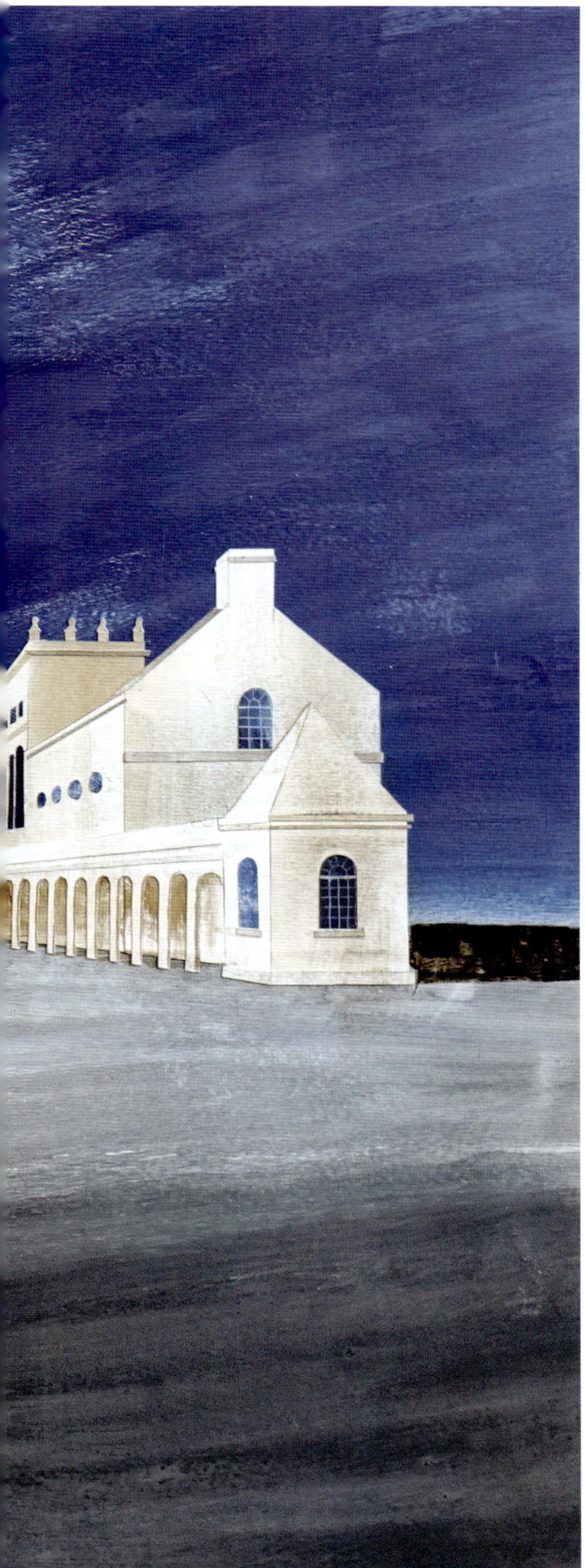

... magnificent, massy and stretching out to a great extent of front with an enormous portico of Doric columns ascended by a stately flight of steps ...

MEMOIRS OF RICHARD CUMBERLAND, WRITTEN BY HIMSELF, 1806

View of the West Façade of Eastbury Park, *paper collage and mixed media, 2017. Detail shown overleaf.*

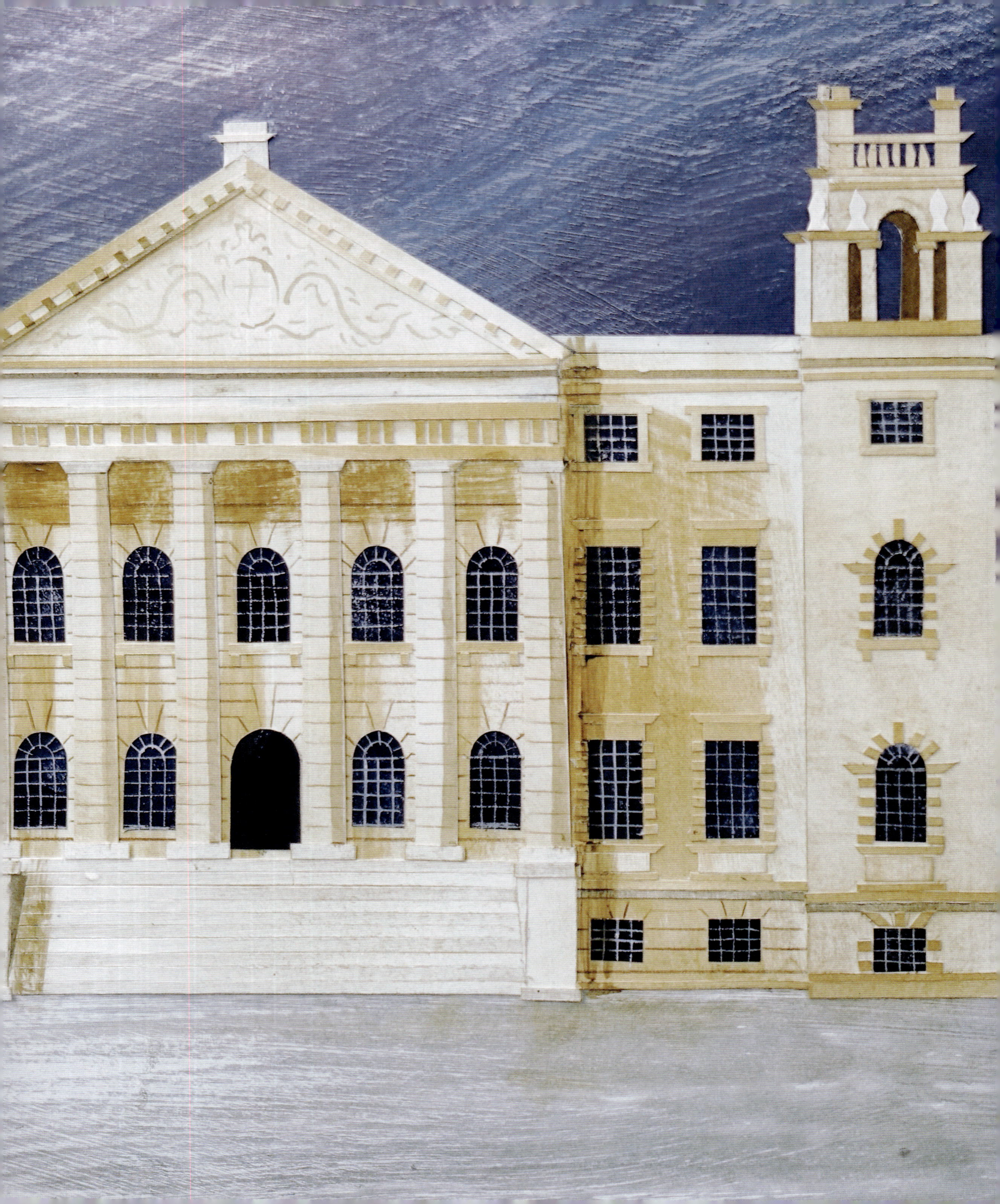

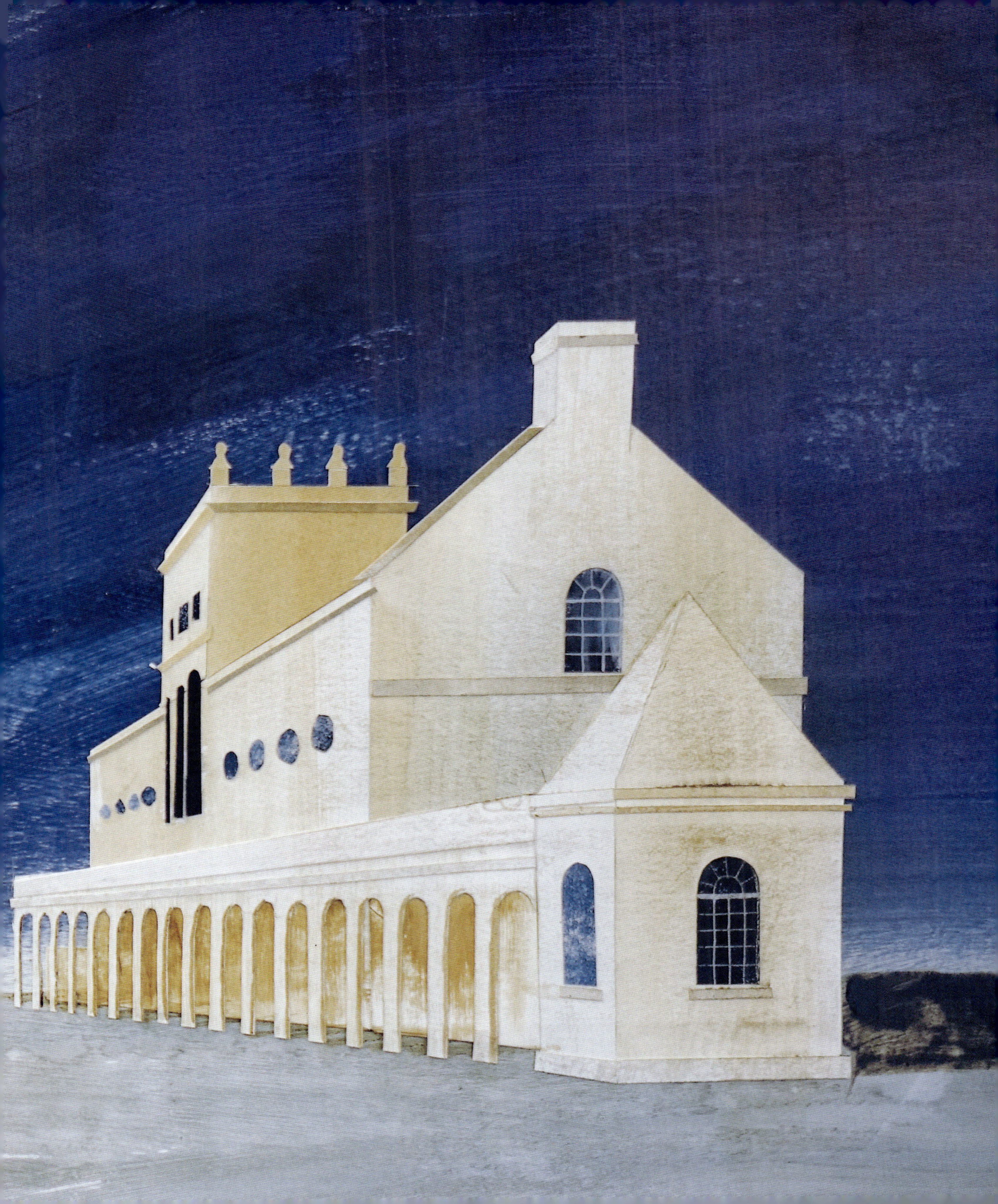

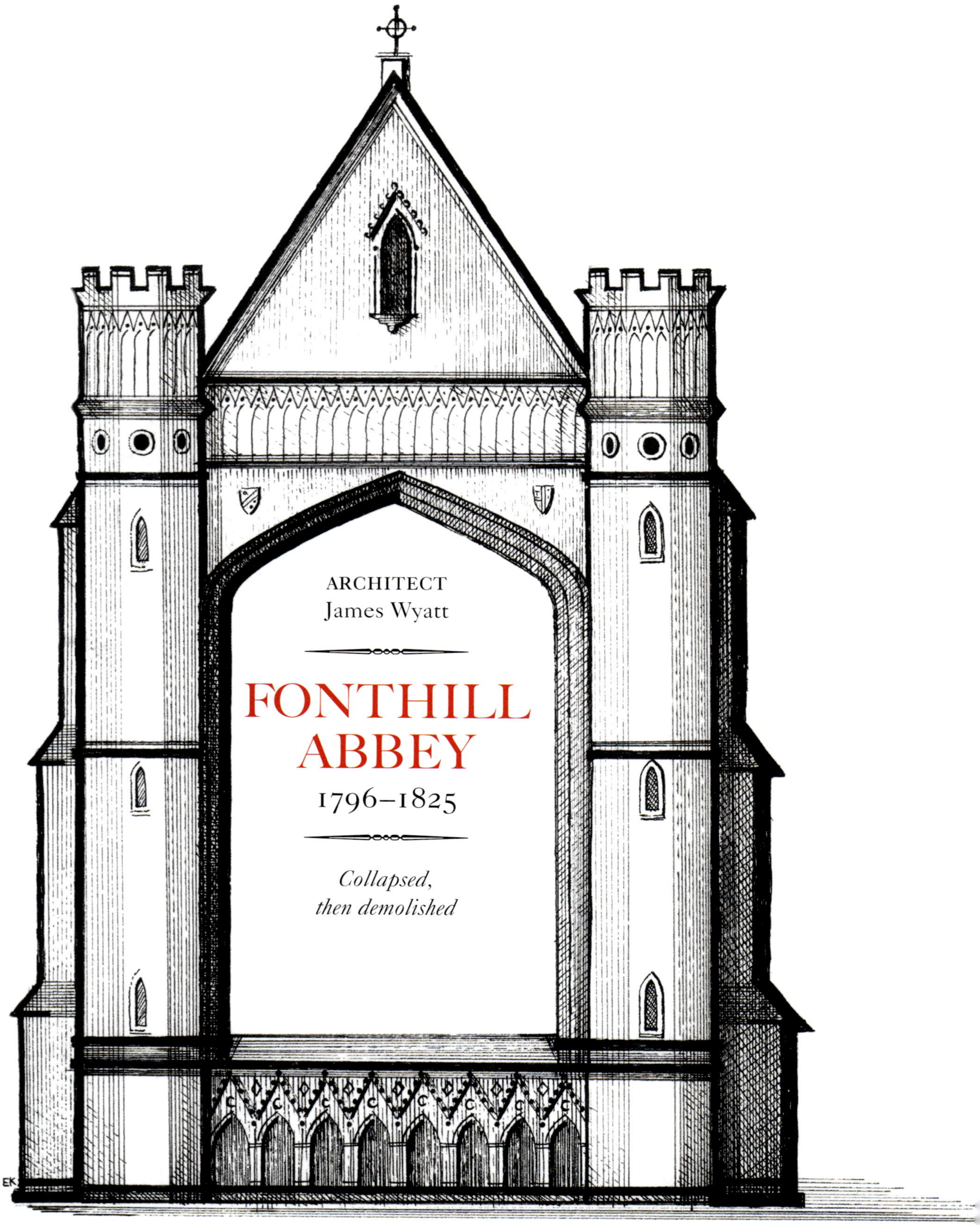

ARCHITECT
James Wyatt

FONTHILL ABBEY

1796–1825

Collapsed, then demolished

Among the auction lots at Fonthill Abbey in 1823 was a painting depicting the construction of the Tower of Babel. Comparisons with Fonthill's own 276-foot-high (84 m) central tower were irresistible. There was, one observer commented, 'something remarkable in Mr Beckford's predilection for towers'.[1] Not only did William Beckford build his own Babel in Wiltshire, but also the anti-hero of his Gothic novel *Vathek* (1786) erected an ostentatious astronomical observation tower. Beckford's precipitous landmark was born not of vanity, but of melancholy: 'Some people drink to forget their unhappiness', he said. 'I don't drink, I build.'[2]

William Beckford (1760–1844) was the son of Alderman William Beckford, a city merchant and twice Lord Mayor of London, who had purchased the Fonthill estate in 1745. The seat was then a mid-seventeenth-century pile built to replace a medieval house that had been destroyed by fire. In 1755 the Caroline incarnation likewise burnt down. Reportedly, Alderman Beckford's phlegmatic response was to call for his pocket book and calculate how much it would cost him to rebuild.[3] The new house, known as Fonthill Splendens, was neo-Palladian, comprising a central block with portico and two pavilions at the end of curved, covered walkways. This was the childhood home of the younger Beckford.

Beckford was only ten years old when his father died. He was educated at home and through a continental Grand Tour, but his most extensive travels were the result of his ostracism and exile following a scandal in 1784 over his homosexual relationship with William 'Kitty' Courtenay. Even before he returned to England in the late 1790s, he was communicating with James Wyatt (1746–1813), who had recently rebuilt Lee Priory, Kent, and was recognized as the most successful executor of modern Gothic. After some preliminary ideas to enlarge the existing house, Beckford determined that he would build anew, resulting in the demolition of all but one wing of Fonthill Splendens, which he saved as a memento.

Building began in 1796; the following January, a celebratory fete marked the project's inception. Wyatt himself proposed a toast: 'May the great works at Fonthill be successfully accomplished and long enjoyed by their present owner!'[4] In fact, the construction period outlasted Wyatt, who died in 1813. He had, however, been an absentee architect, and it was always Beckford's vision that drove the project. Beckford was intimately involved in the design, and it was said to be 'one of his principal amusements' to supervise the workmen on the scaffold.[5] At one point, to make swifter progress, he even had them toil through the night, illuminated by moon- and torchlight.

The abbey was cruciform in plan, with the tower at its heart. Particular friends to whom Beckford permitted access entered via an enormous arch into a hallway, then proceeded up a long flight of steps into the central octagon – the architectural and aesthetic apogee. Formed by clustered columns and lit through stained glass copied from the medieval monastery at Batalha (known to Beckford from his time in Portugal), the walls rose vertiginously to a lantern with a vaulted roof. The abbey's interiors were rich with tracery, further stained glass, panelling and elaborate floors, not to mention a vast collection of pictures, hangings and furniture.

Below: Ticket to the Fonthill Abbey sale of 1823 signed by the auctioneer, Harry Phillips. The engraving, by Thomas Higham after a drawing by Stedman Whitwell, depicts the eastern and central towers.

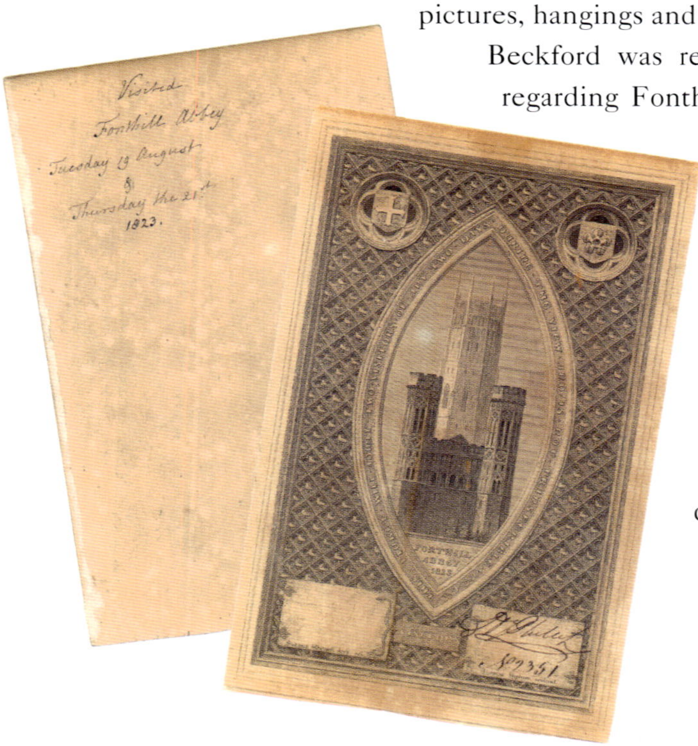

Opposite: Samuel Rawle, Fonthill Abbey Wilts, *engraving, early 19th century.*

Beckford was renowned for his eccentricities: his secrecy regarding Fonthill lent a mythic status to the house itself. In spite of his substantial wealth, high expenditure and a lack of stewardship of his West Indian estates led to financial difficulties. In 1822 Beckford had to put up the house for public auction. 'Fonthill Fever' gripped the country as thousands of visitors rushed to pay a guinea and see its hidden halls.[6] At the last moment, the sale was called off in favour of a private deal with John Farquhar, a Scottish-born

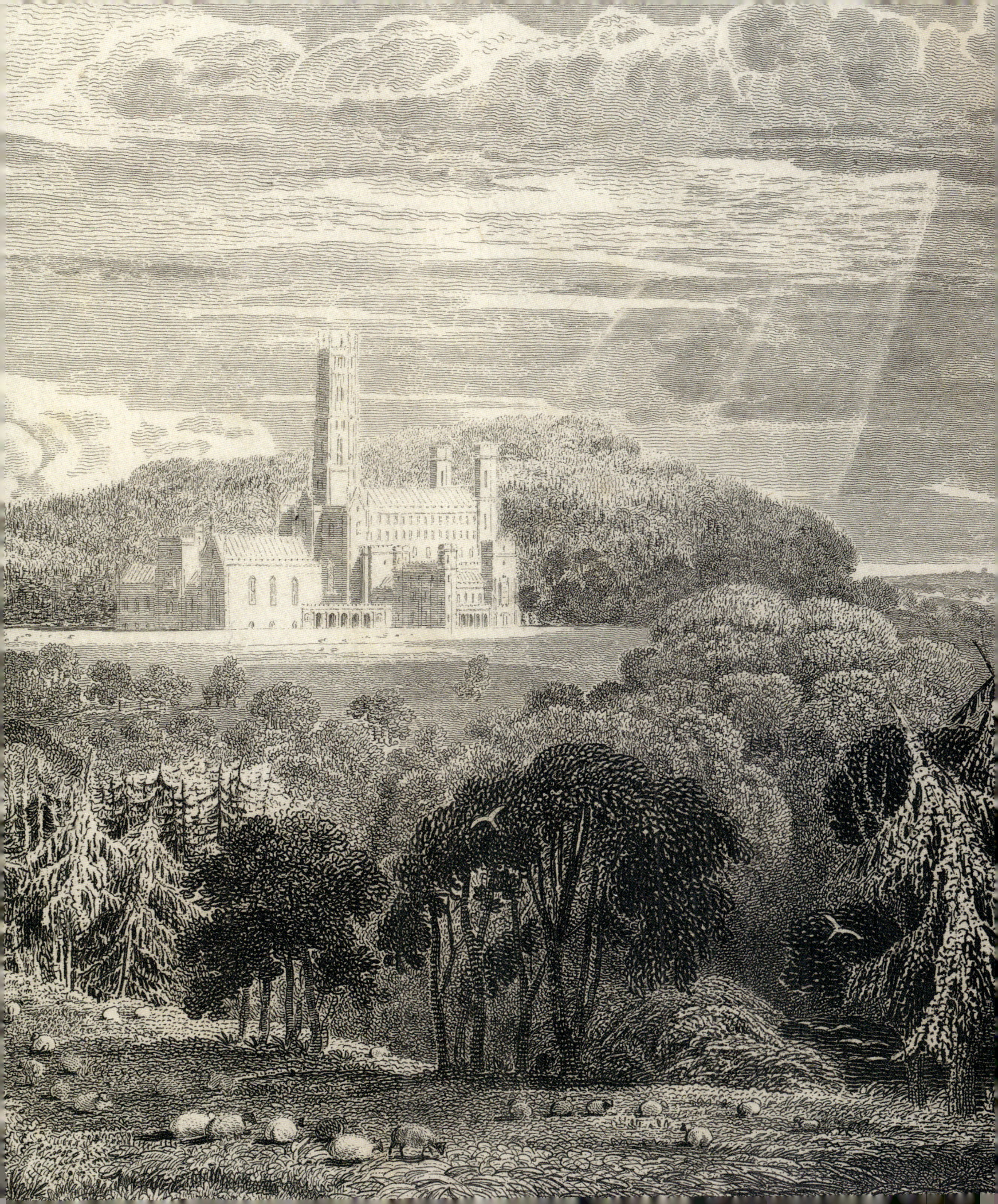

gunpowder contractor who had spent many years in India. Farquhar was known as a 'sordid miser', and the condition of his Baker Street house, 'distinguished by its dingy appearance, uncleaned windows and general neglect', augured badly for Fonthill.[7] Although Farquhar purchased the abbey in its entirety, he held his own auction in 1823, when the majority of the collection was dispersed.

At 3 o'clock in the afternoon of 21 December 1825, the inhabitants of Fonthill heard an extraordinary sound. It was the tower collapsing, taking with it the hall, the octagon, and most of the north and south galleries. Mr Farquhar was apparently not alarmed, as he had expected it. Indeed, there had been an earlier collapse in 1800, caused by the speed of construction and the unorthodox materials employed. The surprise on this occasion was the exposure of the foundations, which were so slight as to make it remarkable that the tower had not crumbled sooner. Amid the rubble, a statue of William Beckford's father remained in its niche, unharmed – as if, an observer reported, 'to point to the ruins of his son's ambition'.[8]

Right: Pictorial relief of Fonthill Abbey from the southwest, c. 1818–23.

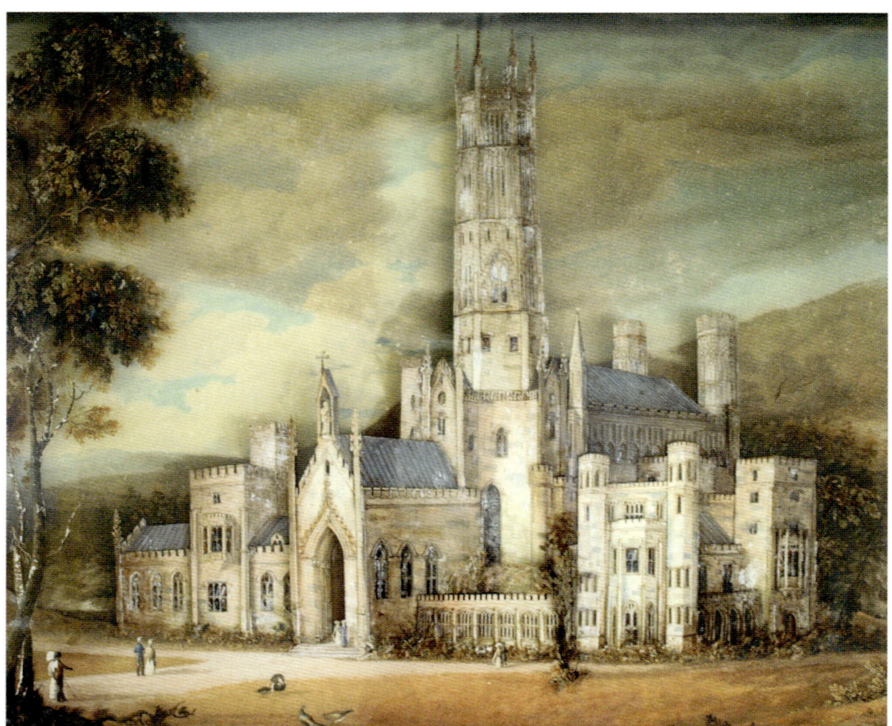

Opposite: John Britton, Fonthill Abbey, Octagon, Looking South East, *engraving published in* Graphical and Literary Illustrations of Fonthill Abbey, Wiltshire, *1823.*

Pages 136–37: William Westall, after a drawing by John Buckler, Ruins of Fonthill Abbey, *lithograph, c. 1825.*

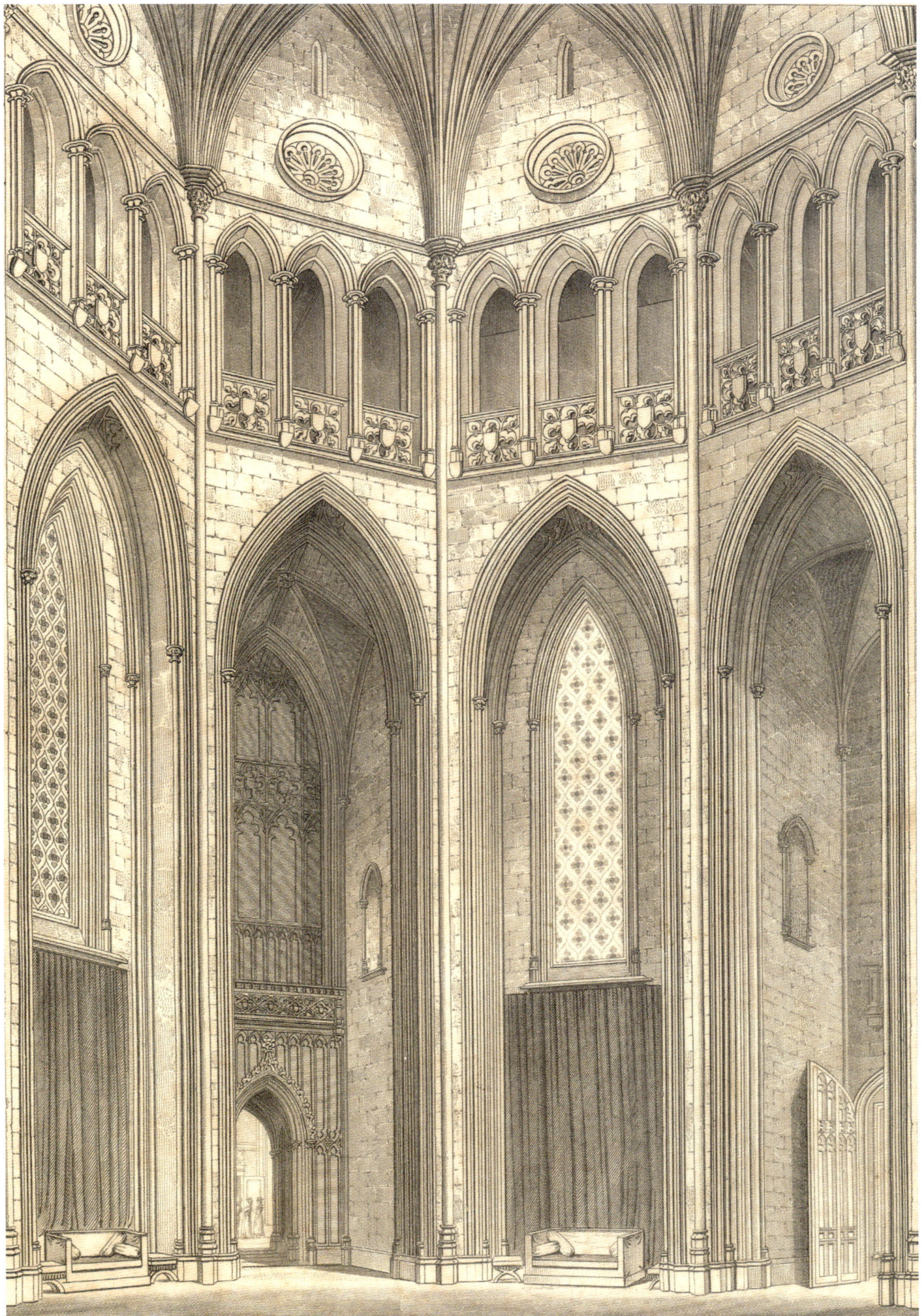

FONTHILL ABBEY

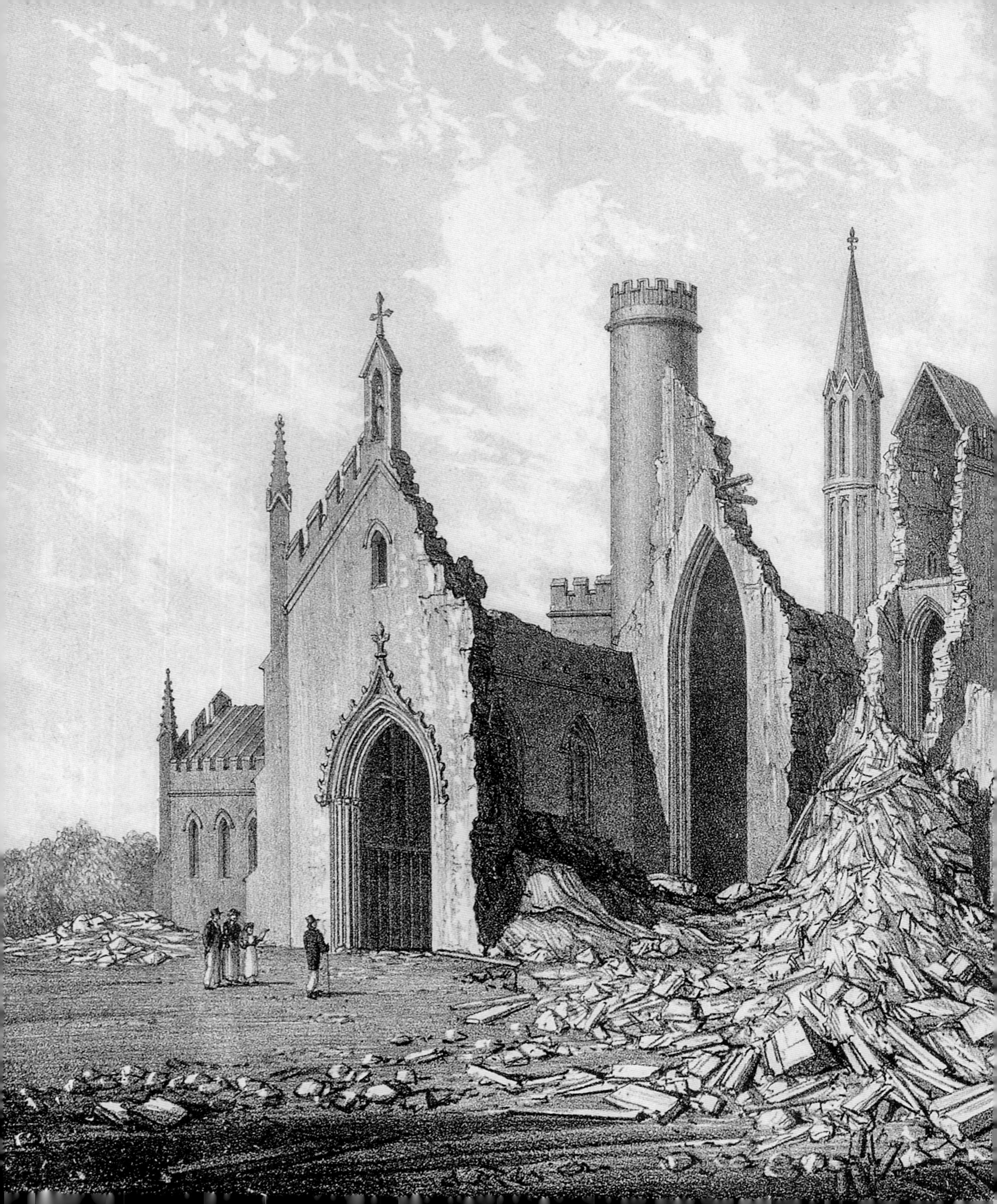

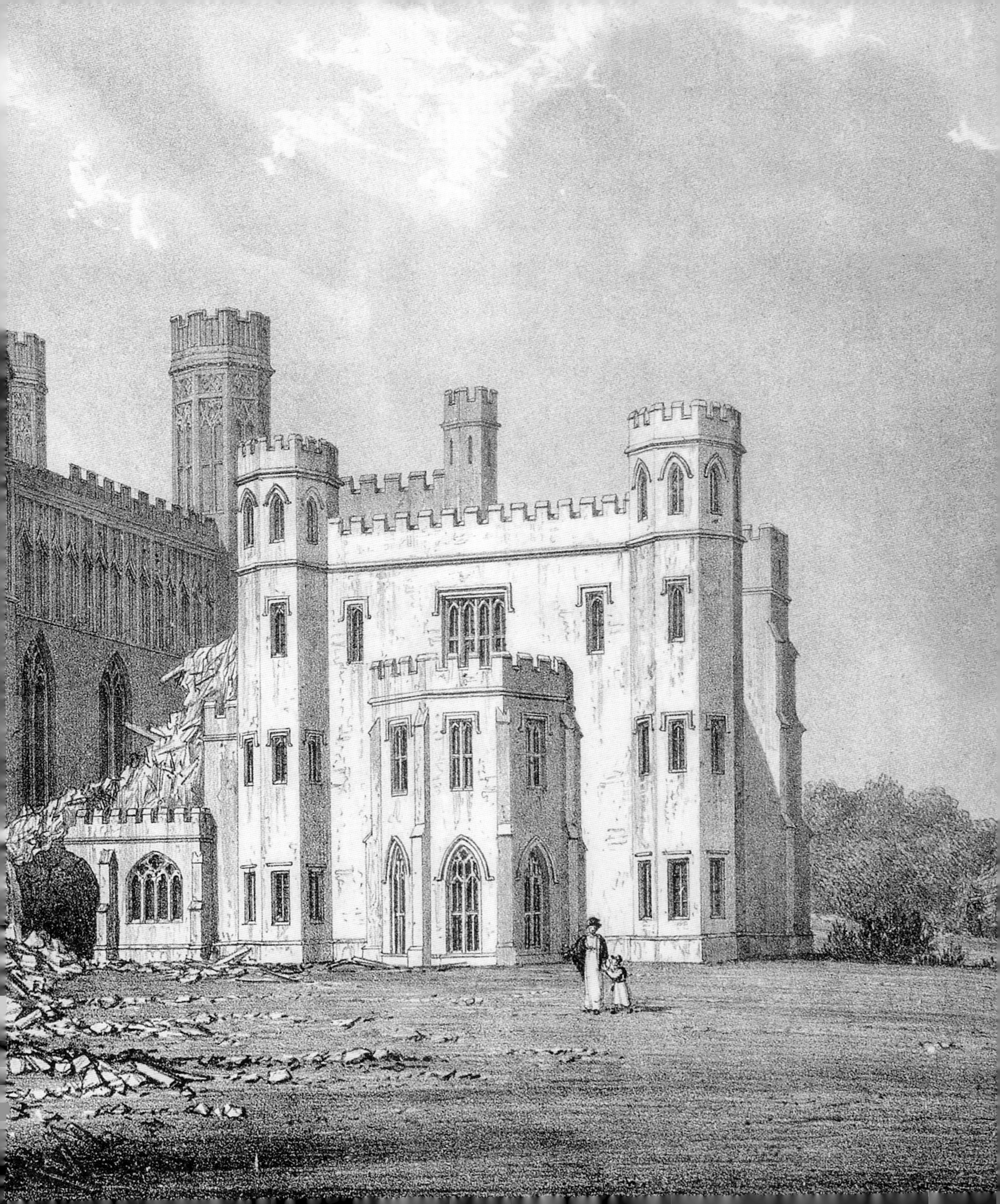

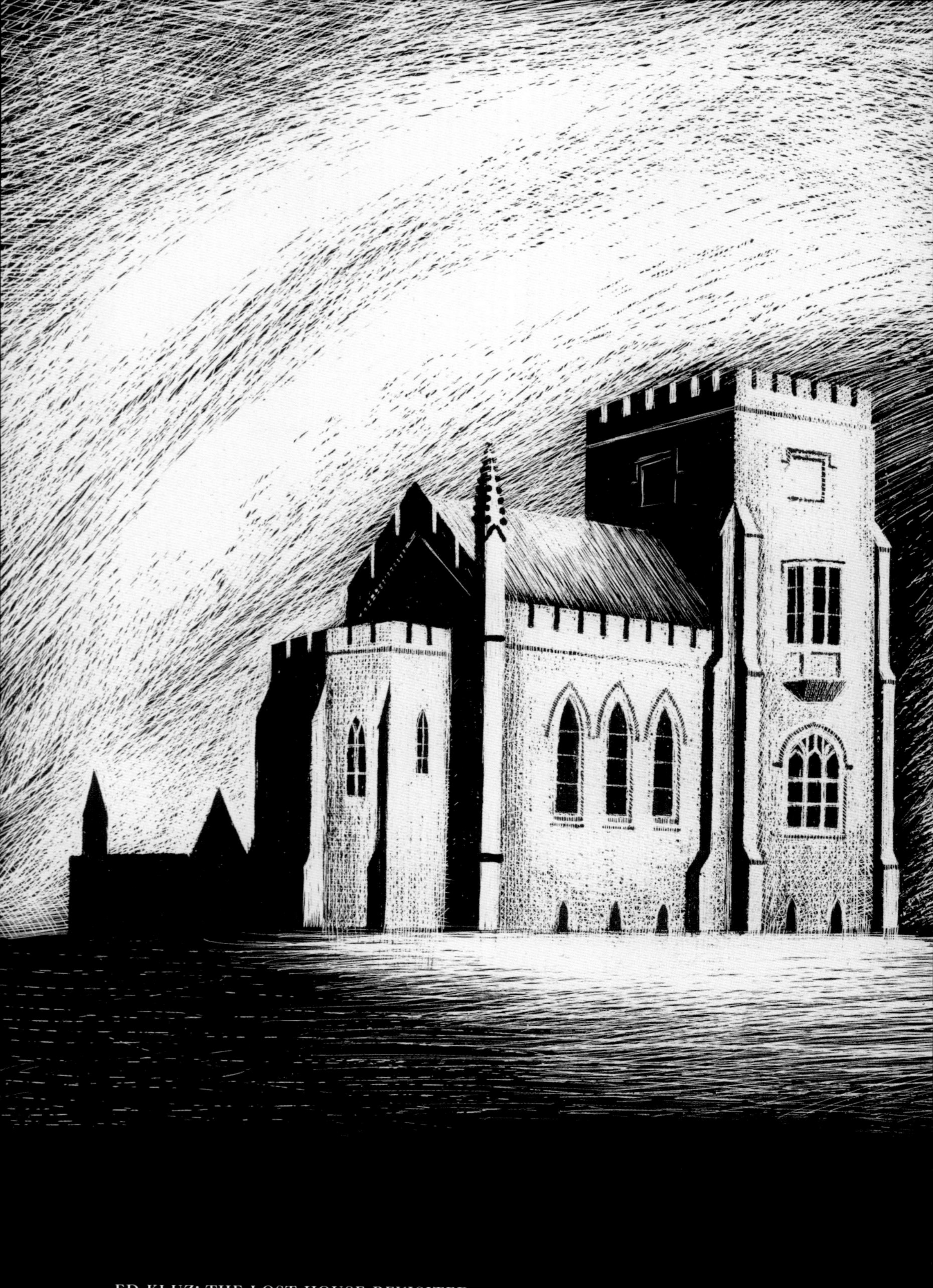

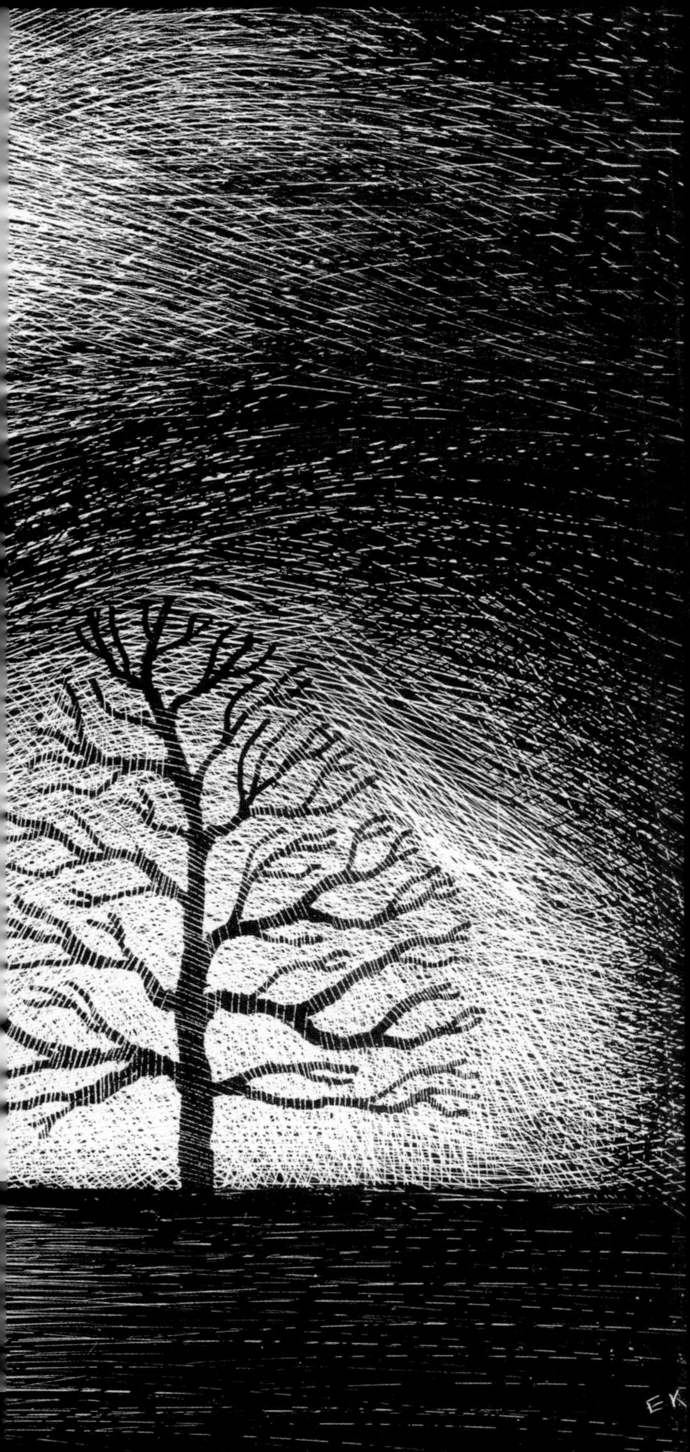

View of the Last
Remaining Portion
of Fonthill Abbey,
scraperboard, 2017.

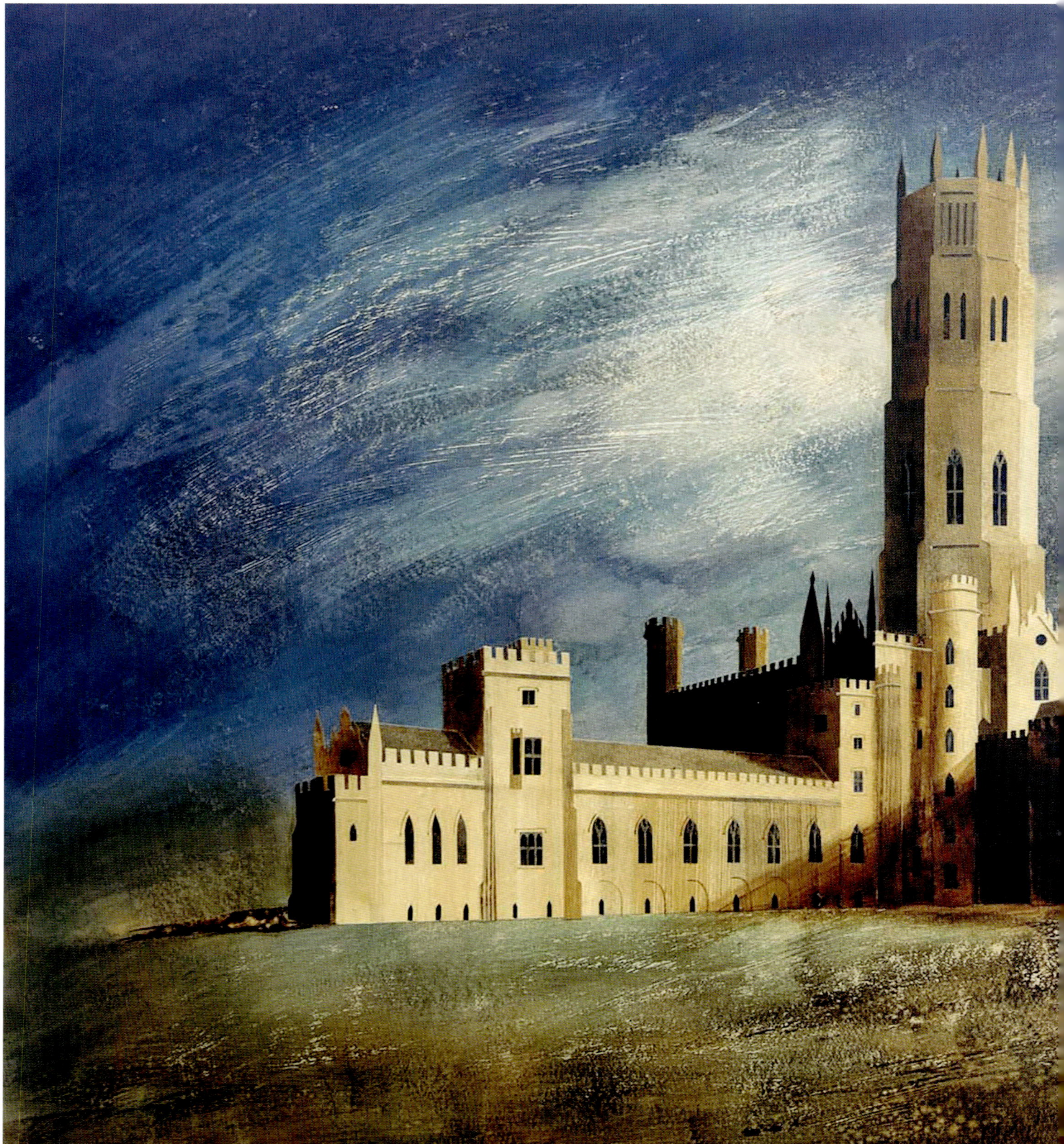

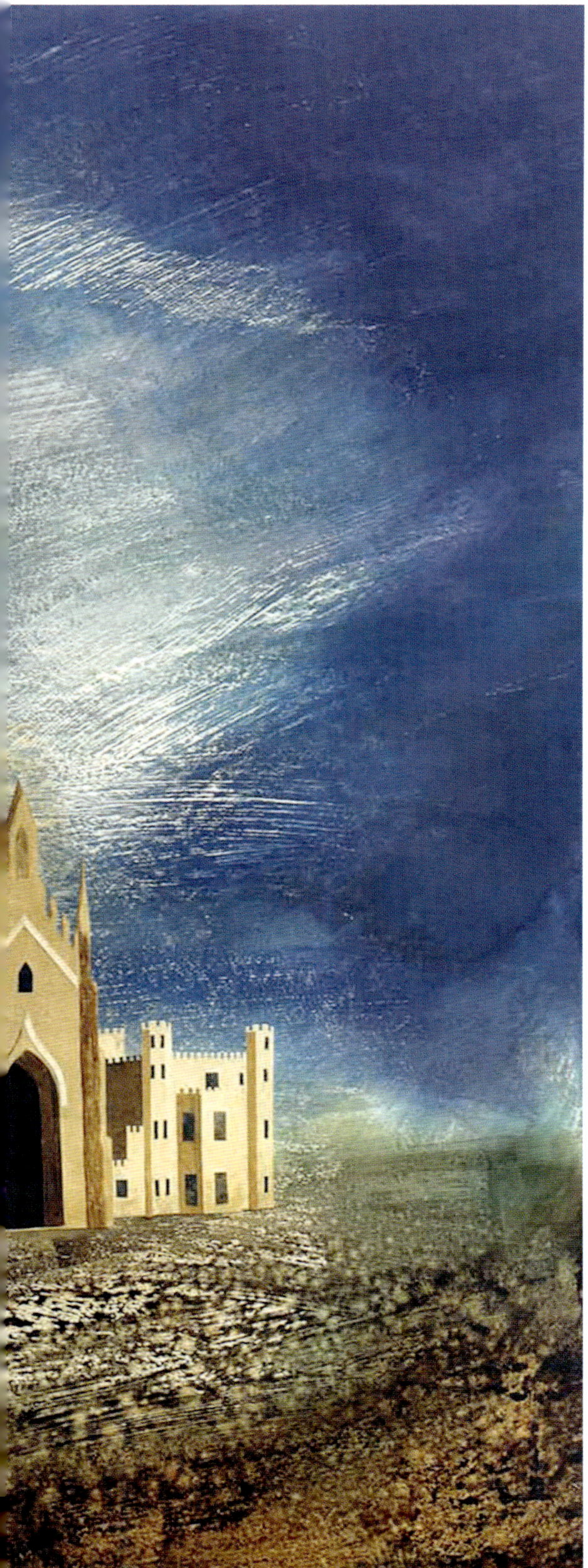

Yes, FONTHILL, yes; pre-eminent, unvied,
Thy splendors beam, all rival works to chide;
Alone, unequall'd, to a wond'ring World,
Thy endless glories all have been unfurl'd;
Thy view, like some giant-ensign, high array'd,
Throws Tow'rs, Cathedrals, Castles, into shade,
And, save the remnants of old GREECE or ROME,
Or BU'NAROTTI'S boast, or WREN'S high dome,
No age, no land, no genius e'er brought forth,
A nobler fane to gild the breathing Earth.

FROM JOHN JEFFERSON, *FONTHILL: A POEM*, 1824

Prospect of Fonthill Abbey, *paper collage and mixed media, 2014.*

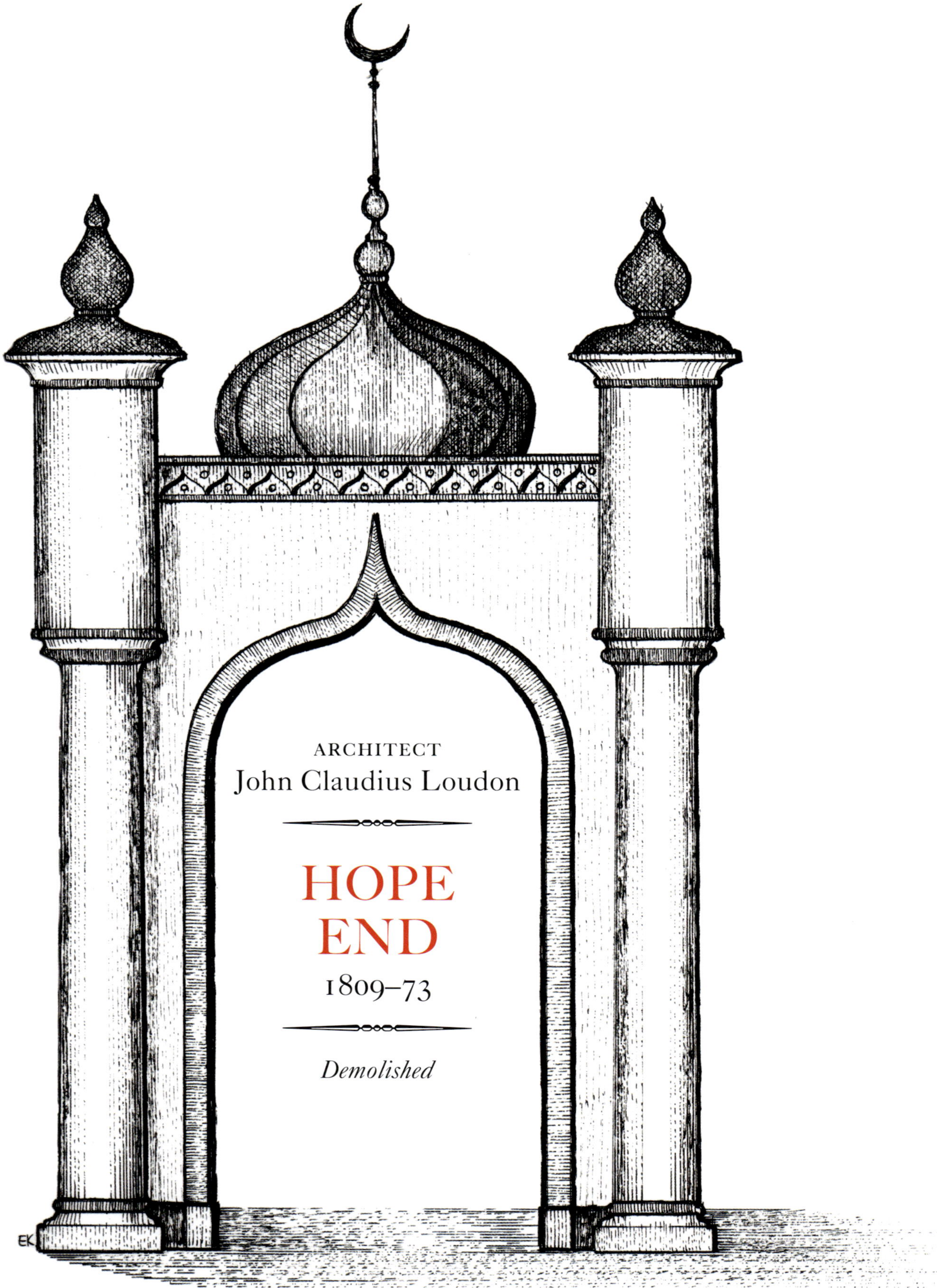

ARCHITECT

John Claudius Loudon

HOPE END

1809–73

Demolished

What enchanting bedtime stories must have been told under the eaves of Hope End! Twelve children spent their early years there, surrounded by exotic towers, chasing one another through doors inlaid with mother-of-pearl, and looking out through windows impossibly positioned over fireplaces. The most famous of this brood is better known by her married name, Elizabeth Barrett Browning. She was only three years old in 1809, when her father conjured this extraordinary house in an unremarkable Herefordshire valley.

Before Edward Moulton-Barrett (1785–1857) acquired the estate, Hope End was 'a small but very pleasant seat'.[1] He found a simple, mid-eighteenth-century, double-fronted house of three storeys, which he reduced in height and turned into a stable block, building a new, exotic house next to it and incorporating part of the old fabric. A history of the area published shortly after the completion of Hope End describes the house as 'in part, a modern structure'.[2] When Moulton-Barrett sold it, the house was lauded as 'a chef-d'oeuvre, unrivalled in this kingdom' and 'the chief ornament of the surrounding country'.[3]

The distinguishing characteristic of Hope End was that it was 'in the Eastern style' – an indistinct classification (interchangeable at that time with 'Moorish' and 'Hindoo') that indicated an eclectic combination of features including ogee-headed Gothic windows, oculi, turrets and domes.[4] John Claudius Loudon (1783–1843), best known as a landscape gardener, claimed credit for the work, stating that the house and grounds were 'recently improved from our designs'.[5]

An extensive carriage drive leads through the grounds, which are laid out in a park-like style, to an enclosed portico, with vaulted roof, folding doors, filled with stained glass, a noble vestibule supported by columns ... a Magnificent Drawing Room ... elegant Cornice, Doors and Windows painted white, and finished with gilt Mouldings, beautiful marble Chimney-piece, richly ornamented with Or-molu.

HOPE END SALE CATALOGUE, 1832

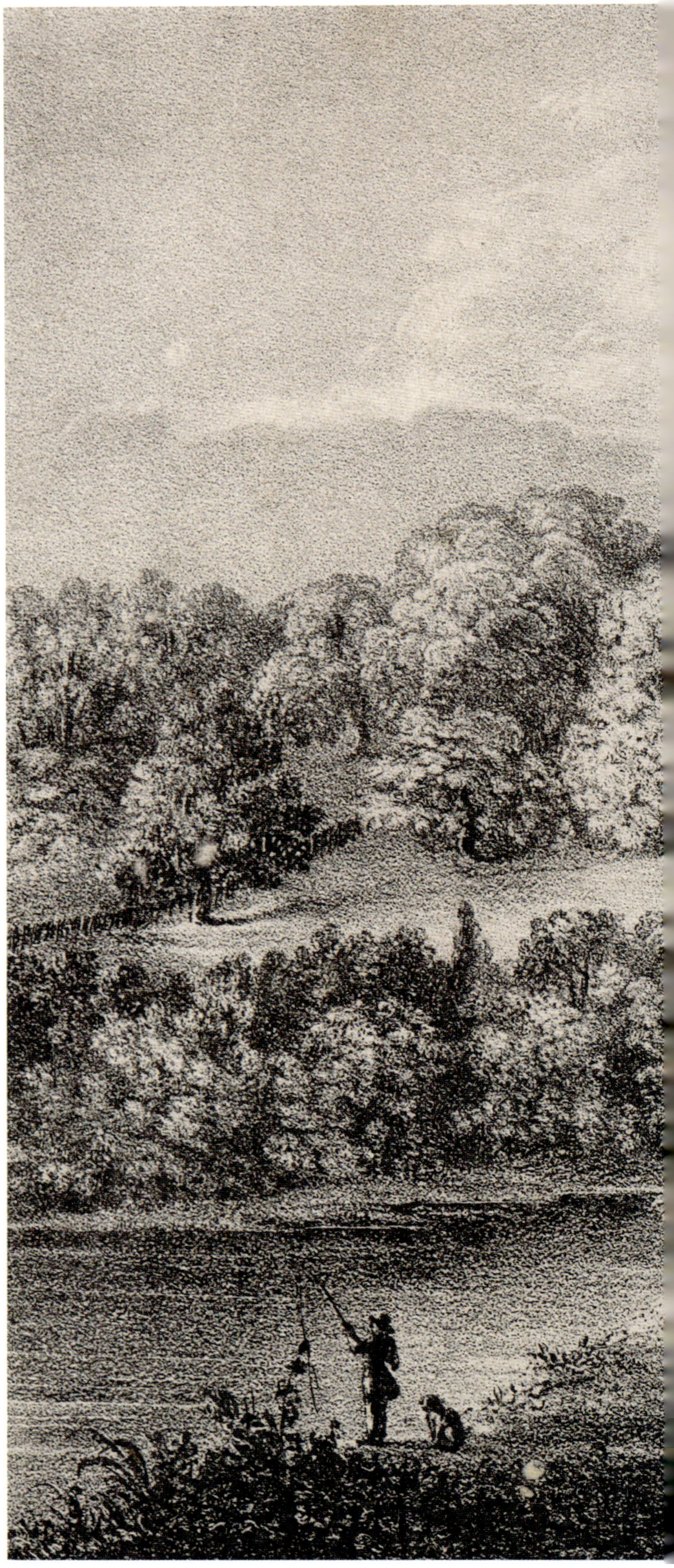

Mrs Heywood, Hope End, near Ledbury, *lithograph, 1810.*

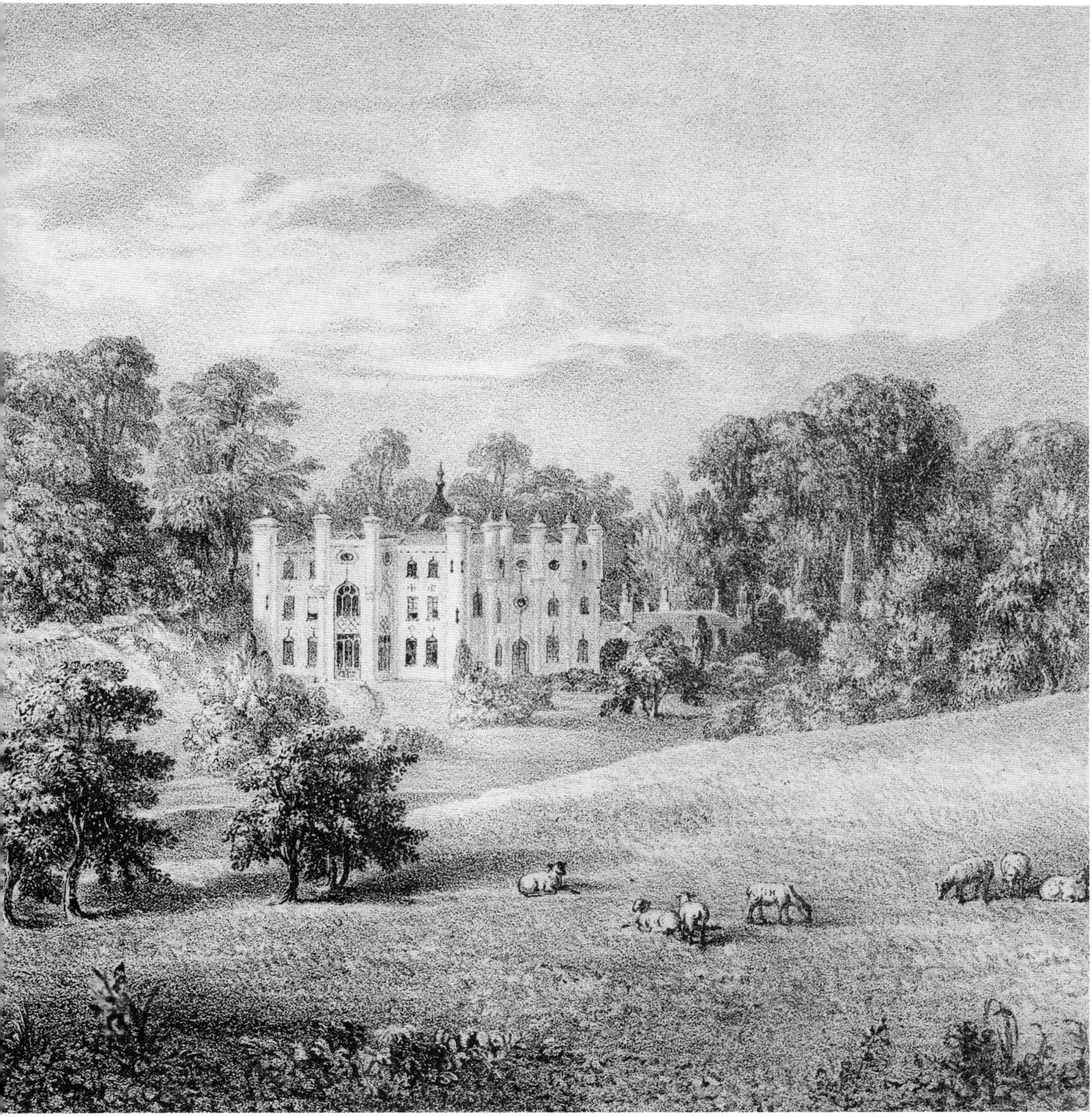

HOPE END

Loudon's work at Hope End owed much to Humphry Repton's unrealized proposals for the Royal Pavilion at Brighton, published in 1808. The similarities between the schemes are striking, particularly the slim turrets, the ogee-arched windows, the onion dome and the lavish interiors – although one must admit that Hope End is a slightly lumpen cousin. Loudon admired Repton and quoted his analysis of English domestic architecture, noting that the architect had identified 'the Hindoo' as a modern addition to the stylistic repertoire that was 'likely to become fashionable'.[6]

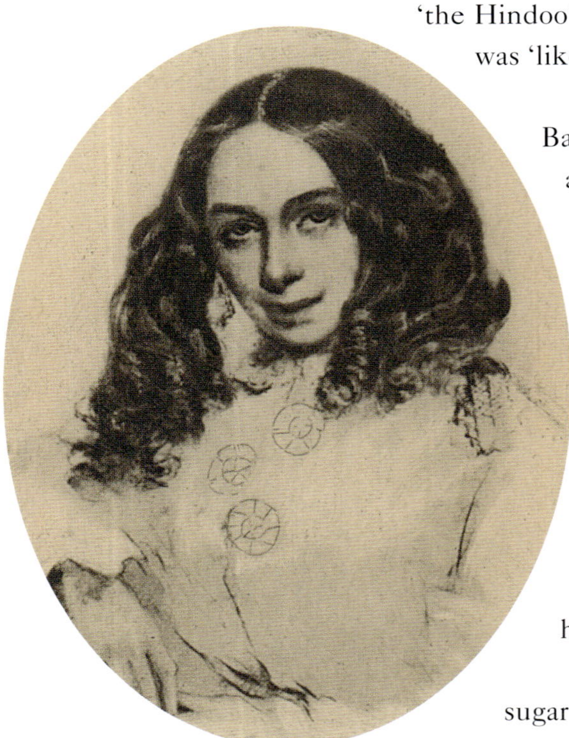

Left: Portrait of Elizabeth Barrett Browning, published in Aurora Leigh, a Poem, *1899.*

Records do not relate the impetus behind Moulton-Barrett's decision to clothe his home in Turkish garb and to decorate it internally in a variety of modes, including Chinese and Gothic. It was a surprising choice for someone who was known for being devoutly religious and reserved in character. Yet that was his tenor in later life. At the time of acquiring Hope End, he was a man barely out of his minority with a young wife who, as the daughter of a wealthy northern businessman, doubtless had expectations of her own. The promise of being pioneers of taste may have been all that it took to convince them to adopt what was (and remained) a highly unusual style.

Edward Moulton-Barrett's fortune derived from sugar plantations in Jamaica. The house at Cinnamon Hill where he was born survived the Slave Revolt of 1831, but the unrest damaged the family's finances and led to the sale of Hope End in 1832. It was purchased first by the antiquary Thomas Heywood and then again in 1867 by Charles Archibald Hewitt.[7] It was under Hewitt that the playful extravagance of the house was crushed. In 1873 he demolished Loudon's confection and built a larger, modern mansion on higher ground (see p. 175). All that survives of Moulton-Barrett's whimsical home are the stables, a gateway and a lone minaret.

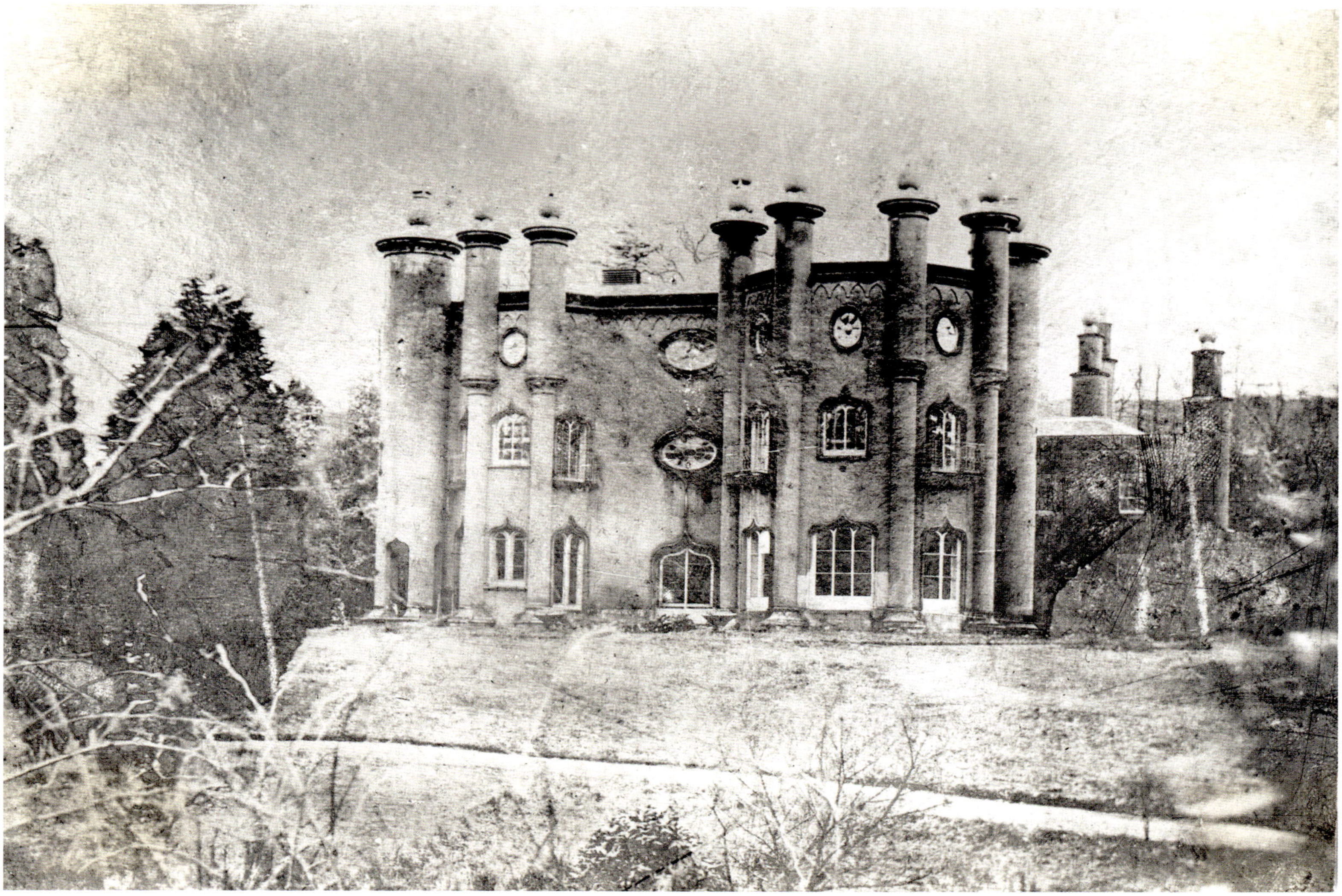

Hope End, photographed in the mid-19th century.

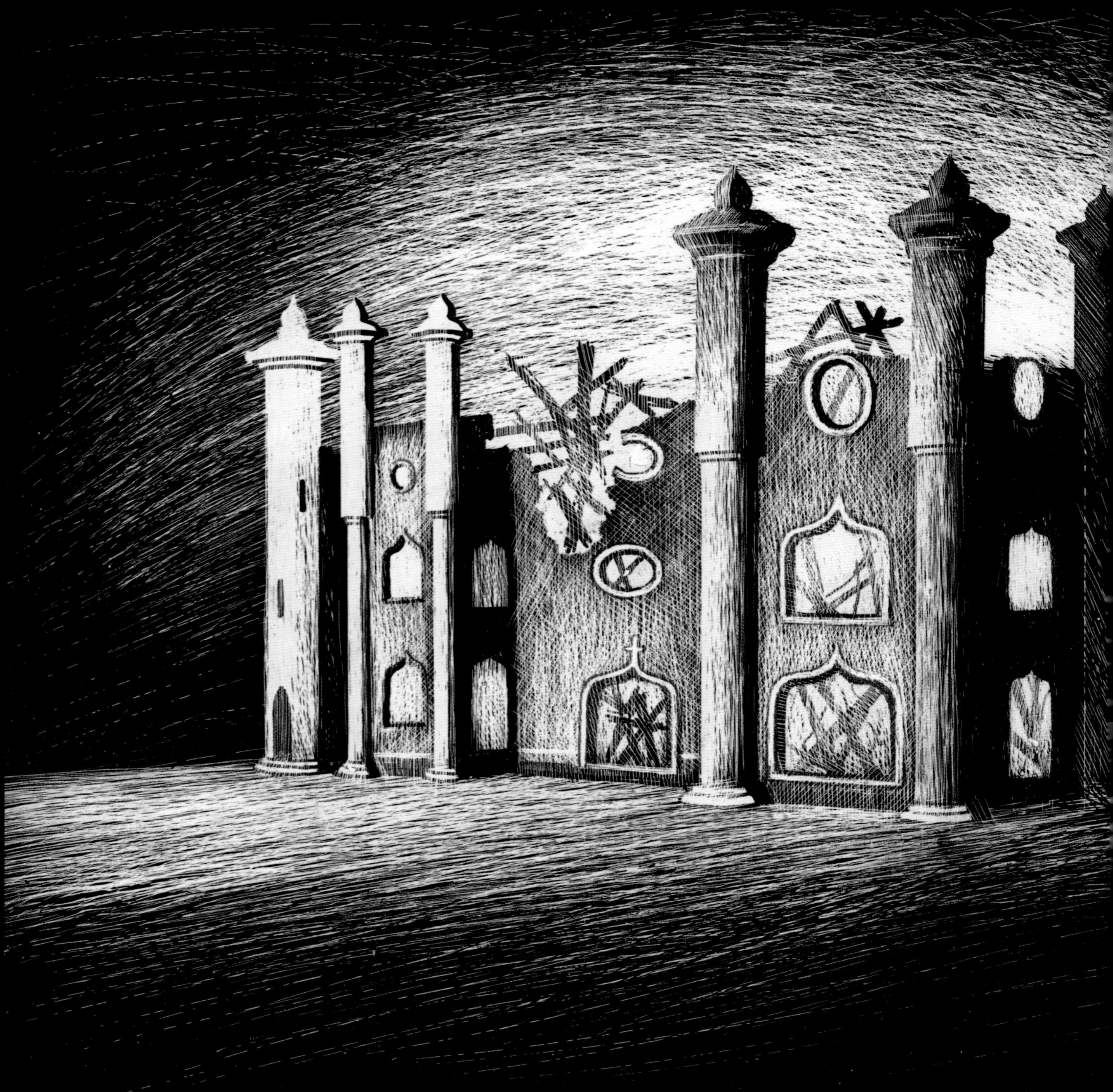

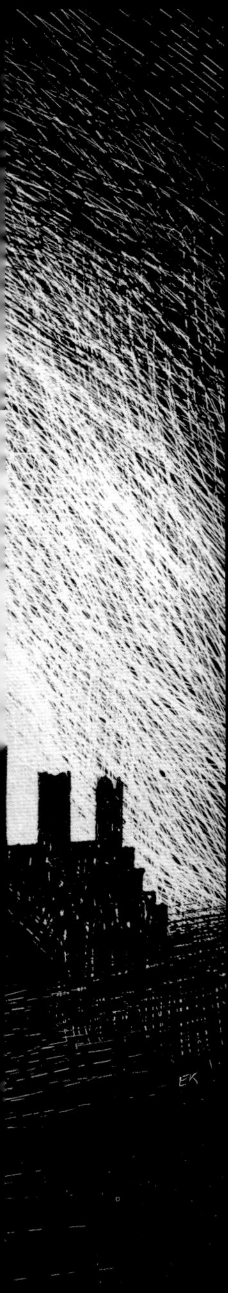

View of Hope End during Demolition, *scraperboard, 2017*.

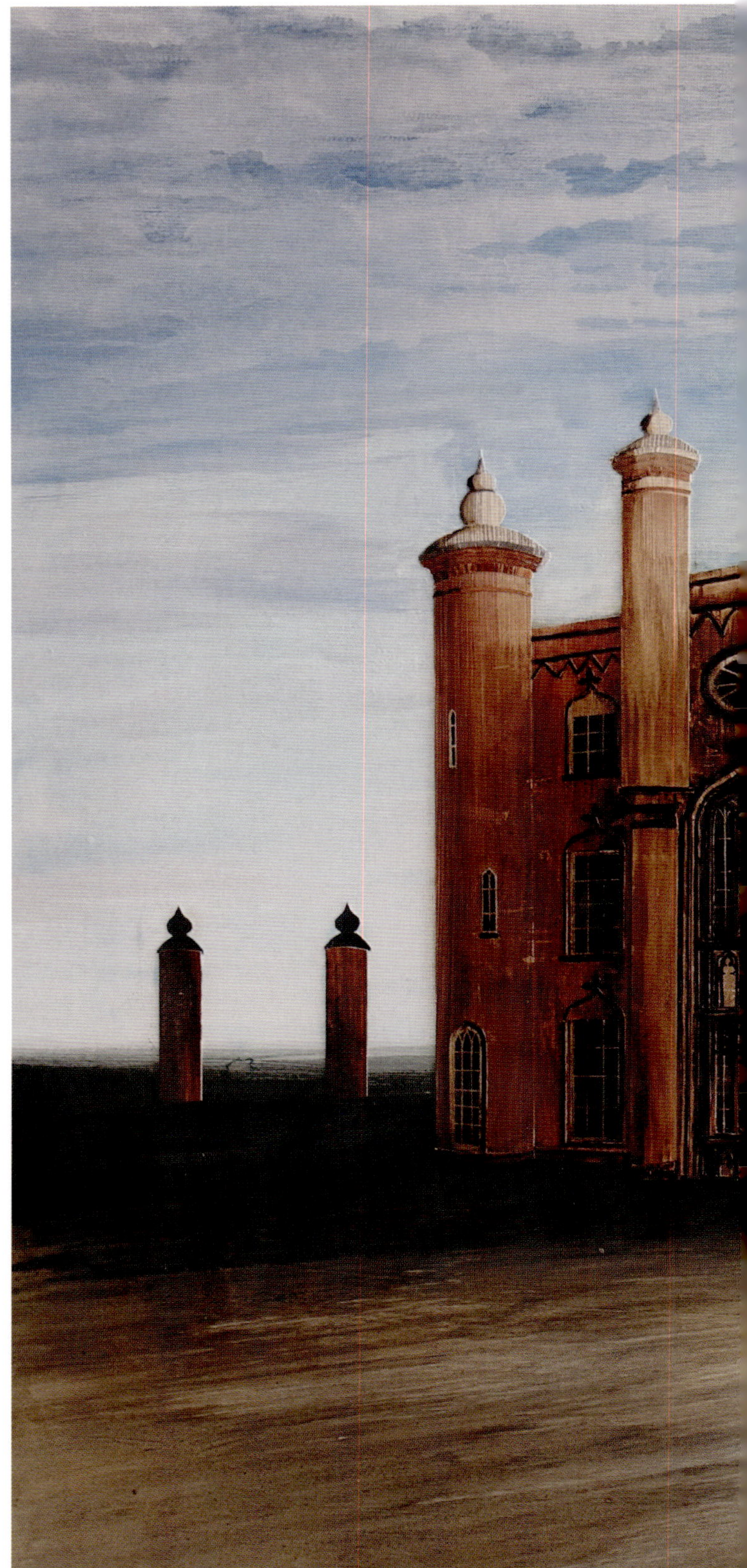

Prospect of Hope End, *paper collage and mixed media, 2017. Detail shown pages 152–53.*

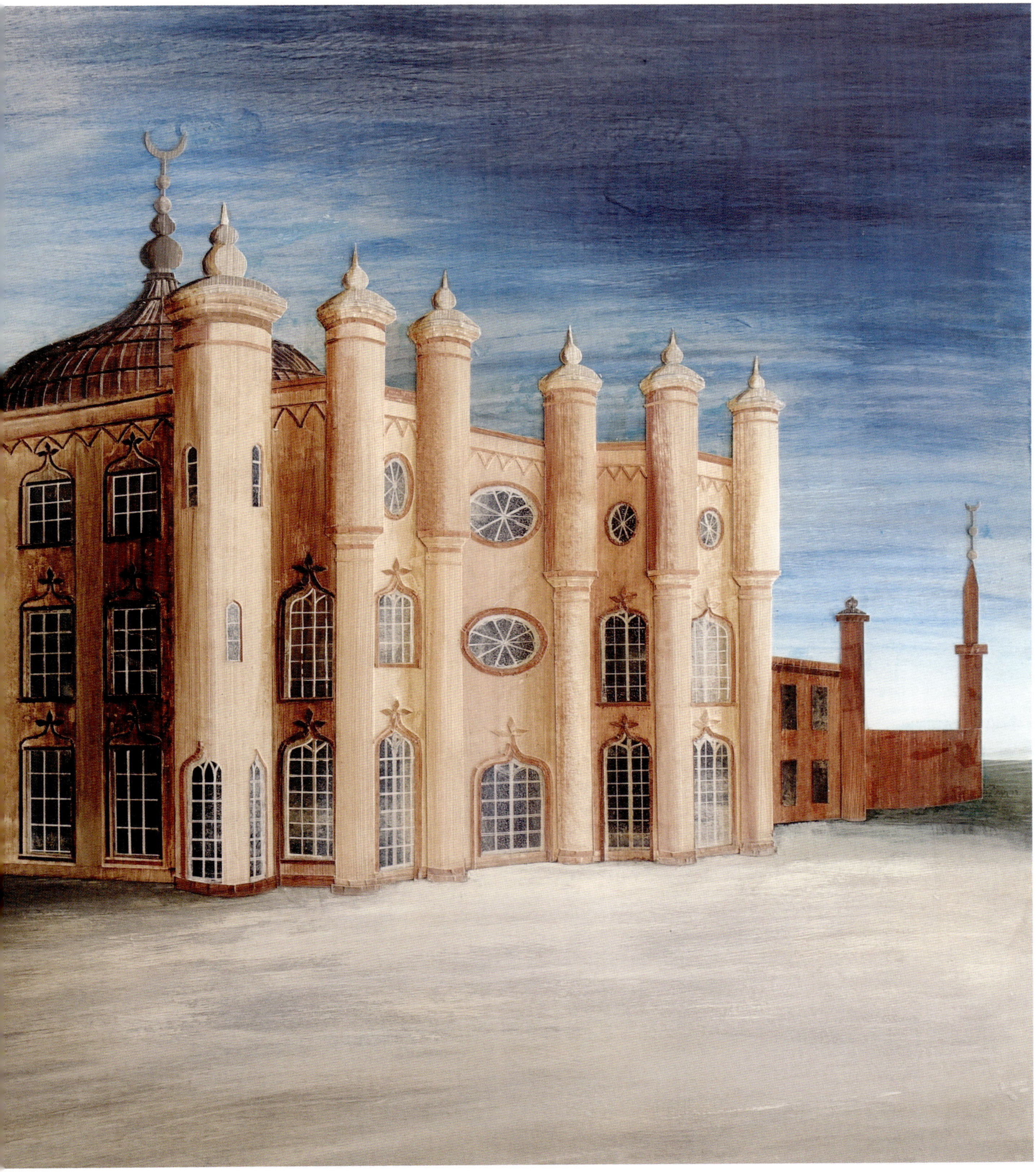

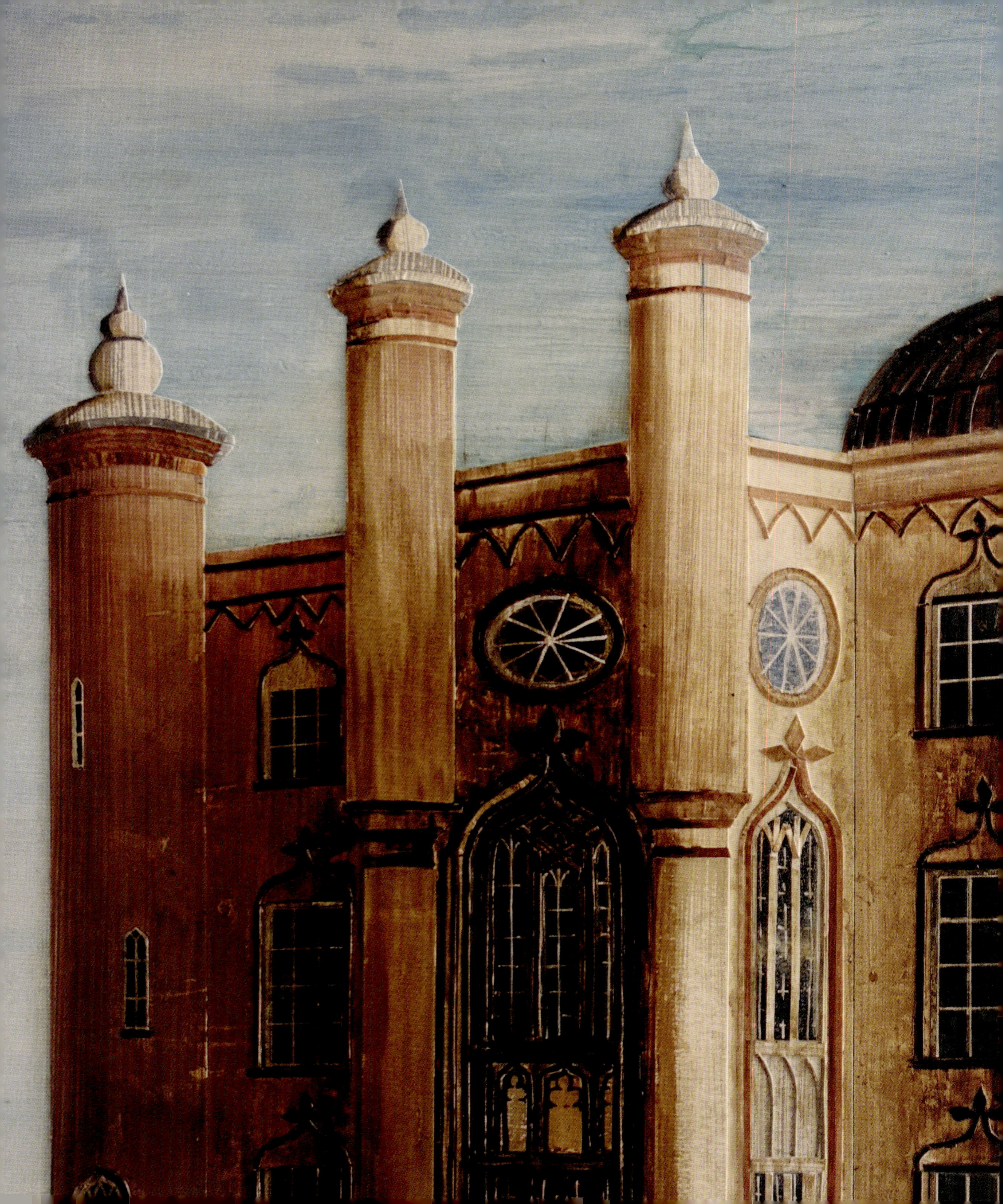

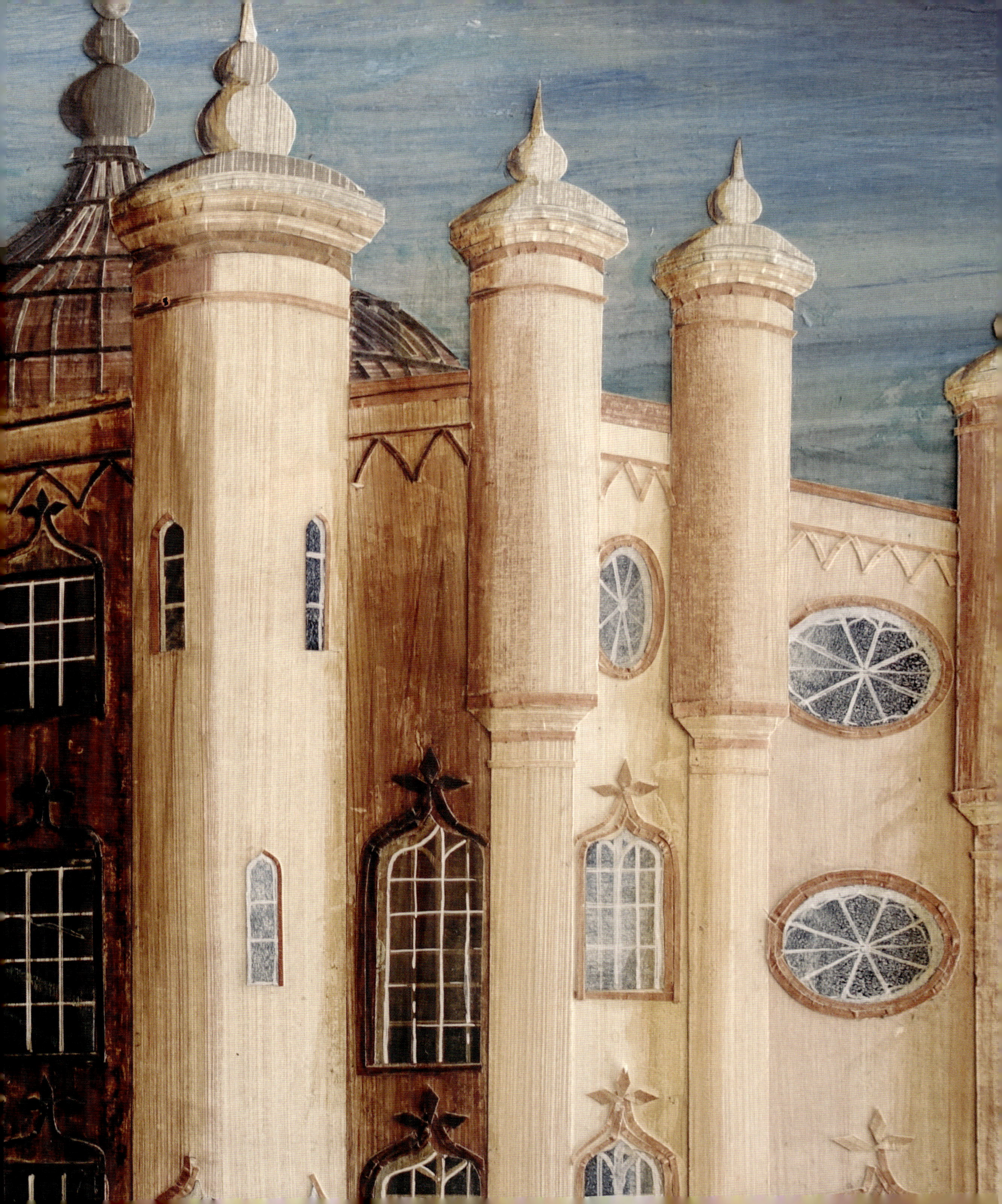

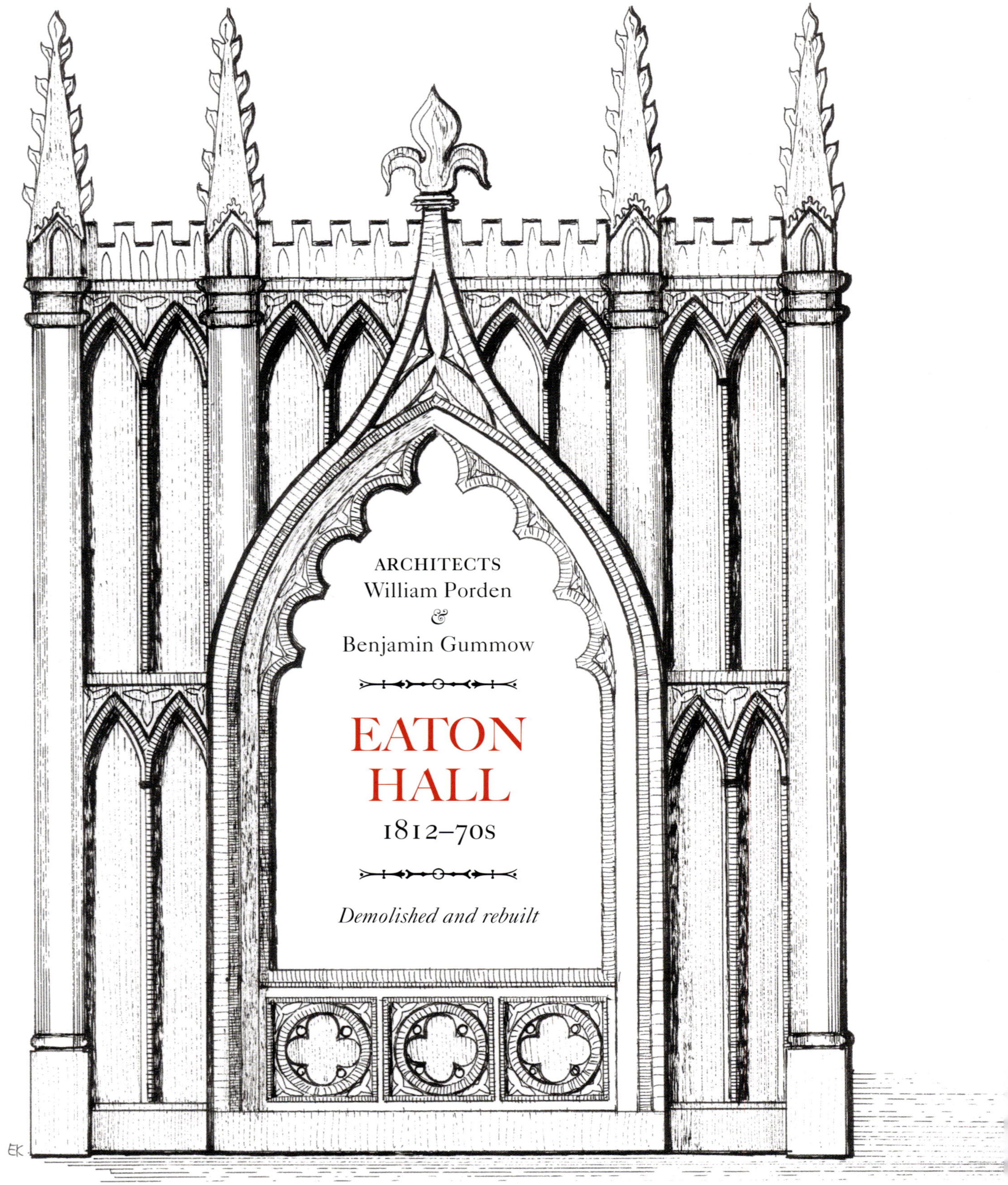

ARCHITECTS
William Porden
&
Benjamin Gummow

EATON HALL

1812–70s

Demolished and rebuilt

When Dr Syntax (a comic invention of the satirist William Combe) viewed 'the architect'ral pageantry' of Eaton Hall in 1820, he admired its 'Monkish' form.[1] It was right, he declared, that when an ancient family built a modern house, 'The new rais'd structure should dispense/The stile of old magnificence'.[2] William Porden's pinnacled confection for Lord Grosvenor accomplished this with delicacy. Were it not for changing taste, it would be a rare manifestation of Regency medievalism. Instead, it was consumed by the voracious appetites of the late nineteenth-century Gothic revival.

Porden's Eaton Hall itself effaced the previous building on the Cheshire site: a brick house built between 1675 and 1683 by Sir Thomas Grosvenor to designs by William Samwell (see pp. 156, 157). By 1768, when Robert Adam proposed renovations, it was in a state of considerable disrepair, but nothing was done; by 1802, when the 2nd Earl Grosvenor (1767–1845) succeeded his father, modernization was urgently required. Rather than turning to a fashionable architect, he appointed Porden, surveyor of the family's London estates since 1789.

Porden (*c.* 1755–1822) conjured up a confident vision for Eaton, swiftly abandoning his initial proposals to encase the existing house in the classical dress that was 'seen everywhere' in preference for Gothic, which he considered more exclusive, because its 'expensiveness, or the opinion of it being so, has prevented it from becoming common'.[3] Gothic could also convey the ancient nobility of the family (they were descended from William the Conqueror's nephew) by appearing 'as the work of our Ancestors and not of yesterday'.[4]

Porden's sources ranged from medieval cathedrals (particularly York Minster, which he regarded as his architectural cradle) to the late eighteenth-century Donington Hall near Derby and the early nineteenth-century castellated palace at Kew. Retaining only the basement of Samwell's house, Porden doubled its footprint to create a three-storey turreted block with single-storey wings that looked like chantry chapels. The entrance front sported a triple-arched porte cochère, while the garden front offered a cloister walk overlooking terraces by the landscape designer John Webb. The house was completed in 1812, but by 1814 expansion was already projected. With Porden unwell, his long-term clerk of works, Benjamin Gummow (1766–1844), oversaw the addition of two asymmetrical wings: one containing two libraries, the other housing a chapel and a pair of bedrooms.

Porden was as exacting about the building's interiors as he was about its shell. Notable features were heraldic stained-glass windows and elaborate vaulted plaster ceilings (that of the salon incorporated two roundels from the earlier house). The rich colours and textures of these schemes, as well as the specially designed furniture, were captured in J. and J.C. Buckler's 1826 views of Eaton Hall (see pp. 158–59). By 1825 expenditure on the house had spiralled from an anticipated £15,000 to some £100,000, funded by the Grosvenors' lead mines in North Wales.

Over the next fifty years Porden's creation was swallowed up. In 1846, just twenty years after its enlargement, the 2nd Marquess of Westminster enlisted William Burn to modify the house. He removed wings to make it less picturesque and reworked pinnacles to strike a more convincingly Tudor note. The final obliteration was ensured in the 1870s with Alfred Waterhouse's remodelling. This aggrandizement produced a muscular High Gothic ensemble, complete with gatehouse and free-standing chapel.

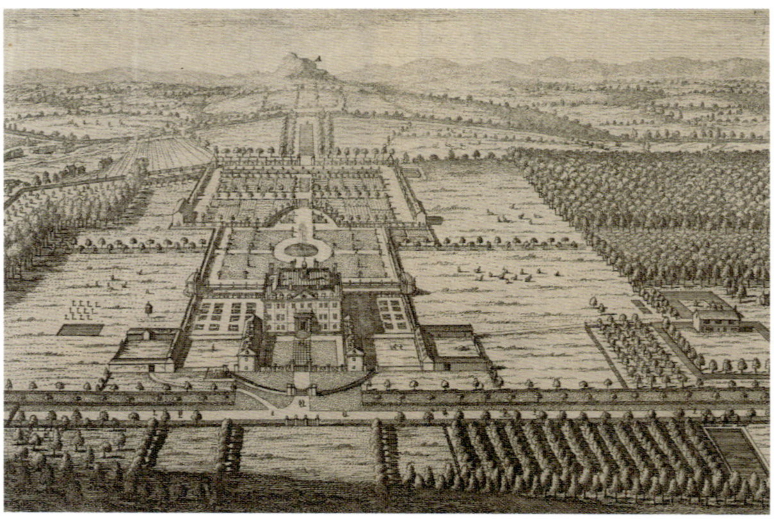

Pieter van der Aa, after Johannes Kip, Eaton Hall on the River Dee, near the City of Chester in Cheshire, *engraving published in James Beeverell,* Les Délices de la Grande Bretagne et de l'Irlande, *1707.*

Even Waterhouse's Eaton Hall, however, was not immune from changing taste. In 1961 the Army's lease on the house expired, but the trustees of the Grosvenor estate, in consultation with the family, decided that the cost of restoration and maintenance would be prohibitive.[5] Demolition was judged the only alternative. After about a decade, the 5th Duke determined to rebuild, and commissioned John Dennys to design a smaller house, completed in 1971, in a peculiar retro-modern style redolent of commercial buildings of the 1930s. Its appeal swiftly waned, and in 1989 it was extended and clad in dusky-pink sandstone to create the appearance of a French château. With that, the succession of houses has – for the moment – reached a standstill.

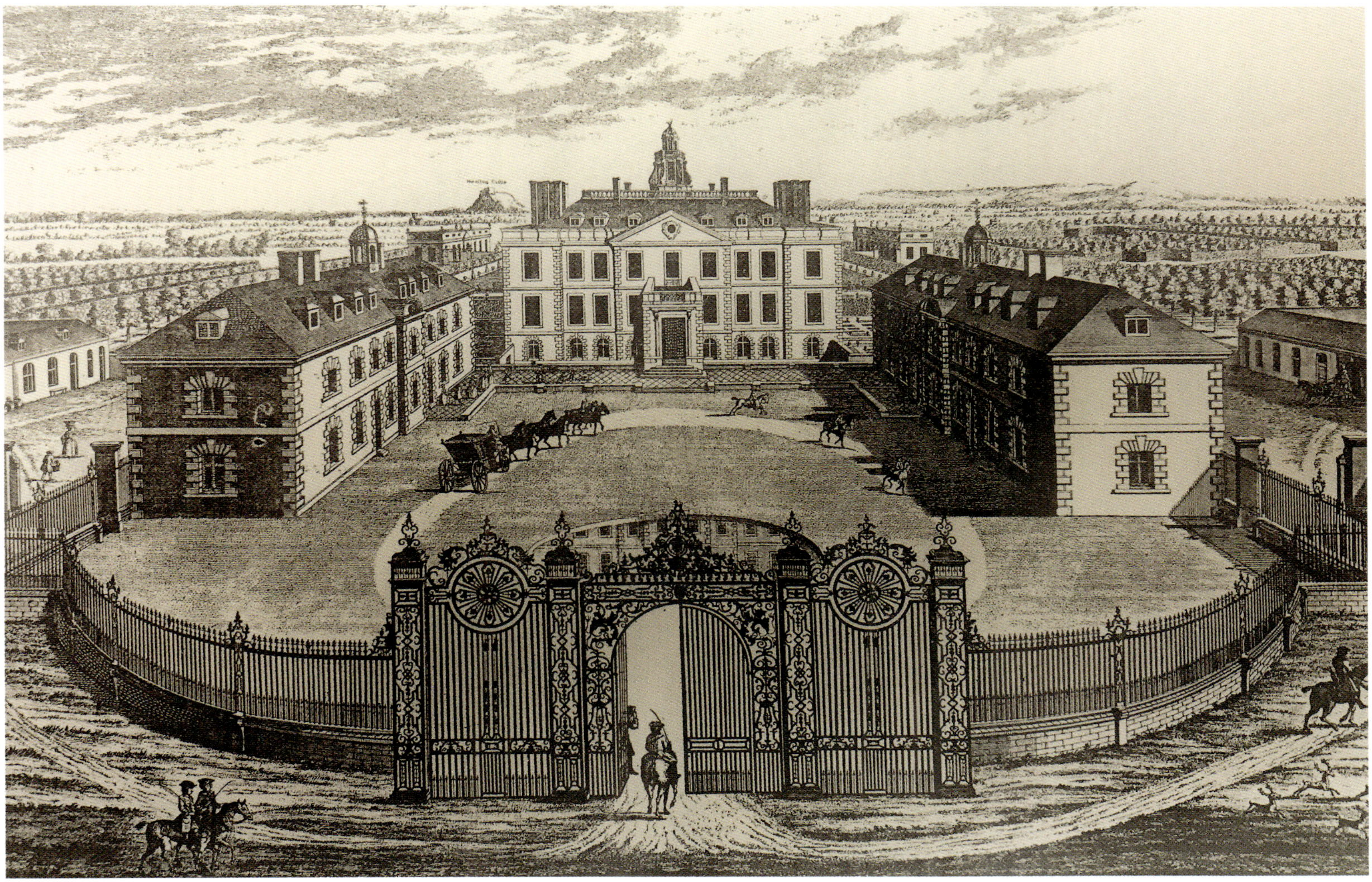

Thomas Badeslade, Eaton Hall, Cheshire, c. *1740*, *engraving published in* English Houses and Gardens in the 17th and 18th Centuries, *1908*.

Eaton Hall is
the magnificent seat
of Earl Grosvenor.
It is built of white stone,
in the florid gothic style,
from designs by Mr. Porden,
and is richly ornamented.
It contains a complete suit
of rooms, not excelled in
the empire for taste
and splendour.

J. H. H[ANSHALL], *THE STRANGER IN CHESTER, GIVING AN ACCURATE SKETCH OF ITS LOCAL HISTORY*, 1816

Right: John Buckler, The Library, *lithograph published in* Views of Eaton Hall in Cheshire, *1826.*

Pages 160–61: George Batenham, West Front of Eaton Hall, the Seat of the Right Honourable Earl Grosvenor, *hand-coloured engraving, 1827.*

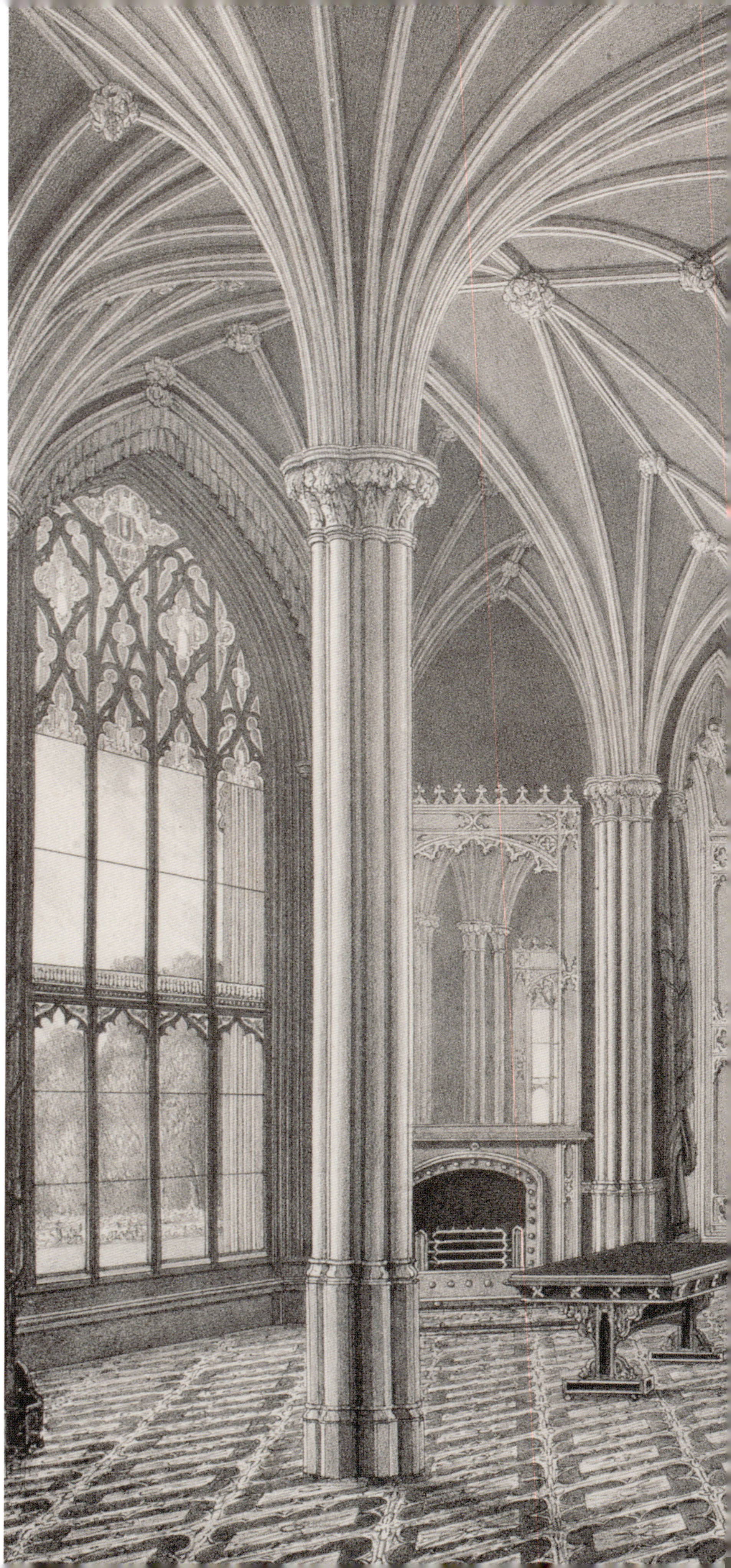

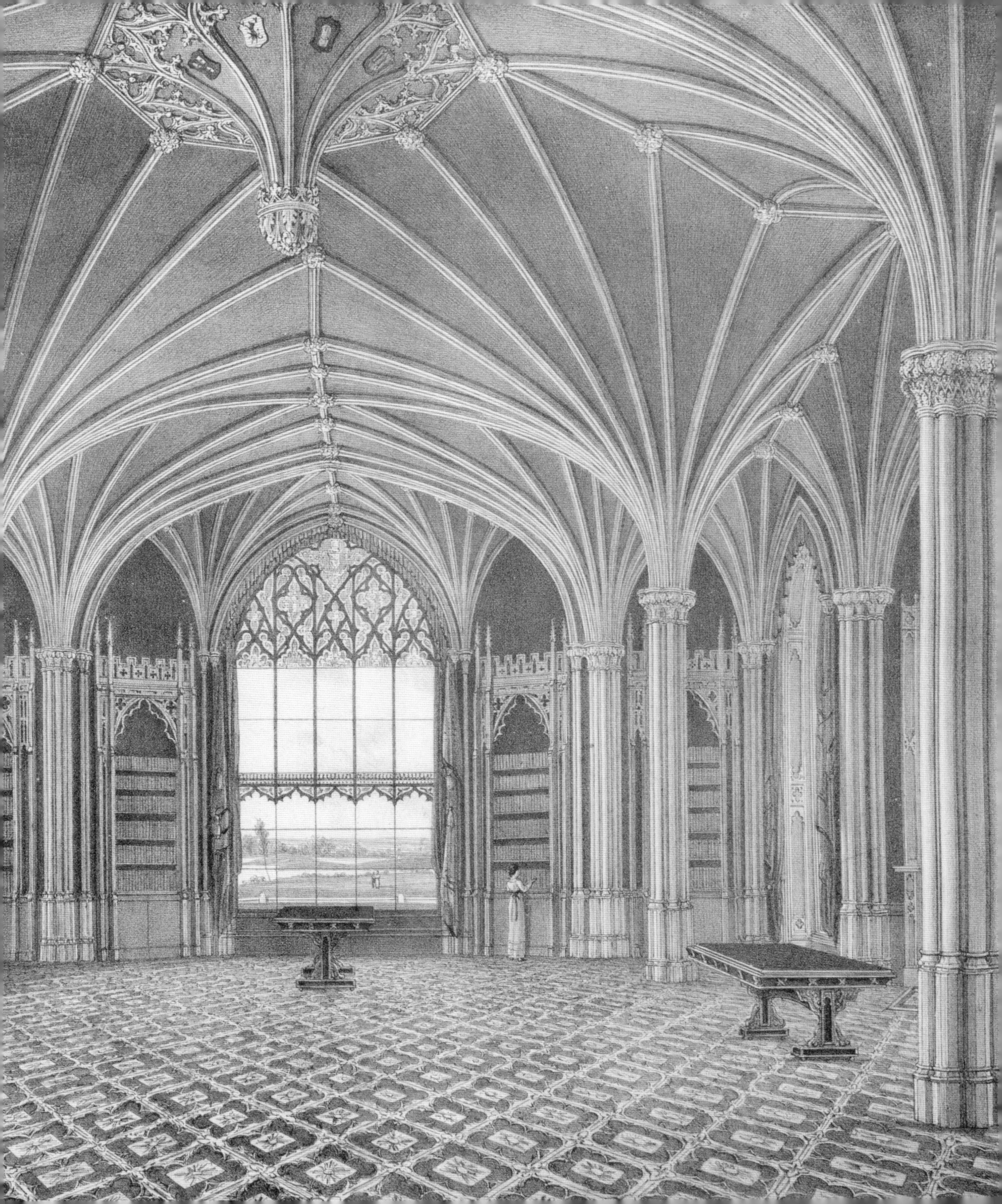

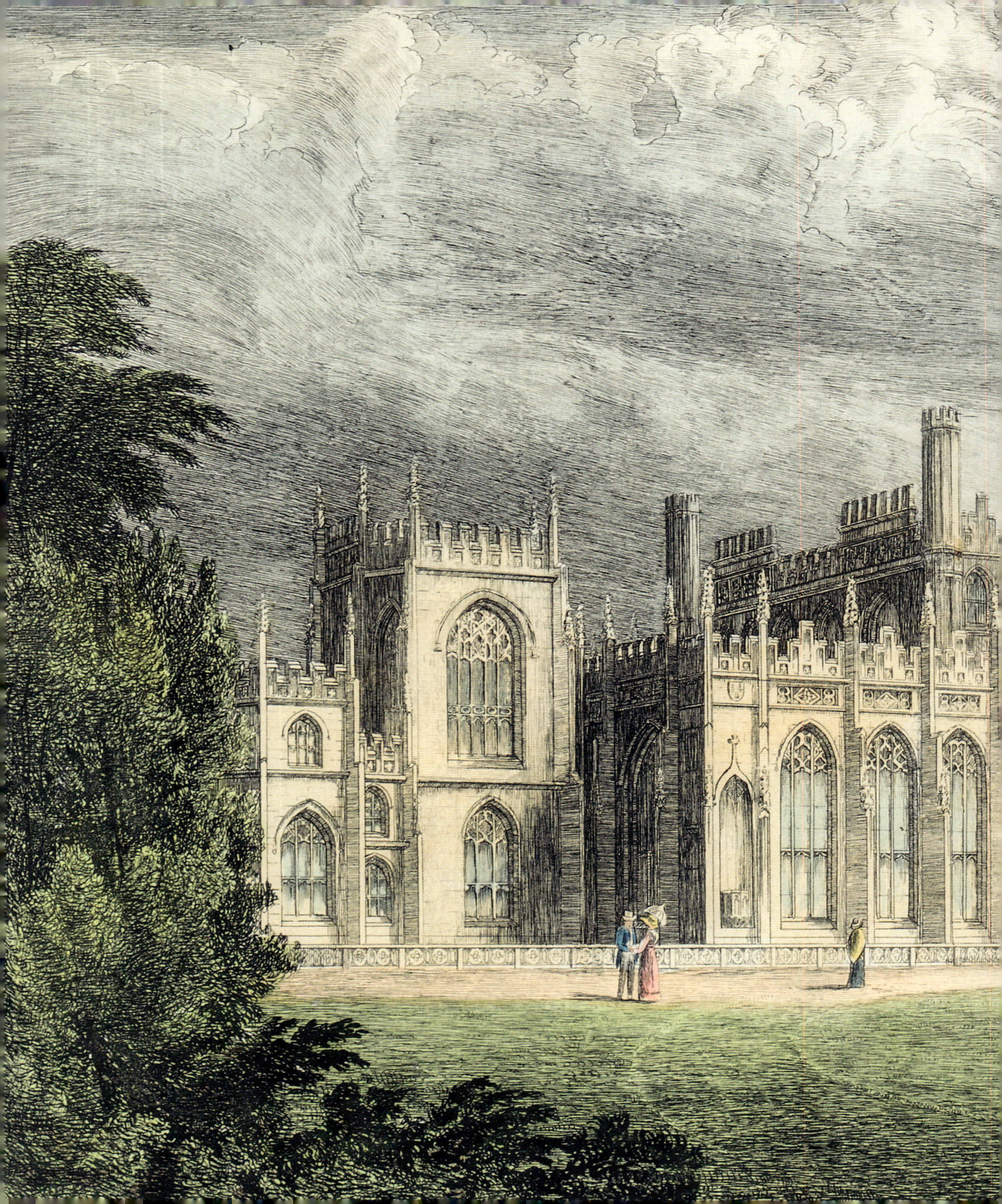

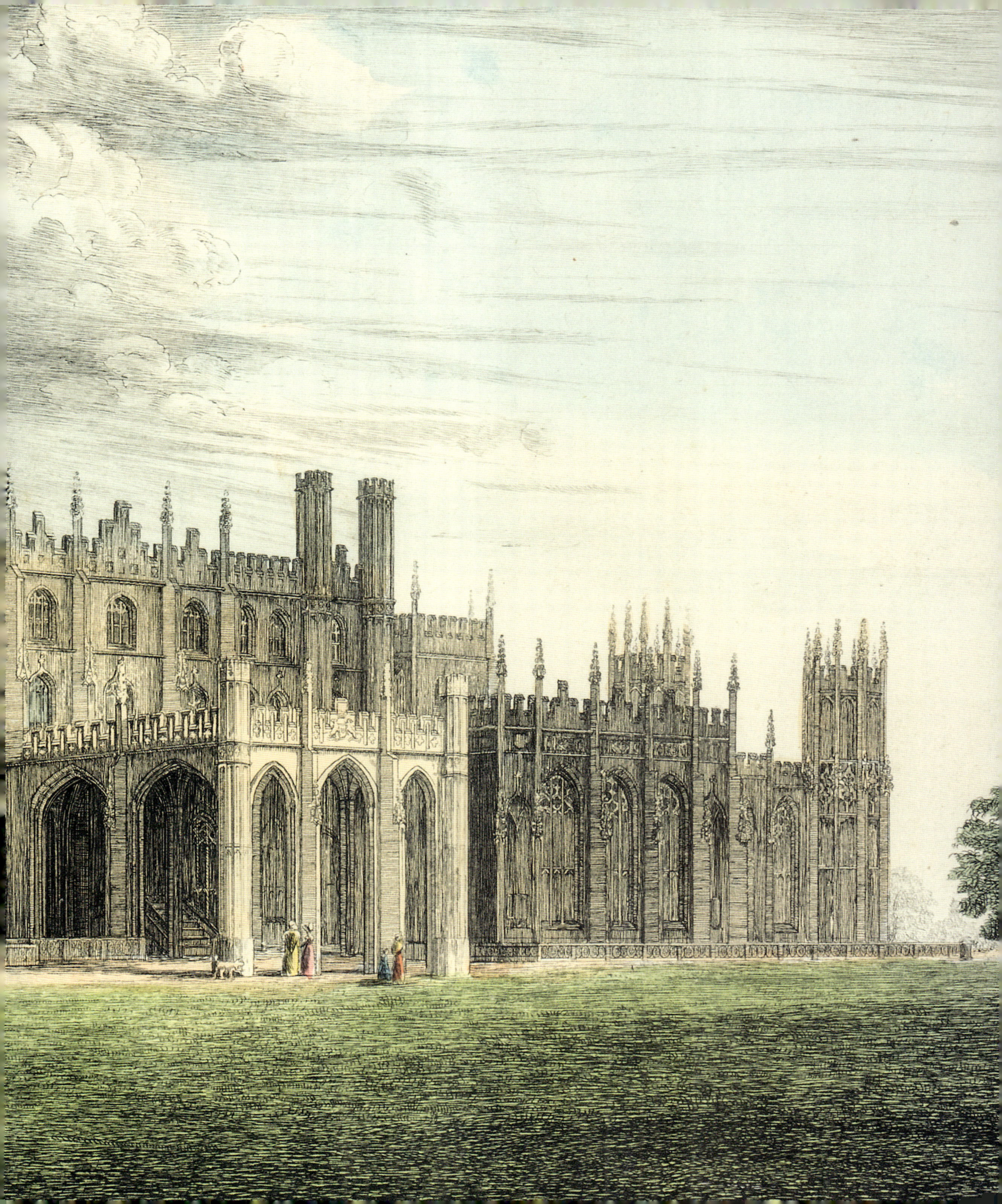

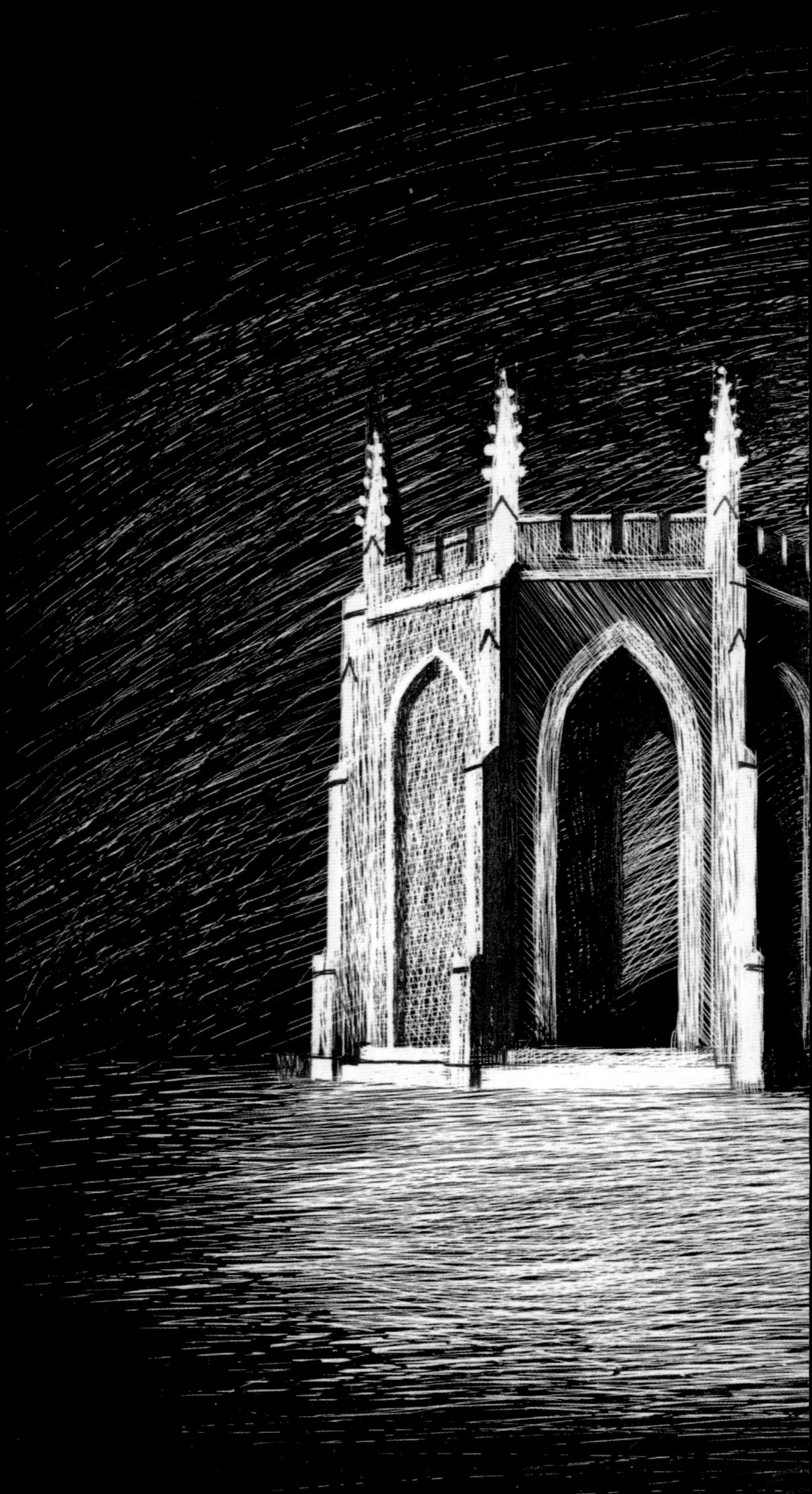

View of Eaton Hall from
the Gothic Temple,
scraperboard, 2017.

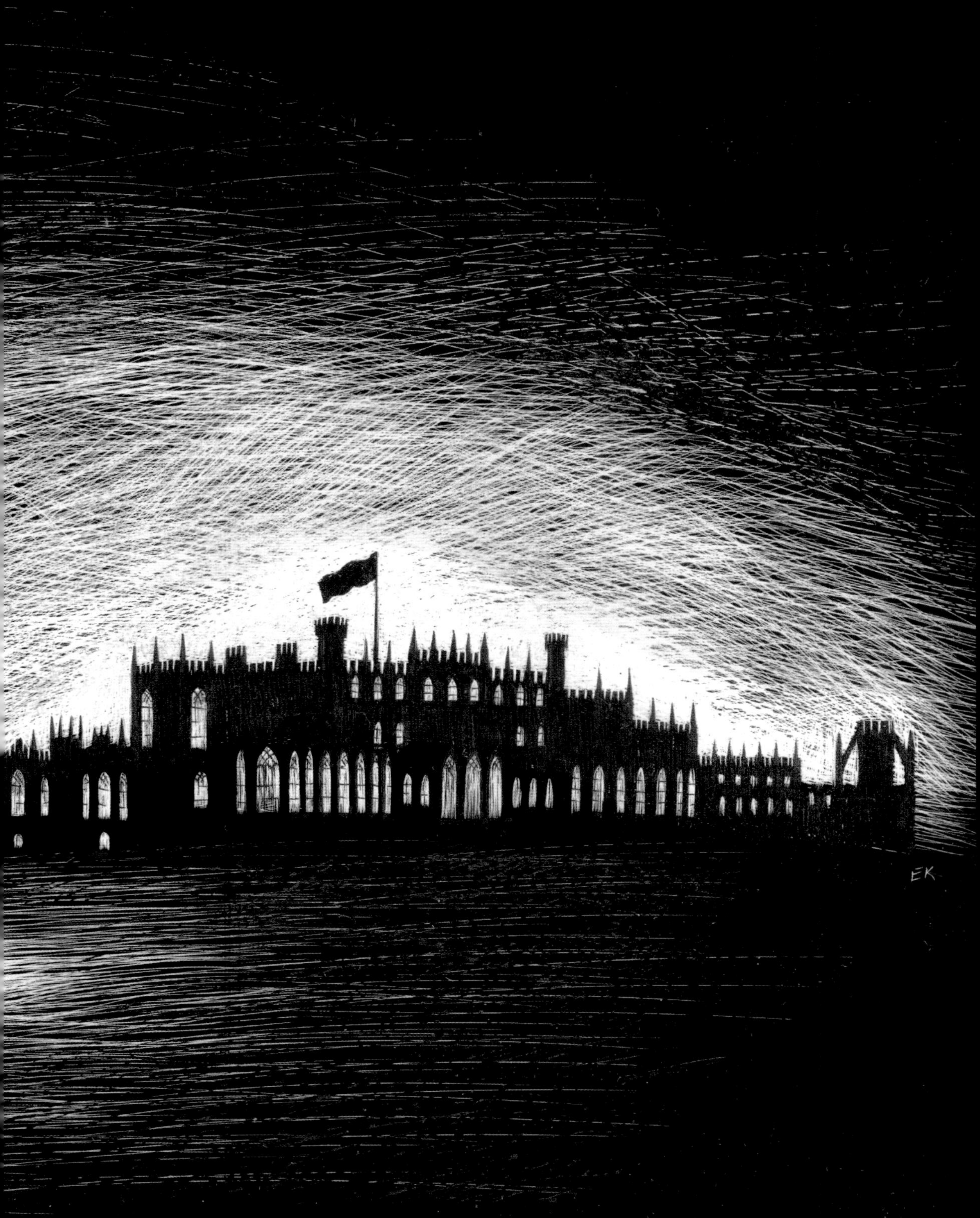

EATON HALL

Prospect of Eaton Hall,
paper collage and mixed media, 2014.

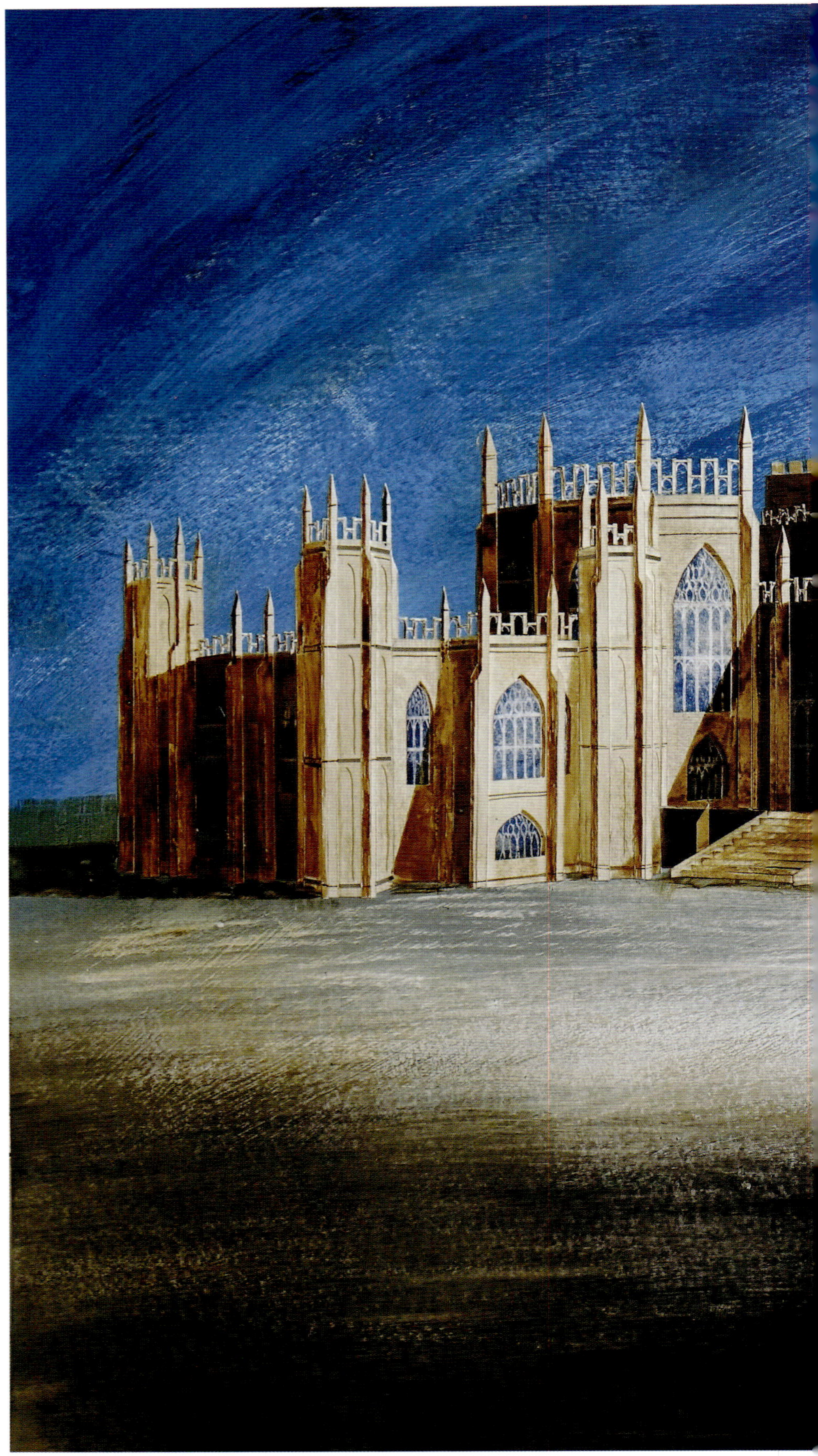

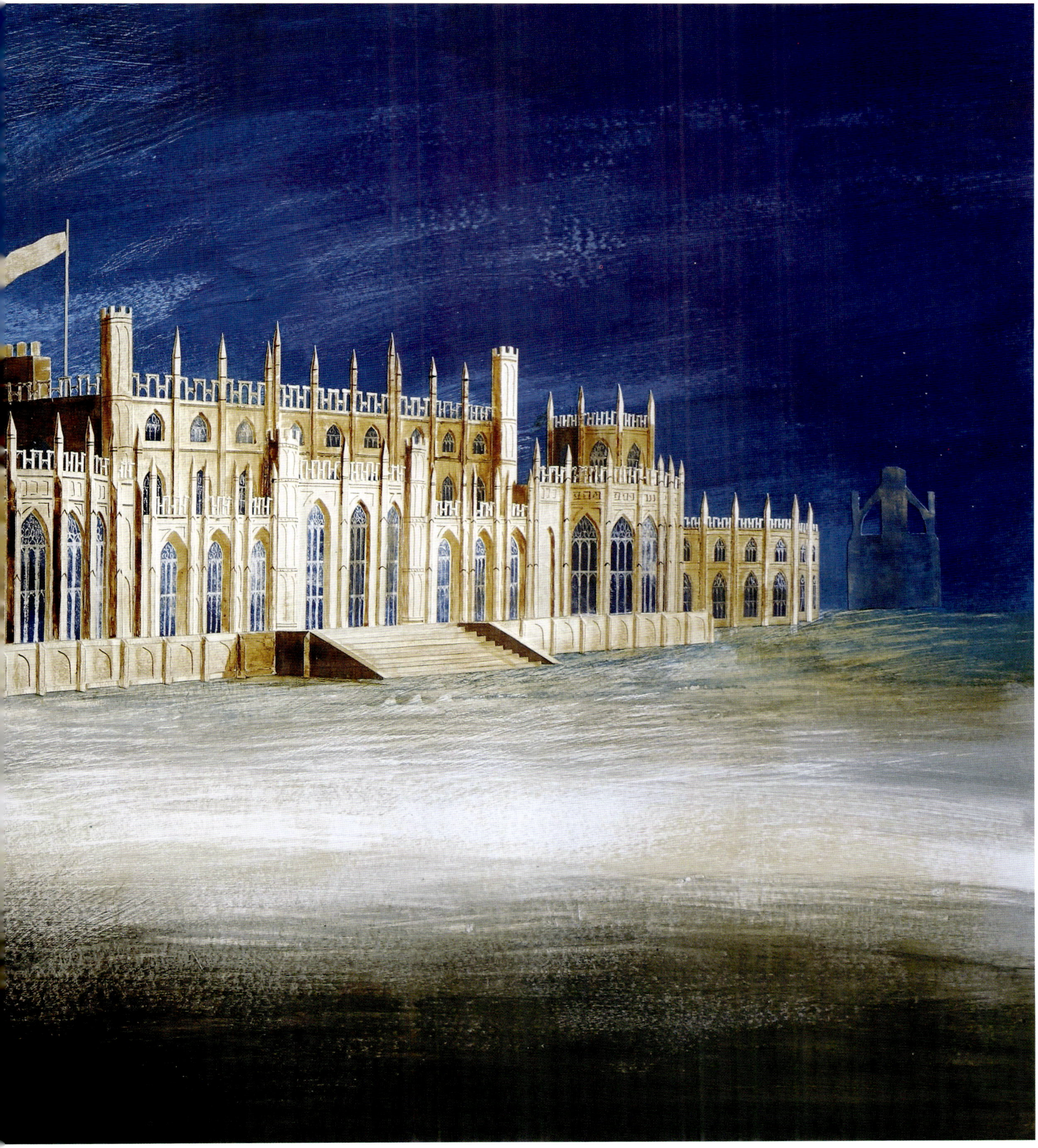

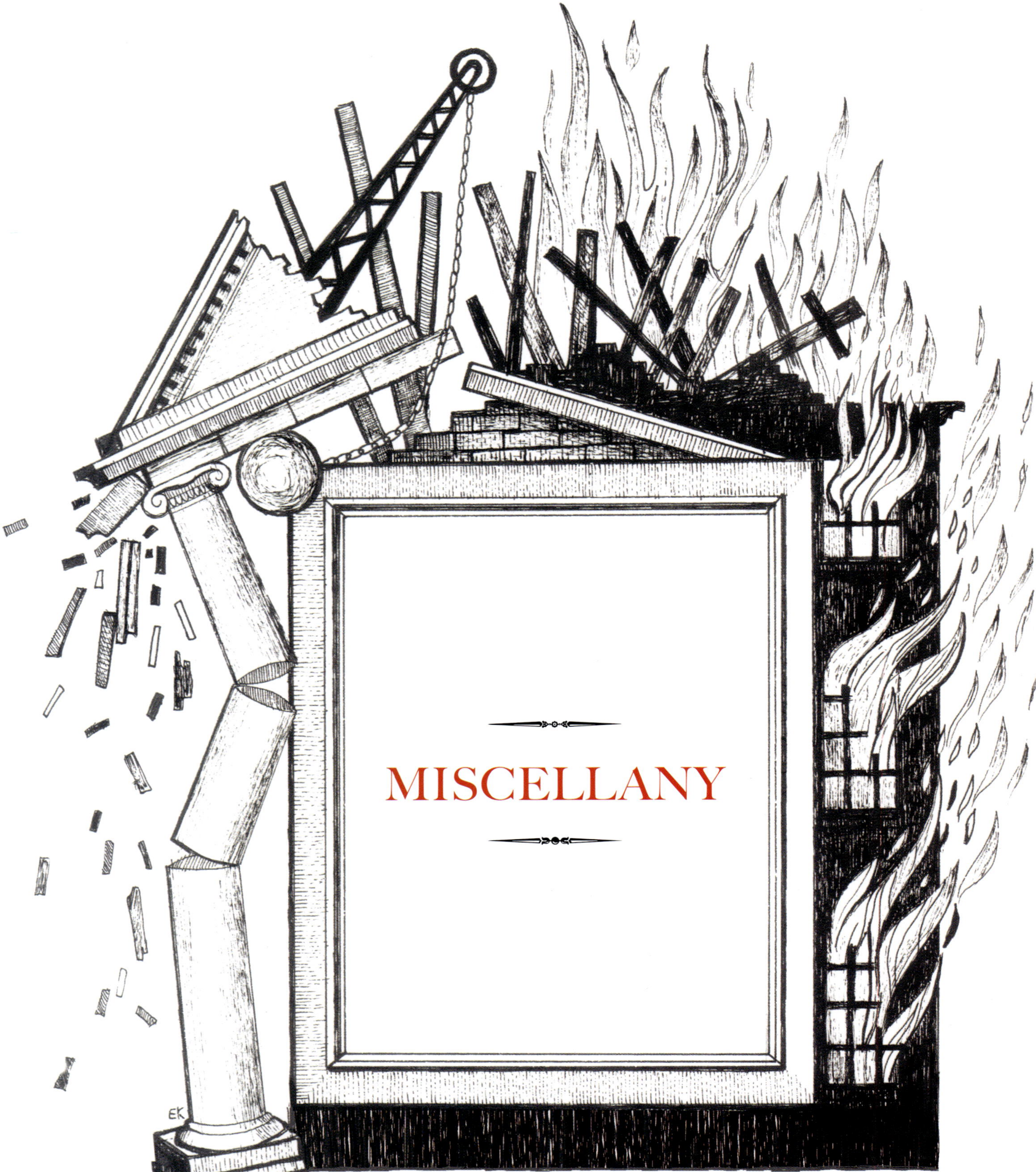

MISCELLANY

Since the year 1800 almost 2000 architecturally and historically significant houses have been demolished in England (and many have been lost in Scotland and Wales, too). If we were to delve back further over the centuries, a few hundred more could be added to this figure. Fire, civil war, changing tastes and requirements, death, loss of fortune, social and political change, redevelopment, wartime damage – all have led to the destruction of houses. A large number vanished so long ago and so completely without trace as to have faded from memory entirely; however, evidence of the existence of hundreds of lost houses endures in the form of engravings and photographs. The images on the following pages comprise but a mere fraction of the wealth of visual material that survives. Some of the works in Kluz's first 'Lost House' series, created in 2014, are also shown in this chapter.

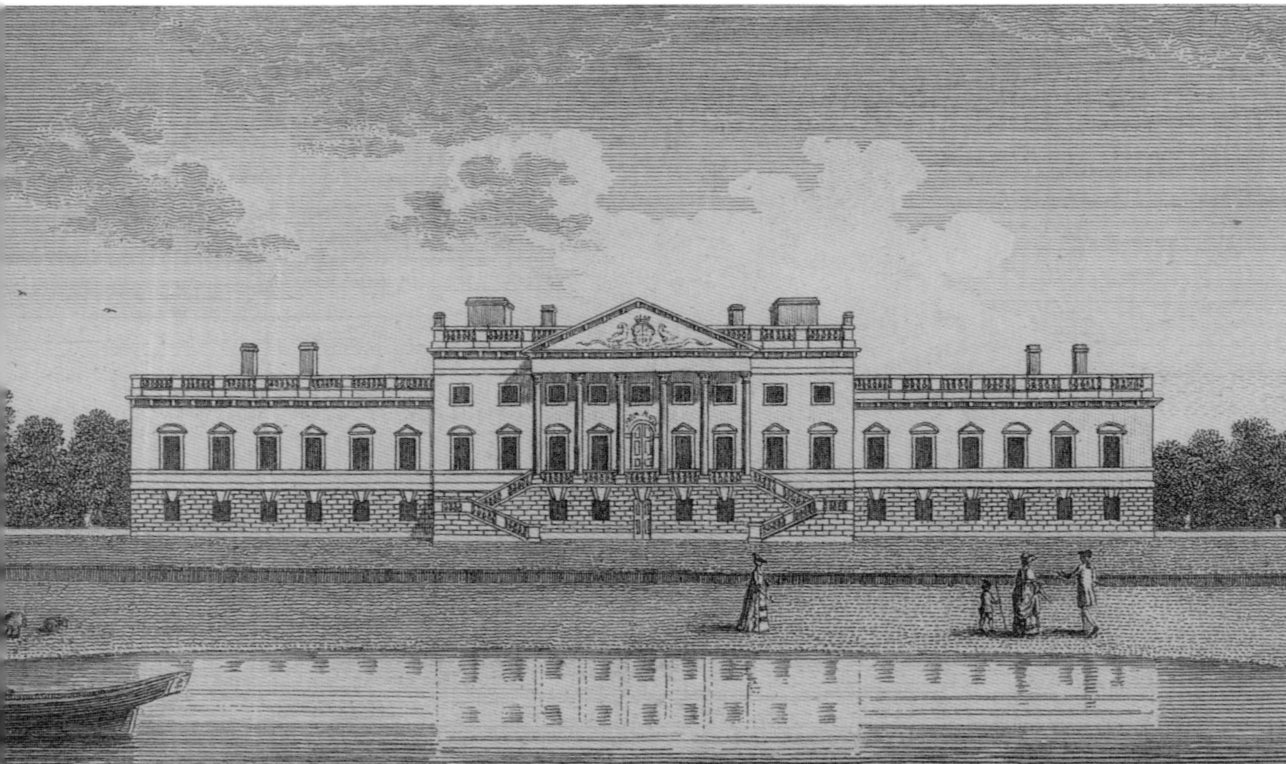

Left: Wanstead House, Essex, the Seat of the Earl of Tylney *engraving published in* The Complete English Traveller, c. *1790*. *Demolished 1824*.

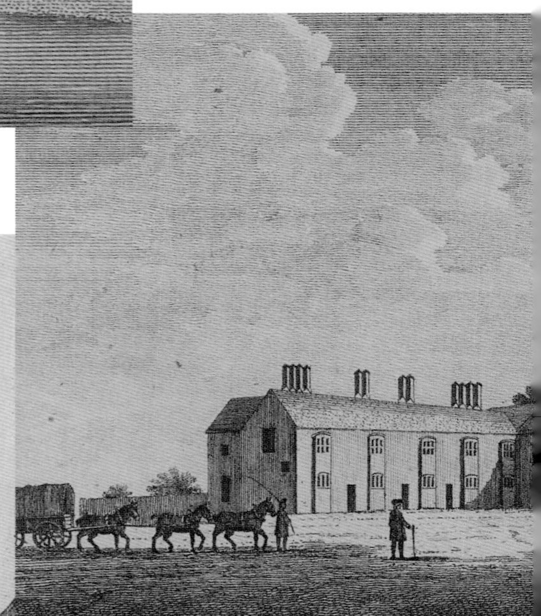

Below: Cassiobury Park, Hertfordshire, the Seat of the Earl of Essex, *engraving published in* The Complete English Traveller, c. *1790*. *Demolished 1927*.

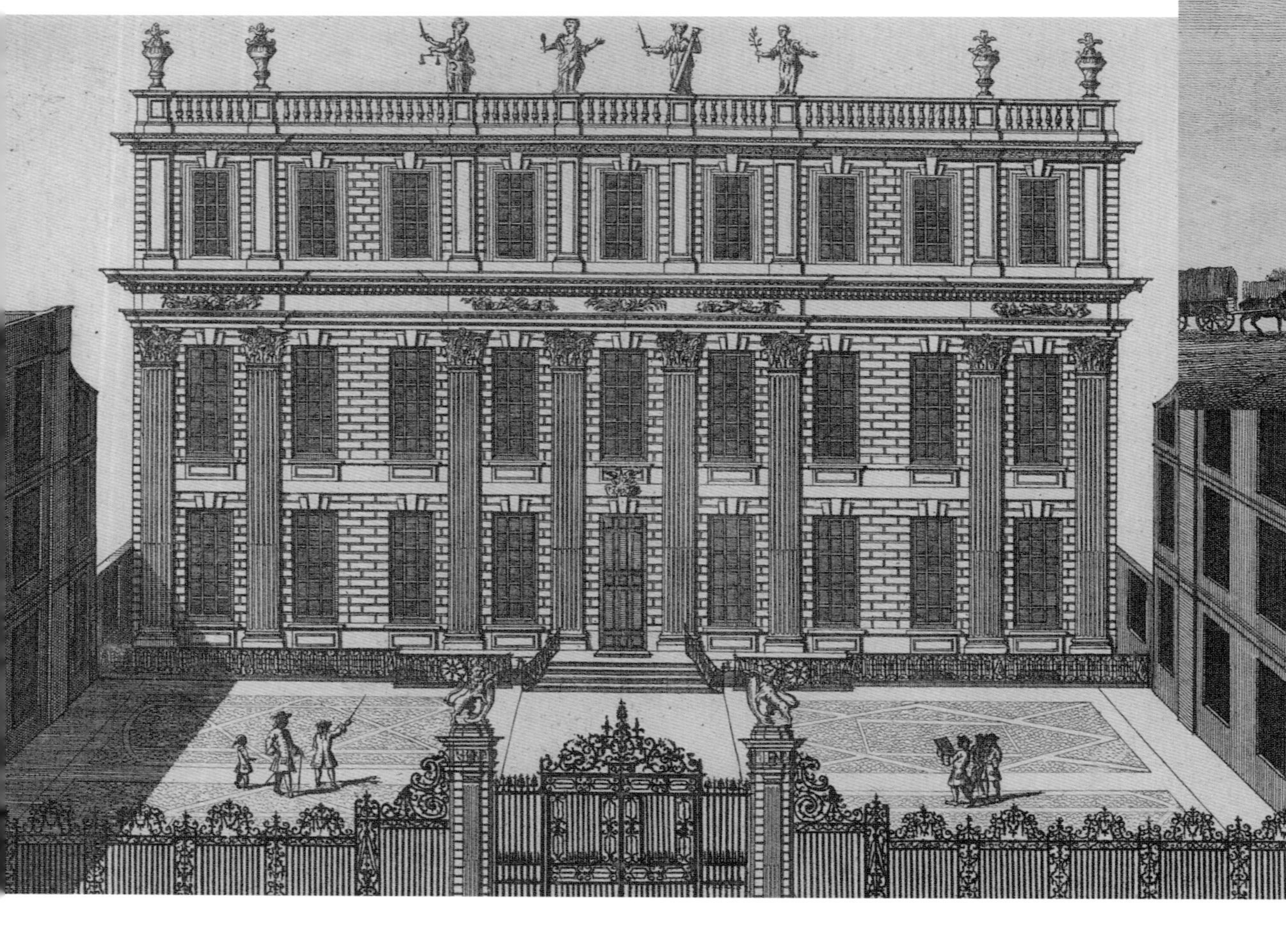

Below, left: H. Terasson, Powis House in Ormond Street, London, *engraving*, *1714*. *Demolished* c. *1780*.

Opposite, top: James Collins, A Prospect of Lodge, the Seat of ye Right Hon.ble Lord Teynham at Linstead in Kent, *engraving*, c. *1720*. *Mostly demolished 1829, small surviving central portion.*

Opposite, bottom: Victor Marie Picot, The Gateway, Clifton House, Dorset, *engraving*, *mid-18th century. Mostly demolished 1786*.

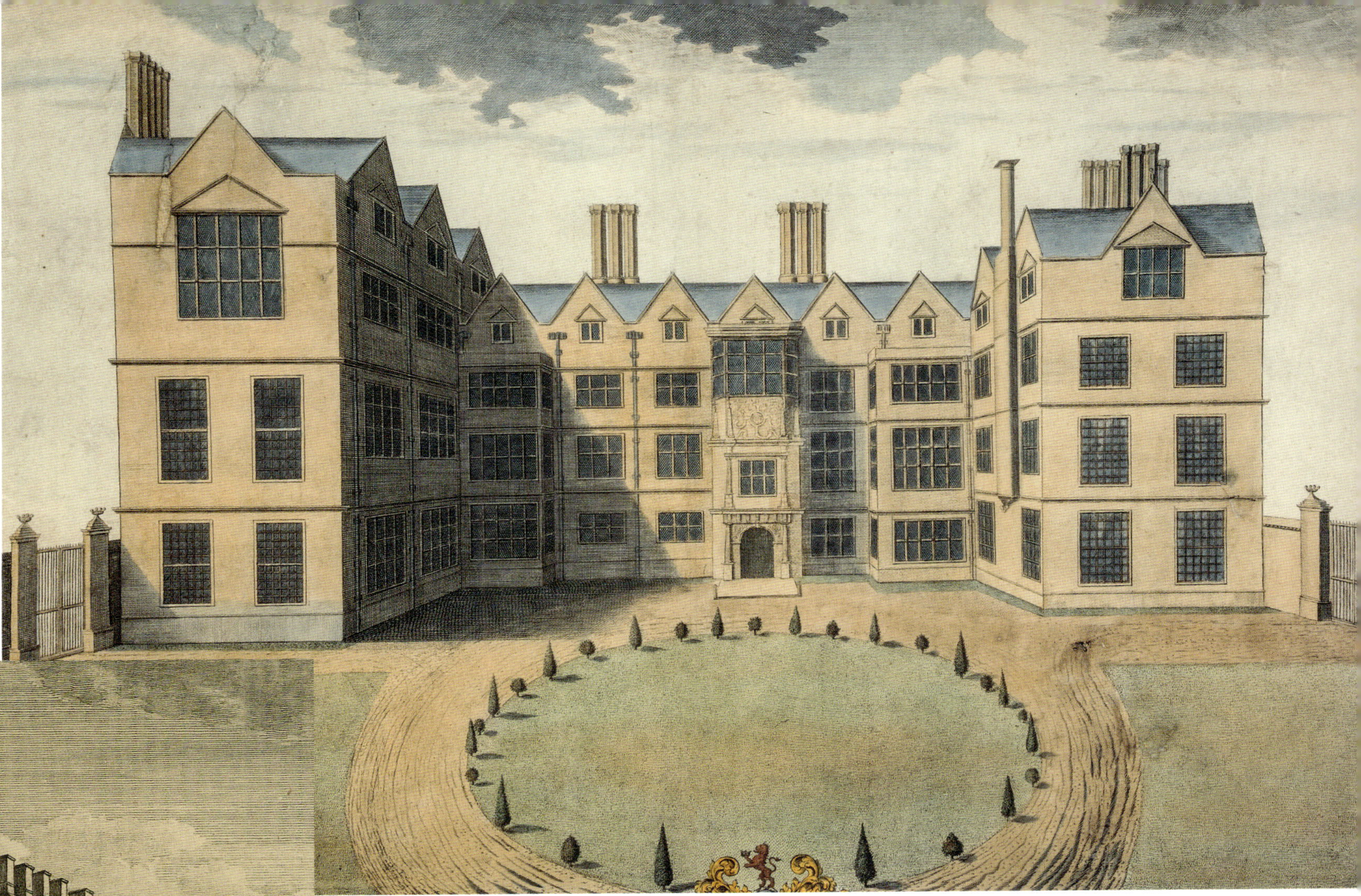

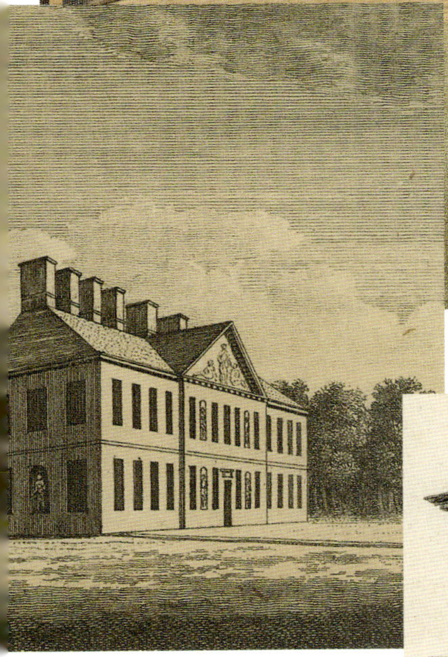

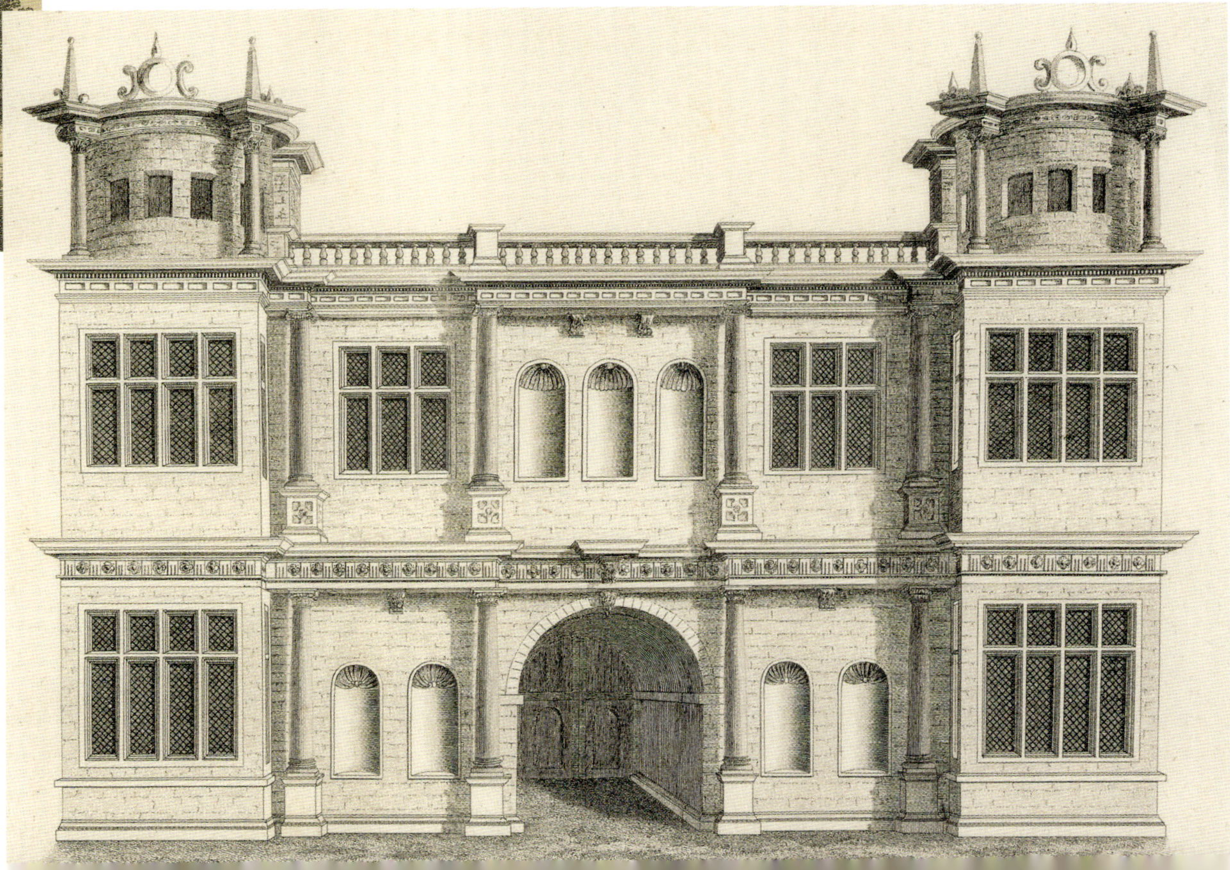

Right: Holland House, Kensington, *engraving published in Edward Walford,* Old and New London, *vol. V, 1878. Bombed in 1940 during the Blitz.*

Below, left: Monmouth House, Soho Square, *engraving published in Walter Thornbury,* Old and New London, *vol. III, 1878. Demolished 1773.*

Below, right: William Skillman, after a painting by Johann Spilberg II, The South Front of Albemarle House, previously called Clarendon House, Piccadilly, London, *engraving,* c. *1680. Demolished 1683.*

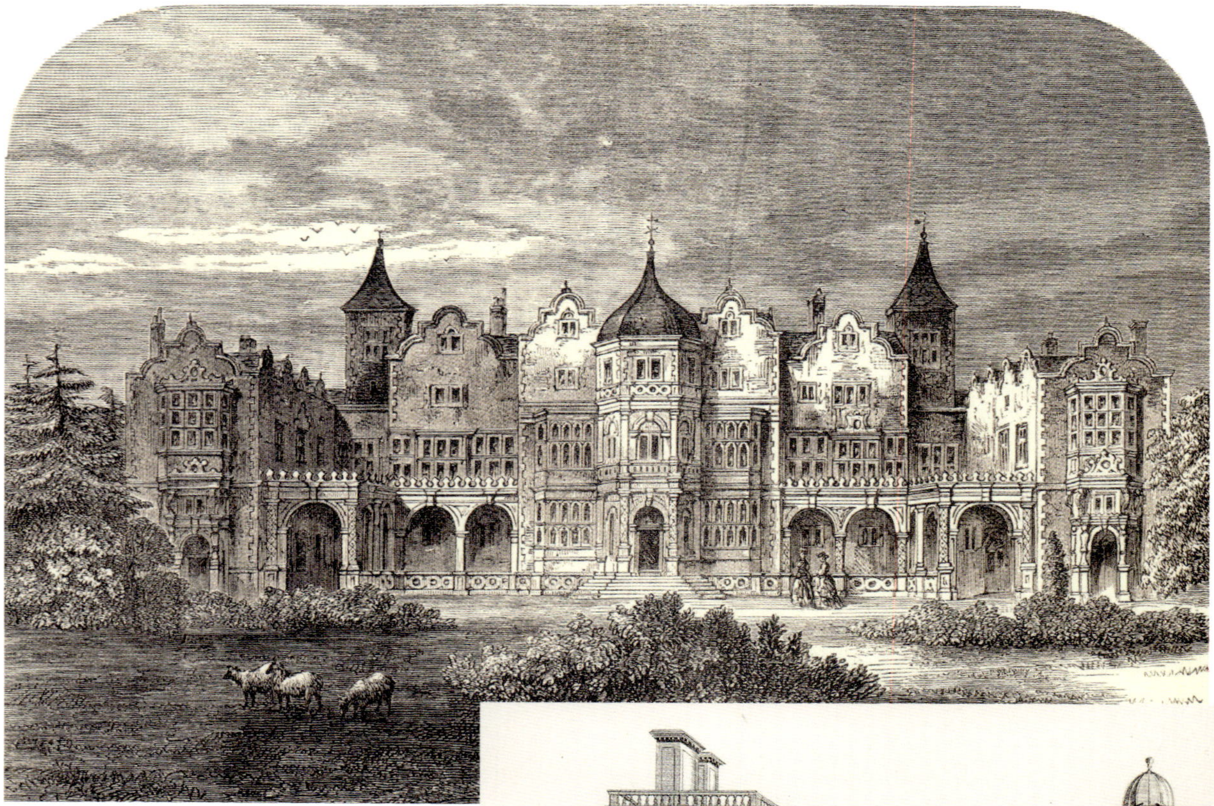

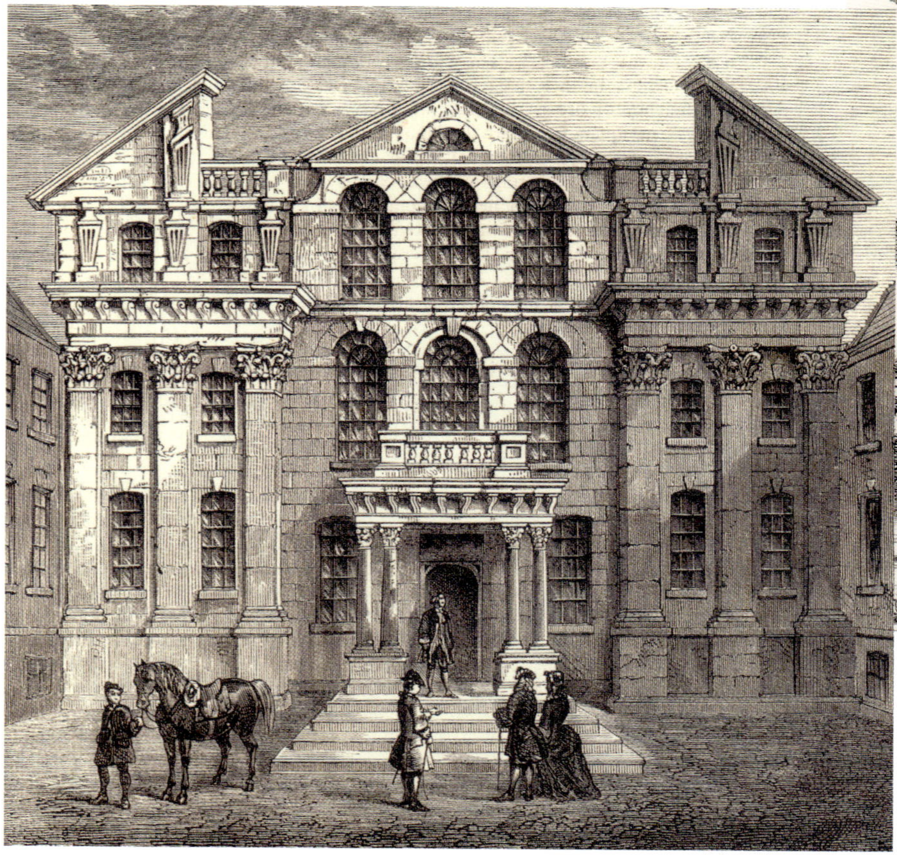

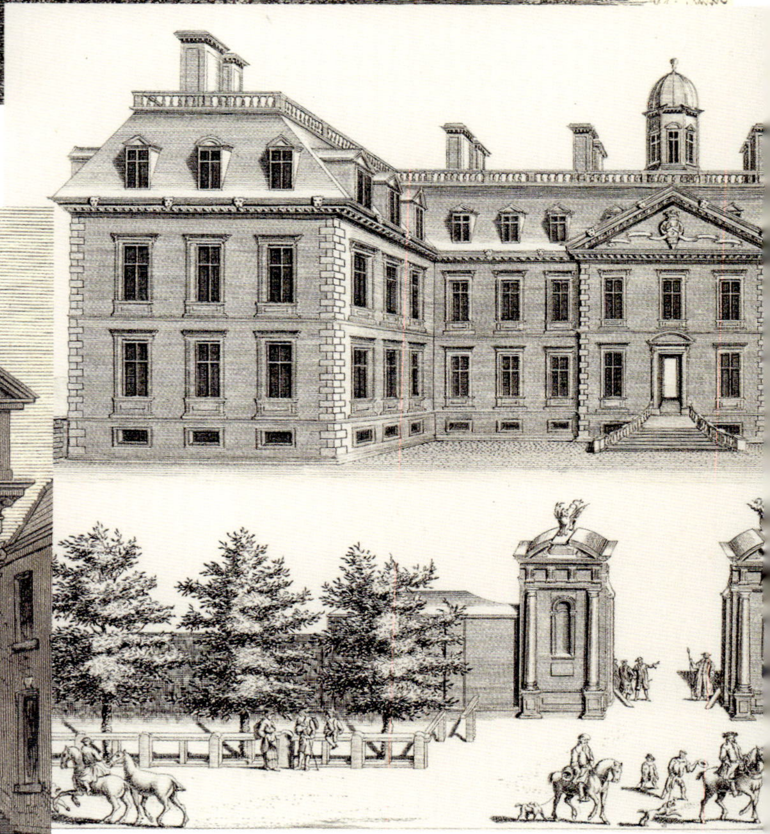

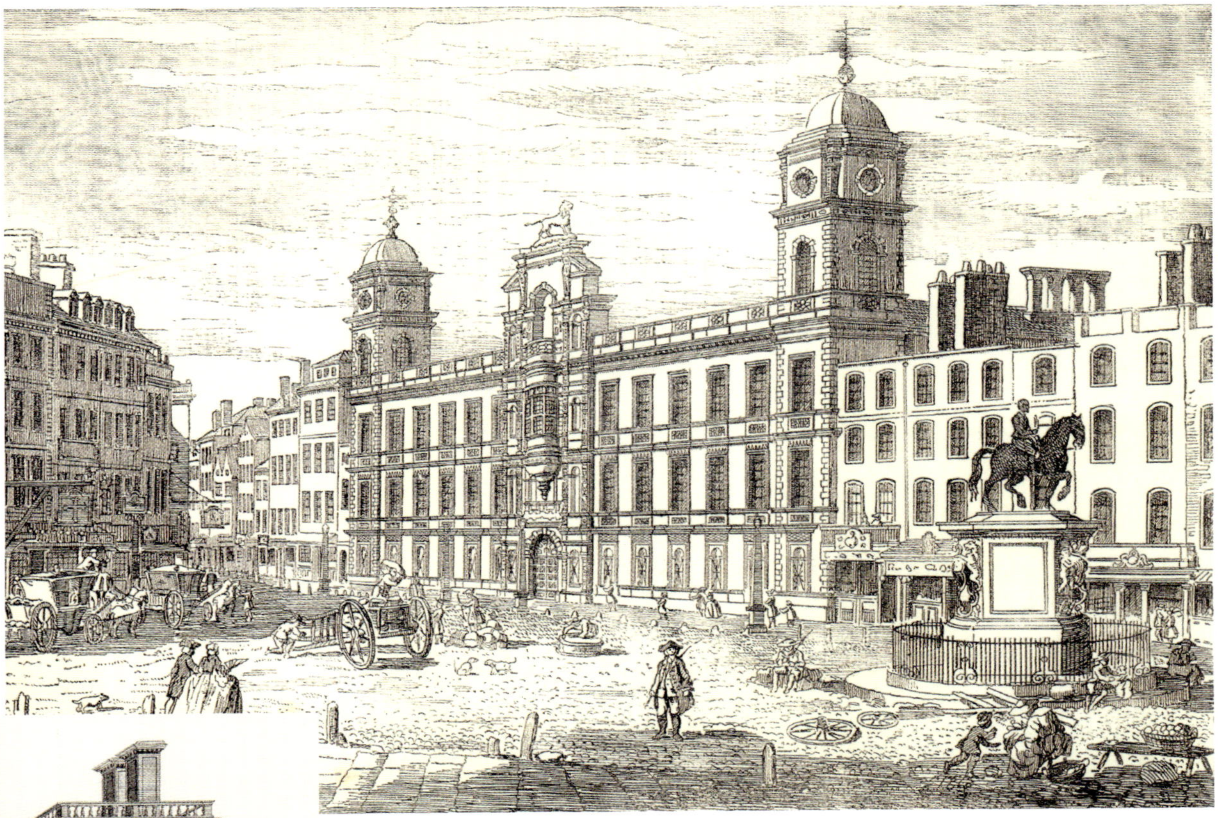

Left: Northumberland House, Charing Cross, *engraving published in Walter Thornbury,* Old and New London, *vol. III, 1878. Demolished 1874.*

Below: Montagu House, Great Russell Street, *c.* 1830, *engraving published in Edward Walford,* Old and New London, *vol. IV, 1878. Demolished 1840s.*

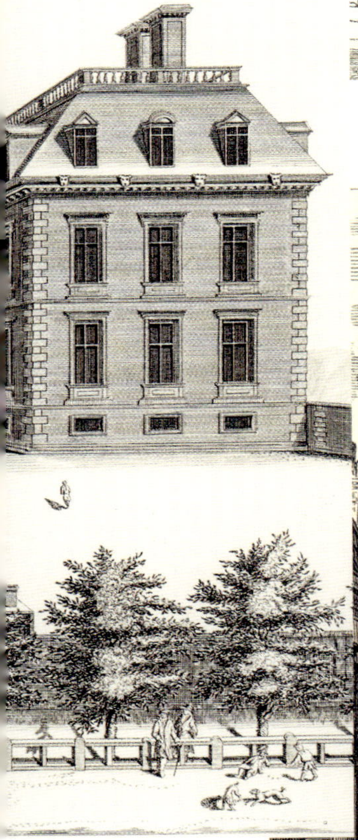

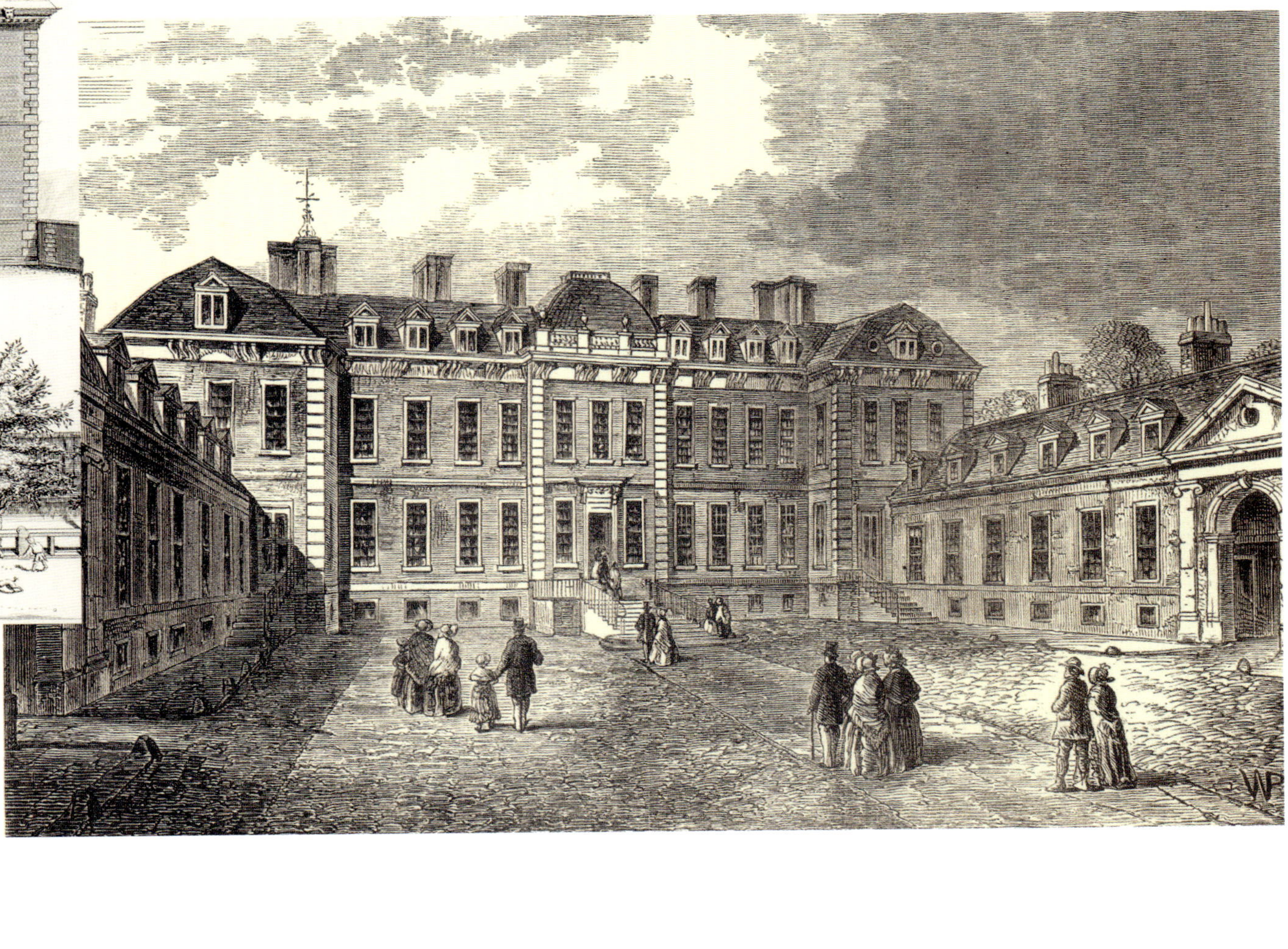

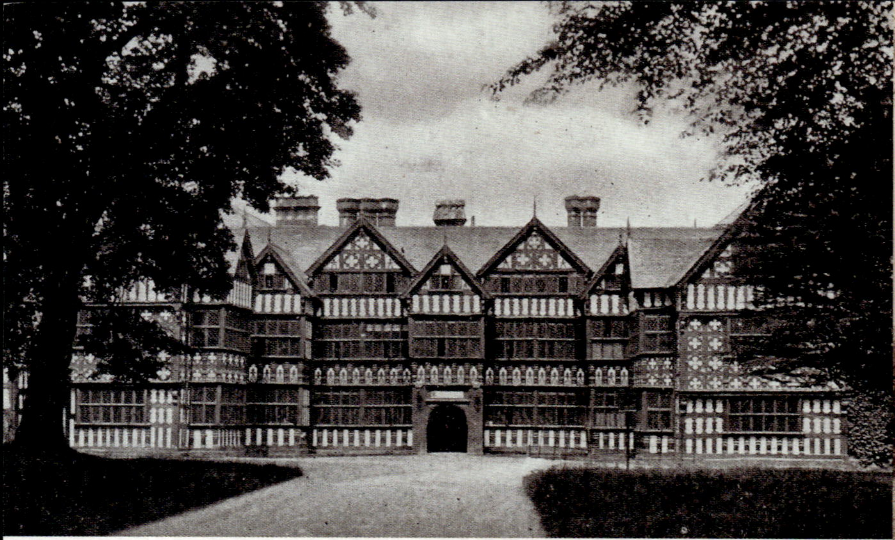

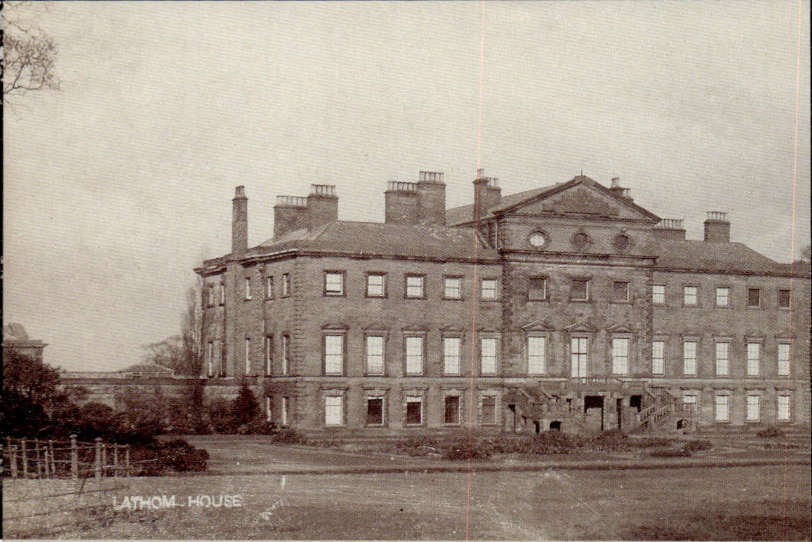

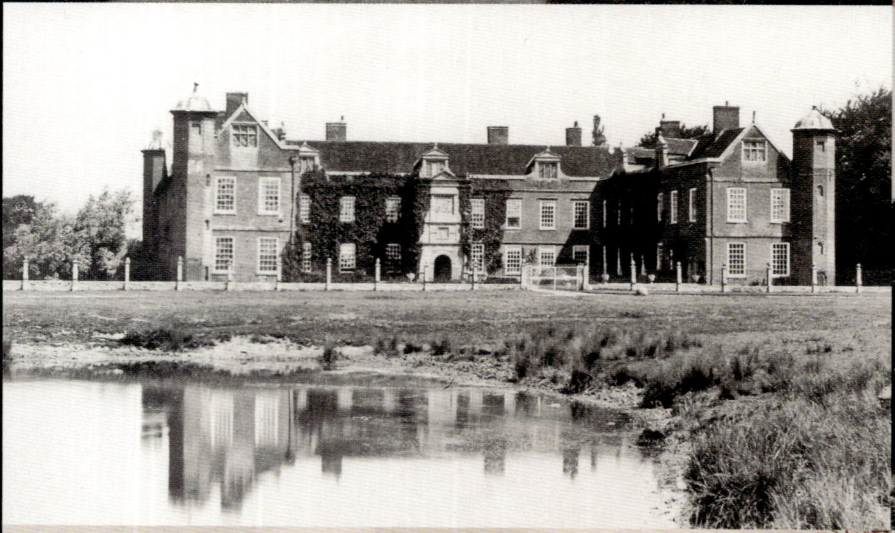

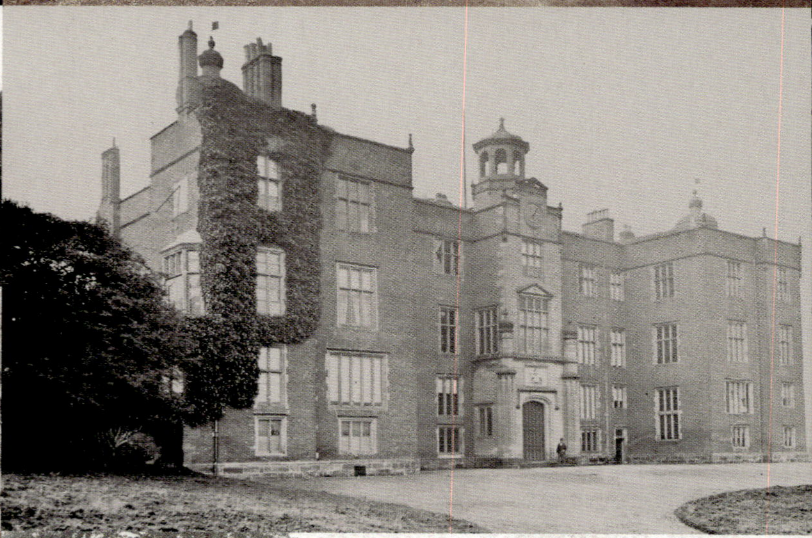

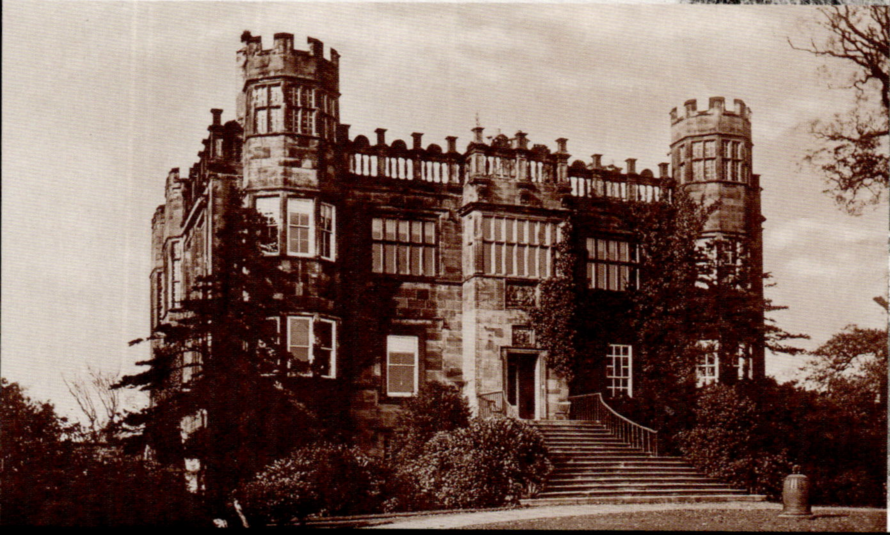

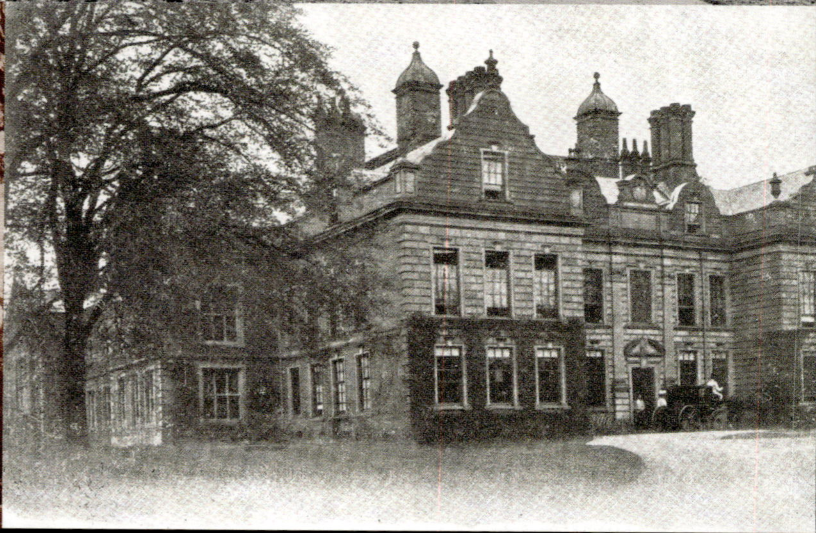

Park Hall, Shropshire; demolished 1918 post-fire.
Rushbrooke Hall, Suffolk; demolished 1961 post-fire.
Heath Old Hall, West Yorkshire; demolished 1961.

Lathom House, Lancashire; demolished 1925.
Beaudesert Hall, Staffordshire; demolished 1935.
Willesley Hall, Leicestershire; demolished 1953.

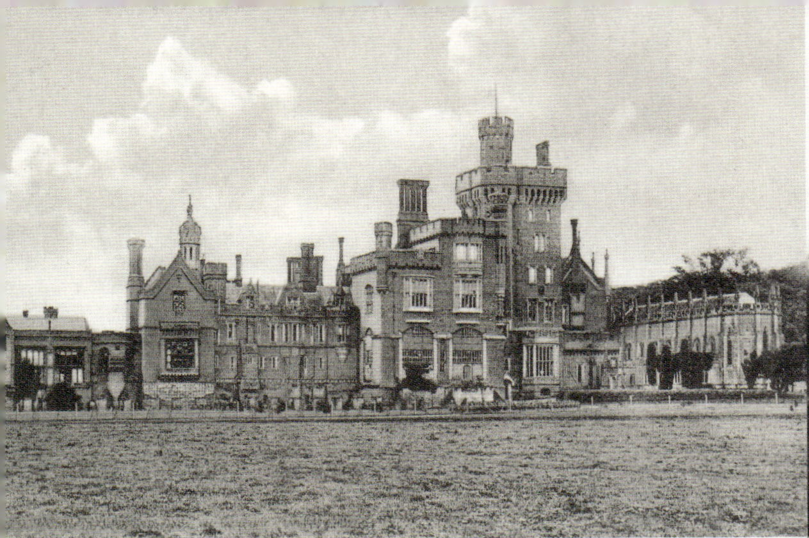

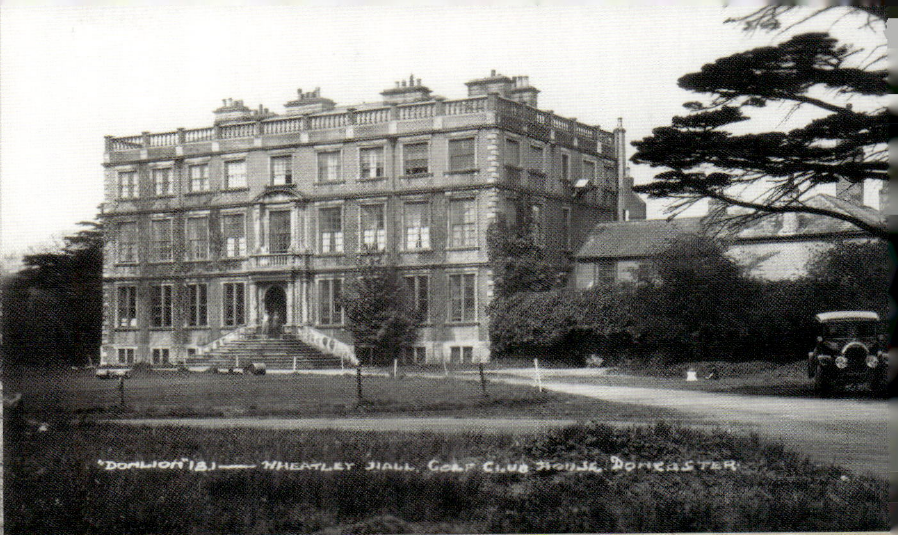

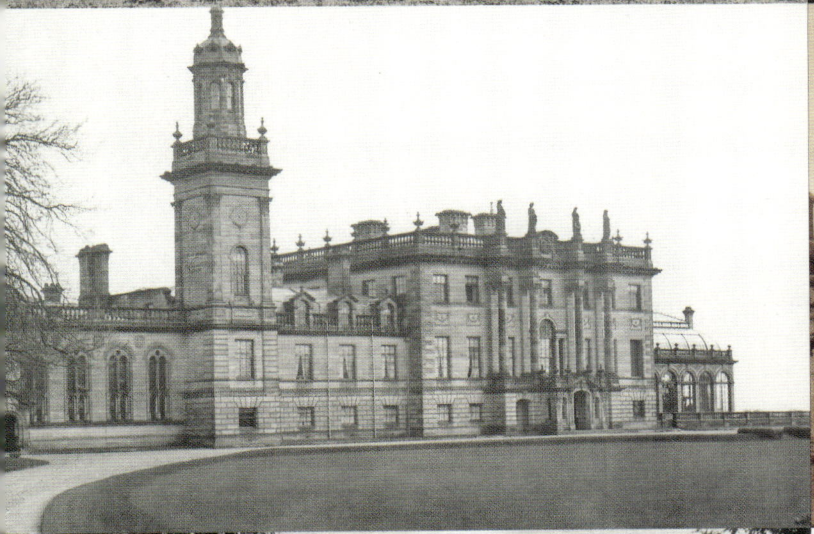

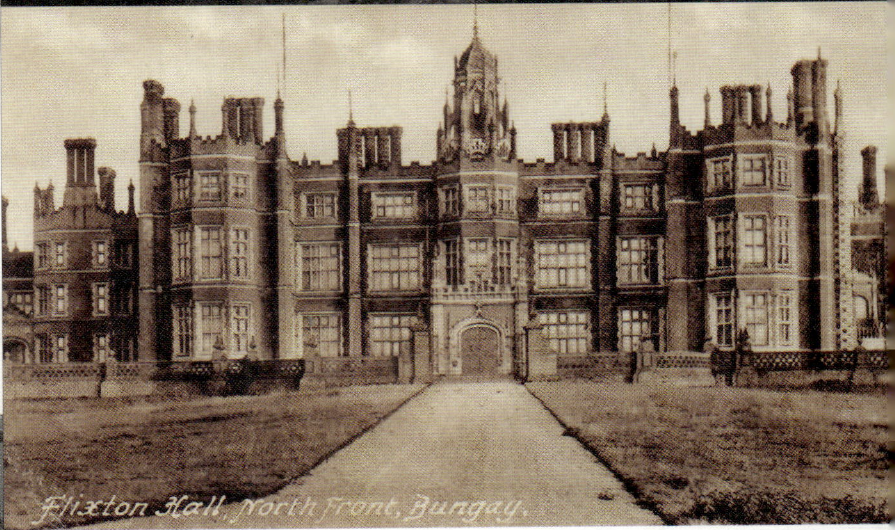

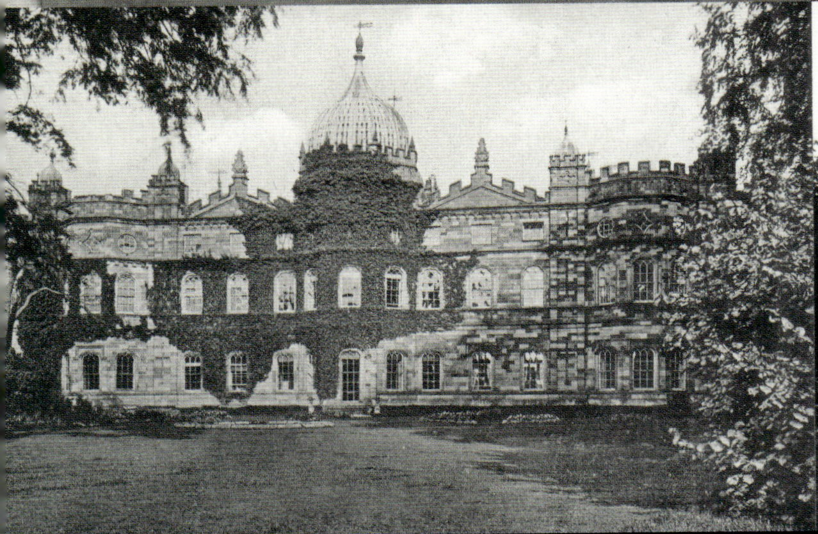

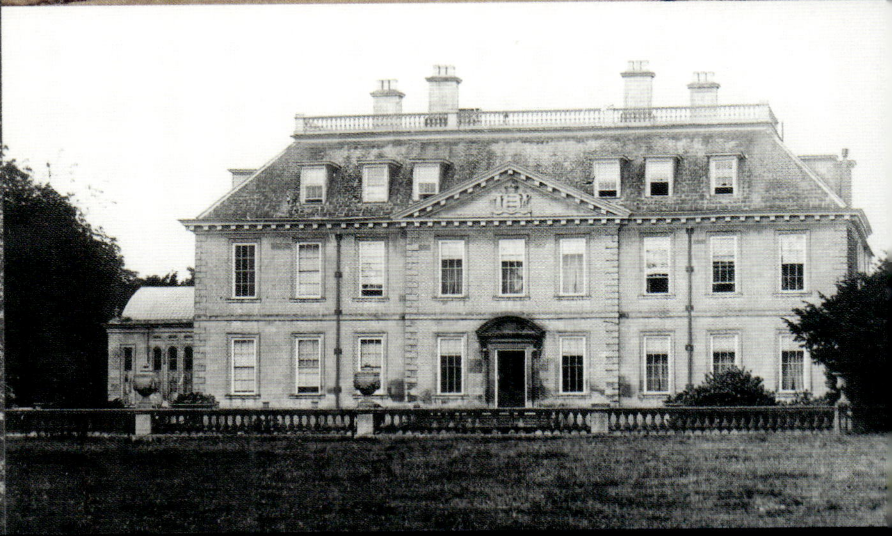

Costessey Hall, Norfolk; demolished c. *1918–20.*

Hooton Hall, Cheshire; demolished 1932.

Tong Castle, Shropshire; demolished 1954.

Wheatley Hall, South Yorkshire; demolished 1934.

Flixton Hall, Suffolk; demolished 1953.

Uffington House, Lincolnshire; destroyed by fire 1904.

Top row, left to right: Baginton Hall, Warwickshire, after the fire of 1889, demolished 1926; Hague Hall, West Yorkshire, collapsed 1910; Glossop Hall, Derbyshire, during demolition, 1959; unidentified house after fire of unknown date.

Centre row, left to right: Denton Manor, Lincolnshire, after the fire of 1906; Foxley Hall, Cheshire, during demolition, c. *1950s; Uffington House, Lincolnshire, after the fire of 1904; unidentified house after fire of unknown date.*

Bottom row, left to right: Wingerworth Hall, Derbyshire, during demolition, 1927; Hazelwood House, Hertfordshire, after the fire of 1908; Hope End, Herefordshire, after the fire of 1910 (the third house on the site, built by Charles Archibald Hewitt in the 1870s after the demolition of the Moulton-Barrett house); Hazelwood House, Hertfordshire, after the fire of 1908.

Pages 176–77: Further houses among the many hundreds that have been demolished in Britain since the early 19th century.

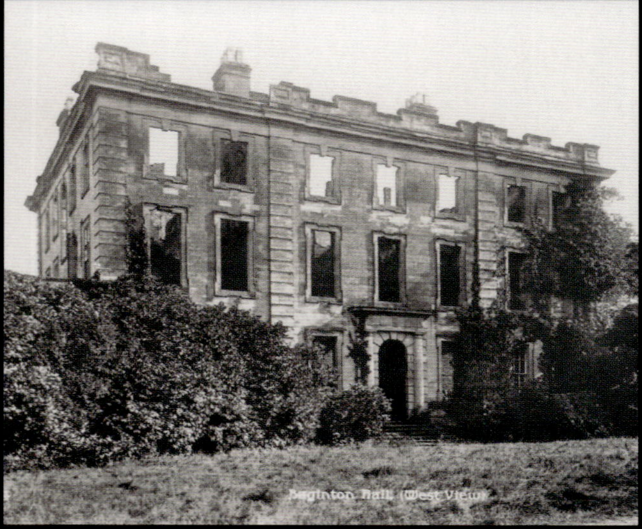

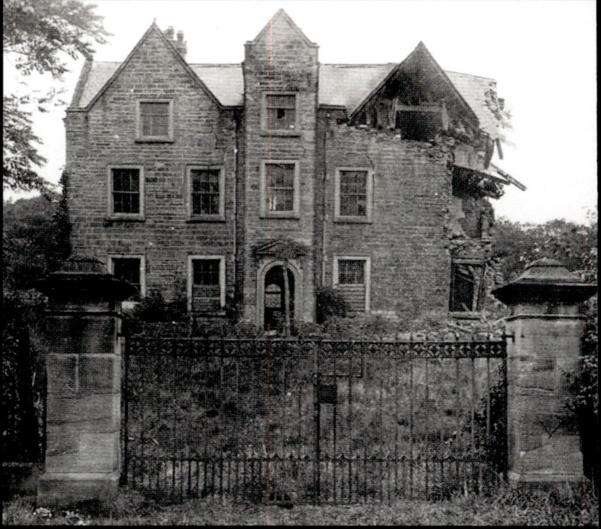

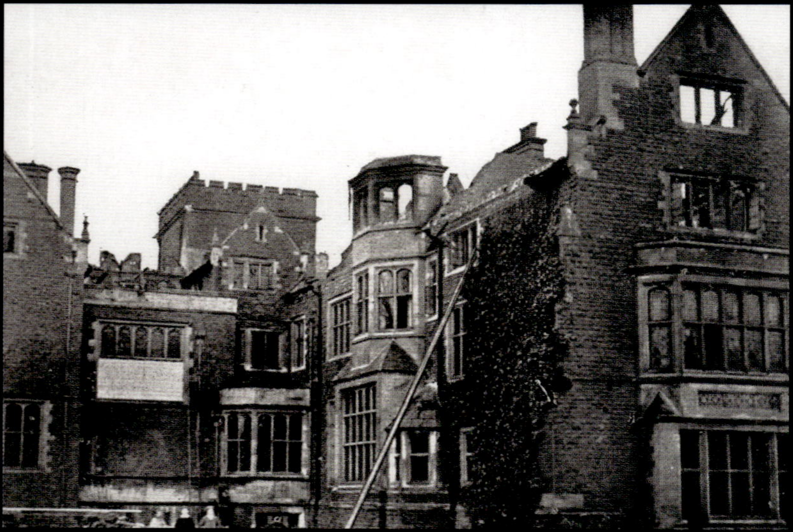

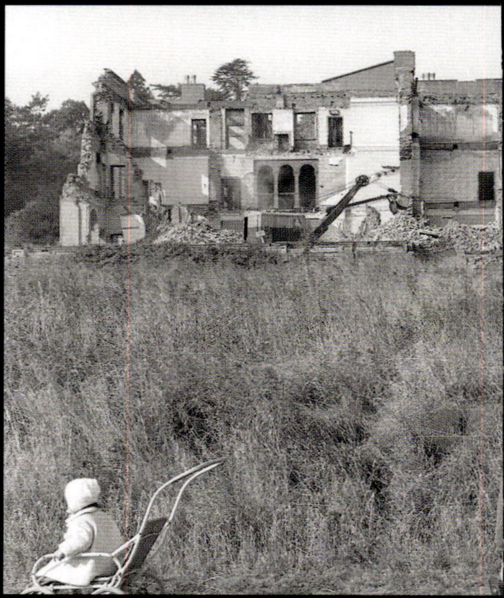

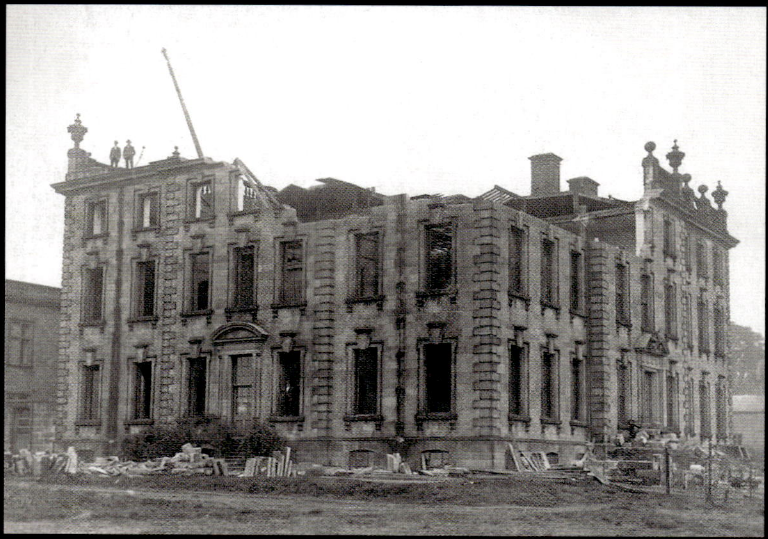

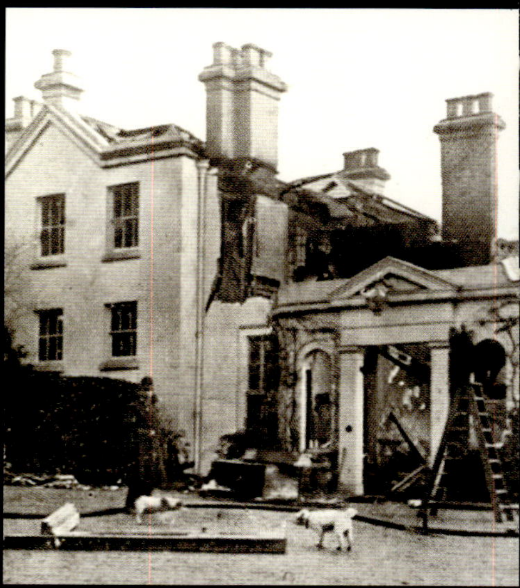

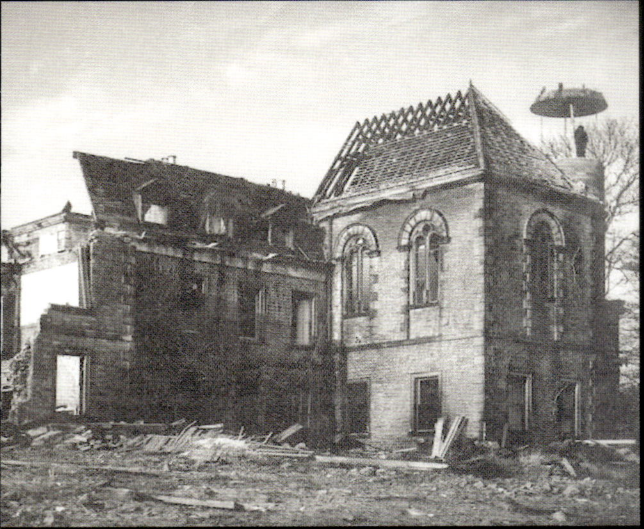

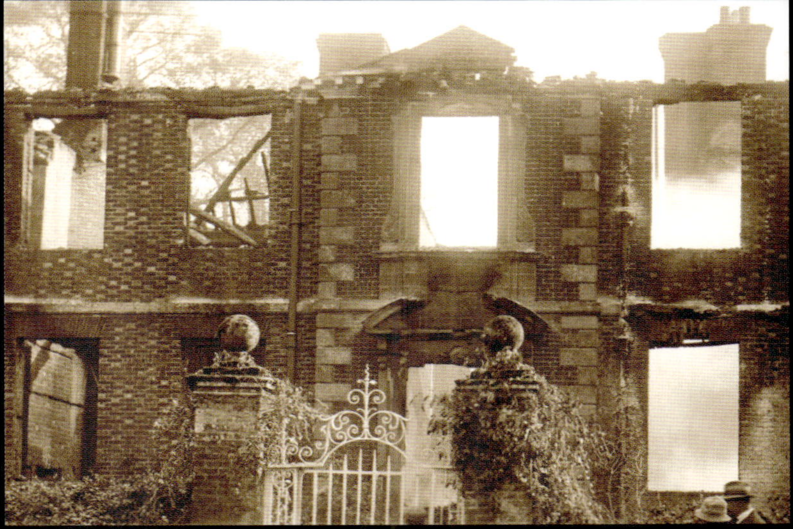

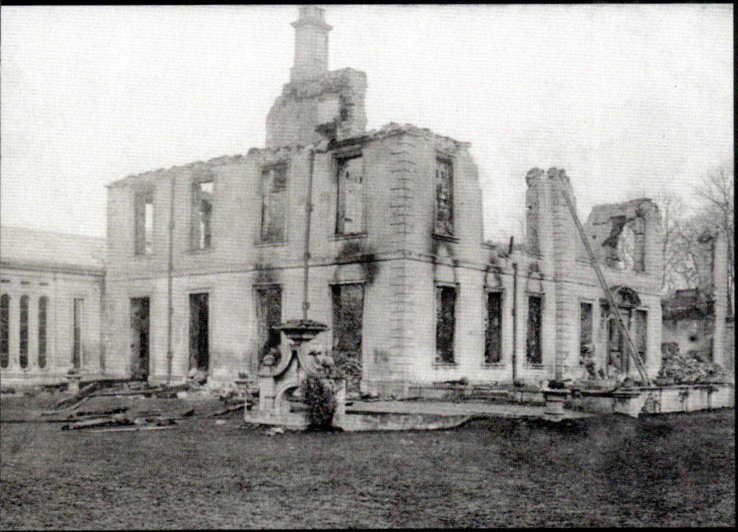

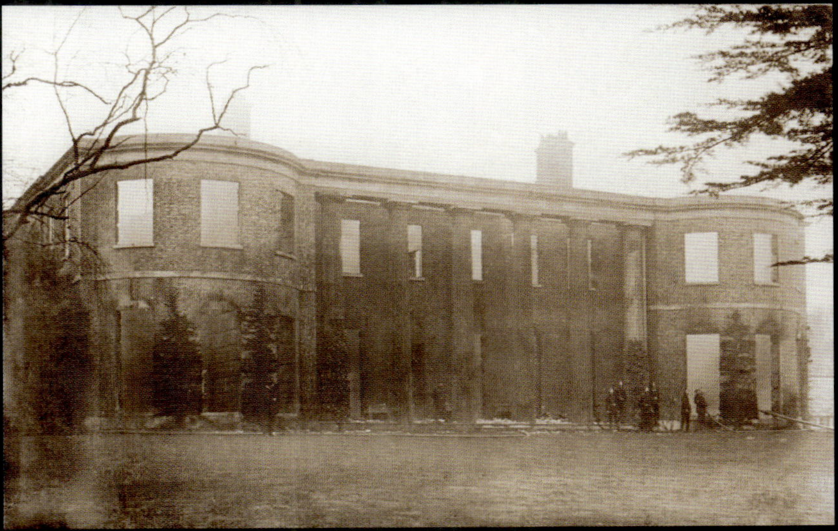

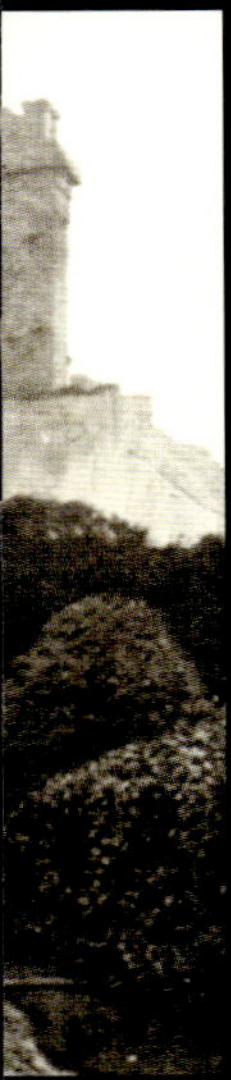

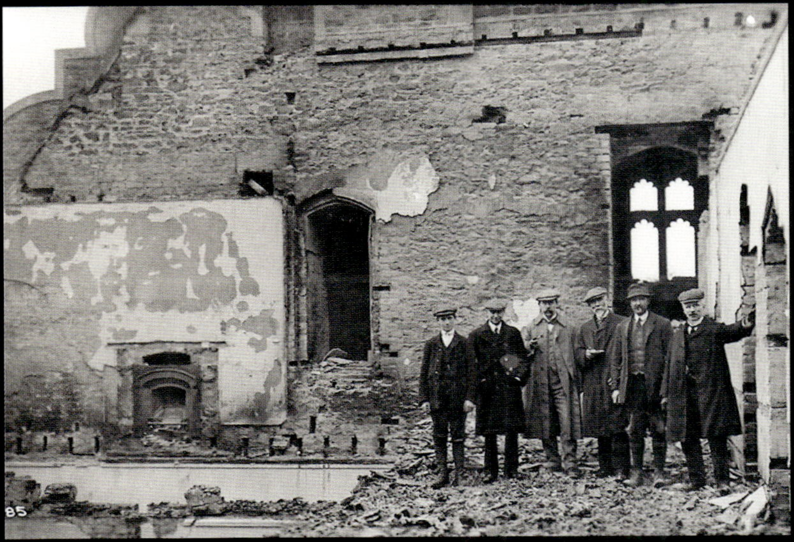

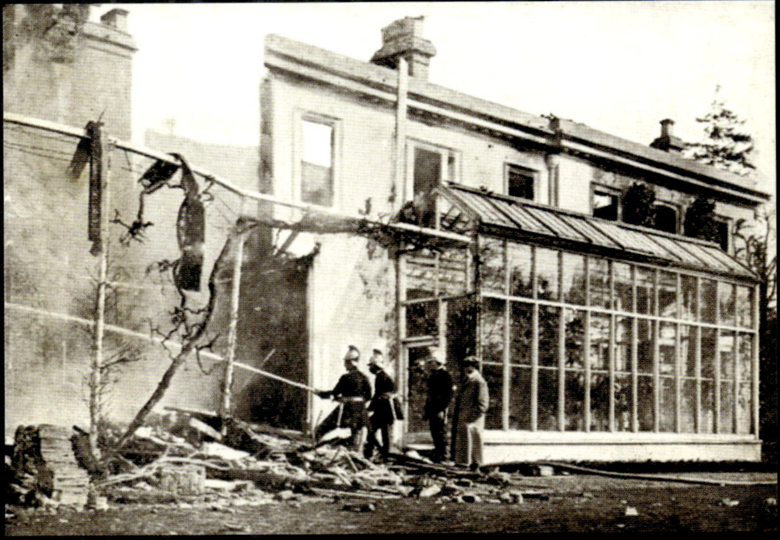

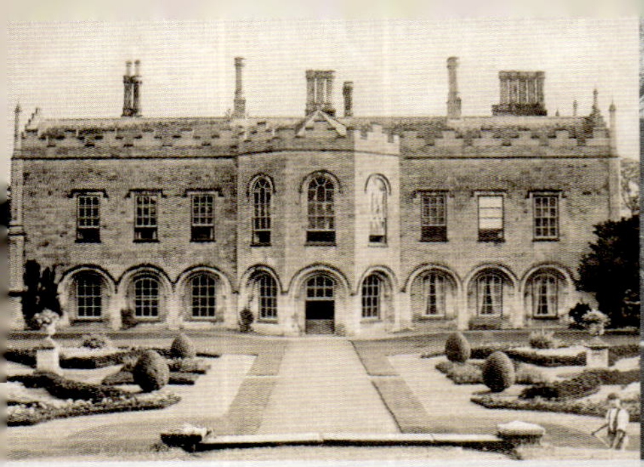
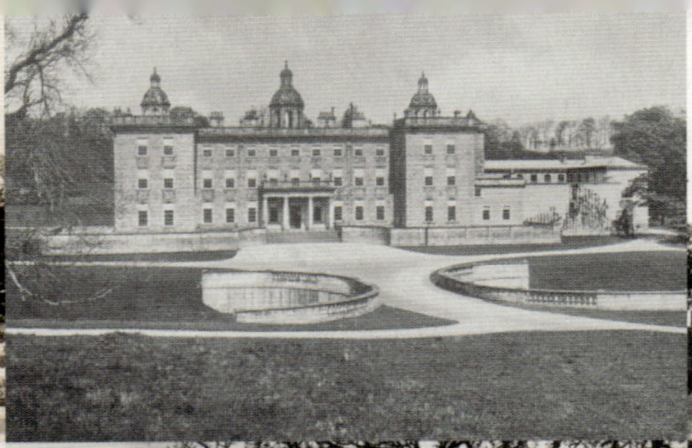
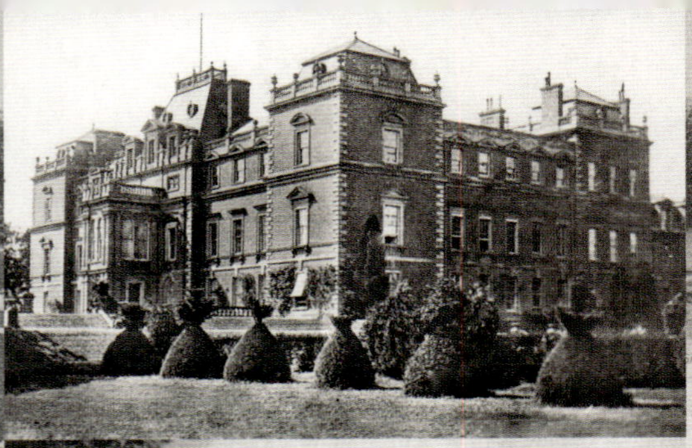
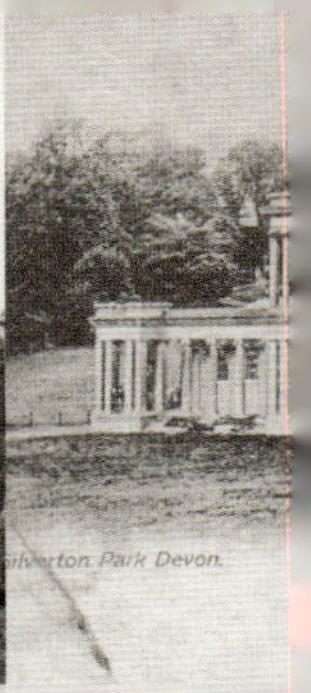
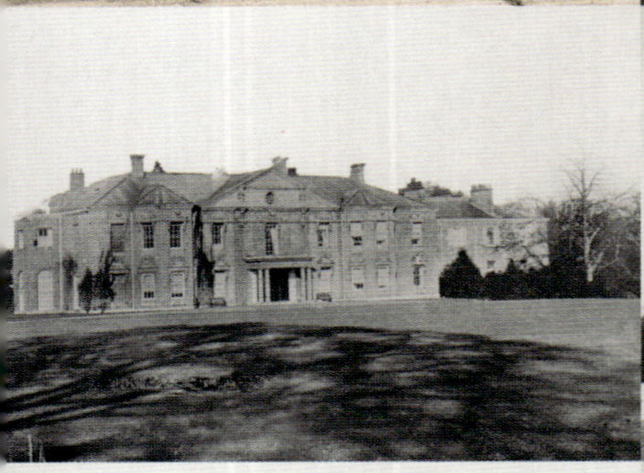
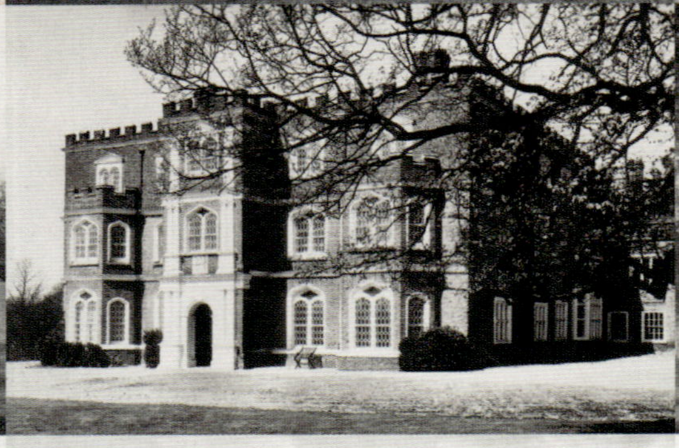
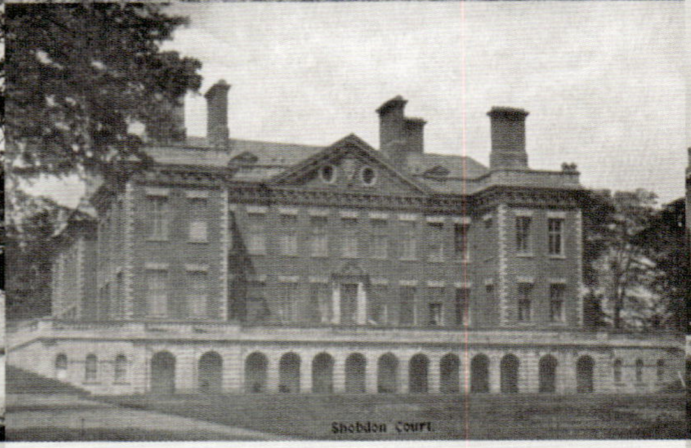
Shobdon Court
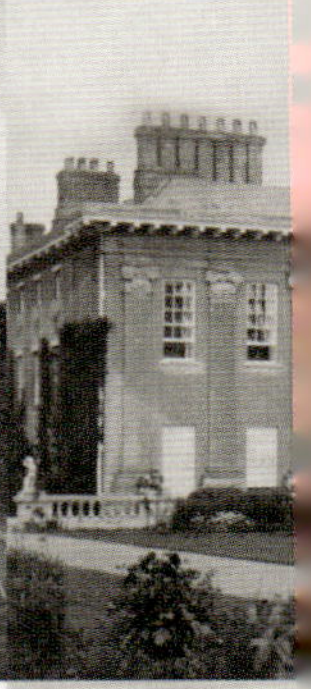
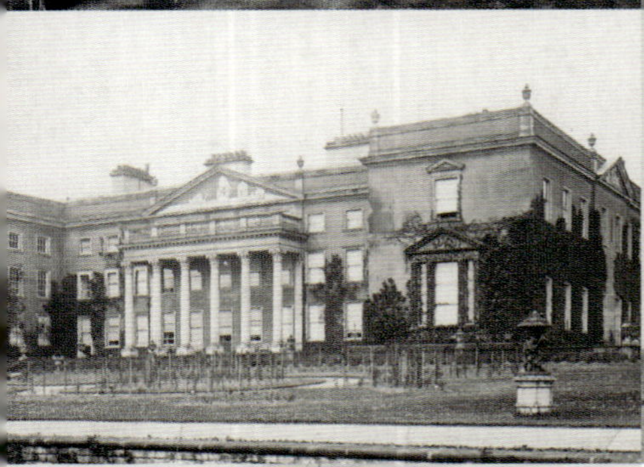
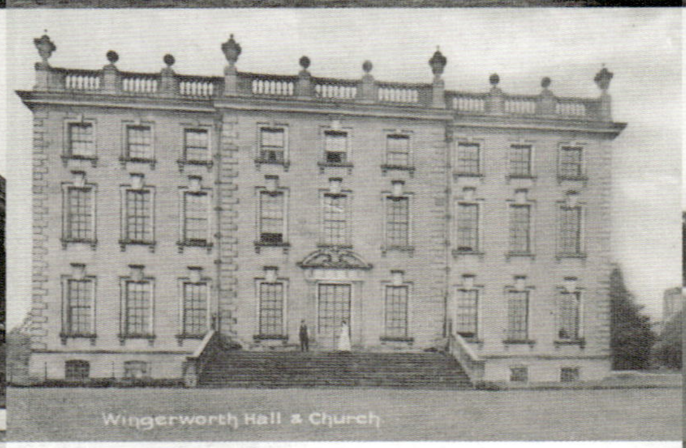
Wingerworth Hall & Church
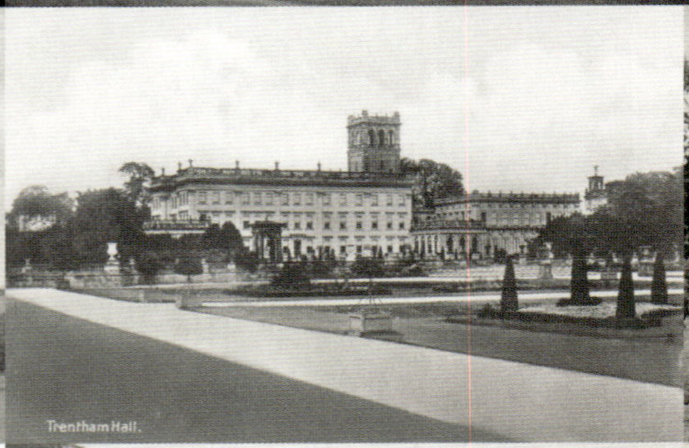
Trentham Hall.
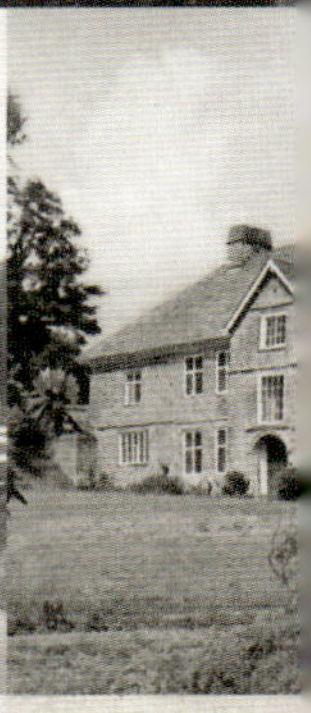
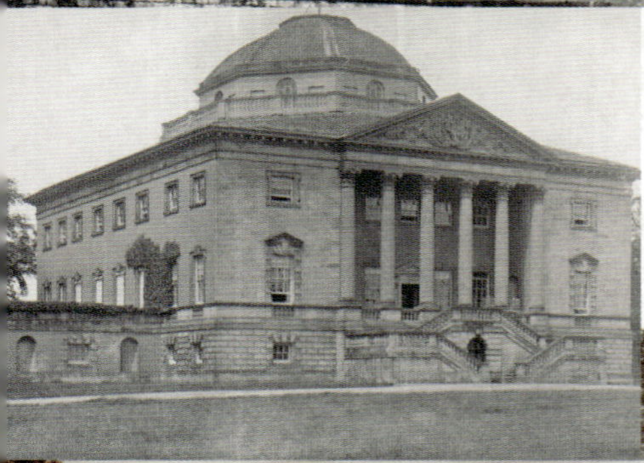
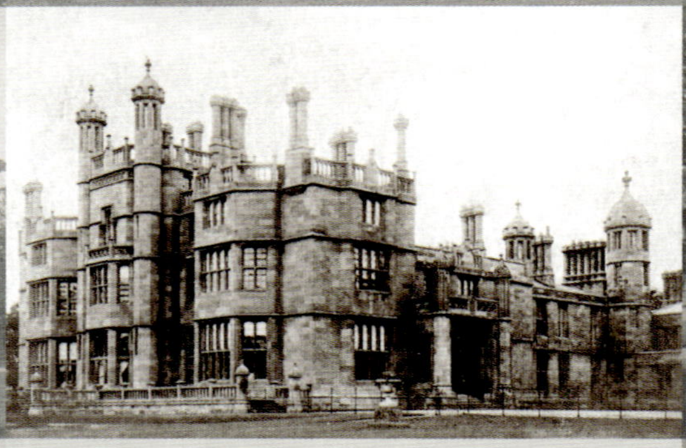
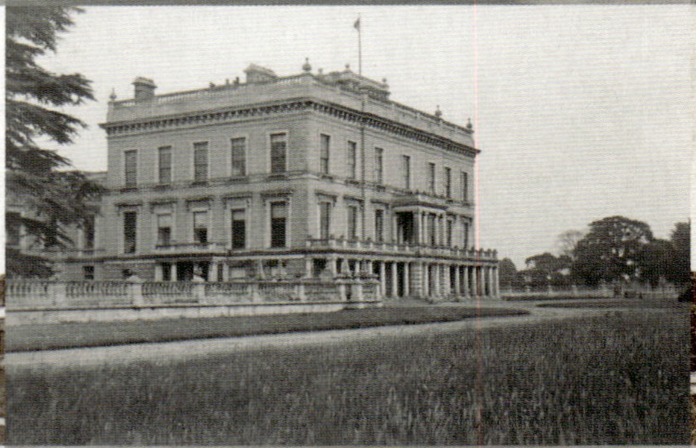
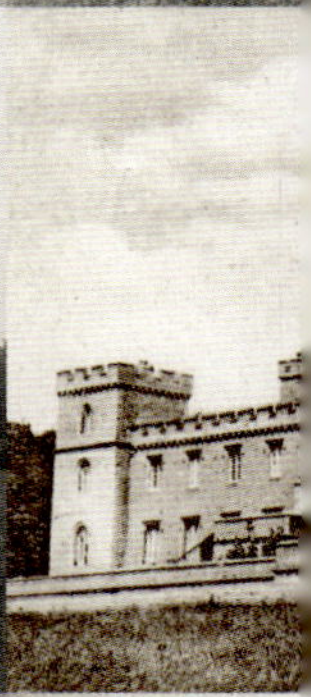
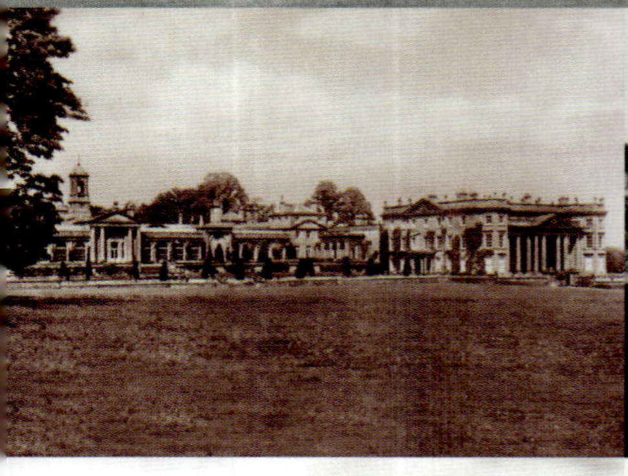
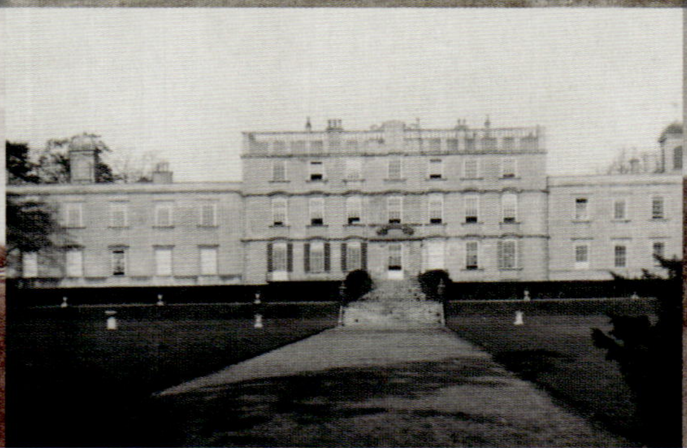
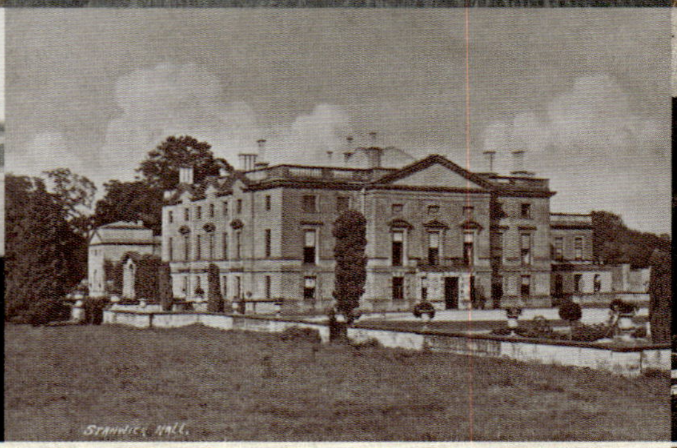
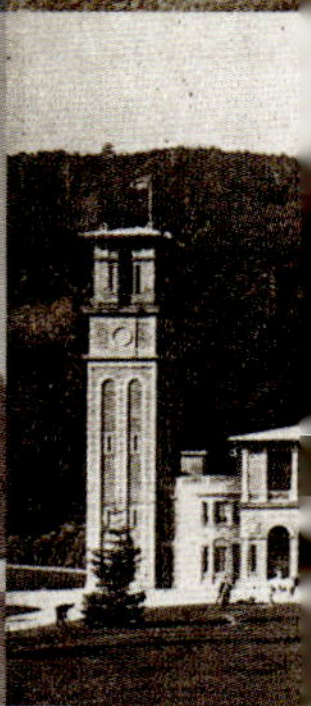
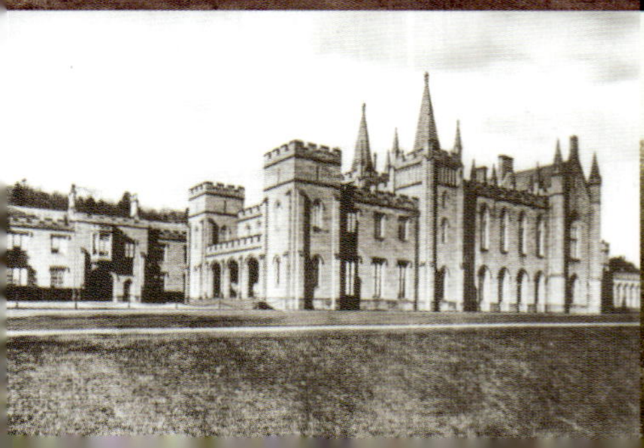
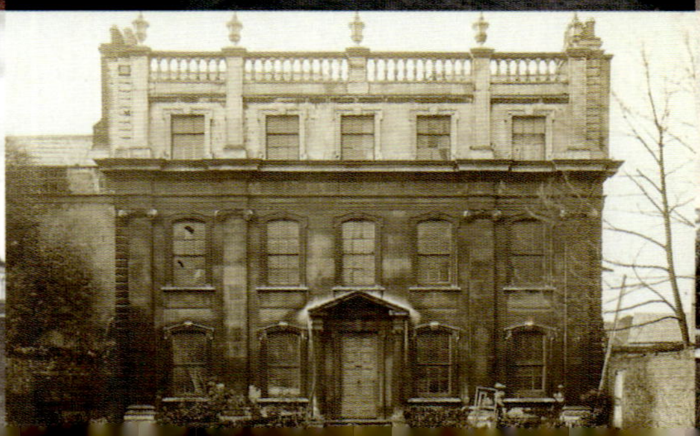
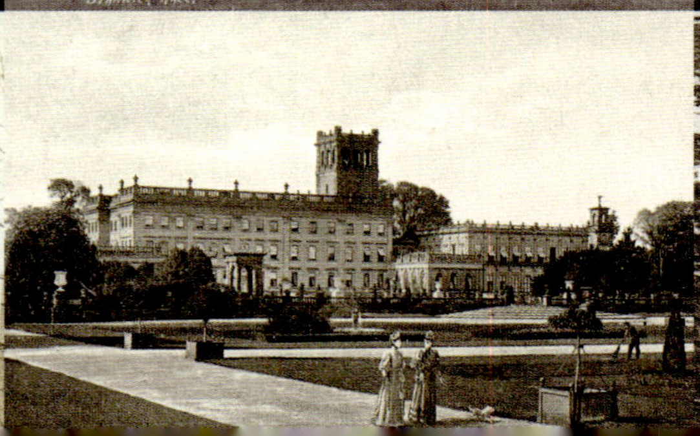
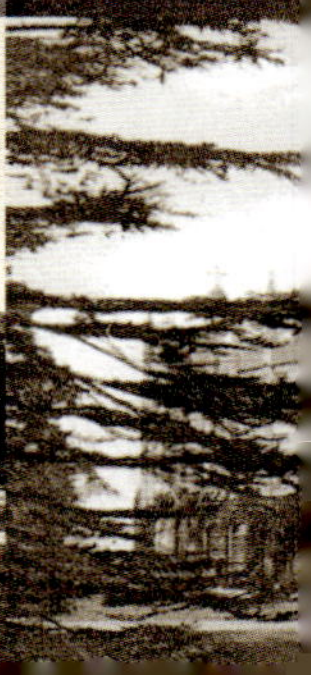

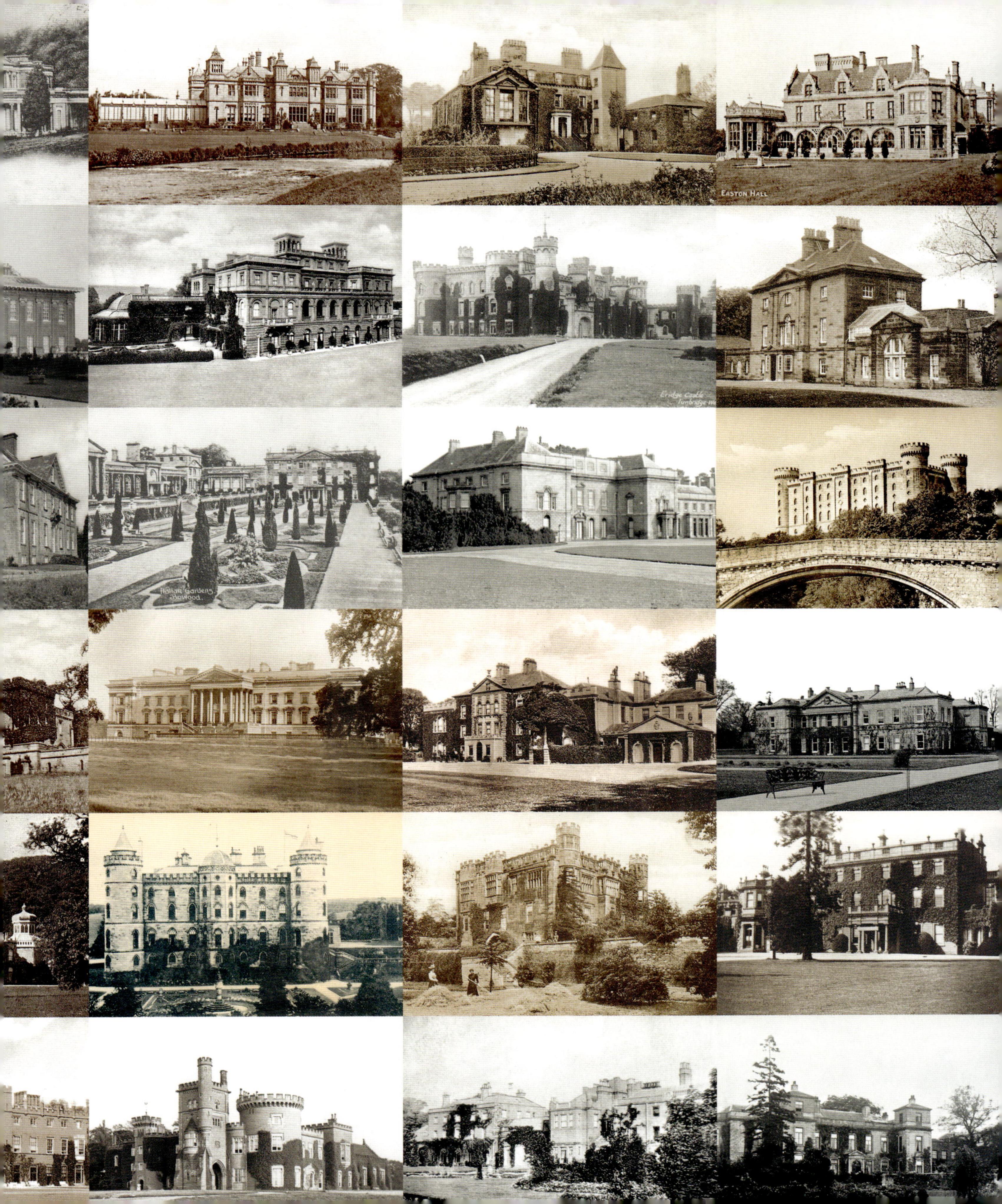
EASTON HALL
Eridge Castle
Tunbridge
Italian Gardens,
Bowood.

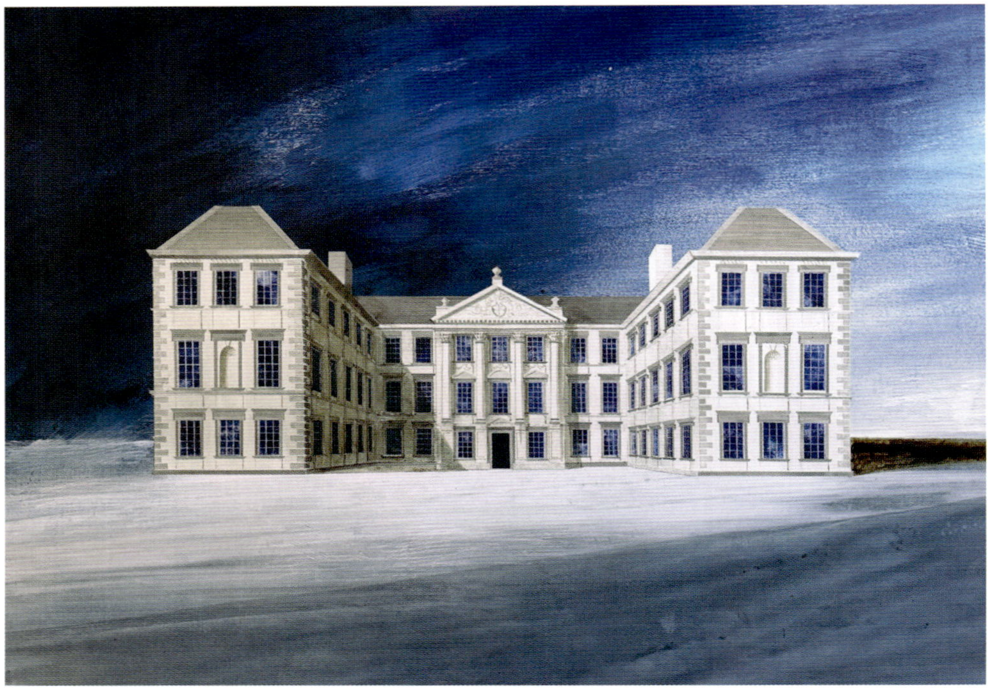

Hamilton Palace, Scotland *(demolished 1927)*
Paper collage and mixed media
2014

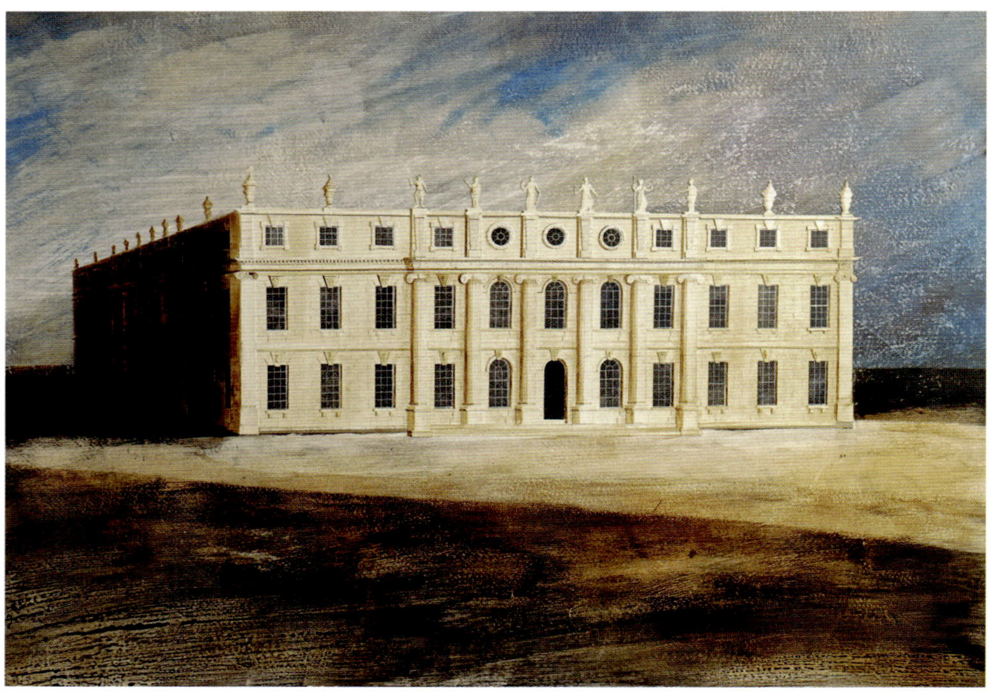

Canons House, Middlesex *(demolished 1747)*
Paper collage and mixed media
2014

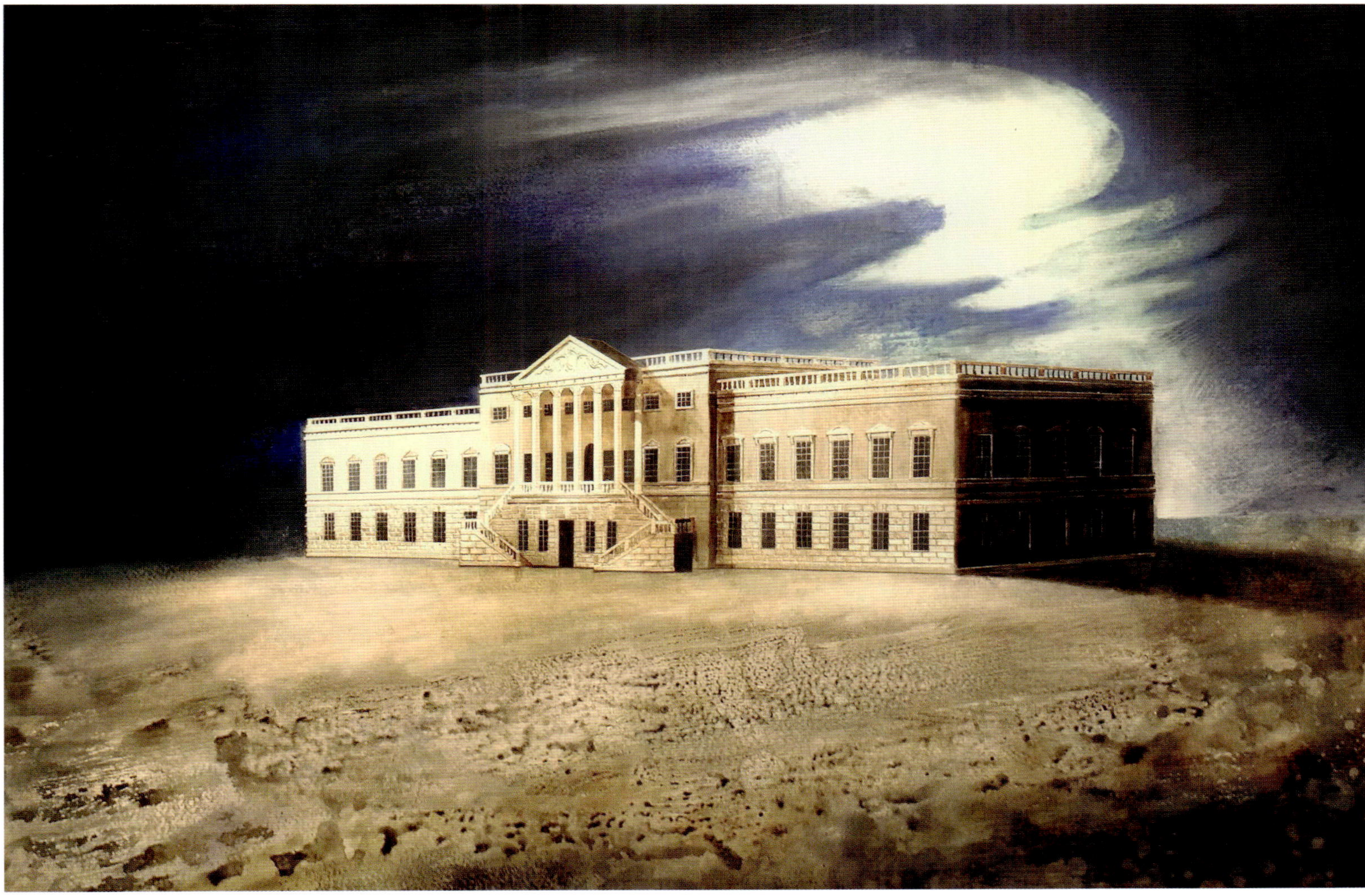

Wanstead House, Essex *(demolished 1824)*
Paper collage and mixed media
2014

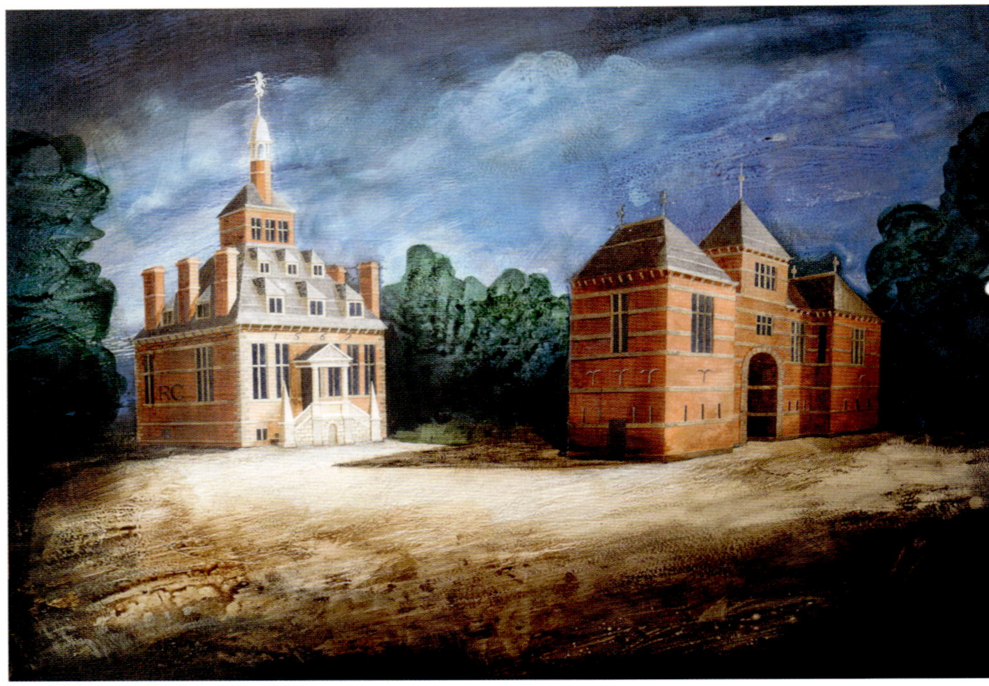

Bach y Graig, North Wales *(demolished 1817)*
Paper collage and mixed media
2014

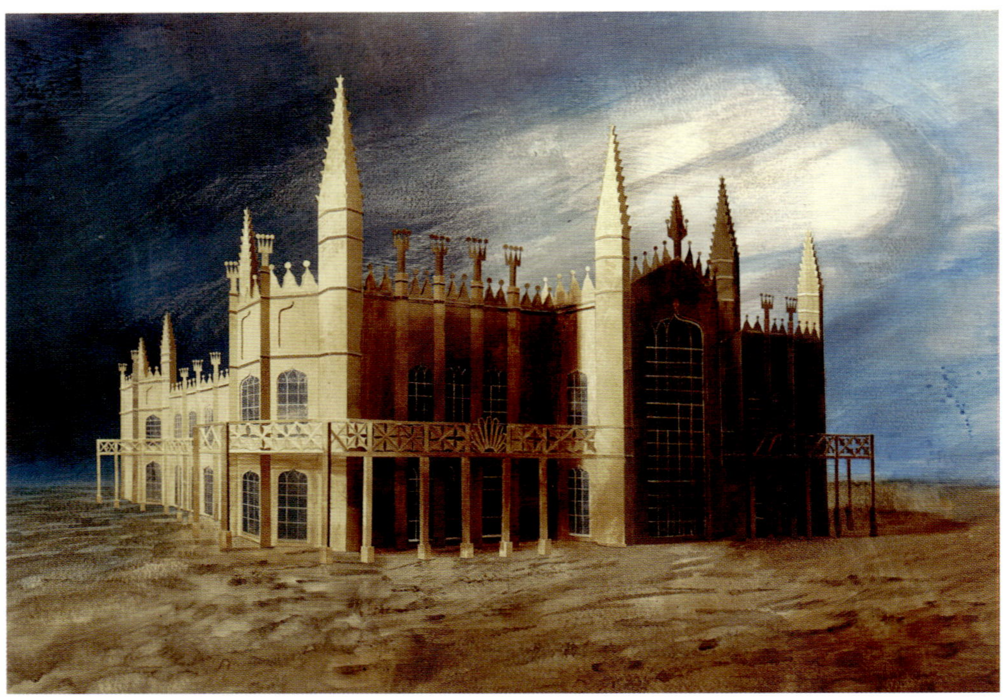

Garth Hall, Guilsfield, Wales *(demolished 1947)*
Paper collage and mixed media
2014

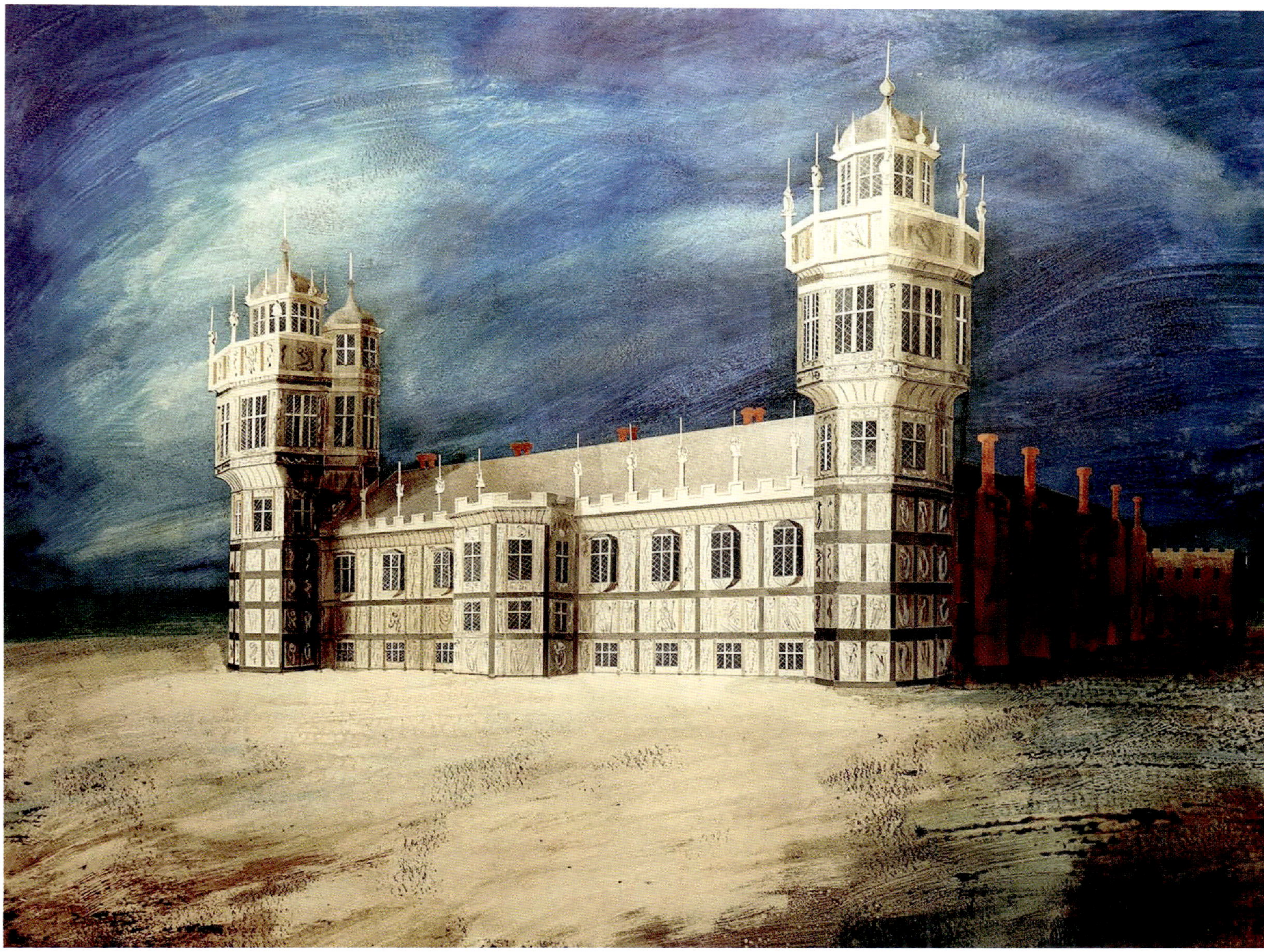

Nonsuch Palace, Surrey *(demolished 1682)*
Paper collage and mixed media
2014

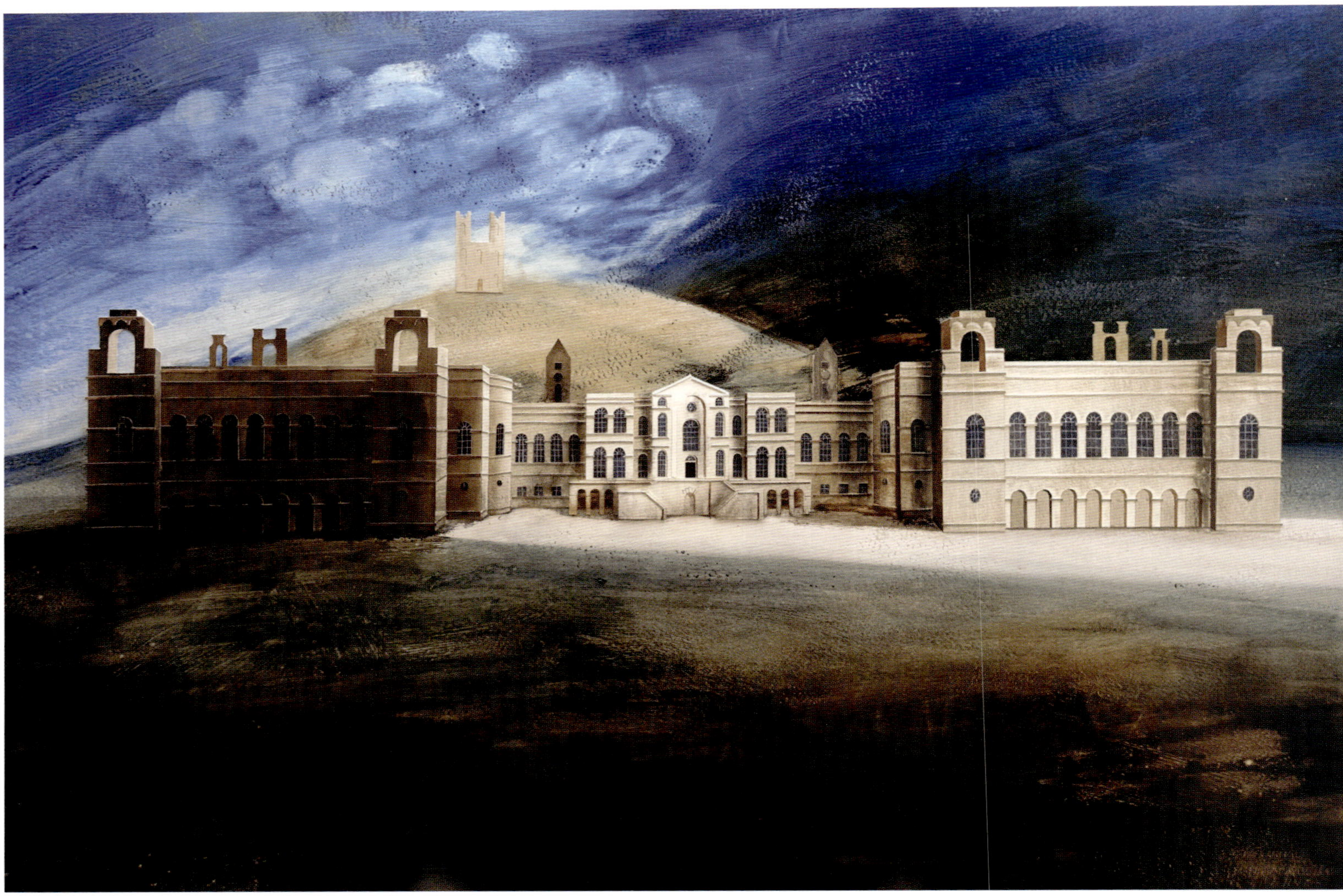

Claremont House, Surrey *(demolished 1769)*
Paper collage and mixed media
2014

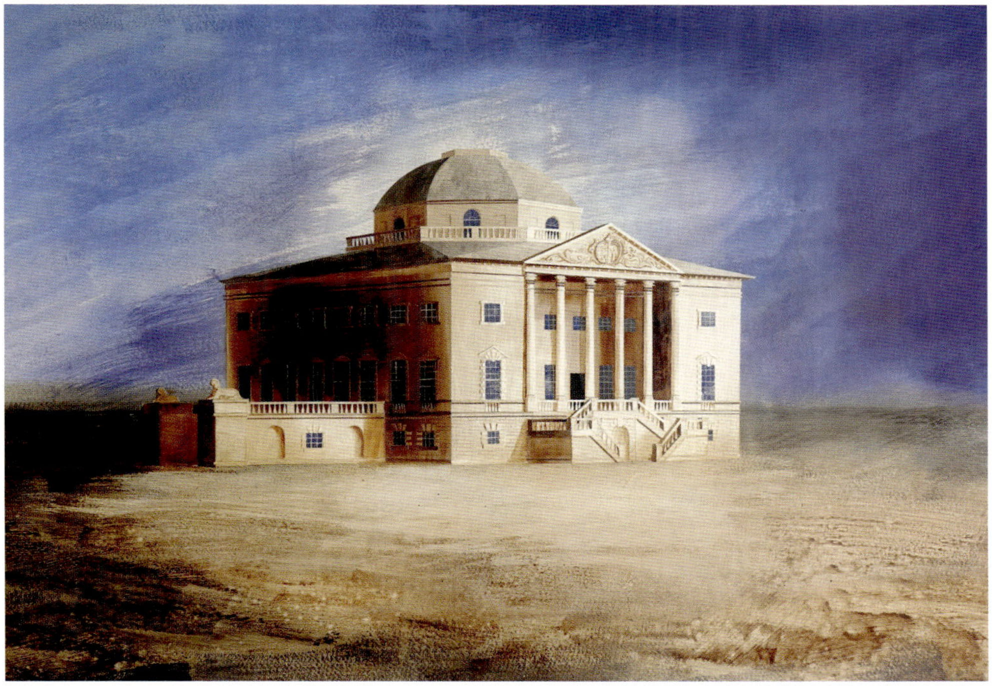

Nuthall Temple, Nottinghamshire *(demolished 1929)*
Paper collage and mixed media
2014

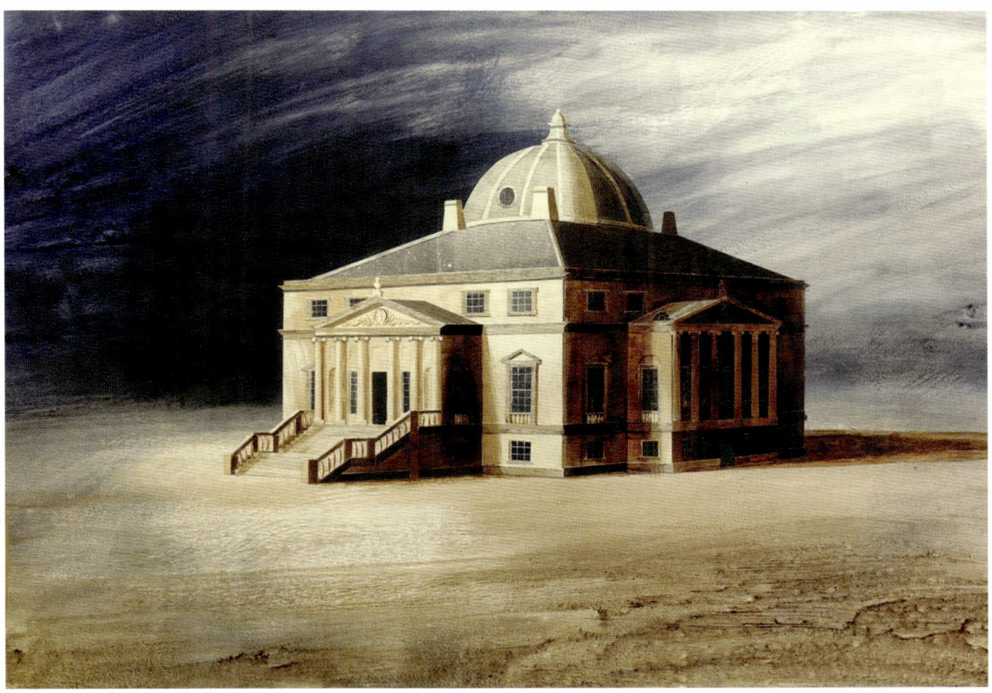

Foots Cray Place, Kent *(demolished 1950 post-fire)*
Paper collage and mixed media
2014

Notes

HOLDENBY HOUSE

1 Joseph Wright, *The English Dialect Dictionary*, 4 vols., London 1905, III, p. 213: 'Holmby'.
2 Quoted in Emily Sophia Hartshorne, *Memorials of Holdenby*, London 1868, p. 16.
3 Quoted *ibid.*, p. 14.
4 Quoted *ibid.*, p. 15.
5 Quoted *ibid.*, p. 17; John Norden, *Speculi Britanniae Pars Altera; or, A Delineation of Northamptonshire*, London 1720, p. 50.
6 William Bray (ed.), *The Diary of John Evelyn*, 2 vols., New York and London 1901, II, p. 105.
7 Thomas Fuller, *The History of the Worthies of England*, London 1662, p. 280.

WORKSOP MANOR

1 John Pendleton, *A History of Derbyshire*, London 1886, p. 265.
2 Lucy Toulmin Smith (ed.), *The Itinerary of John Leland in or about the Years 1535–1543*, vol. IV, part VII, London 1909, p. 17.
3 The screen and survey drawings are in the collection of the Royal Institute of British Architects: London, RIBA Collections, SC231/I/26 and SC238/III/17, respectively.
4 Quoted in Mark Girouard, *Robert Smythson and the Elizabethan Country House*, New Haven, Conn., and London 1983, p. 113.
5 *The Gentleman's Magazine*, vol. 31, November 1761, pp. 531–32.

OLD CAMPDEN HOUSE

1 London, RIBA Collections, SC116/6 recto.
2 London, British Library, Maps K.Top.13.75.3.
3 Henry Peacham, *The Compleat Gentleman*, London 1622, p. 138.
4 Daniel Parsons (ed.), *The Diary of Sir Henry Slingsby*, London 1836, p. 144.
5 *The Weekly Account*, London, 12 May 1645.

HAMSTEAD MARSHALL

1 Oxford, Bodleian Library, MS. Gough Drawings a. 2, ff. 24v–25r.
2 John Ogilby, *The Relation of His Majestie's Entertainment Passing Through the City of London to His Coronation*, London 1661, p. 39.
3 Balthazar Gerbier, *Baltazar Gerbier Knight, To All Men That Loves Truth*, [Paris] 1646, p. 3.
4 Robert Latham and William Matthews (eds.), *The Diary of Samuel Pepys: A New and Complete Transcription*, IV: *1663*, London 1995, p. 162.
5 Bodleian Library, MS. Gough Drawings a. 2.
6 Edward William Gray, *The History and Antiquities of Newbury and Its Environs*, Speenhamland 1839, p. 297.

COLESHILL HOUSE

1 Quoted in Henry Avray Tipping, *English Homes: Late Stuart, 1649–1714*, London 1929, p. 5.
2 R.T. Gunther (ed.), *Sir Roger Pratt on Architecture*, Oxford 1928, p. 253.
3 Christopher Morris (ed.), *The Illustrated Journeys of Celia Fiennes, 1685–c. 1712*, Stroud 1995, p. 47.

EASTBURY PARK

1 Alexander Chalmers, *The General Biographical Dictionary*, rev. edn, vol. XII, London 1813, p. 155.
2 Quoted in John H. Ingram, *The Haunted Homes and Family Traditions of Great Britain*, London 1897, p. 444.

FONTHILL ABBEY

1 *The London Literary Gazette*, no. 293, 31 August 1822, p. 556.
2 Quoted in Boyd Alexander (ed.), *Life at Fonthill, 1807–1822, with Interludes in Paris and London: From the Correspondence of William Beckford*, London 1957, p. 128.
3 Daniel Defoe, *A Tour thro' the Whole Island of Great Britain*, 6th edn, 4 vols., London 1761–62, II, p. 48.
4 Quoted in *The Times*, 20 January 1797, p. 4.
5 'Account of the Works Now Executing at Fonthill', *The European Magazine*, vol. 31, February 1797, p. 107.
6 *The Times*, 5 December 1822, p. 3.
7 *The Times*, 11 October 1822, p. 3.
8 *The Times*, 24 December 1825, p. 3.

HOPE END

1 John Britton and E.W. Brayley, *The Beauties of England and Wales; or, Delineations, Topographical, Historical, and Descriptive, of Each County*, VI: *Hampshire, Isle of Wight, Herefordshire*, London 1805, p. 596.
2 John Chambers, *A General History of Malvern, Embellished with Plates*, Worcester 1817, p. 223.
3 'Hope End Sale Catalogue', 1832, published in P. Kelley and R. Hudson (eds.), *Diary by E.B.B.: The Unpublished Diary of Elizabeth Barrett Browning, 1831–1832*, Athens, Oh., 1969, p. 325.
4 *Ibid.*
5 J.C. Loudon, *An Encyclopaedia of Gardening*, London 1822, p. 1238.
6 *Ibid.*, p. 1172.
7 *The London Gazette*, no. 25798, 20 March 1888, p. 1696.

EATON HALL

1 William Combe, *The Second Tour of Dr Syntax, in Search of Consolation: A Poem*, London 1820, pp. 161, 163.
2 *Ibid.*, p. 164.
3 Quoted in G. Acloque and J. Cornforth, 'The Eternal Gothic of Eaton, I', *Country Life*, no. 149, 11 February 1971, p. 305.
4 Quoted *ibid.*
5 *The Times*, 22 March 1960, p. 6.

Further Reading

Bennett, J.D., *Vanished Houses of Leicestershire*, Leicester 1971

Binney, Marcus, John Harris and Emma Winnington, *Lost Houses of Scotland*, London 1980

Binney, Marcus, and Emma Milne (eds.), *Vanishing Houses of England: A Pictorial Documentary of Lost Country Houses*, London 1982

Davies, Damian Walford, and Siân Melangell Dafydd, *Ancestral Houses: The Lost Mansions of Wales*, Llandysul 2012

The Destruction of the Country House, exhib. cat. by Roy Strong, Marcus Binney and John Harris, London, Victoria and Albert Museum, October–December 1974

Faulkner, Thomas, and Phoebe Lowery, *Lost Houses of Newcastle and Northumberland*, York 1996

Gow, Ian, *Scotland's Lost Houses*, London 2006

Harris, John, *The Artist and the Country House: A History of Country House and Garden View Painting in Britain, 1540–1870*, London 1979, rev. edn 1985

——, *No Voice from the Hall: Early Memories of a Country House Snooper*, London 1998

——, *Echoing Voices: More Memories of a Country House Snooper*, London 2002

——, *Moving Rooms: The Trade in Architectural Salvages*, New Haven, Conn., and London 2007

Lauder, Rosemary Anne, *Vanished Houses of North Devon*, Callington 1981

——, *Vanished Houses of South Devon*, Bideford 1997

Leach, Terence R., and Robert Pacey, *Lost Lincolnshire Country Houses*, 6 vols., Burgh-le-Marsh 1990–2010

Lloyd, Thomas, *The Lost Houses of Wales: A Survey of Country Houses in Wales Demolished Since c. 1900*, London 1986, rev. edn 1989

MacDonnell, Randal, *The Lost Houses of Ireland*, London 2002

Meadows, Peter, and Edward Waterson, *Lost Houses of County Durham*, Welburn 1993

Neave, David, and Edward Waterson, *Lost Houses of East Yorkshire*, Hull 1988

Roberts, W.M., *Lost Country Houses of Suffolk*, Woodbridge 2010

Robinson, John Martin, *Felling the Ancient Oaks: How England Lost Its Great Country Estates*, London 2011

Sproule, Anna, *Lost Houses of Britain*, Newton Abbot 1982

Waterson, Edward, and Peter Meadows, *Lost Houses of York and the North Riding*, Thornton-le-Clay 1990

——, *Lost Houses of the West Riding*, Welburn 1998

Williamson, Tom, Ivan Ringwood and Sarah Spooner, *Lost Country Houses of Norfolk: History, Archaeology and Myth*, Woodbridge 2015

Worsley, Giles, *England's Lost Houses: From the Archives of Country Life*, London 2002

Acknowledgements

I should like to thank the
many individuals whose shared fascination
for lost houses has helped to feed the flames of my
imagination and enabled this book to come to fruition.
In particular, I thank Olivia Horsfall Turner, Tim Knox and
John Harris, whose passion and ability to bring together ideas
and facts with such colour and vigour underpin this volume.
I am indebted to the generosity of those who have shared their
research and collections. I should also like to thank the many
friends and family members who have provided sensitive
ears and eyes, and sound advice when needed.

Special thanks go to the following: my parents,
Andy and Liz Kluz; Hugh Merrell of Merrell Publishers,
also Nicola Bailey, Claire Chandler and Nick Wheldon;
David Adshead; Matthew Beckett of the Lost Heritage website;
Louise Benson of the Eaton Hall Archive; Peter Boughton
of the Grosvenor Museum; Alun Callender; Laura Campbell;
Phoebe Clive; John Day; Jonathon Egerton-Peters; Dr Amy Frost;
Charlie Gordon-Harris; Grosvenor Prints, London; Eileen Harris;
Jamie Harris; Nathaniel Hepburn and Rebecca Hone of
Mascalls Gallery; Kevin Leslie Knight; Todd Longstaffe-Gowan;
John Martin; Chris Moss; Ann Marie Murphy; Henry Pavlovich;
Jonathan Peacock; Janette Ray; Delphine Ruston;
Caroline Stanford; Robert Tobin;
Michelle Tompkins.

Index

Picture Credits

Key: l = left, r = right, t = top, b = bottom, c = centre

Collection of Matthew Beckett/lostheritage.org.uk: 45, 46t, 172 (all), 173 (all), 174tl; 176–77 (top row, l–r: image 2, Streatlam Castle, Co. Durham; image 4, Silverton Park, Devon; 2nd row, l–r: image 1, Mark Hall, Essex; image 2, Marks Hall, Essex; image 3, Shobdon Court, Herefordshire; image 4, Lees Court, Kent; 3rd row, l–r: image 1, Gopsall Hall, Leicestershire; image 2, Wingerworth Hall, Derbyshire; image 3, Trentham Hall, Staffordshire; image 4, Dunsland House, Devon; 4th row, l–r: image 1, Nuthall Temple, Nottinghamshire; image 3, Henham Hall, Suffolk; 5th row, l–r: image 1, Bowood House, Wiltshire; image 2, Sprotbrough Hall, South Yorkshire; image 3, Stanwick Hall, North Yorkshire); Courtesy of Beckford's Tower & Museum, Bath: 134; Ivan Bell: 174–75t; The Bodleian Library, University of Oxford. MS. Gough Drawings a. 2, f. 25r: 98–99; Courtesy of Peter Boughton, Grosvenor Museum, Chester: 158–59; © British Library Board. All Rights Reserved/Bridgeman Images: 80–81; Alun Callender: 40; Jamie Harris: 48, 49; herefordshirehistory.org.uk: 147; Collection of Ed Kluz: 11t, 11b, 44, 46b, 55, 56–57, 66–67, 68, 78, 94–95, 96, 110, 121t, 121b, 132, 133, 135, 136–37, 146, 156, 157, 160–61, 168t, 168b, 168–69, 169t, 169b, 170t, 170b, 170–71, 171t, 171b, 174tr, 174c, 174–75b, 175t, 175cl, 175cr, 175bl, 175br, 176–77 (all, with the exception of those listed under Matthew Beckett), endpapers; Kevin Leslie Knight: 174b; Todd Longstaffe-Gowan: 8, 17, 18t, 18b, 19, 20; Henry Pavlovich: 174–75c; RIBA Collections: 144–45; © The Society of Antiquaries of London: 122–23; Courtesy/copyright *Swindon Advertiser*: 111t, 111b

The publisher and author have made every effort to trace and contact copyright holders of the illustrations reproduced in this book; they shall be happy to correct in subsequent editions any errors or omissions that are brought to their attention.

First published 2017 by Merrell Publishers, London and New York

Merrell Publishers Limited
70 Cowcross Street
London EC1M 6EJ

merrellpublishers.com

British Library Cataloguing in Publication Data. A catalogue record for this book is available from the British Library.

ISBN 978-1-8589-4662-7

Produced by Merrell Publishers Limited
Designed by Nicola Bailey
Project-managed by Claire Chandler
Additional picture research by Nick Wheldon
Proofread by Barbara Roby
Indexed by Sue Farr

Printed and bound in China

Jacket: *Prospect of Old Campden House*, 2017; see pp. 88–89.
Page 1: Detail of Old Campden House, Gloucestershire; see pp. 76–91.
Page 21: *Carclew House Ruins*, scraperboard, 2017.
Page 51: *Fallen Gate Piers*, scraperboard, 2017.
Endpapers: *Demolition of Northumberland House* (1874), from *The London Illustrated News*, 30 January 1875.

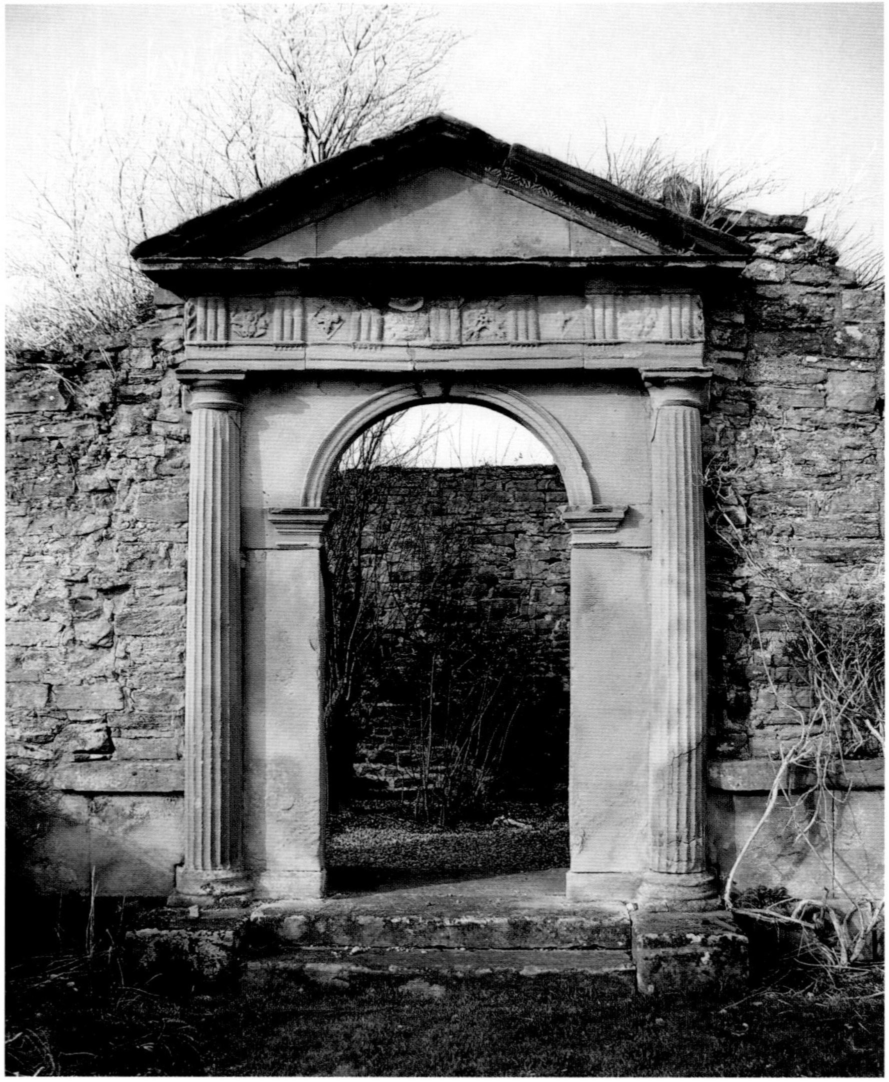

GILLINGWOOD HALL

According to folklore, on the night of St Stephen's Day 1750, after a grand party, Margaret Wharton, co-heiress to the family fortune, maliciously set fire to Gillingwood Hall, North Yorkshire. It had lately been revealed that her deceased brother William had left the estate to another family member. Margaret's drunken rage resulted in the loss of the entire contents of the house, and reduced the building (newly reworked in the Palladian style, probably by Daniel Garrett) almost to its foundations. Today the earthworks of the elaborate terraced gardens surround the vestiges of the house, punctuated by decaying follies; the fine door surround, shored up by the last few stones of the building, stands scorched and reddened by fire in the middle of the lawn. Margaret reputedly lived out the rest of her years as a miser, spending only one penny at a time, thus gaining the nickname Peg Pennyworth. Much like the site at Gillingwood, haunted by echoes of the past, her spectre is said to persist, roaming through an old house in the market town of Thirsk.

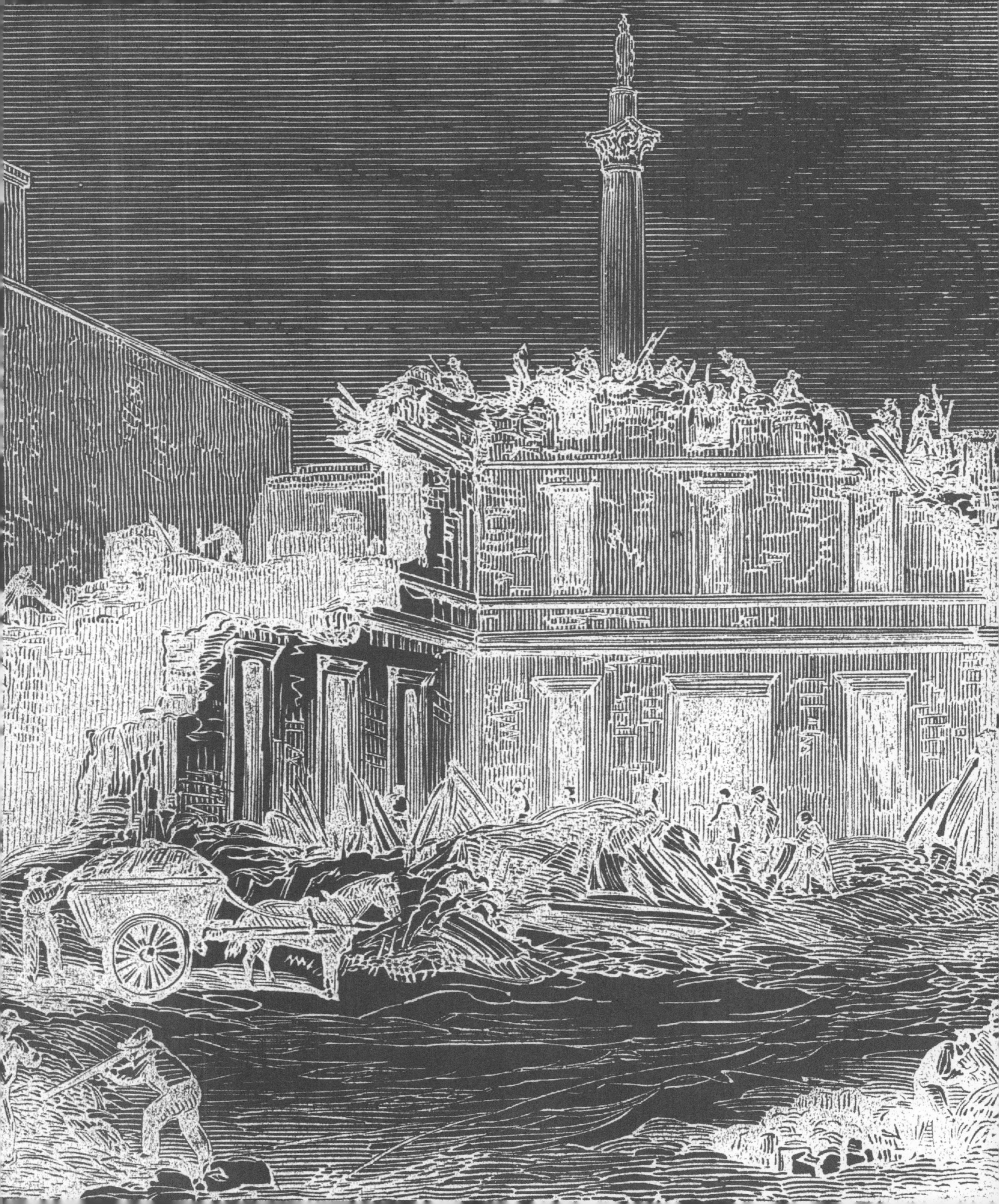